T0329332

Underwriting Services and the New Issues Market

Underwriting Services and the New Issues Market

George J. Papaioannou

Distinguished Professor Emeritus,
Zarb School of Business, Hofstra University,
New York, United States

Ahmet K. Karagozoglu

C.V. Starr Distinguished Professor of Finance and Investment Banking,
Zarb School of Business, Hofstra University,
New York, United States

ACADEMIC PRESS

An imprint of Elsevier

British Library Cataloguing-in-Publication Data
A catalogue record for this book is available from the British Library

Library of Congress Cataloging-in-Publication Data
A catalog record for this book is available from the Library of Congress

ISBN: 978-0-12-803282-4

For Information on all Academic Press publications
visit our website at https://www.elsevier.com/books-and-journals

Working together
to grow libraries in
developing countries

www.elsevier.com • www.bookaid.org

Publisher: Candice Janco
Acquisition Editor: J. Scott Bentley
Editorial Project Manager: Susan Ikeda
Production Project Manager: Poulouse Joseph
Cover Designer: Matthew Limbert

Typeset by MPS Limited, Chennai, India

Dedicated to

My wife, Susan, my children, and my students
George J. Papaioannou

and

My parents, grandparents, and all my teachers
Ahmet K. Karagozoglu

Contents

Foreword

In this book, Papaioannou and Karagozoglu provide comprehensive coverage of securities underwriting that brings together practice and theory. Their unique approach in covering the material is supplemented by an extensive review of the findings of academic research. By doing so they contribute to a more thorough understanding of the securities issuance business among its practitioners and policymakers that leads to more informed decision making.

"*Underwriting Services and the New Issues Market*" is structured to follow the phases of the issuance process, presenting both the activities and decisions that issuers and investment bankers have to execute to facilitate the issuance of securities as well as the theoretical arguments and research findings that shed light on the consequences and the efficacy of the practices applied. Although the literature on underwriting and the new issues market has been available in a vast array of academic and professional journal articles, it has not been organized and integrated with practice in a comprehensive manner within a single source. Papaioannou and Karagozoglu fill this gap with their book. Presentation of the material follows an activity-centered pattern which is familiar to investment banking professionals but also makes it accessible to novice readers and students who are considering investment banking as a career.

The authors enhance the reader's understanding of the underwriting services by incorporating the stock price and operating performance of firms issuing new securities. In this framework, coverage of the empirical evidence produced by academic research is critical for the evaluation of the various activities and services performed in the context of new issues and for gaining an appreciation of their consequences. In addition to the evidence from the domestic U.S. market, the book covers international markets with respect to both offering arrangements and performance outcomes, thus providing a more comprehensive examination of the comparative results of issuance mechanics and their consequences.

Papaioannou and Karagozoglu also present a step-by-step approach to structuring and evaluating new issues. They offer investment bankers as well as corporate finance officers the tools to analyze the financial value of the decision to issue securities as well as the framework for making important choices on various features of securities offerings ranging from public versus private placement, to choosing the listing venue, type of underwriting contract and underwriter characteristics. By supplementing the methodological discussion with theory and empirical findings, the authors provide an indispensable resource that should guide professional decisions and policymaking. While the book is aimed at the professionals involved in the issuance of new securities, its balanced coverage of theory, practice, and research findings makes it well-suited for academics and students as well.

Frank J. Fabozzi
Professor of Finance, EDHEC Business School and
Editor of *The Journal of Portfolio Management*

Preface

One of the most important functions of the financial markets is to facilitate the raising of capital through the issuance of equity and debt securities. This book is dedicated to covering the underwriting services of investment banks and the new issues markets in which these services take place. Despite the importance of the topic and the great body of literature it has spawned, there is a dearth of books that provide a comprehensive coverage of this subject matter.

Underwriting Services and the New Issues Market aims to fill this void by providing a resource that integrates the practice and academic theory as well as evidence on this subject. The exposition of theory and empirical findings presents information that has implications for the practice of underwriting without attempting to provide a critical appraisal of the existing academic literature. Although the conceptual and technical tools that apply to the issuance and underwriting of securities straddle various fields of finance, the book's primary focus is on the activities and decisions that are directly relevant to the issuance process and the pertinent theory and evidence that help assess the consequences and efficacy of those decisions. Thus the book is designed to impart the reader a well-rounded understanding of the underwriting of new issues.

The material of the book is structured to follow the sequence of the various phases of the capital raising process and the activities underwriters perform in each stage of this process. Consequently, coverage of theory and empirical evidence follows this pattern rather than one that could be adopted in an academic research exposé.

The book covers the following topics: Chapter 1, The Underwriting Business: Functions, Organization, and Structure, and Chapter 2, The New Issues Markets, provide, respectively, an overview of the underwriting business and the major new issues markets around the world. Chapter 3, Regulation of the New Issues Market in the United States, reviews important laws and regulations that relate to underwriting services and the new issues markets. Chapters 4−7 discuss the mechanics of the issuance process as well as the activities and services of underwriters and review the various offering methods used around the world. Chapters 8−13 present the theories that have been advanced to explain the pricing of new issues as well as the empirical findings regarding the pricing of new issues and the stock price and operating performance of firms that conduct securities offerings. Chapters 14−16 analyze the decision to issue securities and discuss the choices faced by issuers in relation to structuring new offerings. Although the main focus of the book is securities issuance and underwriting services in the United States, the book provides ample details on offering arrangements in international markets along with the pertinent academic research.

The book is intended for use by practitioners in investment banking, financial analysts, regulators and policy makers, as well as by faculty and students in Master's and doctoral-level courses in investment banking and capital markets. Depending on the reader's objectives, the chapters of the book can be used selectively to study either the mechanics of the issuance process or the conduct of capital markets as it relates to new issues.

The book is based on a graduate course in investment banking taught by George Papaioannou, who wishes to acknowledge the contribution his students made through their thought-provoking and challenging questions and comments. He also thanks his student assistants, particularly Harsiman Singh, Will Gao, and Linshan Qu, for their valuable work.

The authors express their appreciation to Editor Scott Bentley and Editorial Product Manager Susan Ikeda at Elsevier for their encouragement and support in making this book a reality.

George J. Papaioannou, Ahmet K. Karagozoglu

1

The Underwriting Business: Functions, Organization, and Structure

This chapter describes the underwriting business, the firms that provide underwriting services, how these firms organize the underwriting business within the broader scope of their operations, and how they compete in the market for underwriting services.

Functions and Organization

What Underwriters Do

Corporations as well as other entities (e.g., municipalities, universities, etc.) need to raise new capital for various purposes by selling financial claims, like stocks or bonds. Because these issuers come to the market only periodically they lack the expertise required to ensure the new securities are appropriately priced and successfully placed with investors. To overcome these disadvantages, issuers retain financial institutions that operate as investment banks to assist with the pricing, marketing, and placement of their new issues. In full-service underwriting arrangements, the intermediary also assumes the risk of placing the issue. It is this risk bearing service, akin to an insurance policy, that gives the name "underwriting" to these business arrangements and by extension to this business activity. In return, issuers pay underwriting firms a fee to compensate them for the range of services they receive. Underwriting of new issues is part of the activities that take place in the primary capital markets. This is the segment of the financial markets that facilitates the raising of new capital through the sale of financial claims, like stocks and bonds.

The Underwriting Firms

The firms that engage in the provision of underwriting services are called investment banks. Most investment banks are much more than just underwriting firms. They also run various other securities businesses, including brokerage, trading, wealth management, and corporate advisory services. They may operate as independent investment banks (e.g., Goldman Sachs and Morgan Stanley) or as divisions of other financial institutions, banks or insurance companies (e.g., Merrill Lynch is part of the Bank of America).

Underwriting Services and the New Issues Market. DOI: http://dx.doi.org/10.1016/B978-0-12-803282-4.00001-8

The Functions of Underwriters

As intermediaries in the capital raising process, underwriting firms perform several valuable functions that help issuers offer new securities at higher prices and lower cost than otherwise.

Valuation and Pricing

In many instances, a firm approaches the public capital markets for the first time. This is the case of a firm selling stock in an initial public offering (IPO) or the case of a firm issuing a bond for the first time. In these cases, there is no prior history to serve as a guide about the value of the firm. Even in instances when an issuer has publicly traded securities but lacks wide recognition and active trading of its securities there may not be full agreement on the value of the firm's securities. By operating in the capital markets and engaging in repeat new issue deals, underwriting firms acquire the expertise to collect the appropriate information and arrive at a more credible estimate of value than the issuing firm. Arriving at an appropriate value is not, however, sufficient for the successful placement of a new issue. Even more important is to set the right price at which the new securities will be accepted by investors—i.e., the offer price. Informational frictions between sellers (issuer and underwriter) and buyers (investors) can cause the latter to be reluctant to pay the full value of the security for fear of overpaying—a condition called adverse selection. Valuing and pricing a new issue may also require that regular investors be engaged in the production of information relevant to the price discovery process. It is the function of the underwriter to organize this information production by incentivizing investors and finding efficient methods of compensation, as, for example, though price discounts.

Certification

The ability of underwriters to convince the market about the fairness of the offer prices of new issues depends on the underwriter's reputation and track record. Since the underwriter's revenue stream depends on repeat business, underwriters have an incentive to maintain a reputation as credible intermediaries. This is how they build reputation capital. The greater this capital is the greater the certification power of the underwriter. Thus, as certifiers of new issue values, underwriters facilitate the placement of new securities into the capital markets and contribute to the financing of new investments.

Marketing

Underwriting firms have extensive contacts and networks of retail and institutional clients to whom they can pitch the new securities. Through person-to-person contacts or group presentations in the so-called roadshows, underwriters can communicate vital information that helps investors to become informed about the new issue.

Distribution

The distribution of new offers is the culmination of the pricing and marketing activities of the underwriting process. Distribution includes both the sale of the new securities as well as the scope of investor clienteles to whom the new securities will be sold. The sale of new issues requires human capital, especially an experienced salesforce, and tangible assets ranging from brick-and-mortar facilities to information and computer technology resources. Investor networks are valuable in securing the sale of new securities to investor clienteles favored by the issuer or dictated by the conditions of the market.

Valuable Competencies in Underwriting

To perform the above functions efficiently and to succeed in the underwriting business, underwriting firms must possess several competencies.

Ability to Originate Deals

This is the most important competitive advantage an underwriting firm must possess. Receiving mandates to serve as the lead manager of new issues is critical in maximizing revenues from new issue deals and building reputation. Since the lead manager is engaged in all services under the underwriting contract and also retains the lion's share in the allocation of the offers, he/she receives the bulk of the underwriter compensation. As lead manager, the underwriter also selects the comanagers and other syndicate members thus establishing the conditions of reciprocal invitations to participate in other deals. Investment banks develop the origination advantage by cultivating and maintaining relationships with many prospective issuers. Such contacts and networks are built on reputation and a wide-ranging scope of operations that can be of use to issuers (e.g., providing services in M&A deals and other corporate finance decisions and transactions).

Ability to Design and Price New Issues

Capital markets expertise enables successful underwriters to advice issuers on the appropriate type of new securities to offer (e.g., stocks or bonds) and design the terms of new securities so that they are compatible with market conditions and dynamics, investor appetite, and other institutional arrangements. This kind of expertise is most important in the case of bond issues. Debt instruments can have many different features in terms of maturity, callability, and convertibility to mention a few. Part of the ability to advise on financial instruments is also the ability to assess their relative risk-return appeal to different investor clienteles.

Ability to Place Securities

Underwriting starts with origination and ends with placement. Successful placement of the new issue under the terms of issuance (i.e., offer price and quantity offered) is the necessary outcome to prove the underwriter's competence in organizing and executing the new issue mandate. Without access to investor capital even a firm strong in origination is likely to fail.

Ability to Intermediate Client Interests

The overarching ability of successful underwriting firms is to smooth out informational frictions and the conflicting interests of issuers and investors. Information frictions can prevent issuers and investors to come to terms on mutually acceptable prices for new issues. Issuers seek to maximize proceeds from the new issue by selling at the highest offer price possible, whereas investors seek to maximize returns by buying at offer prices below the fair market value of the new securities. Underwriting firms can ill-afford to disappoint either side of their clients since both are needed for survival in the underwriting business. This leads underwriters to strike implicit contracts with both sides that allow the parties to meet their goals, usually over several deals with the same underwriter. For example, an issuer may be willing to accept a lower offer price for the opportunity to get better quality analyst coverage in anticipation of a follow-on issue. Or investors may accept to buy less promising new issues for the opportunity to participate in future "hot" issues managed by the underwriter. These *quid pro quo* agreements are not explicitly articulated in the underwriting contracts but they are understood to have force because they are backed by the underwriter's reputation capital at stake (Morrison and Wilhelm, 2007). To deliver on these implicit obligations and enforce nonopportunistic behavior, especially on the side of investors, underwriting firms need to have a steady deal flow. The implicit contracts can work if investors understand that violators will be frozen out of future good deals and lose their long-run benefits.

Supporting Activities for Successful Underwriting

Underwriting services are not organized and offered in a vacuum. To possess the competencies described above requires that investment banks run a number of secondary and primary market activities. These supporting activities can be profit centers on their own, but also engender significant synergies that benefit underwriting. In some of these activities investment banks assume the role of an agent, that is, they execute transactions for their clients without assuming any market risk, as in brokerage and asset management. In other activities, they act as principals, that is, they put their own capital at risk, as with underwriting, trading, and merchant banking.

Brokerage

Brokerage business involves the execution of orders on behalf of customers. This enables the firm to establish and grow networks of retail and institutional investors. These networks provide immediate access to an investor base to whom the new securities can be pitched and eventually sold.

Trading

Underwriting firms operate trading floors for the execution of trades for their account as well as the accounts of clients (investors). When they trade as a counterparty to a client's order, they act as a principal and bear the risk that comes with price volatility. On the plus side, trading cultivates relationships with investors and offers the investment bank the opportunity to hone its valuation skills and develop a deeper understanding of market dynamics.

Market Making

Market makers stand between buyers and sellers and support one or the other side when there is an imbalance between buy and sell orders. This service places an investment bank in a strong position to provide and support liquidity in the early aftermarket of new unseasoned securities (like IPOs and first-time bond issues). Without the presence of market makers, trading on these issues could become possible only if buyers paid more or sellers accepted less, thus jeopardizing the liquidity of the securities.

Wealth Management

Advising or running mutual funds or managing other pools of money provides the investment bank with placement capabilities. Although there is a reputation risk at stake because of conflicts of interest, when well done, these activities can be of mutual benefit to the investment fund and the underwriting business in the case of well-priced securities. The investment bank gains access to new financial products, whereas the placement of new issues finds a more receptive investor outlet.

Analysis and Research

Successful underwriting firms are supported by strong research departments and top quality analysts. As with market making, research output and analyst coverage are extremely important in the aftermarket, especially for first time issuing firms. These firms need to build their investor base and attract attention to the firm's business. In many cases, it is only the underwriter's firm that provides analysis and recommendations that investors can use to consider investing in the firm. Since the mid-1990s, analyst quality and coverage have become critical factors in the issuers' selection of underwriters. Accordingly, investment banks have used their strength in this area to gain entry into the group of comanagers which is the first step for eventually graduating to the position of lead manager (Ljungqvist, Marston, and Wilhelm, 2009). Reputable analysts are also prized for their power to attract new clients to the underwriting firm (Clarke, Khorana, Patel, and Rau, 2007).

Corporate Finance Services

Besides managing new issues and operating in the securities business, investment banks also serve as advisors to corporations in regards to various transactions on the assets and liabilities side. As such, investment banks advice clients on mergers and acquisitions, leveraged and management buy-outs, spin offs of assets and equity carve outs, stock repurchases, debt refinancing, and other corporate finance matters. The advantage of acting as a corporate finance advisor is the opportunity to maintain ongoing contacts with corporate clients and to promote the underwriting business when some of these corporate transactions require the issuance of new securities. Therefore, corporate finance services can be critical to the origination of underwriting deals.

Merchant Banking

Investment banks also risk their own capital by taking positions as lenders in bridge loans and as partners in private equity and hedge funds. Acting as lenders, investment banks facilitate the interim financing of corporate clients engaging in asset restructurings or M&A transactions. The bridge loans are eventually paid off through issues of securities in which the lending investment bank is very likely to serve as underwriter. In private equity funds, investment banks engage in the purchase and restructuring of promising private firms sold later through an IPO. Thus, both types of activities can generate synergies with corporate finance as well as underwriting. However, participation in private and hedge funds has been severely curtailed under the Dodd-Frank or Wall Street Reform and Consumer Protection Act of 2010.

Financial Engineering

Financial engineering is the design of financial instruments with new and unique features that help finance complex projects or overcome frictions on the issuer or the investor side. Financial innovation is vital to investment banks. It gives them the advantage to pitch new products to clients—both issuers and investors—and acquire skills in the design of securities.

Conflicts of Interest

The joint production of services can create serious conflicts of interest that diminish the potential benefits from operational complementarities. Conflicts of interest arise when a party acting as the agent of a client can take action that benefits the former but hurts the latter. For example, an investment bank that functions as an underwriter of new securities and asset manager can reduce its placement costs by placing low quality (e.g., overvalued) securities in the investment accounts of clients. Or a commercial bank acting as an underwriter can conceal the true value of the issuer's securities in order to raise funds that are purposed to repay the client's bank loan.

These conflicts of interest came to the fore in the years 1999–2000 when many IPOs of technology, especially internet-based, stocks came to the market at very high discounts relative to their ensuing market prices in the secondary market. Specifically, investment banks were accused for *quid pro quo* deals that favored their investors or the executives of issuing firms. These accusations were settled in the 2003 Global Analyst Research Settlement at a total cost of $1.4 billion. The settlement involved initially 10 and later 2 more of the biggest investment banks, including First Boston, Goldman Sachs, Merrill Lynch, and Morgan Stanley.

Two areas that have attracted interest in the study of conflicts of interest are analyst recommendations and the performance of mutual funds operated by investment banking firms. The promise and actual delivery of aggressive analyst recommendations has been used to attract to the underwriting business issuers eager to achieve better prices for their stocks. Dumping less promising new securities into mutual funds operated by the parent investment bank can facilitate the placement of these issues. Empirical research has produced evidence of conflicts of interest in both of these areas. Bias in recommendations by affiliated analysts has been documented in Barber, Lehavy, and Trueman (2007) and Kadan, Madureira, Wang, and Zach (2009), whereas Berzins, Liu, and Trzcinka (2013) find evidence of underperformance in mutual funds operated by investment banks.

Conflicts of interest can be mitigated by concerns of loss of reputation in the businesses entangled in the joint operations. For example, Ljungqvist, Marston, and Wilhelm (2006) find that the risk to their professional status and the standing of the parent firm restrains very reputable analysts from issuing aggressive recommendations to help the underwriting arm of their firm. Conflicts of interest can be also mitigated by competition from organizations with simpler business models that are free of conflicts of interest, like boutique investment banks. Another mitigating factor is the price discount clients can impose on the seller if the latter is known to mishandle conflicts of interest. Or investors aware of the bias in analyst recommendations may discount their impact on asset values. Closer monitoring by outside investors can also check conflicts of interest. For example, Ljungqvist, Marston, Starks, Wei, and Yan (2007) point out that the analysts' behavior is restrained when stocks are held by the usually better-informed institutional investors. Analysts employed by reputable underwriting firms with more loyal underwriting clients are found to be less aggressive in their recommendations.

Chen, Morrison, and Wilhelm (2014) argue that the development of reputation follows a cycle that initially favors aggressive behavior which is followed by more restrained behavior in order to preserve the reputational capital of the firm. Thus, investment banks are more likely to place their interests ahead of those of their customers when the former need to develop a "type" of reputation for possessing certain skills in the execution of deals. Once this reputation has been established investment banks start to build "behavioral" reputation that puts the interests of the client ahead of those of the investment bank.

Industry Structure and Competition

Brief Historical Perspective

Throughout the 19th century and until the 1930s, underwriting was organized as part of the securities business run by commercial banks and independent securities firms. Following the Glass−Steagall Act of 1933, securities business was separated from commercial banking and as a result underwriting of corporate securities was exclusively left in the domain of the securities industry. The gradual relaxation of the Glass−Steagall Act started in the mid-1980s, when the Federal Reserve Board expanded the powers of Section 20 affiliates of commercial banks[1]. Section 20 affiliates were permitted to underwrite and trade in debt securities in 1989 and a year later in equities as long as the revenue from these activities did not exceed 10% of the revenue of the Section 20 affiliate. This revenue limit was raised to 25% in 1996 and the same year the "fire wall" separation between the securities business and the

---

[1] Section 20 of the Glass−Steagall Act had allowed commercial banks to conduct some nonbanking activities (but not corporate underwriting) as long as they were not the affiliate's principal business.

commercial banking business was lifted. These relaxations were important because they afforded commercial banks greater scale and scope of operations. That is, the underwriting business had more room to grow and the communication between securities business staff and commercial lending staff gave banks an informational advantage over their security firm rivals.

The Glass-Steagall Act was finally repealed in 1999 by the Gramm-Leach-Bliley Financial Services Modernization Act.

Although the intent of deregulation was to expand the number of players in the securities business and the new issues markets, it ushered in a large wave of industry consolidation as the largest banks moved quickly to takeover established independent investment banks. Eventually, with the exception of Goldman Sachs and Morgan Stanley, all the large independent investment banks were absorbed into commercial bank conglomerates. Thus, for example, Salomon Brothers was absorbed into Citigroup, Merrill Lynch into Bank of America, Bear Sterns into J. P. Morgan Chase, First Boston and Donaldson, Lufkin and Jenrette into Credit Suisse (Switzerland), Paine Webber into UBS (Switzerland), and Alex Brown into Deutsche Bank (Germany). The acquisitive strategy followed by the commercial banks was primarily motivated by the difficulty commercial banks had faced in the organic (i.e., de novo) development of the competitive competencies required for expansion into investment banking.

Along with changes due to the evolving regulatory environment, underwriting firms and their parent investment banks underwent other significant changes over the years. The most important was the gradual abandonment of the partnership form of ownership in favor of the public corporate form. This change was driven mainly by the fast-rising need for capital as the securities business became capital intensive. This was the result of expanding volumes of trading and underwriting as well as the need to provide real-time analysis and execution through the use of elaborate information and computer technology. Also, the introduction of accelerated offerings through Rule 415 ushered in the practice of the "bought deal"[2]. Underwriters had to commit to the purchase of a new issue before they had time to form a syndicate and canvass the market's demand for the new securities. That meant putting large amounts of capital at risk that should be backed by a strong balance sheet.

An important consequence of adopting the public corporate form was the breakdown of the partnership model which in turn led to a more fluid labor force that was less dependent on mentoring by senior partners and less committed to the reputation of the firm for long-term compensation benefits (Morrison and Wilhelm, 2008).

Industry Structure

The makeup of the underwriting industry is a mirror image of the makeup of the investment banking industry. Underwriting (and investment banking) firms can be classified by various criteria.

---

[2] Rule 415 adopted in 1982 gave relatively large issuing firms a window of two years after obtaining approval from the SEC during which they could offer new securities with a very short notice.

By Affiliation

Independent securities firms: These are investment banks that remain independent of any affiliation with other financial institutions. As of 1985, all top US investment banks operated as independent securities firms without ties to banks. By 2015, almost all top ranked investment banks were controlled by commercial banks or operated as subsidiaries of banks. Currently, Goldman Sachs and Morgan Stanley are the only remaining independent firms among the top ranked investment banks (see Table 1.2).

Commercial-bank-controlled firms: These are investment banks that have either evolved organically within commercial banks or were acquired by banks. Top ranked investment banks that came under the control of commercial banks are: Alex Brown, Bear Sterns, First Boston, Merrill Lynch, Paine Webber, Salomon Brothers, Smith Barney.

Subsidiaries of other financial or industrial firms: These are investment banks owned by other types of firms, most usually, insurance companies. An example of such a securities firm was Dean Witter which was controlled by Sears, Robuck & Co. and later merged with Morgan Stanley. Prudential (an insurance firm) used to operate Prudential Securities before it sold it to Wachovia Bank.

By Ownership

Privately owned: These are investment banks that are privately owned and usually organized as limited partnerships. This was the traditional form of ownership before capital needs started to exceed the ability of partners to capitalize their firms. With the exception of First Boston, Merrill Lynch and Paine Webber, the top ranked investment banks were privately held as of 1985. As of 2015, all top ranked investment banks were publicly traded corporations (see Table 1.2).

Publicly owned: These are investment banks with publicly owned and traded equity. With few exceptions of small boutique investment banks, all major investment banks are now publicly held. The "going public" trend among large investment banks took hold in the mid-1980s as Alex Brown, Bear Stearns, Morgan Stanley, Salomon Brothers, and Shearson Lehman Hutton (predecessor of Lehman Brothers) went public within a few years. Goldman Sachs was the only holdout among top securities firms that eventually went public in 1999.

By Scope of Operations

Integrated investment banks: Integrated investment banks are firms that have integrated their operations across segments of the capital markets, investor clienteles, and sectors of the securities business. Traditionally, securities firms have been classified into national full-line firms and large investment banks. National full-line firms operate in all types of securities business, including brokerage, trading and market making, asset management, research and analysis, as well as underwriting and corporate finance. These firms were traditionally strong in retail securities business. Large investment banks were those operating in underwriting corporate finance and wholesale securities business (i.e., they catered to high-end clients). Over time, the lines between retail and wholesale securities firms have become less clear as investment banks pursued an integrative strategy that aimed at placing them in all areas of the securities business. Thus, Merrill Lynch started as a retail securities firm and later developed wholesale operations. Morgan Stanley integrated its wholesale business with retail business by merging with Dean Witter. Goldman Sachs is an example of a well-diversified firm that has retained most of its wholesale orientation.

The culmination of the integrated investment banking model in the United States has been the emergence of the commercial plus investment banking model as a result of the deregulation of 1999. Under this model, securities business (including underwriting) is combined with corporate lending thus creating new information advantages.

Specialized investment banks: There are limited scope investment banks, called boutique banks, which specialize in the provision of a limited menu of securities services, like advisory services in M&A (mergers and acquisitions) deals and underwriting of new issues in specific industries. These firms derive their market advantage from in-depth expertise in a few products, close relations with clients and the absence of major conflicts of interest that can afflict multiservice investment banks. As a result, they enjoy advantages in providing more objective research and analyst coverage and advisement in corporate finance deals. Examples of boutique investment banks are: Cowen Group, Evercore Partners, Morgan Keegan, and WR Hambrecht.

By Reputation

In past years, underwriting firms would announce their new issue deals in the form of the so-called tombstone advertisements that appeared in various print media. They were so named because they were very terse and matter of fact in their content due to regulations that prohibit the solicitation of buy orders prior to the approval of a new issue by the Securities and Exchange Commission (SEC). The names of the underwriting firms would be listed in order of importance in the syndicate, from the lead manager down to the smallest members of the underwriting syndicate. Based on this hierarchy, underwriting firms came to be grouped in order of reputation into:

Bulge (or special) bracket: These are firms that frequently appear as lead managers (e.g., Goldman Sachs, Morgan Stanley, Merrill Lynch, Salomon Brothers, First Boston, Lehman Brothers). Currently, the bulge bracket is occupied by the banks that acquired securities firms, like JP Morgan, Bank of America (Merrill Lynch), and Citi, in addition to Goldman Sachs and Morgan Stanley.

Major bracket: These are firms that usually serve as comanagers alongside the lead managers and receive large allocations of new securities for underwriting and placement. Examples of major bracket firms are: Jefferies Group, RBC Capital Markets, Wells Fargo, and HSBC.

Submajor bracket: These are firms that receive considerable allocations of new securities but have infrequent presence in the ranks of lead managers or comanagers.

Mezzanine and lower bracket: These firms receive smaller allocations of new issues and have infrequent participation in underwriting syndicates. Many of these firms are regional broker-dealer firms and have mostly selling responsibilities.

Industry Competition

The Impact of Scope of Operations

Expanding and integrating operations across different securities markets brings significant complementarities and synergies to the parent organization. As noted above, brokerage and trading help maintain networks of investors; market making, analysis and research support the creation of new secondary markets for newly issued securities; and corporate finance helps in the origination of new deals for the flotation of securities. The success of the underwriting business within an investment bank is critically affected by how the parent organization utilizes the different services to generate positive synergies and minimize costs from negative synergies that come mostly from conflicts of interest.

Client Relationships and Competition

Developing and maintaining relationships with both sides of the underwriting market, issuers and investors, are a critical component of intraindustry competition. Investment banks maintain relationships with issuing clients through corporate finance advisory deals and underwriting deals. Relationships with investors are being sustained through brokerage services, trading and market making and asset management. Traditionally, issuers would maintain relationships exclusively with a core investment bank or more eclectically with a core group of banks (Eccles and Crane, 1988). With greater competition among underwriters in relation to indirect services, like analyst coverage and market making support, relationships have become more fluid.

Following the entry of commercial banks into the underwriting business, a new type of relationship was introduced, that of corporate lending. As noted above, an investment bank that is also a lender can accumulate information and become much more knowledgeable about the operations, and, hence, the quality of the loan client. This inside information can then be used to more credibly certify the value of a new issue by a loan client than if an independent underwriter manages the deal. However, the dual role of the commercial plus investment bank can create the perception of a conflict of interest when the proceeds of the issue are used to repay the bank loan.

Empirical research has shown that the certification advantage of combining lending with underwriting more than offsets the negative effects from the perception of a conflict of interest. The case in favor of the certification advantage is stronger in the issuance of lower quality debt where the lending bank is better placed to screen the risks of the issuers and certify the value of their debt issues. In other cases, when the perception of a conflict of interest has to be avoided, banks cede the role of lead manager to an investment bank without prior lending relationships with the issuer (Song, 2004). The evidence also shows that both prior lending and underwriting relationships can influence the choice of underwriter (Ljungqvist, Marston, and Wilhelm, 2006; Bharath, Dahiya, Saunders, and Srinivasan, 2007).

A more direct example of a joint deal to the same client is the concurrent provision of lending and underwriting services. That means the investment bank underwrites the firm's new issue and at the same time lends the issuer. These "pay for play" joint deals have grown from 1% of seasoned equity offerings in the early 1990s to 20% in the early 2000s (Drucker and Puri, 2005).

Syndicate Structure and Competition

While underwriting firms are fiercely competitive, at the same time, they work together in the flotation of new issues. They do so by forming syndicates which underwrite and place the new issues to the market. Each syndicate is formed at the initiative and discretion of the lead manager (the firm that has received the mandate) and includes one or more comanagers, the underwriting syndicate members and the selling group. The comanagers' role is to assist the lead manager in the preparation of the new issue and its pricing and marketing to investors. The managing group comprised of the lead manager and comanager(s) and the syndicate members bear responsibility for underwriting the issue (i.e., guarantee its proceeds) and placing the issue in the market. The selling group members are only responsible for the sale of the securities.

The reasons that support collaboration through syndicates are related to capacity constraints and risk bearing. Underwriting deals are executed in real-time and follow a job-shop production model (Eccles and Crane, 1988). Unlike tangible goods, underwriting services cannot be produced in advance and stored for later sale. Each underwriting deal is also unique in regards to the features of the product and servicing the particular client's needs. This means each deal may require a different set of skills, not all found in the lead manager's firm. Individually considered, investment banks have limited capacity, especially in human resources, to produce alone multiple deals at a time. Similarly, there are capacity limits in a single firm's ability to reach out to sufficient numbers of investors in order to place the new issue. Finally, large new issues can very well exceed the investment bank's capacity to bear the underwriting risk on the entire issue. The syndicate model is an efficient way to overcome these capacity constraints and meet the needs of the production model that applies to underwriting services.

Collaboration also creates mutually beneficial relationships among investment banks that increase deal flow and generate side benefits for other businesses within investment banks. In addition to the above benefits, issuers value syndicates for their role as monitors of the lead manager's commitment to fulfill the contractual obligations. Lead managers are compelled to perform as expected lest they lose future deals to comanagers. Since the composition of syndicate members is quite stable over time, the lead manager's reputation relies on how well they are perceived by the syndicate members through ongoing collaboration (Pichler and Wilhelm, 2001). Recognizing the benefits of strong and large syndicates, issuers have been willing to pay higher underwriting fees (Corwin and Schultz, 2005).

Participation in underwriting syndicates is very important to investment banks for building a name and eventually winning mandates from issuers. To this end, investment banks utilize various competitive advantages. In the 1970s, Merrill Lynch used its extensive retail brokerage business to enter syndicates at a time when wholesale firms had placement difficulties because of lack of interest from institutional investors. Salomon Brothers also used its prowess in bond valuation and trading to establish itself as a bulge bracket underwriter

Table 1.1 Four-Firm Concentration Ratios for Selected Underwriting Markets[a]

Panel A: US Markets				
Underwriting Market	**1985**	**1995**	**2005**	**2015**
US seasoned equity offerings	48.99	49.82	43.11	41.94
US initial public offerings	54.33	48.16	38.69	38.55
US investment grade bond offerings	67.12	53.34	42.20	42.72
US high-yield bond offerings	78.11	55.68	48.57	39.00
Panel B: Global Markets				
Underwriting Market	**2000**		**2005**	**2015**
Global seasoned equity offerings	48.75		35.72	32.90
Global initial public offerings	54.34		32.56	22.97
Global bond offerings	51.61		39.17	40.84

[a]The data for 1985 and 1995 are from the League Tables published by Investment Dealers' Digest. The data for 2000, 2005, and 2015 are from Bloomberg Professional terminal.

(Hayes, 1979). In other instances, investment banks use their strength in analyst quality and research to elevate themselves within syndicates.

Market Structure

The underwriting markets have always shown evidence of considerable concentration. Table 1.1 shows the four-firm concentration ratio (FFCR)[3] in the US underwriting markets for SEOs, IPOs, investment grade bond offerings and high-yield bond offerings in the years 1985, 1995, 2005, and 2015. Although concentration ratios have remained generally high, there is a clear pattern of declining concentration, especially after the repeal of the Glass–Steagall Act in 1999. The most dramatic decline has taken place in the underwriting markets for corporate debt. This can be directly attributed to the entry of commercial banks into these markets because of the relatively greater informational advantage they enjoyed over securities firms thanks to their lending relationships.

Panel B of Table 1.1 presents concentration ratios for global underwriting markets in SEOs, IPOs, and bond offerings. Since 2000, concentration has fallen dramatically in all three markets. The main reason is the entry of new firms from abroad, especially China, that rushed to take advantage of the growing volume of new issues in their own countries.

Table 1.2 lists underwriting firms that ranked top 10 by market share in the US underwriting markets for investment grade bond offers, SEOs, and IPOs in 1985, 1995, 2005, and 2015[4]. The year by year comparisons reveal that the top ranks of underwriting firms in the United

---

[3] In the case of underwriting markets, the four-firm concentration ratio is the ratio of the sum of the gross proceeds from a particular category of new issues (say, IPOs) produced by the top four underwriting firms to the total gross proceeds of all new issues in the same category (i.e., IPOs) in a given year.

[4] Firms are included in Table 1.2 if they ranked top 10 in any of the three markets for investment grade bond offers, seasoned equity offers and initial public offers. Hence, the annual lists may include more than 10 firms.

Table 1.2   Top Managers in US Investment Grade Bond, SEO, and IPO Markets[a]

1985	1995	2005	2015
Dean Witter	Alex Brown	Bank of America—B	BoFA Marrill Lynch—F
Dillon Reed	Bear Stearns	Citi—B	Citi—B
Drexel Burnham Lambert	Donaldson Lufkin Jenrette	Credit Suisse First Boston—F,B	Goldman Sachs
First Boston	First Tennessee Bank—B	Goldman Sachs	JP Morgan—B
Goldman Sachs	Goldman Sachs	JP Moran—B	Moran Stanley
Kidder Peabody	JP Moran—B	Lehman Brothers	Wells Fargo—B
Lazard Freres	Lehman Brothers	Merrill Lynch	Barclays—F,B
Lehman Brothers	Merrill Lynch	Morgan Stanley	Credit Suisse—F,B
Merrill Lynch	Montgomery Securities	Wachovia Corp.—B	Deutsche Bank—F,B
Morgan Stanley	Morgan Stanley	Deutsche Bank—F,B	HSBC—F,B
Paine Webber	Paine Webber	HSBC—F,B	RBC Capital Markets—F,B
Salomon Brothers	Salomon Brothers	UBS—F,B	
Daiwa Securities—F	Smith Barney		
Nikko Securities—F	Stephens		
Nomura Securities—F	First Boston—F,B		

The data for 1985 and 1995 are from the League Tables published by Investment Dealers' Digest. The data for 2005 and 2015 are from Bloomberg Professional terminal.
[a]Firms are listed in alphabetical order with foreign banks listed last. F denotes foreign firm; B denotes commercial bank.

States have been occupied quite steadily by the same firms. Top underwriters like Alex Brown, Donaldson Lufkin and Jenrette, First Boston, Salomon Brothers, and Smith Barney do not appear any more in the rankings but only because they have been acquired by large commercial banks, which used the market share of the acquired firms to climb to the top of the league tables.

Reasons for High Concentration

The principal reason for the relatively high concentration in the underwriting markets is the high cost of building the specialized resources needed for successful competition and the enduring value of these resources. Not only the requisite resources are costly to build but once they are in place, the outcomes they produce, like reputation and certification power, are long-lived.

First, underwriting thrives within multiservice organizations that support origination of mandates, quality execution in marketing, price discovery and placement, and the provision of valuable secondary market services, like market making and analyst coverage. Second, building networks of investors and issuers takes time and requires quality across the investment bank's business segments, not just in underwriting. Third, reputation takes time to develop, and once built, it becomes a formidable competitive advantage and barrier to entry because of the certification power it endows upon the investment bank. Though not negligible, the demand for capital is less important as a barrier to entry and as a factor that explains the high concentration in underwriting markets. The emergence of commercial banks in the top ranks of underwriting business through an acquisitive rather than organic growth strategy speaks to the importance of intangible barriers like reputation and relationship networks. Although commercial banks had heavy balance sheets, they opted to use them to acquire investment banking operations rather than build them de novo.

Factors Explaining Market Share

Despite the relative stability in the ranks of underwriting firms across time, there is considerable variability in the market share of individual firms. Dunbar (2000) finds that changes of market share in the gross proceeds of IPOs is primarily affected by industry specialization and secondarily by changes in analyst quality and underwriting spreads. Whereas narrow industry specialization and excessive underwriting fees impact market share negatively, improvement in analyst quality did not appear to have a significant positive effect on market share changes. This may be due to the sample period (1980s and early 1990s) when analyst coverage was not as strongly sought after by issuers as in subsequent years. Using a more recent sample, Clarke, Khorana, Patel, and Rau (2007) find that investment banks that raise the quality of their analysts gain additional market share in the IPO and SEO markets but not in the bond offerings market. This confirms the documented pursuit of aggressive analyst coverage by issuers in recent years.

Commercial Banks versus Securities Firms

Following their entry into the underwriting markets, commercial banks gradually started to raise their market share, especially in the market for debt offers. By 1999, the year the Glass–Steagall Act was repealed, the share of commercial banks was 19.52% in debt offers, 10.20% in SEOs, and 5.21% in IPOs. Following a string of acquisitions of securities firms, the commercial banks' share in the same markets had climbed to 43.09%, 30.37%, and 24.17%, respectively, by 2004 (Kim, Palia, and Saunders, 2008). As predicted, the commercial banks were most successful in capturing market share in the debt markets because of their lending relationships with many of those issuers and their superior credit analysis skills. The slower progress of commercial banks in the equity markets, especially IPOs, was due to the importance of superior skills in valuation and analyst coverage as well as secondary market operations possessed by securities firms.

The success of commercial banks in capturing market share in underwriting is shown in Table 1.2. In 1995, only two US commercial banks were ranked among the top 10 underwriters in investment grade bond offerings, SEOs and IPOs. These were J. P. Morgan and First Tennessee Bank. First Boston was also operating under the control of Credit Suisse (Switzerland) by that year. By 2015, all top 10 underwriters were commercial banks with the exception of Goldman Sachs and Morgan Stanley.

An interesting question is whether the market share gains of commercial banks were over and above what could be attributed to their acquisitions of securities firms. That is, was the market share of the acquiring bank, including the acquired securities firm(s), in the postacquisition year greater than the sum of the market shares of the combined firms in the year prior to the acquisition? Papaioannou (2011) finds evidence that, after adjusting for acquisition effects on market share, the mean market share of commercial banks in bond and equity underwriting markets during 2000−2004 was not significantly different than their mean market share in the years 1997−1999. This implies that commercial banks had increased their market share primarily by acquiring established underwriting firms from the securities industry.

Internationalization and Foreign Competition

The internationalization of underwriting services started with the birth of the Eurobond market in Europe in the 1960s (Hayes and Hubbard, 1990). It was further driven by the internationalization of US corporations that needed to raise capital abroad where their operations were located. Thus, by following their clients, US investment banks started to establish overseas operations in the large international financial centers, including London and Tokyo.

Starting in the mid-1980s, a wave of financial liberalization across Europe and Japan made it possible for US investment banks to find new opportunities in international markets. The growth of American Depositary Receipts that allow foreign companies to list their stocks and even raise capital in the US markets gave additional impetus to the internationalization of the underwriting business. Finally, the creation of a secondary market for privately placed securities (many of them by foreign entities) under Rule 144A in 1990 was another major boost to the international depth of the US underwriting markets. Another important development that facilitated the globalization of the underwriting industry was the eventual adoption of US underwriting methods like the fixed-price bookbuilt offering by foreign markets. This made the transfer and application of "technology" in the issuance of securities more efficient across international markets.

Although foreign banks in Europe and less so in Japan were free to operate in the investment banking area under the universal banking model, underdevelopment of capital markets and various restrictions had not given them the opportunity to develop skills in the primary and secondary markets similar to those of US firms. In addition, US investment banks were favored by the preeminence of the US dollar as an international currency, the strong demand of securities by domestic US investors and the presence of supporting services in the legal, accounting, and information technology fields (Hayes and Hubbard, 1990). This explains the early dominance of US investment banks in the global underwriting markets. Although Japanese securities firms were initially successful in dominating the Eurobond market in the 1980s, eventually their aggressive pricing damaged their profitability and forced them to retrench from both Europe and the United States.

Gradually, European banks first and Chinese banks later started to emerge as serious competitors of the US banks primarily in their home countries. The establishment of a more homogeneous new issues market across member states of the European Union (EU) gave European banks the space to expand their investment banking operations aggressively across national markets. Following the example of their US commercial bank rivals, European banks also used acquisitions to build their securities business in their local markets and in the United States.

Clearly, the big winners of the internationalization of the investment banking industry were the large universal banks. In the United Kingdom, one by one the old merchant (investment)

Table 1.3   Top Managers in Global Bond, SEO, and IPO Markets[a]

1987	1995	2005	2015
First Boston	Bear Stearns	Merrill Lynch—B	BoFA Merrill Lynch—B
Drexel Burnham Lambert	Donaldson Lufkin Jenrette	Citi—B	Citi—B
Goldman Sachs	Goldman Sachs	Goldman Sachs	Goldman Banks
Lehman Brothers	JP Morgan—B	JP Morgan—B	JP Morgan—B
Merrill Lynch	Lehman Brothers	Lehman Brothers	Moran Stanley
Morgan Stanley	Merrill Lynch	Moran Stanley	Wells Fargo—B
Salomon Brothers	Morgan Stanley	Barclays—F,B	Barclays—F,B
Daiwa Securities—F	Salomon Brothers	Credit Suisse First Boston—F,B	Credit Suisse—F,B
Nikko Securities—F	First Boston—F,B	Deutsche Bank—F,B	Deutsche Bank—F,B
Nomura Securities—F	SBC Warburg—F,B	HSBC—F,B	HSBC—F,B
		Nomura Securities—F	RBC Capital Markets—F,B
		UBS—F,B	UBS—F,B

The data for 1987 and 1995 are from the League Tables published by Investment Dealers' Digest. The data for 2005 and 2015 are from Bloomberg Professional terminal.
[a]Firms are listed in alphabetical order with foreign firms listed last. F denotes foreign firm; B denotes commercial bank.

banks were taken over by US and European investment and commercial banks. Thus, Schroders was bought by Citigroup; Smith Court by Merrill Lynch; Baring Brothers by ING (Holland); Cazenove by Chase; Morgan Grenfell by Deutsche Bank; and S. G. Warburg by SBC (Switzerland). Several US investment banks were also taken over by European universal banks. For example, Donaldson Lufkin Jenrette was acquired by Credit Suisse First Boston, Paine Webber by UBS (Switzerland), Dillon Reed by SBC (Switzerland), and Alex Brown was eventually absorbed into Deutsche Bank when the latter bought Bankers Trust.

Tables 1.2 and 1.3 offer a good glimpse into the competitive inroads foreign banks have made in the United States as well as the global underwriting markets[5]. As of 1995, there was only one foreign bank (i.e., First Boston controlled by Credit Suisse) listed among the top 10 underwriters in the United States underwriting markets for investment grade bond offers, SEOs and IPOs. In 2005, four foreign banks were among the top 10 underwriters in these markets. 10 years later, half of the top 10 underwriters were foreign banks (Table 1.2). In 1987, only three, all Japanese, firms were listed among the top underwriters in the global markets for bond and equity issues. By 2005, their number had climbed to six, the same number as in 2015 (Table 1.3).

It is interesting to note that the same US investment banks that dominated in the global markets in the 1980s were also dominant 30 years later but under different parent firm names. For example, Salomon Brothers was under Citi, Merrill Lynch under Bank of America, and First Boston under Credit Suisse. After the demise of Drexel and later Lehman Brothers and the retrenchment of Japanese securities firms, their market positions had been captured by the large European universal banks.

---

[5] Firms are included in Table 1.3 if they ranked top 10 in any of the three markets for global bond offers, global seasoned equity offers and global initial public offers. Therefore, the annual lists may include more than 10 firms.

The New Issues Markets

This chapter provides an overview of the new issues markets and the structure and operations of the secondary markets that facilitate the trading of securities. The goal is to familiarize the reader with concepts and terms that are used in the subsequent chapters.

Primary and Secondary Markets

Corporations and other entities (e.g., state and local authorities) raise capital through the issuing of new financial instruments, like equity and debt, which they sell to investors. This capital raising activity takes place in primary markets. Thus, the function of primary markets is to facilitate the issuance and selling of new securities. Previously issued securities are sold and bought by investors in secondary markets. The function of secondary markets is twofold: (1) to establish prices for newly issued and traded securities and (2) to enable investors to revise their portfolios and liquidate their holdings. Hence, secondary markets are an important complement of primary markets.

Public and Private Markets

Public markets refer to the issuance and trading of securities in open markets with no restriction to the number or type of investors. To ensure fair practices and informed trading, public markets require extensive disclosure of information and impose penalties for violations. Firms that issue or list securities for public trading must register with a capital markets authority [e.g., the Securities and Exchange Commission (SEC) in the United States] and comply with periodic information disclosure requirements. The advantages of public markets include continuous pricing of securities, ease of buying and selling, and the presence of large pools of investors. The disadvantages include costly information disclosure, compliance with various rules and procedures, and lack of flexibility in the design of securities.

Private markets allow the sale of new issues to limited numbers of investors or investors deemed knowledgeable or financially strong to bear the risks of trading under conditions of possibly less information and regulatory supervision. Private markets also impose restrictions in the resale of securities. The advantages of private markets include quick approval for sale, low cost of information disclosure, confidentiality of critical information, flexible design of securities to meet the needs of issuers and investors, ability to renegotiate the terms of the security (i.e., recontracting), and close monitoring of firm operations to ensure efficient utilization of capital. The disadvantages include lack of liquidity due to resale restrictions, infrequent pricing, and limited transparency of prices.

Underwriting Services and the New Issues Market. DOI: http://dx.doi.org/10.1016/B978-0-12-803282-4.00002-X

Depending on whether an issuer chooses to issue into the public or private market, the new issues are referred to as public or private offers or placements, respectively.

Equity and Debt Markets

Equity markets are those that refer to the market mechanisms that facilitate the issuance and trading of equities, i.e., stocks. Similarly, the debt markets refer to the issuance and trading of various debt instruments.

Equity Markets

The new issues market for raising equity capital are distinguished into the market for initial public offerings (IPOs) and the market for seasoned equity offerings (SEOs).

Initial public offering: An IPO refers to the initial sale of equity (stock) into the public market by a corporation that has no publicly traded equity. Following an IPO, the shares are traded in the secondary market where the stock has been listed.

Seasoned equity offering: A SEO refers to the issuance of additional shares of stock by corporations that have outstanding shares traded in public secondary markets. SEOs have the advantage that the issuer is an already publicly traded corporation which has a history of information disclosure and presence in the public markets.

Primary and secondary offerings: IPOs and SEOs can have a primary as well as a secondary portion. The shares issued as part of the primary offering increase the number of outstanding shares and the proceeds are paid to the firm. Thus, the proceeds increase the equity capital of the firm. The shares sold as part of the secondary offering belong to existing shareholders and raise proceeds that are paid to the selling shareholders. Thus, secondary offerings enable current shareholders to liquidate part of their equity holdings in the firm. Secondary offers can also be executed independently of a primary offering.

Bond Markets

The bond markets comprise a wide variety of debt instruments that can differ considerably with respect to various features. Below we define the most commonly used types of bonds.

Straight bonds: A straight bond pays a fixed rate of interest (the coupon interest) in fixed intervals (e.g., every 6 months) and a maturity payment (the maturity or face value) at some finite future point in time.

Zero-coupon bonds: A zero-coupon bond does not pay periodic interest but pays the face value at its maturity time. These bonds are issued at a price below the maturity value and the income on the bond consists of the difference between maturity value and issuance value.

Callable bonds: A callable bond gives the issuer the right to call back, that is buy back, the bond at a predetermined price. Callable bonds allow refinancing at a lower interest rate.
Convertible bonds: A convertible bond gives the investor the right to exchange the bond with a predetermined number of equity shares. Convertible bonds enable an investor to profit from the rise of the value of the stock.
Floating rate bonds: A floating rate bond allows the issuer to reset the coupon interest rate the bond pays in accordance with the fluctuation of a reference interest rate (e.g., the Treasury Bill rate).

Bonds are also classified by their risk level into investment grade bonds and noninvestment grade bonds depending on the rating they receive from rating agencies, like Moody's and Standard & Poor's (S&P).
Investment grade bonds: An investment grade bond has moderate to very low risk of defaulting on the interest and/or maturity value. In regards to bond ratings, investment grade bonds are those rated from AAA to BBB.
Noninvestment grade bonds: A noninvestment grade bond has a more than moderate to a very high likelihood of defaulting on the interest and/or maturity value. In rating terms, noninvestment grade bonds are those with a below BBB rating. Because of their relatively high risk, these bonds carry high interest rates or yields to maturity. For this reason, they are also referred to as "high-risk" or "high-yield" or even as "junk" bonds.

When an issuer issues a public bond for the first time this bond issue is called BIPO, i.e., bond initial public offering.

Negotiated and Competitive Offerings

New equity and debt issues can be placed in the market through a negotiated or competitive underwriting arrangement. In a negotiated offering, the issuer negotiates with several investment banks and chooses the underwriting firm that becomes responsible to organize the issuance and placement efforts. In a competitive offering, the issuer chooses the underwriting firm among those that bid to buy the new securities at the highest price.

Growth of US New Issues Markets

Table 2.1 presents the gross proceeds raised through underwriting in selected categories of new issues markets in the United States. The figures show the dramatic growth of the new debt issues markets during the last 15 years. The main reason is the very low interest rate environment that prevailed in the years following the financial crisis of 2008 and the Federal Reserve's aggressive monetary policy in order to stimulate the US economy. The new markets for IPOs and convertible securities, on the other hand, have not returned to their high levels of 2000, a year associated with the dot-com era that saw a frenzy of new equity issues by technology and especially internet-based firms.

Table 2.1   Total Gross Proceeds Raised in Selected US New Issues Markets and Years[a]

Security Type	2000	2005	2010	2015
US equity IPOs	61,095	36,405	38,153	33,325
US equity seasoned offerings (SEOs)	155,752	115,354	164,641	201,448
US domestic bonds	833,294	1,309,014	1,782,498	2,088,962
US corporate bonds	545,839	863,399	1,121,536	1,604,319
US investment grade corporate bonds	488,376	725,488	811,968	1,291,065
US high yield corporate bonds	39,672	94,265	275,963	274,919
US convertible bonds	46,297	29,338	22,931	19,394
Yankee bonds	250,682	510,967	810,734	950,413

[a]Gross proceeds are in millions of nominal US dollars. Data source is the Bloomberg Professional terminal.

Structure of Global New Issues Markets

Equity and debt securities can be issued in national, international, and supranational markets. The distinction is important because it prescribes the regulatory compliance that applies to new issues. The distinction also has implications for the scope of the issuance process and effort.

National Markets

The term national market for new issues refers to the issuance and placement of securities within the home country of the issuer. National market issues are placed with residents of the home country and are subject to the regulations of the country of issuance (e.g., the SEC in the United States). An example of a national market new equity issue is the IPO of a US firm for exclusive placement within the United States.

International Markets

The international markets for new equity and debt issues refer to new issues of securities which are sold to international pools of investors or are executed in a national market other than the national market of the issuer.

International New Equity Issues Markets

The following are examples of international equity issues:

Foreign equity issues: A foreign equity issue is the issuance of equity in a national market outside the home country of the issuer. Such issues are usually denominated in the currency of the national market within which they are placed. Such issues are subject to the regulations of the country of issuance. For example, a US firm, which is also listed on the London Stock Exchange (LSE), issues equity denominated in UK pounds for distribution in the United Kingdom.

American depository receipts: A special case of foreign equity issues is the American Depository Receipts (ADRs). ADRs are certificates that represent ownership on the shares of foreign firms. ADRs allow foreign firms to have their stocks traded in the national exchanges or the over-the-counter (OTC) market in the United States and also to raise capital through the placement of new ADRs in the US market. When a company issues equity for placement in various countries, through the use of depository receipts, the new securities are represented by Global Depository Receipts (GDRs) and are underwritten by international syndicates. To facilitate secondary market trading, GDRs are listed in several major national markets around the world.

Euro-equity issues: The term Euro-equity issue refers to equity issues denominated in a currency other than the one of the country of placement and simultaneously distributed in several national markets. Euro-equity issues are underwritten by international syndicates and are usually listed and traded in several markets outside the home country of the issuer. An example of a Euro-equity issue is the issuance of dollar-denominated new shares by a US firm for placement across countries of the European Union and/or in Asia.

International New Debt Issues Markets

International bond issues refer to bonds which are issued and traded outside the home of the issuer.

Foreign bonds: Foreign bonds are issued by foreign issuers in a foreign national market and are denominated in the currency of that market. Foreign bond issuance is regulated by the rules of the host national market. An example of a foreign bond is a bond denominated in US dollars issued by a German company in the United States. Foreign bonds bear distinct "street" names by which they are recognized as being traded in a particular country. Examples of foreign bonds are: Yankee bonds traded in the United States, Bulldog bonds traded in the United Kingdom, Samurai bonds traded in Japan, and Matador bonds traded in Spain.

Eurobonds: A Eurobond is a bond issued outside the home country of the issuer through an international syndicate and sold to investors residing in various countries. Eurobonds are usually denominated in a currency other than that of the country of placement. An example of a Eurobond is a bond denominated in US dollars issued by a US firm and placed in European and/or Asian countries. The Eurobond market is often referred to as a supranational market because Eurobonds are issued simultaneously by international syndicates of underwriters under loose regulation across many countries. Eurobonds are traded in various exchanges, but mostly in the LSE.

Growth of the Global New Issues Markets

Table 2.2 reports gross proceeds raised through underwriting in various new issues markets around the world. As in the case of the US new issues markets, the most rapid growth has been in the new issue markets for various types of debt. IPOs and SEOs have grown much

Table 2.2   Total Gross Proceeds Raised in Selected Global New Issues Markets and Years[a]

Security Type	Currency	2000	2005	2010	2015
Global bond offerings	USD	402,453	519,444	734,179	1,062,836
Global corporate bonds	USD	521,190	566,974	1,270,278	1,903,407
Global equity IPOs	USD	384,410	154,247	265,298	193,142
Global seasoned equity offerings (SEOs)	USD	609,038	443,138	710,162	631,489
International bonds	USD	1,351,849	2,742,572	3,627,822	3,607,578
European bonds	EUR	800,572	1,425,035	1,777,309	1,630,063
Euro currency bonds	EUR	601,134	1,065,167	1,288,576	1,258,639
Eastern European bonds	USD	5,780	55,108	107,463	57,047
Sterling bonds	GBP	60,189	85,586	89,217	93,477
EMEA equity IPO	USD	108,000	54,290	38,425	67,957
EMEA seasoned equity offerings (SEOs)	USD	205,538	159,151	121,451	193,686
Emerging market bonds	USD	118,971	292,047	720,068	1,241,457
African bonds	USD	3,228	6,870	24,792	27,901
Chinese equity IPO	CNY	41,919	3,835	483,301	155,983
Chinese seasoned equity offerings (SEOs)	CNY	51,222	18,281	517,075	798,860
Chinese corporate & debenture bonds	CNY	5,800	61,400	333,653	977,829
Japanese equity IPO	JPY	1,148,152	1,434,510	263,535	1,925,886
Japanese seasoned equity offerings (SEOs)	JPY	3,469,677	5,727,964	3,407,547	4,119,219
Latin American bonds	USD	49,778	77,552	122,636	104,778
Latin American seasoned equity offerings (SEOs)	USD	7,579	11,437	90,368	9,819

[a]Gross proceeds are reported in millions for each currency used and are nominal figures. EMEA: Europe, the Middle East and Africa. Data source is the Bloomberg Professional terminal.

less or not at all. Both Tables 2.1 and 2.2 provide evidence of the growing importance of new issues markets as mechanisms for raising capital and more particularly of the importance of new debt issues as a reliable and growth-oriented sector within the underwriting business.

Trading in the Secondary Markets

This section describes the trading mechanisms and intermediaries that facilitate the buying and selling of securities in secondary markets.

Trading Mechanics and Intermediaries

Depending how trading proceeds, secondary markets are classified into order-driven and quote-driven markets. In order-driven (auction) markets, prices are determined by the flow of orders to buy or sell securities. Transactions in order-driven markets take place between buyers and sellers of securities without dealers providing intermediation. Order-driven markets can operate as continuously order-driven markets or periodic call auction markets. In periodic call auction markets buy and sell orders are collected at predesignated times during a trading day, for example at the opening and closing, and all are executed at a marker-clearing price.

In quote-driven (dealer) markets, dealers stand ready to buy a security at their bid price quote and sell a security at their ask price quote. That is why they are referred to as market makers. Order-driven markets may also have intermediaries with the responsibility to act as market makers, who, in this case, are referred to as designated market makers (DMMs) or specialists.

Organized exchanges may operate as order-driven or quote-driven markets while all OTC markets are quote-driven (dealer) markets. Since almost all fixed-income securities (e.g., bonds) are traded OTC, they are traded in quote-driven markets.

Order Types

Investors may place orders with brokers or into electronic trading platforms. Brokers are intermediaries that simply execute orders submitted by their customers and brokerage firms. A market order is an order to buy or sell a security at the best prevailing price when the order reaches the market. A limit order is an order to transact at a specified (limit) price. While market orders provide for quick execution (immediacy), limit orders provide price selectivity since orders are executed if the limit price or a better one can be obtained. Outstanding limit orders are recorded in a limit order book that is maintained by DMMs or by the exchange for all market participants, in which case it is referred to as the central limit order book.

In electronic order-driven markets, a new market order is matched against other standing orders or against limit orders previously placed into the limit order book. In quote-driven markets a new market order is matched against the dealers' posted quotes.

Bid and Ask Prices

In quote-driven markets, bid price is the price at which a dealer is willing to buy a security while ask price is the price at which a dealer is willing to sell a security. The dealer's bid price is always lower than his/her ask or offer price so that the dealer can be compensated for "making the market," i.e., facilitating the trading among investors. The difference between the bid and ask prices is referred to as the bid−ask spread. Factors that determine the bid−ask spread include information asymmetry, inventory carrying costs, and dealer competition. Information asymmetry about the intrinsic value of a security increases the risk that the dealer's bid−ask spread is not aligned with the "true" price of the security. Dealers also bear the cost of financing their inventory of securities. Finally, the more dealers make a market in a security the smaller the spread is. In order-driven markets, the prevailing bid−ask spread is the difference between the lowest price among all existing limit sell orders (analogous to the dealer's ask) and the highest price among all existing limit buy orders (analogous to the dealer's bid).

The bid−ask spread is often used as a measure of liquidity of a security in the market. Lower spreads imply that buyers face lower ask prices and sellers face higher bid prices than otherwise. Therefore, narrow spreads encourage trading. Another measure of liquidity is the market depth with higher depth indicating more liquidity. Market depth (in the limit order book or in dealer quotes) refers to the existence of orders to buy and sell at many different prices that are away from the current price of a security. Furthermore, in more liquid markets larger quantities can be transacted at different prices. Therefore, larger market orders can be executed without significantly impacting the price level in more liquid markets.

New issues benefit from more liquid secondary markets because more investors are encouraged to trade at lower costs thus creating an active secondary market for the new securities.

Gray Markets

Within the context of primary markets, a "gray market" refers to the sale of securities that have not yet officially been issued by a firm. For this reason, gray markets are also referred to as "when issued" markets. Gray market prices serve as a good indicator of the demand for a new issue in the public market and help underwriters to more accurately price a new issue.

Main Secondary Markets Around the World

Structure of the US Securities Markets

Secondary public markets for the trading of stocks in the United States consists of national and regional security exchanges which are required to register with the SEC, alternative trading systems (ATSs) regulated by the SEC since 1998, and OTC markets. ATSs are venues for matching buy and sell orders of their subscribers for stocks listed on an exchange or for trading when national exchanges are closed, i.e., after-hours trading.

National Exchanges

The two major stock markets in the United States have been the New York Stock Exchange (NYSE) and the National Association of Securities Dealers Automated Quotation system (Nasdaq). The American Stock Exchange was the third major exchange until it was acquired by the NYSE in 2008. To be traded on a national exchange, a security must be listed on the exchange, provided it meets the listing requirement of the specific marketplace.

Ever since stock exchanges around the world abandoned their mutual ownership structures and became corporations, there have been numerous realignments of national exchanges within and across national markets. The NYSE, for example, currently operates under the Intercontinental Exchange (ICE)-NYSE that was formed from the merger of ICE with NYSE Euronext in 2013. The parent company of the NYSE had previously merged with Euronext that comprised three European exchanges, the Paris Bourse, the Brussels Exchange, and the Amsterdam Exchange.

The NYSE is a hybrid continuous order-driven market with periodic call auctions at the opening and closing of each trading day. Providing market liquidity in the NYSE is the responsibility of DMMs, called specialists. Each stock is assigned to one or more specialists who maintain bid and ask quotes. The specialists conduct the auction process by crossing investors' orders and maintaining a limit order book for their designated stocks. They are required to buy and sell their designated stocks for their own account in order to bridge temporary imbalances between sell and buy orders to ensure "orderly markets."

The Nasdaq, originally founded in 1971 by the National Association of Securities Dealers as an electronic OTC stock market, was spun off to become the Nasdaq National Market in 2000. Since 2006, the Nasdaq Stock Market is a nationally registered exchange for the trading of its listed stocks. After merging with OMX (which operates seven Nordic and Baltic stock exchanges in Europe), the Nasdaq Market became the Nasdaq OMX Group. The Boston Stock Exchange, the Philadelphia Stock Exchange, and the International Securities Exchange (bought from Deutsche Bank) are now also operated by the Nasdaq OMX Group which was recently renamed Nasdaq, Inc. The Nasdaq, Inc. operates the Nasdaq Stock Market LLC for the trading of Nasdaq listed securities and the Nasdaq BX, Inc. for the trading of securities on the Nasdaq, the NYSE, the NYSE MKT, and other regional exchanges.

The Nasdaq is a quote-driven market which also runs a call auction at the opening of trading in each day. The Nasdaq-approved dealers make markets in Nasdaq-listed stocks as they choose and are under no obligation to act as DMM for specific stocks. The Nasdaq Stock Market has three market tiers for listed securities: Nasdaq Global Select Market, for large-cap stocks that meet the most stringent initial listing standards; the Nasdaq Global Market, for mid-cap stocks that meet less stringent initial listing standards; and the Nasdaq Capital Markets, for small-cap stocks.

Regional Exchanges
Stock trading in the United States also takes place in smaller stock exchanges also known as regional exchanges including the Chicago Stock Exchange, Inc. and the National Stock Exchange, Inc. (formerly the Cincinnati Stock Exchange).

Alternative Trading Systems
The term alternative trading systems (ATS) refers to trading systems that include proprietary trading systems, broker-dealer trading systems, electronic communication networks (ECN), and crossing networks. ECNs provide their subscribers continuous, anonymous, and automated trading via a central limit order book. Crossing networks are trading systems that allow participants, usually institutional investors, to enter large buy and sell orders without specifying a price to be matched or "crossed" at specified times at prices derived from another market. Dark pools are public crossing networks where bid ask prices as well as quantities are not visible to investors before they place orders. In general, ECNs provide bid ask prices and quantities prior to order submissions and disclose price and quantity information on executed orders. Therefore, ECNs are also known as light pools or LIT markets.

Over-the-Counter Markets

The OTC Bulletin Board (OTCBB) is an electronic interdealer quotation system that is used by subscribing FINRA (Financial Industry Regulatory Authority) members to reflect market making interest in OTCBB-eligible securities (as defined by FINRA Rule 6530). The OTCBB displays real-time quotes, last-sale prices, and volume information for many OTC equity securities that are not listed on a national securities exchange. Under the OTCBB's eligibility rule, companies that decide to have their securities quoted on the OTCBB must file current financial reports with the SEC or with their banking or insurance regulators.

Table 2.3 presents the market capitalization of listed securities for selected national markets around the world.

Structure of the European Securities Markets

The London Stock Exchange

The LSE Group, formed when the London Stock Exchange acquired Italy's main stock exchange Borsa Italiana in 2007, operates three trading venues for its Main Market and its Alternative Investment Market (AIM). Stock Exchange Electronic Trading Service (SETS) is

Table 2.3 Selected National Markets Around the World and Market Capitalization of Listed Securities[a]

Europe		
Exchange	**Country**	**Listed Value**
London Stock Exchange	United Kingdom	3,272
Euronext	Europe	3,379
Deutsche Böerse	Germany	1,738
Nasdaq OMX Nordic Exchange	Scandina via	1,253
SIX Swiss Exchange	Switzerland	1,479
Asia Pacific		
Exchange	**Country**	**Listed Value**
Japan Exchange Group	Japan	4,910
Shanghai Stock Exchange	China	4,460
Shenzhen Stock Exchange	China	3,424
Hong Kong Exchanges & Clearing	Hong Kong	3,165
Korea Exchange	South Korea	1,265
Australian Securities Exchange	Australia	1,139
North America		
Exchange	**Country**	**Listed Value**
ICE-NYSE	USA	18,486
Nasdaq, Inc.	USA	7,449
TMX Group	Canada	11,697

[a]Listed values (market capitalization) are in billions of nominal US dollars. Data source is the World Federation of Exchanges monthly report-November 2015.

the LSE's premier electronic trading service that combines electronic order-driven trading with integrated market maker liquidity provision. SETSqx (SETS for quotes and crosses) is a trading service for less liquid securities than those traded on SETS. SETSqx combines a periodic electronic auction book with a standalone nonelectronic continuous quote-driven market making system. SEAQ (Stock Exchange Automated Quotation) is the LSE's nonelectronically executable quotation service that allows market makers to quote prices for its AIM securities, which are not traded on SETS or SETSqx, as well as for a number of fixed interest securities. The LSE Group also maintains a pan-European Trade Reporting service for the nonliquid securities in EU Regulated markets and SIX Swiss Exchange equities. The LSE also operates the International Order Book, a dedicated electronic market for trading in GDRs. The LSE Group markets provide listing and trading in equities, fixed-income as well as derivative instruments.

Euronext

Euronext is a pan-European market structured as an order-driven electronic market for trading in stocks listed across five European exchanges in Amsterdam, Brussels, Paris, Lisbon, and AlterNext (EnterNext). Euronext also serves as a trading venue for Electronic Traded Funds (ETFs), bonds, and derivative securities. Euronext N.V. operates the London International Financial Futures and Options Exchange. Alternext is a listing and trading venue for small and mid-class companies in the Eurozone, while EnterNext is specifically designed for listing and trading equity securities of small and medium-size enterprises.

The Deutsche Börse Group

The Deutsche Börse Group is a market for listing and trading equity securities as well as structured instruments. The Group consists of the Frankfurt Stock Exchange, the electronic trading platform Xetra, the Eurex Exchange for derivatives trading, the Eurex Clearing as well as the Clearstream clearing house. Similar to the NYSE, the trading structure of the Frankfurt Stock Exchange is a continuous order-driven market with specialist designations. The Xetra platform provides trading in equities, ETFs as well as exchange-traded commodities and notes. The equities trading in Xetra is structured as a hybrid continuous order-driven market with periodic call auctions at the opening and closing of each trading day.

Nasdaq OMX Nordic Exchange

The Nasdaq Nordic Exchange, formerly the Nasdaq OMX Nordic, is a subsidiary of the US-based Nasdaq, Inc. and operates exchanges in Denmark, Finland, Iceland, Sweden as well as in several Baltic countries. The Nasdaq Nordic is a market for listing and trading for all Nordic equities including the First North and QUOTE MTF, an alternative market. Across its exchanges, the Nasdaq Nordic offers trading in equities, derivatives, fixed income and ETFs. As its parent Nasdaq, it operates as a quote-driven market with a call auction at the opening of trading in each day.

Almost all other European markets are electronic hybrid continuous order-driven markets with periodic call auctions at the opening and closing of each trading day.

Structure of Asian Securities Markets

The Japan Exchange Group

The Japan Exchange Group was formed when the Tokyo Stock Exchange (TSE) and Osaka Securities Exchange (OSE) merged in 2013. The formerly known as JASDAQ Securities Exchange was acquired by the OSE in 2010. The TSE is the main secondary market for trading in equities, while the OSE is the trading venue for derivative instruments. In addition to equities, the TSE provides trading for fixed-income securities, ETFs, and Japanese Government Bonds. The TSE is a hybrid continuous order-driven market with periodic call auctions at the opening and closing of the morning and afternoon sessions.

The Shanghai and Shenzhen Stock Exchanges

The Shanghai Stock Exchange (SSE) provides listing and trading of stocks, ETFs, fixed-income and derivatives instruments in China. The Shenzhen Stock Exchanges (SZSE) is mainly for the trading in stocks of subsidiaries of state-owned enterprises. In addition to the Main Board Markets of the SSE and SZSE, the Small and Medium Enterprise Board facilitates trading in smaller cap stocks. In 2009, the SSE launched ChiNext a market for the listing and trading of "new economy" stocks.

The SSE and SZSE list and trade two types of shares. A-shares are denominated in the Chinese currency, the Renminbi, and trading was originally restricted to domestic investors. Since 2003, Qualified Foreign Institutional Investors are also allowed to trade with certain limitations on A-shares. B-shares are denominated in US dollars and were originally available for trading only to foreign investors; since 2001, domestic investors are also permitted to trade on B-shares. Both the SSE and SZSE are hybrid continuous order-driven markets with periodic call auctions at the opening and closing of the morning and afternoon sessions.

Hong Kong Exchanges and Clearing

The Hong Kong Exchanges and Clearing Limited (HKEx) operates the Stock Exchange of Hong Kong Limited (SEHK) and the Hong Kong Futures Exchange Limited as well as four clearing houses. The SEHK is a venue for listing and trading equity securities. The HKEx provides a market for trading depository receipts, debt instruments, ETFs as well as derivative securities. The SEHK is a hybrid continuous order-driven market with periodic call auctions at the opening and closing of each trading day.

Almost all other Asia-Pacific markets are electronic hybrid continuous order-driven markets with periodic call auctions at the opening and closing of each trading day.

3

Regulation of the New Issues Market in the United States

This chapter provides an overview of the regulation of the securities markets in the United States. The primary focus is on the regulation of the new issues (i.e., primary) markets and those aspects of secondary market regulation that are relevant to new issues. Familiarity with the regulatory framework is important because it affects the issuance process, and in turn, the risks and costs faced by issuers and underwriters.

Regulation of Primary and Secondary Markets

The main regulatory laws that govern the issuance of new securities (i.e., the primary market) and the trading of securities (i.e., the secondary markets) in the United States are, respectively, the Securities Act of 1933 and the Securities Exchange Act of 1934. The regulatory agency that oversees the enforcement of these laws is the Securities and Exchange Commission, commonly referred to as the SEC.

Regulation of the securities markets was not uniform across different states prior to the 1930s. In 1911, Kansas passed the first "blue sky"[1] law to regulate securities markets within its state borders. The law required the filing and granting of approval of a registration statement before the sale of new securities and imposed penalties for fraudulent practices. Other states followed with their own "blue sky" laws. The alleged abuses in the securities markets during the go-go years of the 1920s, and the large losses investors suffered in the Great Crash of 1929 finally influenced Congress to pass the securities acts and establish the SEC as a regulatory enforcer[2].

Since their original inception, the securities laws and regulations have undergone extensive rewriting and modernization in order to keep up with the evolution of financial markets and technology in securities trading.

The Securities and Exchange Commission

The SEC was established by the 1934 Act to function as an independent, bipartisan, quasi-judicial agency of the United States government. The main purpose of the SEC is to ensure that the sale of new securities to the public and the trading of securities in public markets are conducted with "full and fair" disclosure of information to investors. The intent is not necessarily to prevent speculative and risky securities from being issued and/

---

[1] The term "blue sky" comes from the practice of securities brokers to promise investors all but a "blue sky."

[2] The main sources of material on the history and features of US securities markets regulation is Skousen (1983) and Afterman (1995).

Underwriting Services and the New Issues Market. DOI: http://dx.doi.org/10.1016/B978-0-12-803282-4.00003-1

or traded, but to ensure that investors be provided with adequate and fair information so they can form their own opinions about the value of financial instruments. Besides overseeing compliance with the securities laws, the SEC also has the power to initiate litigation in cases of fraud and to impose penalties for violations of the laws and regulations under its authority.

The Securities Act of 1933

The purpose of the Securities Act of 1933 (hereafter referred to as the 1933 Act) is to regulate the issuance and placement of new securities in interstate offerings. An interstate offering is the sale of new securities to investors residing in multiple states within the United States. The 1933 Act has two objectives: (1) to provide investors with material financial and other information concerning securities offered for public sale and (2) to prohibit misrepresentation, deceit, and other fraudulent acts and practices in the sale of securities generally (whether or not they are required to be registered). The objectives of the 1933 Act are met through the registration requirement, restrictions on untimely sale and public communications, and the parties' obligation for due diligence.

The Registration of New Offerings

The cornerstone of the 1933 Act is the requirement that issues for public sale must be registered with the SEC. The SEC must confirm that the registration statement is complete and all required information has been disclosed in accordance with applicable laws and regulations. The SEC's approval is not an endorsement of the new issues.

Part I of the registration statement, also referred to as the prospectus, contains the basic information about the issue that allows investors to form an opinion about the value of the new issue. In general, it includes:

- The financial position of the firm over the past few years. This includes financial statements for the past 2 to 5 years depending on the regulation that applies to the firm. These statements, unless an exemption applies, must be audited and follow the US Generally Accepted Accounting Principles (GAAP).
- Background on the issuing organization, including its business lines, research and development, recent and impending acquisition activity, and any legal matters.
- How the proceeds of the issue will be used.
- Key management executives, their compensation and stockholdings.
- The particular features of the issue.

Part II of the registration statement contains supplementary and procedural data. The formal sale of the new securities is not permitted to commence before the SEC has examined the registration statement and granted its approval.

The 1933 Act exempts from registration several classes of offerings for which the registration costs would make public offering economically burdensome or information disclosure is less critical because of the sophistication of prospective investors.

Restrictions on Public Communications

To avoid aggressive promotion of new issues, which may not reflect accurate information and may unduly influence investors, the Act imposes restrictions on public communications around the period the new issue is under SEC review and is being offered to the public.

The prefiling period: This is the period between the time the firm decides to issue a new security and the time of filing the registration statement with the SEC. During this period, public references to a new issue which is about to be registered are restricted, and there should be no attempt to sell the new securities.

The waiting period: This is the period between the filing of the registration statement with the SEC and the time at which the registration statement becomes effective. A registration statement becomes effective when the SEC has completed its review and has approved the new issue for public sale. Once the SEC has approved the preliminary prospectus (also called "red herring"), the issuer (and the underwriter) may distribute it to investors and use it to market the pending offer of the new securities. New rules enacted in 2005 have allowed additional latitude in the use of communication means and content to supplement information contained in the prospectus. The new provisions apply mostly to large seasoned issuers that qualify as "well-known seasoned issuers" (WKSIs)[3]. The restrictions on public communications extent beyond the time of the formal offer (i.e., sale) of the new issue and together with the waiting period comprise the "quiet period." A recent rule adopted by the SEC and the Financial Industry Regulatory Authority (FINRA) has shortened the quiet period to 10 days after the offer day for initial public offerings (IPOs) and to 3 days for seasoned equity offerings. The significance of the postoffer quiet period is that analysts associated with the underwriting firm must abstain from releasing forecasts and recommendations about the newly issued security.

Due Diligence

Since the registration itself does not guarantee the accuracy of the registration statement, Section 11 of the 1933 Act establishes that the parties involved in the offering share an obligation for due diligence. The liable parties are: the issuing entity; the officers and directors of the issuer; the underwriters; and the independent accountants. Section 11 grants investors the right to recover, through the courts, any losses incurred as a result of false or misleading registered materials.

Most importantly, each of the parties is jointly and severally liable for a registration statement found to be defective. This means that aggrieved investors can sue any one party or all for indemnification of losses. By creating a shared responsibility, the law puts the parties in an adversarial relationship that compels each party to produce and submit all relevant information.

---

[3] Seasoned issuer is a firm that has issued public securities in the past and as a result reports periodically financial and other information to the SEC.

The Securities Exchange Act of 1934

The purpose of the Securities Exchange Act of 1934 (hereafter referred to as the 1934 Act) is to regulate securities trading in the secondary markets as well as the brokers and exchanges that facilitate the trading of securities. Its intent is to establish fair and honest practices in the trading of securities. This Act also established the SEC to police the securities markets and their participants.

The most consequential provision of the 1934 Act for the new issues market is the obligation of issuers that conduct public offerings to register with the SEC and submit periodic reports. These filings include annual financial reports, referred to as 10-K, and quarterly financial reports, referred to as 10-Q.

Reporting Firms and Registered Securities

A reporting firm is one that has registered with the SEC and has the obligation to file periodic reports, like 10-K and 10-Q, under the 1934 Act. The registration obligation arises when (1) a firm lists a class of securities (e.g., common stock) on a national exchange (e.g., New York Stock Exchange or Nasdaq Market); (2) a firm with total assets greater than $10 million has a class of securities with more than 500 holders; and (3) a firm has received SEC approval to sell new securities into the public market. Under the Jumpstart our Business Startups (JOBS) Act of 2012, the reporting requirement takes effect when the firm has at least 2,000 shareholders if less than 500 are nonaccredited investors.

The term "registered security" refers to a class of securities (e.g., stock or bonds) the firm has outstanding and has registered with the SEC. Registration of securities is mandatory for public placement and trading in public markets. It is possible for a firm to be a reporting firm and issue unregistered securities as in the case of a private placement.

A firm can voluntarily delist its securities from a national exchange and also seek deregistration of its securities under the 1934 Act. In general, deregistration is allowed if the number of shareholders of record falls below 300. For example, many small firms abandoned their public (reporting) status and "went dark" following the adoption of the Sarbanes–Oxley (SOX) Act in 2002 in order to avoid the cost of additional regulation.

Short Selling Restrictions

Regulation M of the 1934 Act (as amended by the SEC in 2007) makes it unlawful for a person to short-sell shares before a stock offering and then cover the short by purchasing the security from the underwriter or the dealers involved in the offering of the security. The restriction applies to short sales conducted within 5 business days before the offer day or within the period between the filing of the registration statement and the pricing of the issue, whichever is shorter. Short sales in these restricted periods are allowed if the short seller fully covers the short by purchasing the securities before the day of pricing. Selling shares short can depress their prices and thus force the sale of new equity at lower prices than otherwise possible. Assume, for example, the market share price is $20 and short sales push the price to $19.50. If the underwriter planned to offer the new shares at a discount of $0.50 from the last trading price, the offer price would be $19 per share compared to $19.50 without the short sale. By having to cover the short prior to the offer, the price can potentially recover to its previous level of $20 and allow the offer to be completed at $19.50.

There is no short-sale restriction on debt securities as they are less susceptible to price manipulation. Securities issues which are not conducted on a firm commitment basis are exempted from the short-sale restriction. In a firm commitment arrangement, the underwriter buys the securities from the issuer at a fixed price and offers them to the public at a higher fixed offer price.

State "Blue Sky" Laws

Securities issuers must also comply with the registration laws of the individual states in which the securities will be offered for sale. Thus, the registration statement filed with the SEC must be also filed with the appropriate state authorities. Similar to the federal laws, "blue sky" laws mandate that companies accurately disclose information to help investors make informed decisions.

State registration of federally registered securities is usually simplified under the rules of coordination and notification adopted by most states. Thus, under Federal law, states are not permitted to impose their own registration requirements on new securities listed on organized exchanges.

Registration with FINRA

A new offering cannot be completed without the "no objection" opinion by FINRA that the proposed underwriting and other terms and arrangements of the offer are fair and reasonable. The issuer is obliged to submit to FINRA the registration statement or offering memorandum in the case of private placements and the terms of the underwriting agreement between issuer and underwriter and the terms and agreements that apply to the working of the underwriting syndicate.

FINRA has significant influence in determining what is deemed to be a fair and reasonable compensation for the underwriting services delivered by investment banks. To ensure that issuance fees are set competitively, FINRA requires that fees fall within a range that meets industry guidelines and conforms to past practices. Both direct compensation in the form of a gross spread as well as indirect compensation, such as warrants, stock options and expense reimbursements come under the review of FINRA. To avoid collusion, FINRA does not publicize its benchmarks for underwriting compensation. It is recognized though that the underwriting compensation or gross spread (stated as a percentage of the dollar amount of the offering proceeds) can vary with the type of securities being offered, the amount of risk to be assumed by the syndicate members and the dollar amount of the offering proceeds.

Exempted from FINRA review are shelf registered issues offered on a continuous basis under Rule 415 and issues underwritten through a competitive bid as provided by the Public

Utility Holding Company Act. Prior to 2007, the FINRA review was conducted by its predecessor, the National Association of Securities Dealers[4].

Rule 415 and the Integrated Disclosure System

The Securities Act of 1933 stipulated that the registration statement of new securities offerings should include financial statements freshly produced for the purpose of the filing. The original intent for this requirement was to strengthen the price discovery process through the production of up-to-date financial information. In its effort to harmonize the disclosure requirements of the two Acts (of 1933 and 1934) and reduce the cost of raising new capital, the SEC took steps toward integrating the two disclosure systems.

The process started in 1967 when the SEC allowed qualified issuers with a current reporting status to incorporate information contained in SEC filings under the 1934 Act. This meant that financial statements in recent 1934 Act filings could be also included in the registration statement under the 1933 Act. Finally, the SEC adopted the three-tier integrated disclosure system (IDS) on a probationary basis in March 1982. The new system was permanently introduced in January 1983. Initially, the system introduced three levels of required forms: S-1, S-2, and S-3. The flexibility regarding the incorporation of information was least for S-1 filers (e.g., private firms going public) and greatest for S-3 filers (large, publicly held firms).

Concurrently with the three-tier system, the SEC also adopted Rule 415 or shelf registration that extended continuous issuance privileges to filers of Form S-3. Over the years, the SEC has enacted a series of rules that have simplified the disclosure requirements of issuers and has extended the benefits of IDS to smaller firms.

Features of the Integrated Disclosure System

The principal feature of the IDS is the harmonization of the information content required by the SEC under the Acts of 1933 and 1934. Two significant implications of this streamlining are (1) the periodic reports filed under the 1934 Act present information about the filer consistent in content with the information originally required by the 1933 Act and (2) information filed under the 1934 Act can be incorporated in the filings of the 1933 Act by reference. By reference means that the registration statement refers interested parties to already filed information (such as financial statements) the issuer has submitted under the 1934 Act. Thus, filing firms do not have to incur the direct and indirect costs of producing such materials anew.

The kind of information firms must disclose under both Acts can be found in Regulation S-X and Regulation S-K. Regulation S-X covers the form and content of financial statements included in forms filed under the Acts of 1933 and 1934. Regulation S-K covers textual (non-financial statement) information about the firm.

The Multitier System

The 2005 reforms of securities laws reduced the initial three-tier system to a two-tier system comprised of Forms S-1 and S-3.

[4] See www.FINRA.org.

Form S-1: This form is used by issuers who sell securities to the public for the first time (e.g., IPOs) as well as by issuers who sell securities in subsequent offerings but do not qualify for Form S-3. A Form S-1 filing requires that all company-specific information must be included in the prospectus. This information must be produced specifically for the occasion of the registration filing. Thus, issuers who have a filing record with the SEC cannot use statements recently filed under the Act of 1934 to satisfy the information disclosure requirement of the 1933 Act. Since 2005, the SEC has permitted reporting firms which are in good standing with their periodic disclosure requirements to file Form S-1 and incorporate information from recent reports by reference. Firms that file in relation to an IPO must use Form S-1 and submit all required information.

Form S-3: Originally, firms eligible to file Form S-3 were required to have a common stock float of at least $150 million. The float requirement was lowered to $75 million in April 1990. To qualify for Form S-3 the issuing firm must satisfy the following general registrant eligibility requirements:

- It has a class of securities registered with the SEC and is a reporting firm in good standing under the Act of 1934.
- It has filed in a timely manner the required reporting materials for at least 12 months prior to filing Form S-3.
- It has not defaulted on preferred dividends and debt or lease payments.

In 2008, the SEC enacted new rules that allowed firms to register with Form S-3 without regard to the $75 million float requirement in the following cases:

- The issuer has a class of common equity securities listed and registered on a national securities exchange.
- The issuer does not sell more than the equivalent of one-third of its public float of shares in primary offerings over the previous period of 12 calendar months.
- The offering is for investment-grade nonconvertible (debt) securities provided there is a rating by a nationally recognized rating agency.
- The issue is a secondary offering, i.e., the proceeds go to the selling security-holders and the firm is listed on a national exchange.
- The issue is completed through a rights offering.
- The issue refers to an offering of investment grade asset-backed securities.
- The issue is an offering of nonconvertible securities (other than common equity) and the issuer (1) has issued at least $1 billion of nonconvertible securities (other than common equity) over the prior 3 years; (2) has outstanding at least $750 million of nonconvertible securities (other than common equity) registered with the SEC; or (3) the issuer is a wholly owned subsidiary of a WKSI—as defined below.

Form S-3 filers must make all information incorporated by reference available to buyers of the offered securities at no cost.

To satisfy the additional information needs of the 1933 Act, both Forms, S-1 and S-3, require the inclusion of information about the offering itself, namely, the description of the security, the purpose of the proceeds, and the underwriting arrangements. Furthermore, both forms must include, whether by incorporation or by reference, balance sheets for each of the latest 2 years and income statements and cash flow statements for each of the three most recent years.

Shelf-Registration or Rule 415

Rule 415, titled "Delayed or Continuous Offering and Sale of Securities," was also adopted in 1982. It permits firms that qualify to register with Form S-3 to put registered securities on the "shelf" and offer them into the public market as they deem appropriate within a future period of time. Since 2005, the Rule permits firms to offer the registered securities within a 3-year period of the effective date of the original registration without obligation to reregister the offering.

The amount of shelf-registered securities an issuer can issue within a given year is limited in the case the issuer does not satisfy the public float requirement of $75 million. Securities must be offered via underwriter(s) acting as principals or agents; and underwriter(s) must be named in the prospectus that is distributed at the time of sale.

The Rationale for Adopting Rule 415

Adoption of Form S-3 and Rule 415 by the SEC was a practical outgrowth of the mounting evidence that securities markets are informationally efficient. Formally, the capital markets efficiency hypothesis states that securities prices reflect all available information (public and private). An implication of informational efficiency is that information contained in already published (financial and nonfinancial) statements becomes stale and of no use to investors. This is so because investors react promptly to any new piece of information. Hence, there is no more useful information to be extracted from past news releases or financial statements that could affect the current price of a security.

This view of capital markets leads to two important implications. First, the reproduction of recent filings under the 1934 Act is redundant; past information is not relevant for current prices. Second, the underwriter's price discovery skills are not unique vis-à-vis those of other investors. If information is uniformly available to all market participants, the underwriter should not possess any superior information advantage in pricing the firm's securities. As new information becomes available, investors revise their expectations and adjust the prices of securities accordingly. Notwithstanding the views in favor of the efficient capital markets hypothesis, the SEC adopted the more conservative approach and extended the privilege of shelf registration to large seasoned issuers that also met criteria for broad stock ownership.

Benefits of Rule 415 for Issuers

Rule 415 offers qualified reporting firms the opportunity to register and then offer their securities through a fast-track process. The Rule allows firms not only to make continuous offerings of the registered securities over a 3-year period, but, in addition, to change certain features of the securities without the obligation to refile. This flexibility as well as the simplified preparation and registration translate into significant cost savings for issuers.

Second, Form S-3 shortens the waiting period for the SEC review and the time it takes to declare the registration effective and the issue eligible for sale. Therefore, Rule 415 affords issuers the advantage to quickly bring new securities to the market when market conditions are favorable, meaning stock prices are high or interest rates are low.

Implications of Rule 415 for Underwriters

For underwriters, Rule 415 means greater competition, in the form of lower compensation, and a shorter time to exercise due diligence. The continuous offering pattern allowed by Rule 415 compels investment banks to be ready to take new issues "off the shelf" at a time chosen by the issuer. The time to engage in information search and price discovery is very restricted in this environment as the time to collect information is severely curtailed. Nonetheless, the underwriter is still liable for due diligence. The need to issue quickly into a continuous market has forced investment banks to adopt the "bought deal" method, that is, to buy the whole issue from the issuer and then try to sell it through their in-house distribution facilities or a quickly formed syndicate. The result is that distribution capacity and capabilities have become more important than marketing in managing shelf-registered issues.

Registration Exemptions and Simplifications

The original 1933 Act permitted issuers to offer new issues through a private placement without registration with the SEC. These offerings were permitted in the case the number of buying investors is limited or the investors are deemed sophisticated enough to pursue investments in new securities without relying on the publicly available information contained in the registration statements. Subsequent laws and regulations have expanded the permissible exemptions and simplifications for new issues.

The intent behind these registration exemptions and simplifications is to: (1) reduce the issuance costs of small issuers or small offerings and thus lower the cost of external financing; (2) increase smaller firms' access to broader pools of capital other than traditional lenders, like banks; and (3) facilitate the negotiation of better financing terms in the case of complex projects whose terms of financing cannot be easily standardized for the purpose of a public offering.

The implications are both positive and negative for issuers and investors. Issuers enjoy significant cost savings associated with the preparation and filing of forms. There is also a time advantage since there is no waiting period while the SEC staff reviews the statements filed for a public offering. Finally, a private placement can better suit firms which need to issue securities with complex features or when there is significant informational asymmetry between issuer and investors and more direct exchange of information (normally disallowed in a public offering) is needed to bridge the information gap. In other cases, the cost of disclosing and disseminating all relevant information to the market is inordinately high or undesirable to the issuer for business strategic reasons. The disadvantages of private offerings for issuers come in the form of (1) a limited investor base and (2) less market liquidity for the new securities.

Both of these limitations can have a negative effect on the valuation of the firm's securities and increase the required return (cost of capital) investors demand.

On the investor side, the benefits of privately placed issues mostly accrue to institutional investors, who dominate this market. They have the opportunity to buy securities with risk and yield characteristics not necessarily found in the public markets. The most common disadvantage comes in the form of the resale restrictions and, hence, the resultant loss of liquidity. However, the lack of marketability and the acceptance of unusual terms in certain private offerings is compensated by a higher yield than what could be expected from the purchase of securities in public offerings. Moreover, certain institutional investors (e.g., insurance firms) often have investment horizons that match the maturities of privately placed securities. Hence, the liquidity constraint is not binding.

The most important exemptions and simplifications in regard to registration requirements are set forth in Sections 4(2) and 4(6) of the 1933 Act and Regulations A and D of the same Act. The Small Business Investment Incentive Act of 1980 expanded registration exemptions to small business securities offerings. Further simplifications were adopted in the Small Business Initiatives of the SEC of 1992 and 1993[5].

Accredited and "Sophisticated" Investors

Exemptions and simplifications regarding the registration requirement often demand that buying investors meet the criteria of an accredited or sophisticated investor.

Accredited investors: The term applies to institutional investors (e.g., banks, insurance companies, pension plans), employee benefit plans, individuals with a minimum net worth or income, entities owned entirely by accredited investors, and directors, executive officers, or general partner of the issuer. An individual is currently deemed to be an accredited investor if annual income exceeds $200,000 and has a minimum net worth of $1 million.
Sophisticated investors: These are nonaccredited investors who along with their purchase representatives have enough knowledge and experience in financial and business matters to be capable to evaluate the merits and risks of the offered securities. The usual wealth and income criteria of "sophistication" include a net worth of $2.5 million or earnings in excess of $250,000 in the past 2 years. Accredited investors are considered to be "sophisticated."

Private Placement Exemptions

Section 4(2) Exemption
Section 4(2) of the Securities Act of 1933 exempts from registration "transactions by an issuer not involving any public offering." To qualify for this exemption, which is sometimes referred

---

[5] The section on private offers and resale restrictions draws from Blowers, Griffith, and Milan (1999) and SEC releases in www.sec.gov.

to as the "private placement" exemption, the purchasers of the securities must meet the criteria of a sophisticated investor and agree not to resell or distribute the securities to the public. They are entitled to be furnished with information normally provided in a prospectus for registered offerings. Such information is provided in the "offering memorandum."

Section 4(6) Exemption

Section 4(6) of the 1933 Act was adopted in 1980 and refers to the private placement of offerings not in excess of $5 million to an unrestricted number of purchasers provided they are all accredited. This type of offering is available to all issuers, who in addition have no explicit obligation to disclose information or to furnish specified financial statements. Issuers cannot engage in solicitation and advertising and, in addition, the offered securities have resale restrictions.

Regulation A Offerings

Regulation A (Reg A) applies to offerings of an amount not in excess of $5 million by a single issuer in any 12-month period. These offerings are available for sale to an unlimited number of accredited as well as nonaccredited investors even if the latter are not sophisticated. Entities eligible under Reg A are only US and Canadian companies which must not be reporting companies.

The offering must satisfy information disclosure requirements, including unaudited financial statements for the last 2 years prior to the offering. In addition, issuers of Reg A offerings are permitted to engage in solicitation and advertising in reference to the sale of the offered securities. Issuers are not obligated to report to the SEC following the public offering.

Buyers of Reg A offerings do not receive restricted securities, meaning they can resell them in the secondary market.

"Test the Waters" Provision

A small issuer, especially one filing for the first time, runs the risk the issue will not be well received by investors and thus fail despite a costly effort. The "testing the waters" provision permits Reg A issuers to get a sense of the investors' interest before they file the registration statement with the SEC. Specifically, issuers are allowed to conduct oral presentations and advertisements through newspapers and other forms of media. In this case, all materials used to "test the waters" must be filed with the SEC and are not exempted from the SEC's antifraud provisions. Moreover, the materials should avoid the solicitation of money before formal sale is allowed.

A company that finds the outcome of the "test the waters" efforts disappointing may not file any documents with the SEC and cancel its offering. In the opposite case, the firm must proceed with the filing of the required forms under Reg A. After such filing, the firm must discontinue its promotion of the offering, and allow 20 days to elapse from the last solicitation until the sale of the securities. If, after "testing the waters" a firm ascertains the potential for a larger offering than permitted under Reg A, the SEC, under certain conditions, can allow the firm to file a registration statement and disregard the use of "test the waters" materials. In such cases, 30 days must elapse from the last solicitation before the firm is allowed to file a new registration statement.

Regulation A+ Offerings

In March 2015, the SEC adopted Regulation A+ (Reg A+) that allows small investors (not necessarily accredited or sophisticated) to participate in equity offerings of up to $50 million by a single issuer within a 12-month period conducted under the less burdensome provisions of Reg A. Issues that raise more than $20 million (referred to as Tier 2) must have audited financial statements and submit annual and semiannual financial statements. Tier 2 issues are also subject to certain participation limits by nonaccredited investors. Importantly, the "test the waters" provision of Reg A applies to Reg A+ issues as well. The significance of the new rules is that they open up new investment opportunities to small investors and enable firms to raise new funds by tapping a much broader pool of capital suppliers.

Regulation D Offerings

Regulation D, adopted by the SEC in 1982, grants issuers exemption from the registration provisions of the 1933 Act for limited and unlimited amounts of new offers under specific conditions. The qualifications of offerings, terms and conditions are included in Rules 504, 505, and 506 of Regulation D.

Rule 504: It applies to offerings of up to $1 million in any 12-month period. The Rule is available to nonpublic as well as to reporting companies. Purchasers of such offerings are not limited by number or qualifications. The issuers are under no specific requirement to disclose information or to file or furnish specific financial statements. Issuers are not permitted to engage in general solicitation and advertising in relation to the sale of securities. Securities bought in Rule 504 offerings have resale restrictions.

Rule 505: The size of the offering should not exceed $5 million in any 12-month period, and the nonaccredited purchasers are limited to 35. Rule 505 may be used by both reporting and nonreporting firms. An unlimited number of accredited investors is allowed to participate in the purchase of Rule 505 offerings. Information disclosure to nonaccredited investors is necessary only if issuer discloses information to the accredited investors. Rule 505 prohibits the solicitation and advertising prior to sale and imposes resale restrictions.

Rule 506(b): Securities offered under Rule 506(b) have no offering size limit nor do they limit the number of accredited investors. However, the number of nonaccredited investors cannot exceed 35 and they must, in general, be sophisticated investors. Nonaccredited investors must be given disclosure documents similar to those used in a registered offering. Other information disclosed to accredited investors must be also shared with nonaccredited investors. The issuer must also refrain from general solicitation and advertising. Similarly, the resale of the offered securities is restricted.

Rule 506(c): Rule 506(c) was adopted as a result of the JOBS Act of 2012 and for the purpose to allow general solicitation and advertisement, provided all investors are accredited and the issuer has taken steps to verify accredited status.

Intrastate, State, and Federal Offerings

Offerings of securities to residents of a single state are exempted from the registration requirements of the 1933 Act. The criteria determining eligibility and compliance with this exemption are contained in Rule 147 adopted by the SEC in 1974. Rule 147 imposes no limit on the size of the offering or the number and qualifications of the purchasers, except that they must be residents of the state of the offering. Furthermore, there are no specified disclosure requirements or financial statements. Intrastate issuers are not prohibited from soliciting and advertising, but the offered securities cannot be resold without restrictions.

Offerings of securities by municipal authorities, states and the federal government are exempted from the registration requirements of the 1933 Act.

Resale Restrictions

Securities issued privately under various provisions [e.g., Section 4(2), Section 4(6), Regulation D] are subject to resale restrictions.

Resale restrictions are intended to disallow privately placed securities from entering the public markets without satisfying the public disclosure requirements of the 1933 and 1934 Acts. Such a practice would defy the intent of the law to make publicly traded securities subject to the requirement for fair and honest disclosure of information.

Rule 144 sets a holding period before resale is permitted and limits the quantity of securities that can be resold after the holding period expires. The amount allowed for resale in any 3-month period is generally the greater of 1% of the total securities outstanding or, if securities of the same class are traded, the average weekly reported volume during the most recent 4-week calendar period. In February 2008, the SEC shortened the holding periods and relaxed some other requirements. The rules distinguish between reporting and nonreporting firms and between nonaffiliated investors (i.e., other than firm directors, executives, owners) and affiliated investors (i.e., company insiders). Affiliated and nonaffiliated investors of reporting firms are subject to a holding period of 6 months but are free to resell 1 year after the offer. Some volume restrictions apply in the period of six to 12 months[6]. In the case of nonreporting firms, the holding period is 1 year and unlimited (limited) resale is permitted for nonaffiliated (affiliated) investors thereafter.

By shortening the mandatory holding period, especially for nonaffiliated sellers, the new rules improve the potential liquidity of privately placed offerings and thus help reduce the required rate of return (or cost of capital) for such securities.

Rule 144A: A Secondary Market for Privately Placed Securities

In 1990, the SEC amended the 1933 Act and adopted Rule 144A to address the lack of marketability in private offerings. The rule allows the operation of a secondary market for privately placed securities provided the market participants meet the criteria of a Qualified

---

[6] For example, nonaffiliated investors can resell if the firm continues to meet its reporting obligations, whereas affiliated investors are subject to volume limits.

Institutional Buyer (QIB). Investors that qualify as QIBs include asset management companies with a minimum size of assets under management (currently $100 million); banks and thrift institutions with a minimum size of capital (currently $25 million); and dealers with at least $10 million of capital (as of this writing).

Issuers that place new securities privately in the Rule 144A market have the right to declare upon issuance that the securities will be registered with the SEC (usually within 90 days of the issue date) and thus become eligible for public trading. To protect the existing secondary markets, Rule 144A is not available for the trading of already listed securities traded on exchanges or the over-the-counter (OTC) market.

By creating a secondary market for privately placed securities, the SEC increased the liquidity of this market, thus making it attractive to domestic and especially foreign issuers who need to raise capital in a timely fashion without the full disclosure requirements of public offerings. Enhanced liquidity can also help reduce the required rate of return of privately offered securities.

To streamline and stimulate secondary trading under Rule 144A, the Nasdaq has developed the PORTAL Market—an electronic, screen-based market for automated quotations, clearance, and settlement operations.

International Offerings by US Issuers

US issuers can offer securities abroad without SEC registration if they intend to sell the securities only to non-US citizens and they refrain from promotion and sale activities in the United States. According to Regulation S of the 1933 Act, US firms can conduct international offerings if the sale is completed through a so-called offshore transaction without an offer made to investors in the United States; and the issue is not promoted in the United States. To prevent Regulation S securities from flowing back into the US market without registration, the law imposes a holding (also called the distribution compliance) period before they are eligible for resale in the United States. In the case of equity securities, the holding period is 6 months for reporting firms and 1 year for nonreporting firms.

US issuers undertaking global offerings from within the United States must also register the tranche of the offering which is for placement and sale to investors residing in the United States.

Recent Laws and Regulations

Several laws enacted over the past 15 years have introduced significant new rules that affect the new issues market in the United States.

The Sarbanes–Oxley Act of 2002

The SOX Act of 2002, which was passed in the aftermath of the burst of the dot-com bubble of 2000 and the alleged abuses in the issuance and trading of securities, has implications for the new issues markets because it imposes new regulations on publicly traded firms. It requires the presence of independent directors on the audit committee, imposes internal control processes that must be certified by the Chief Executive Officer and Chief Operating Officer of the firm (with serious penalties in case of violation) and prohibits conflicts of interest between the firm and its auditors. It also established the Public Company Accounting Oversight Board (PCAOB) to oversee the conduct of public auditing of firms and reduce incidents of conflicts of interest in auditing firms that can be harmful to investors. Firms going public via an IPO must comply with the SOX provisions and have internal controls in place at least 1 year in advance. Although SOX has raised the cost of being a public firm it has also improved the quality and transparency of firm information. Since firms that go public are relatively unknown, the additional care with which executives must approach financial and internal control systems and disclosure should have a beneficial effect on both the quality of disclosed information and the corporate governance of firms. If this is so, then the valuation and pricing of new issues should have become more efficient. One academic study reports evidence that IPOs executed after SOX have lower degree of underpricing (i.e., lower discount from first-day market prices) and higher returns in the first postissue year (Johnston and Madura, 2009).

The Securities Offerings Reforms of 2005

In July 2005, the SEC introduced several Releases as part of a comprehensive securities offering reform initiative. These Releases relax the regulation of the flow of information on behalf of the issuer and the securities offered so that the timing, scope and methods of communicating information are in step with recent innovations in information technology and enable issuers to provide more timely and relevant information to investors. Among other provisions, the new Releases:

- Amended the Rules regarding the quiet period (when release of information outside of what is included in the prospectus is not allowed) by permitting more information dissemination prior, during and after the registration period.
- Provided definitions of graphic and written communications that allow the conduct of live roadshows and contacts with investors by electronic and other means without the restrictions that govern the statutory registration statements.
- Created a new type of issuers, the WKSI who enjoy increased privileges with respect to information dissemination and the acceleration of their registration approval for new issues. WKSIs are seasoned firms (i.e., have outstanding publicly traded securities) which are eligible to use Form S-3 (if domestic) or Form F-3 (if foreign). In addition, they must have either a minimum equity capitalization of $700 million (not held by affiliates) or must have issued in the last 3 years at least $1 billion of nonconvertible securities, other than common stock.

The JOBS Act of 2012

The Jumpstart Our Business Startups (JOBS) Act enacted in April 2012 relaxed several provisions of the securities laws for the purpose of facilitating the raising of capital by small to mid-size issuers. Below are the most important provisions of the JOBS Act:

- It recognizes a new type of firms that can qualify as Emerging Growth Companies (EGCs). EGC is a firm with less than $1 billion of revenues during its most recent fiscal year. A firm that qualifies as EGC enjoys relief from several previous requirements, including:
  - Disclosure of financial statements for two instead the customary 3 years prior to the IPO.
  - Confidential treatment of information submitted to the SEC prior to the IPO. This relieves the firm from releasing information that may be useful to competitors or information about accounting and other irregularities before the firm has time to rectify them.
  - No obligation to have an auditor attest its compliance with the SOX Section 404(b) regarding internal controls.
  - Exemption from regulation regarding auditor rotation and changes in auditor reporting as promulgated under PCAOB regulations.
  - More limited executive compensation disclosure.
  - Permission to "test the waters" by initiating contacts with prospective investors to gauge demand for the issue.
- Small firms may raise up to $50 million (up from $5 million) under Regulation A + .
- The obligation to register with the SEC now applies to firms with 2,000 shareholders of record provided less than 500 of them are nonaccredited investors. These counts exclude "crowdfunding" investors and firm employees who receive shares under a compensation plan.
- Banks and bank holding companies must register with the SEC if they have 2,000 (instead of 500) shareholders of record and may seek deregistration if they have 1,200 shareholders instead of only 300 before.

A recent study has found evidence that the JOBS Act has contributed to a surge of IPOs in the United States mostly fueled by biotech and pharma firms which have more to risk by disclosing proprietary and strategic information. The main motivation is the relaxed rules of filing than the lower costs (Dambra, Field, and Gustafson, 2015).

Crowdfunding

The JOBS Act required the SEC to develop new rules permitting capital raising by "crowdfunding." Crowdfunding is a means to raise money by attracting relatively small individual contributions from a large number of investors. In October 2015, the SEC adopted final rules governing crowdfunding. The rules allow a nonreporting firm to issue up to $1 million of new stock within a 12-month period through crowdfunding. Issuers are required to release the terms of the offer and financial information. In addition, investors are limited in the amount they may invest in each offering ($2,000 or 5% of the lesser of annual income or net worth if either is less than $100,000 and 10% of the lesser if both are equal or exceed $100,000). An issuer may not allow an investor to invest more than $100,000 in crowdfunding offerings.

Regulation of Offerings by Foreign Issuers

The regulation of foreign issues sold and traded in the US securities markets is also covered by the 1933 and 1934 Acts. The regulations define a firm as a foreign private issuer (FPI) if less than 50% of its outstanding voting stock is held by US residents. Otherwise other conditions must apply. A firm that qualifies as a FPI is subject to the same registration and disclosure requirements as domestic US entities. An FPI must register its US public offering under the 1933 Act and become a reporting entity under the 1934 Act. Any security offered globally, including the United States, must be registered under the 1933 Act before it is sold to investors in the United States.

The IDS also applies to foreign issuers and the applicable forms are known as F-1 and F-3. (Form F-2 like its domestic counterpart Form S-2 has been discontinued.) Form F-1 applies to foreign entities which are first-time issuers in the United States. As of 2005, F-1 filers, which are reporting firms in good standing, may incorporate information filed for periodic reporting purposes by reference. Originally, the SEC set a minimum public (worldwide) float of $300 million as a condition for Form F-3. This minimum was reduced to $75 million in 1994. As of 2008, the SEC allows foreign issuers that qualify for Form F-3 to bypass the minimum public float limit of $75 million if the class of securities to be offered is listed and registered on a national securities exchange and they do not sell more than the equivalent of one-third of their public float over 12 calendar months. An FPI that qualifies as a WKSI can use Form F-3 for its securities offering and enjoys automatic effectiveness of its registration statement.

FPIs that qualify as "emerging growth firms" under the JOBS Act enjoy benefits similar to those granted to domestic US firms.

Compliance with US Accounting Standards

Prior to 2008, the SEC required that FPIs submit financial statements prepared in accordance with the GAAP or be reconciled with GAAP. Since 2008, the SEC has allowed FPIs to submit financial statements prepared in accordance with International Financial Reporting Standards (IFRS) issued by the International Accounting Standards Board. Acceptance of the international accounting standards was precipitated by the global competition among securities exchanges for listing and the risk of the US capital markets losing ground to foreign exchanges. Furthermore, US investors are presumed to be familiar with foreign securities by following them in their home markets and they are better protected if these foreign securities are traded in the United States where additional information must become available.

Rights offerings of foreign firms are allowed in the United States by filing with the SEC the same documents as those required by the home country and without reconciliation with GAAP.

Private Offerings by Foreign Issuers

Foreign issuers that decline to comply with IFRS or GAAP can offer their securities in the United States through a private placement. Most frequently used are provisions in the 1933 Act Sections 4(a)(2) or Regulation D. The same resale restrictions applicable to domestic US issues also apply to foreign private issues. Since its introduction in 1990, the Rule 144A market has become the market of choice for the private placement of foreign issues.

Depository Receipts

A foreign firm may choose to register its original shares on its home market or in a foreign market. A firm with a home market listing can also crosslist its shares on a foreign market through an instrument called Depository Receipt. Depository Receipts represent ownership claims on shares of a foreign stock, which serve as the underlying asset. When Depository Receipts are created to be issued and traded in multiple national markets, they are called Global Depository Receipts. Depository Receipts used to list foreign shares in the United States are called American Depository Receipts (ADRs).

ADRs may be sponsored or unsponsored. A sponsored ADR requires the consent of the foreign firm and a US depositary bank (like the Bank of New York Mellon) to serve as custodian. The depositary institution provides safekeeping of the underlying shares, record keeping, distribution of dividends and other services. An unsponsored ADR is created by a broker/dealer, like Morgan Stanley, without consent of the foreign firm and usually for the purpose of establishing a market for the trading of the foreign shares in the United States through the vehicle of an ADR. Unsponsored ADRs trade in the OTC market only.

There are three levels of ADRs. Level 1 ADRs are accorded only trading privileges and are quoted on the OTC market. They must be registered with the SEC but have no reporting requirements. Level 2 ADRs allow the foreign firm to list and trade its shares on a national stock exchange. They must be registered upon creation and use Form 20-F for periodic reporting. Finally, Level 3 ADRs are used by foreign firms to list and trade their shares on a US national exchange and, in addition, can be used to raise new equity capital by selling ADRs formed from newly issued shares. Level 3 ADRs bear the same registration and reporting requirements as those required of Level 2 ADRs.

Registration and Deregistration of Foreign Firms

Like domestic US firms, a foreign firm comes under the registration and reporting obligations of the 1934 Act (1) when it lists its securities on a national exchange; (2) when a class of its securities is held by more than 300 holders and the security has more than 500 holders worldwide or the firm's assets exceed $10 million; (3) when the foreign firm has a public securities offer approved by the SEC. Previous rules allowed a foreign firm to deregister a class of securities if the number of security-holders fell below 300 US residents. To meet this condition the foreign firm had to undertake the rather arduous task of determining the identity of the individual security-holders of record[7]. In 2007, the SEC approved Rule 12h-6 which allows a foreign company to deregister a class of equity securities, and thus terminate its reporting obligations, if the average daily trading volume in the United States is no greater than 5% of the worldwide average daily trading volume of the security during a recent 12-month period. A foreign firm can delist its securities from the US market where it is traded, but it remains a reporting company as long as the deregistration conditions are not met. Moreover, Rule 12h-6 requires that after deregistration the foreign firm that delists its equity securities in the United States has maintained a listing on at least one foreign exchange that serves as the primary trading market for the issuer's securities (Fernandes, Lel, and Miller, 2010).

---

[7] This counting approach is different from the one that applies to US domestic firms. In the latter case, the firm can count the number of institutions that hold the securities instead of the individual investors who are the beneficiary holders.

4

The Mechanics of the Issuance Process

This chapter describes the mechanics of the issuance process under a fully underwritten arrangement, in which the underwriter is delegated the tasks of preparing and registering the issue, organizing the syndicate, pricing and marketing, and finally placing the new issue. The issuance process is described within the framework of the bookbuilding method practiced in the United States.

Preparation and Registration

The issuance process starts with the issuer conducting a search for an underwriter. This is done in the so-called bake-off meetings with prospective underwriters. The issuer eventually selects an underwriting firm that meets the goals and needs of the issuer with respect to the new issue. Issuers may also consider their needs for future underwriting and corporate finance advisory services in selecting an investment bank[1].

Preunderwriting Conferences

The origination phase begins with preliminary meetings between top officers of the issuer and the investment bank. The object of these contacts is to discuss and assess the financial situation of the issuing firm and its funding needs and to form some preliminary views about the type of security to be issued, tentative terms and size of the issue, and the likely price range. Other topics of interest include the composition of the syndicate, issuer suggestions for comanagers, the type of underwriting contract and the underwriter compensation. The issuer would be also interested in discussing the underwriter's role in the aftermarket in relation, for example, to price support, market making, and analyst coverage. These preunderwriting conferences end with the signing of the letter of intent which provides the underwriter with assurance the issuer will proceed with the issuance and retain the investment bank as the underwriter of the issue. Many of the terms agreed in the preliminary conferences are also included in the letter of intent.

The Underwriting Agreement

The underwriting agreement includes all the terms of the offering: the type of security to be issued; the quantity of the issue offered (e.g., number of shares or bonds); the terms of the

---

[1] The criteria issuers use to select the underwriter are discussed in detail in Chapter 16: New Issue Decisions: The Underwriter, Syndicate, Auditor, and Legal Counsel.

Underwriting Services and the New Issues Market. DOI: http://dx.doi.org/10.1016/B978-0-12-803282-4.00004-3

underwriting contract, including underwriting compensation; the preliminary range of prices at which the new securities will be offered to investors; and the expected proceeds of the issue. However, the underwriting agreement does not include the final offer price. The underwriting agreement becomes final and it is signed when the offer price is inserted in the agreement followed by notification of the SEC. The terms of the underwriting agreement can be modified during the preoffering period. An escape clause allows the issuer and the underwriter, under certain conditions, to exit the agreement and, thus, cancel the offering.

The Underwriter's Investigation

Once the letter of intent has been signed, the underwriter undertakes a thorough investigation of the issuer's business and financial condition. The purpose of the investigation is two-fold: (1) to satisfy the SEC requirement for "due diligence" and (2) to enable the underwriter to form an opinion about the fair value of the securities to be issued. The underwriter's investigation is critical to the price discovery service provided by the underwriter. The physical plant, production facilities, and other assets are checked to determine their economic value as well as their legal status with respect to ownership titles, liens, and any pending legal claims. Business accounts are checked to ensure they provide a fairly accurate picture of the firm's assets, liabilities, and economic results. Compliance with accounting principles is done independently by the auditing firm.

The investigation allows the underwriter to have extensive exchanges with key executives of the firm and become privy of business information otherwise undisclosed to the public. This information includes the business strategies and plans of the firm, retention prospects of key executives and employees, potential risks (both business and legal), and the firm's assessment of competitive threats.

The SEC Registration

With assistance from the legal counsel, the underwriter collects and organizes all the pertinent information that must be disclosed in the registration statement. The nature and amount of disclosure depends on whether the issue must be registered as a traditional or as a Rule 415 (shelf) registration issue. As discussed in Chapter 3: Regulation of the New Issues Market in the United States, a traditional registration (Form S-1) filing requires that all financial statements are produced afresh, whereas a shelf-registration (Form S-3) filing allows such statements to be incorporated by reference. The registration statement includes information that covers the following:

- The financial position of the firm over the last few years.
- Background on the issuing firm, including its business lines, research and development, recent and impending acquisition activity, and any legal matters.
- Planned uses of the proceeds of the issue (e.g., for working capital, to repay debt, etc.).
- Key management executives and their stockholdings.
- The particular features and arrangement of the offering.

The above material comprises the basic information of the registration statement that is known as the prospectus. It is the principal source of information that investors use to assess the value of the offered securities. The prospectus also serves as a marketing document used to promote the new issue.

The SEC Review

The SEC review usually results in the issuance of comments and requests for additional information. This requires amending and refiling the registration statement—sometimes more than once. Concurrent with the SEC's review, the offering documents are reviewed by FINRA (Financial Industry Regulatory Authority) to ensure compliance with FINRA's rules regarding the application of fair practices with respect to the underwriter's compensation and placement of the new issue.

When the SEC has determined that its comments have been satisfied and has been informed that FINRA has no objections, the SEC declares the registration statement ready to become effective. Effectiveness occurs when the final offer price is inserted in the prospectus. At that point, the sale to the public can commence.

Since December 2005, the registration statement and posteffective date amendments filed by "well-known seasoned issuers" (WKSIs) become effective automatically.

The Comfort Letter

Financial statements submitted as part of the SEC registration must be audited and signed by independent accountants. However, during the preoffering period (until the registration becomes effective), there may be business events that result in updated financial statements. Although not mandated by the SEC, the underwriter requests the independent auditor to furnish a "comfort letter" which gives the underwriter and legal counsel negative assurance, that is, assurance the interim statements are in good order. The comfort letter serves as additional evidence the underwriter has discharged the duty of due diligence.

Legal Counsel

The issuer and underwriter retain a law firm that specializes in securities issuance to vet the narrative part of the registration for adequate disclosure and ensure compliance with SEC regulations. The legal counsel is liable under the "due diligence" rules of Section 11 (of the 1933 Act) but is held responsible to a lesser standard than the underwriter and auditor.

Listing of the New Securities

Stocks offered to the public market for the first time through an IPO must be listed with a secondary market, like the NYSE or Nasdaq. This is necessary to ensure that there will be a marketplace for the public trading of the stock. The choice of the market venue takes into consideration various factors (e.g., listing expenses, trading costs, favorable valuation environment) as well as whether the issuing firm satisfies the initial listing standards of the marketplace. In some cases, new bonds are also listed on an organized exchange, otherwise they are expected to trade in the over-the-counter market.

State Registration of New Securities Offers

New securities offerings must also be registered under the "blue sky" laws of the states where they will be distributed. Harmonization of state registration requirements with those of the federal laws eliminates redundant duplication of registration materials.

Approval of the Registration Statement

When the SEC staff has determined that the registration statement complies with the law's disclosure and filing requirements, the issuer submits the final offer price through a pricing amendment. In the pricing amendment, the issuer requests acceleration of the effective date. Otherwise, the SEC can initiate the 20-day waiting period. Obviously, the economic reason for an immediate declaration of effectiveness is to minimize the risk of an adverse market movement after the underwriter and the issuer have been locked into a fixed offer price. For initial public offerings, it is estimated that it takes about 20 weeks for a new issue to reach the point of placement after the decision to issue has been made. Once the registration statement becomes effective, the sale of the securities can commence. (Appendix A presents a typical timeline for an IPO.)

Public Communications

The issuer and underwriter must adhere to the restrictions that apply to public communications during the so-called quiet period. During this period, the content of public pronouncements must be consistent with the information supplied through the prospectus.

Since 2005, issuers have been allowed to use additional written communications under the provisions of the "free writing prospectus" and social media to disseminate information. The use of the "free writing prospectus" is more restricted in the case of IPOs and small reporting issuers than in the case of reporting issuers and WKSIs that are eligible for registration Forms S-3 and F-3, especially in relation to forward-looking information, such as earnings projections.

During the quiet period, the issuer can release information related to the normal course of business, especially if it is a firm reporting to the SEC under the 1934 Act. Announcements of material corporate developments related to the issue may trigger though the need to amend the registration statement or "sticker" the final prospectus after the issue has become effective. Accordingly, the firm and the underwriter must be careful not to "jump the gun" by making impermissible statements. A famous case of "jumping the gun" during the quiet period is that of Google, when its founders gave an interview to Playboy magazine before the registration became effective in August 2004. Although this could have led to a refiling, the offer was allowed to proceed.

Organizing the Underwriting Syndicate

A major function of the underwriter is to guarantee the placement of the issue so that the issuer receives the planned proceeds. To this end, lead underwriters organize syndicates that bear the risk of placement and organize the distribution of securities to investors.

The Underwriting Syndicate

The underwriting syndicate is put in place by the lead manager of the issue. It is comprised of

- the managing group,
- the underwriting group, and
- the selling group.

The Managing Group

It consists of the lead or book-running manager and the comanager(s). The lead manager is the originating underwriter who also puts together the book of informal orders reflected in the expressions of buying interest gathered by syndicate members. With or without input from the issuer, the lead manager may invite other investment banks to serve as comanagers. The role and importance of comanagers has grown over the years. The average number of comanagers has increased from 1.38 per IPO issue in 1981 to over 4 in 2001–2006 (Dong, Michel, and Pandes, 2011). The number of comanagers increases with the size, complexity, and riskiness of the new issue (Corwin and Schultz, 2005).

Issuers benefit from more comanagers through greater publicity and promotion of the issue, greater price discovery effort as well as additional market making and analyst coverage in the aftermarket. Comanagers also contribute to service enhancement because they have an incentive to monitor the performance of the lead manager in order to protect their reputation and interests (Davidson, Xie, and Xu, 2006). There is evidence that comanagers add to the credibility of new issues resulting in higher offer prices and enhance their liquidity in the aftermarket by keeping trading costs (i.e., the bid-ask spread) lower than otherwise (Popescu and Xu, 2011).

The Underwriting Group

This group comprises the syndicate members which, along with the lead manager and comanager(s), share the underwriting risk and the responsibility to sell the issue to investors. The syndicate members are chosen based on their strengths in price discovery, industry specialization, analyst quality, and placement capabilities. Syndicate members are also chosen based on how well they complement the skills and strengths of other syndicate members to serve the needs of a particular issue. For example, when the underwriter is a wholesale investment bank with limited retail capacity, inviting retail securities firms to the syndicate is important for the widespread placement of a new equity issue. Or a lead manager, strong in domestic markets, may invite investment banks with extensive presence in foreign markets in the case of an international offering. Syndicate formation is also influenced by practices of reciprocity whereby members of the syndicate are expected to invite the lead manager to join in future syndicates they organize. Following the entry of commercial banks in the underwriting business (which was first permitted for bond offers in 1989), a new form, that of the "hybrid" syndicate, has emerged in which a commercial bank assumes the role of comanager and invites a firm without lending ties to the issuer to serve as lead manager to avoid conflicts of interest when the issuer is a loan client of the bank (Narayanan, Rangan, and Rangan, 2004; Song, 2004).

The Selling Group

The selling group comprises the members of the underwriting group (including the lead manager and comanagers) as well as other retail brokers/dealers—the latter usually drawn from regional markets. Whereas members of the underwriting group are responsible for both underwriting and placing (selling) the new issue, the selling brokers/dealers are responsible only for placing the issue with investors. Therefore, the selling brokers/dealers are not responsible for any unsold securities. The strength and diversity of the selling group depends on the size of the issue and the need for more or less broad distribution.

Responsibilities of the Syndicate Members

The three groups that form the syndicate perform different and distinct services for which they are compensated accordingly.

The lead manager is responsible for: origination; syndicate formation and management; underwriting a major portion of the new issue; placing the allotted fraction of the issue; conducting the price stabilization activities; serving as the major provider of liquidity (i.e., acting as a market maker) in the aftermarket, and providing analyst coverage. Therefore, the lead manager is involved in the entire going-public process. As the book-runner, the lead manager receives all expressions of buying interest collected by the syndicate members in the preoffer period and builds a book of preliminary orders.

The comanagers may have some involvement with origination and preparation of the registration statement, but their main role is to assist with the price discovery process, the underwriting and marketing of the issue, and finally its placement in the market.

The syndicated underwriters (other than the lead manager and comanagers) are involved only with underwriting and distribution services and are allocated smaller portions of the new issue than those reserved for the lead manager and comanagers. The allotted portions vary in accordance with their position in the hierarchy of investment banks (e.g., bulge bracket, etc.)—with higher rank members receiving greater allocations. Allocations tend to be equal across syndicate members of each rank.

The selling brokers/dealers are responsible only for placement among their clients. They have no underwriting responsibility.

The Syndication Agreement

This agreement describes the rules that govern the activities of the underwriting group. The syndication agreement can be of the divided or undivided type. The divided type makes each member of the underwriting syndicate responsible only for the placement of the portion of the issue allotted to each member. The undivided type makes all syndicated underwriters responsible for the unsold portion of the issue allotted to other members. In the latter case, if a member has difficulty in placing its portion, the lead manager redistributes the unsold portion all over again to all syndicate members in accordance with their initial share.

> **Example:** A syndicate member has been allotted to underwrite and place 50,000 shares which represent 5% of all issued shares but it manages to place only 45,000 shares. In a divided agreement, the firm is responsible for the remaining 5,000 shares and has to hold them or sell them at the going market price but only after the syndicate has been dissolved. In an undivided agreement, the firm will withhold 5% of the 5,000 (or 250 shares) and return 4,750 shares to the lead manager who will reallocate them to the other underwriting syndicate members in proportion to their original allocations. Thus, a firm responsible to place 10% of the issue will receive 500 shares.

The Selling Group Agreement

The operations of the selling group are governed by the selling group agreement. This agreement covers, among other provisions, the selling fee or concession earned by the selling group members, the terms of placement and consequences for selling placed securities back to the syndicate, and the duration of the placement effort. The selling concession compensates syndicate members for their expenses and effort to sell the new securities to investors and is the major fraction of the total underwriting spread the syndicate receives as compensation. The "Rules of Fair Practice" of FINRA prohibit the sale of the new issue at a price other than the offer price specified in the prospectus while the offering lasts. Selling group member that have difficulty placing the new securities (or those that buy them back from a client) may attempt to sell the securities to other syndicate members. To discourage this, selling group members forfeit the selling concession for the portion of their allotted securities they place back with the syndicate. Selling dealers are also responsible to prevent their customers from excessive "flipping" (i.e., selling back the newly purchased securities). Finally, the agreement sets the duration for the placement effort. Selling groups usually last for up to 30 days from the first day of formal sale. The lead manager may sometimes decide to extend the life of the selling group to achieve full placement of the issue or will call the placement off if the market is not receptive enough.

The members of the selling group may reallocate small amounts of the new securities to other brokers and dealers (outside the syndicate) for the purpose of facilitating the distribution of the new issue. This is called reallowance and the compensation received is the reallowance fee. The reallowance fee is a fraction of the selling concession. For example, if the reallowance is $0.20 per share and the offer price is $20 per share, reallowed dealers buy at $19.80 and sell at $20 per share to the public.

Allocation of the Underwriting Compensation

The gross spread or underwriting fee, that is, the difference between the offer price of the security to the investors and the price paid to the issuer, i.e., the bid price, is divided among the lead manager, the comanagers, the syndicated underwriters, and the selling group in accordance to the services they offer for any portion of the issue they are allotted.

The gross spread has three components: the management fee, the underwriting fee, and the selling concession. The management fee is the compensation of the (lead and co-) managers for origination and management of the issue, with the lead or "book running" manager receiving a higher fraction than the other comanagers. The underwriting fee is the compensation of the syndicated underwriters for the underwriting risk they assume. Finally, the selling concession is the compensation for the distribution (placement) effort.

Typically, the lead manager and comanagers collect 20%−25% of the total gross spread as management fee; the syndicated underwriters (including the lead manager and comanagers) collect another 20%−25% of the total spread as underwriting fee; and the selling fee claims the remainder, 50%−60%, of the gross spread. The lead manager, who controls the allocation of the issue, typically earns the lion's share in all three components of the gross spread (Chen and Ritter, 2000). A study of IPOs by Torstila (2001) finds that the lead manager usually receives 50%−75% of the management fee; 35%−60% of the underwriting fee; and 60%−90% of the selling fee. IPOs with larger gross fees allocate higher proportion of fees to the selling concession. (Appendix B presents an example of how the gross spread is allocated to the members of the syndicate and at what prices the securities change hands within the syndicate.)

Pricing and Marketing

Pricing of the new issue refers to estimating the fair value of the new issue and setting the final offer price. In addition to engaging in price discovery, the underwriter utilizes the waiting period to market the new issue to investors.

Pricing Activities

To determine the offer price, the underwriter needs to estimate the expected market value of the offered security on the issue day; hence, the underwriter must engage in price discovery. To this end, the underwriter collects and analyzes firm-specific and market-wide information, as well as information from prospective investors. Seasoned equity offerings (SEO), which have a price history and are continually traded, are easier to price by relying on the last transaction price prior to the offer day. On the other hand, IPOs and bond issues have no price record thus making their price discovery much more complicated and challenging. The pricing process includes the following phases:

- Analysis of firm-specific and other available information for the purpose of setting the initial price range.

- Marketing and information gathering through roadshows.
- Building the book of preliminary orders.
- Setting the final offer price.

Setting the Price Range

The preliminary prospectus must include a bona fide indication of the range of the maximum price of the new issue. According to an SEC announcement in 2012, the acceptable price range can be up to $2 relative to the upper bound for issues valued at or less than $10 or 20% of the upper bound for issues valued at or higher than $10. Previously, the SEC had permitted the price range to be the greater of $2 or 10% of the lower price. A larger range may be used in the case the new issue is offered by the auction method (as e.g., in the case of the Google IPO in August 2004, which had a range of $108 to $135).

Example: If the underwriter anticipates the maximum offer price to be $8, the permissible price range is $6–$8. If the underwriter anticipates the maximum offer price to be $30, then the permissible price range is $24–$30.

The midpoint of the price range is the most direct indication the market receives about the value of the new securities on the basis of the underwriter's valuation. It allows institutional and individual investors to calibrate their own analysis and form preliminary buy positions. Depending on how well the issue is received following the circulation of the preliminary prospectus, the underwriter may amend the initial price range to adjust it to the perceived demand for the issue.

There is evidence that informativeness of the prospectus can affect the credibility of the price range as an estimate of the offer price, especially in offerings of unseasoned securities, like IPOs. Hanley and Hoberg (2010) find that issues with more unique language in the preliminary prospectus have offer prices that are closer to the price range as well as to the actual market price when trading starts. That is, expending more resources in due diligence (including auditing and legal counseling) produces more definitive information and, hence, more credible price estimates. This allows underwriters to set higher offer prices than when the prospectus uses less descriptive language. High-reputation underwriters seem to be more effective in credibly communicating information through the prospectus. Loughran and McDonald (2013) also report that when IPO prospectuses use words connoting uncertain, weak, and negative terms, the offer price undergoes more adjustment (up or down) relative to the original price range, and these issues also have greater postissue price volatility.

Marketing and Information Gathering

Public interest in a new issue may sometimes precede the formal announcement of an SEC filing. This is more important for IPOs than seasoned equity or bond offerings of publicly traded firms. Notable examples of IPOs with a lot of preoffer buzz include Google (in August 2004) and Facebook (in May 2012). It is in the interest of the underwriter and the issuer to see that there is news media coverage and public buzz about the issuer and its business without, however, crossing the boundaries set by SEC regulations on publicity as discussed above. Greater publicity can boost valuation and improve the offer price. It can also generate anticipation for the new issue among retail investors and result in stronger buying interest and higher prices in the aftermarket (Cook, Kieschnick, and Van Ness, 2006).

The underwriter also has an interest in marketing the issue by targeting investors who can reveal information that can help to arrive at a more reliable price for the new issue. To this end, the salesforces of the syndicate member firms start contacting their clients to alert them to the new issue and generate interest. To inform investors about the new issue, the syndicate also circulates the preliminary prospectus or "red herring" and starts to organize meetings with investors in the so-called roadshows. The roadshows offer the underwriter and key executives of the issuing firm the opportunity to present pertinent information and analysis that support the price range shown in the preliminary prospectus. Although the exchange of information must be contained within the scope of the registration statement, roadshows and other informal meetings with investors are useful in enhancing the information content of the preliminary prospectus.

The schedule of roadshows includes major cities around the United States which are financial hubs and usually ends in New York City a few days prior to the formal pricing of the issue. If the issue has a portion slated for international distribution, roadshows are also organized in major financial centers around the globe. Roadshows are usually conducted in person. Since 2005, the SEC has permitted the use of electronic roadshows under certain conditions.

The presentation of the new issue to pools of mostly institutional investors (e.g., mutual funds, pension funds, etc.) allows the underwriter to gather useful information about investor interest in the issue which will be used toward setting the final offer price. Larger investor participation in the roadshows increases the likelihood of acquiring more accurate information about the fair price of the security. Larger roadshows can also support wider distribution of the new issue. In effect, the roadshows enable the lead manager to share the cost of price discovery with informed investors. To the extent, roadshow participants are willing to produce additional information and reveal their valuation, the underwriter faces a less challenging and arduous task in regards to estimating the price of the issue.

Building the Book of Preliminary Orders

The ultimate purpose of the roadshows and other communications with prospective investors is to elicit expressions of buying interest, that is, to generate preliminary (albeit nonbinding) buy orders. These orders, in the form of quantity and price bids, are used by the lead manager to build the book of orders. The book generates a demand schedule that shows at what prices varying quantities of the new issue are likely to be placed in the market. The lead manager uses this information to arrive at the final offer price. The lead manager must also ascertain the strength of commitment behind these informal orders so that the clearing price (i.e., the price at which market demand will match the supply of new securities) can be reliably determined. The expressions of interest come in the form of bids as shown below:

Strike bid: A strike bid indicates interest to buy new securities regardless of the issue price. A strike bid may specify the amount of money or the number of securities. An example of a strike bid is the indication to buy 5,000 shares or a bid to buy shares worth $40,000.

Limit bid: It specifies the maximum price the bidder is willing to pay for the securities requested. For example, an indication to buy 5,000 shares at $50 per share is an example of a limit bid.

Step bid: The bidder expresses interest to buy different quantities at different prices in a step fashion. Example: First step bid: buy 5,000 shares at $50; second step bid: buy 6,000 shares at $45; third step bid: buy 7,000 shares at $40.

Step bids are considered to be the most informative and strike bids the least informative in assisting the underwriter to construct the demand schedule of the new issue. Strike bids are more likely to be submitted by less informed investors who may be more uncertain about the value of the issue or by those who are less willing to reveal their private information. In general, investors who submit preliminary orders run a double risk. If their bids are too generous, they may push the offer price above the fair market value of the issue. If, on the other hand, their bids are too conservative, they may not receive their desired allocation.

Soliciting preliminary expressions of interest from investors presents the underwriter with an incentivization problem. Informed investors who have positive information relative to that reflected in the price range can benefit from not revealing this information so that they can buy a possibly underpriced security, that is, a security whose market opens at a price above the offer price. Consequently, the underwriter needs to incentivize informed investors to share their private information. The "information gathering" model of Benveniste and Spindt (1989) suggests underwriters use underpricing and preferential allocation of securities to induce informed investors to release positive information that can improve the offer price.

Example: Let us assume that in the absence of bookbuilding the underwriter has arrived at a price range of $18 to $20 per share. The range reflects the underwriter's assessment of the expected value of the issue at the offer time. Let us also assume that when it is time to price the issue, the underwriter believes the expected market price is $20; however, the underwriter decides to set the offer price at $18 to better ensure full placement of the issue. Assuming the aftermarket price is indeed $20, an investor that buys 10,000 shares has made a paper profit of $20,000. Let us now introduce bookbuilding. Based on the same initial assessment, the underwriter sets the price range at $18–$20. Following the roadshows and expressions of interest from likely buyers, the underwriter believes the new shares have an expected market price of $24. To reward the investors who shared their positive private information, the underwriter has three options: price the shares so that the anticipated gain is greater than the $2 expected gain in the no-bookbuilding case;

(Continued)

(CONTINUED)

allocate to investors who reveal positive information more shares than what they would receive in the no-bookbuilding case; or do both. With an indicated expected price of $24 per share, the underwriter can satisfy the objectives of the issuer and the investors. For example, choosing a price of $20 improves the offer price and increases the net proceeds to the issuer. At the same time, investors who contributed to the price improvement have the opportunity to gain $4 per share (i.e., the difference between the expected market price of the shares and the offer price).

When the roadshows are over, the syndicate members submit all indications of interest to the book-running (lead) manager. The book-running manager builds the book of preliminary orders by aggregating the bids for various quantity levels and derives the demand schedule for the issue. Ideally, the offer price should be the clearing price that generates demand equal to the supply of the new issue. However, to reward investors who have revealed positive valuation estimates, the underwriter sets the offer price below the clearing price level. Pricing below the clearing price of the book also makes it more likely the issue will be oversubscribed. Oversubscription creates unsatisfied demand which is expected to generate additional buying activity in the aftermarket. This helps maintain the price above the offer price, thus reducing the need for price support, and creates stronger trading (and, hence, more liquidity) in the aftermarket.

An interesting question is how informative bookbuilding is and how it influences the underwriter's decision regarding the offer price. A study of IPOs underwritten in Europe provides useful insights into this question. Specifically, Cornelli and Goldreich (2003) report that

- limit bids have a strong influence on the offer price.
- bids that arrive later in the bookbuilding period have greater influence on the offer price, presumably because they reflect more timely information.
- large bids and bids by frequent investors weigh more in setting the offer price.
- submitted bids tend to include additional information than what is publicly available.
- underwriters do not seem to adjust the offer price as much as it is justified by the degree of oversubscription.

Setting the Offer Price

Choosing the offer price for the new securities is the last important step before formal sale begins. The offering price is agreed upon by the issuer and the underwriter in a special meeting, and then it is inserted into the underwriting agreement and the prospectus. This makes the underwriting agreement final and ready for execution. The final offer price is immediately submitted to the SEC in the form of a pricing amendment, which also requests that the SEC accelerate the effective date of the issue. Once the offering price is incorporated into the registration statement, the SEC declares the statement effective and the sale of the new issue can commence.

To minimize the risk that adverse new information may depress the value of the new securities, the offer price is set as close to the offer time as possible. In the case of Rule 415 (shelf) issues, the offer price is set just after the underwriter takes the issue off the shelf. In traditional registration offerings, the offer price is set the evening before the issue is schedule to go on sale.

If the roadshow has revealed positive information which can improve the offer price, the lead manager will adjust the offer price upwards. The adjustment may, however, be only partial if the underwriter intends to reward informed investors for divulging their private information (Hanley, 1993). For example, if the price range is $18−$20 but the clearing price is believed to be $24, the underwriter will likely set the offer price at the top or even above the price range, but below the implied clearing price. On the other hand, if the information is unfavorable, the offer price will be set lower, even below the price range. A study by Loughran and Ritter (2002) reports that in a sample of IPOs completed in the 1990s, the final price was set below the price range in 27.3% of IPOs, within the price range in 48.4% of IPOs, and above the price range in 24.3% of IPOs. Offer prices tend to reflect more the negative than the positive information generated in the preoffering period. As a result, IPOs that receive positive information have offer prices that fall short of their aftermarket price more than IPOs that receive negative information (Lowry and Schwert, 2002).

When preoffer indications of interest suggest a much stronger or weaker price relative to the price range, the underwriter may amend the initial price range to avoid a large discrepancy between price range and offer price. Updating the price range also serves to notify investors about the current strength or weakness of the new issue so that they can adjust their purchasing plans accordingly. Besides revising the initial price range, the issuer and the underwriter may also decide to revise the offer size. If information about expected demand appears to be strong in the book of preliminary orders, the offer size is revised upward and the reverse if demand seems weak. A study of SEOs whose offer sizes were revised has shown that they realized a positive (negative) market price reaction to upward (downward) revisions but this reaction was statistically significant only for stocks traded on the Nasdaq or the AMEX but not for stocks traded on the NYSE (Galloway, Loderer, and Sheehan, 1998).

Placement

The tasks executed in relation to the placement of the new issue in the market include the allocation of the new securities to different investor clienteles as well as the physical distribution of the securities.

The Allocation Decision

How the new issue is allocated among investors is an integral part of the marketing and pricing activities. The bookbuilding method, followed in the United States and most international offerings, gives the lead manager full discretion in allocating the new securities across classes of investors. The main allocation decision is to determine the relative weights of the institutional and retail investor "pots." Beyond this broad decision, the allocation of the issue is influenced by such factors, like frequency of participation in new issues underwritten by the investment bank, long-term commitment to holding the new securities, and reciprocal business the investors can bring to the underwriter's firm.

Institutional versus Retail Investors

Institutional investors are in general favored over retail investors. Institutional investors are well regarded for the valuation insights they bring to the price discovery process and their purchasing capacity. In addition, institutional investors can be value-added clients in other ways, like directing brokerage and trading business to the underwriter's firm. Greater allocations to institutions also reduce placement costs because institutions buy in large quantities. Underwriters have an interest to cultivate loyalty among institutional investors, who by virtue of their business and resources can be frequent buyers of new issues through good and tough times. This is accomplished through an implicit understanding that institutional investors who buy new issues with weak preoffer demand will be awarded larger allocations in future promising new offers. The preference for institutional investors is reflected in the widely accepted practice of a 70:30 split between institutional and retail investors, at least in the case of IPOs.

Nonetheless, retail investors are also coveted by underwriters because they bring additional pools of money to the new issues market and contribute to a more widespread ownership and investor base which can have a beneficial effect on the market value of the securities (Merton, 1987). Broader ownership in the case of stock issues is also sought by top executives of firms in order to lessen concentration of stock ownership that can increase monitoring of executives and raise the likelihood of future takeover threats.

Studies show that institutional investors are favored with allocations of good-quality new issues which have attractive price discounts and generate better long-run returns (Aggarwal, Prabhala, and Puri, 2002; Boehmer, Boehmer, and Fishe, 2006). Institutional investors who are net buyers of shares in the preoffer period are also awarded larger allocations in SEOs underwritten by reputable underwriters. These investors also tend to remain net buyers in the postoffer period, and they realize better long-term returns on the new issues (Chemmanur, He, and Hu, 2009).

The Prospect of Aftermarket Flipping

An important consideration that affects the allocation decision is the possibility of flipping. This term refers to the resale of the new security by the initial buyers during the early aftermarket period. In general, flipping is regarded unfavorably by underwriters because it has the potential to dampen demand for the new issue and cause a price decline. Flipping is particularly detrimental to the syndicate's interests in the case of cold new issues, that is, issues whose reception by the market is tepid and slow. If flipping causes market price to fall below the offer price, the underwriter will be forced to provide price support which can be costly. On the other hand, when new issues are hot (the market price following the offer significantly exceeds the offer price), flipping is welcome by the syndicate because it generates additional trading activity and brokerage commissions. In general, underwriters prefer to allocate new issues to investors with long-term holding horizons, the so-called "strong hands."

Since June 1997, lead underwriters and syndicate members have used the Depository Trust Company's (DTC) Initial Public Offering Tracking System to monitor flipping with greater reliability and at low cost. Lead managers usually retaliate for unwelcome flipping by reducing or eliminating future allocations to repeat flippers. Also, dealers of the selling syndicate that buy back flipped shares and resell them to the syndicate may forfeit their selling concession.

If underwriters expect their regular large investors to participate in both hot and cold issues, do they treat these investors differently in relation to flipping? The evidence suggests that institutional investors are allowed more latitude than retail investors. Krigman, Shaw, and Womack (1999) find that a significant fraction of early trading consists of block trades, which is a sign of institutional trading. Hot IPOs attract greater volume of block trades but the latter make up a greater percentage of the smaller volume of trading in cold IPOs. These patterns signify that large (institutional) investors participate in the placement of cold IPOs but seek a quick exit to avoid losses.

Aggarwal (2003) also finds evidence of flipping in the early aftermarket of IPOs. Institutions are found to be more prone to flipping when IPOs realize high initial as opposed to low initial returns (given by the difference between market price and offer price). The same pattern is found among retail investors, but their percentages of allotted shares flipped are lower than those of institutional investors. Retail investment banks tend to favor retail clients with larger allocations compared to wholesale banks but they also restrain flipping by retail clients more than wholesale banks.

Chemmanur, Hu, and Huang (2010) also document that institutional investors are active flippers the first 2 days, and they end up selling 70.2% of their IPO allocations by the end of the first year. Furthermore, underwriters seem to poorly enforce antiflipping practices on institutional buyers. Institutional flipping is concentrated within more uncertain and underpriced issues and those with poor long-run prospects. On the contrary, in the case of SEOs, flipping by institutional investors is very low (Chemmanur, He, and Hu 2009). Their evidence shows that institutional investors are successful in identifying good-quality issues; as a result, buying overpriced issues, which they have to flip, is less frequent. According to Ellis (2006), the first-day trading is related more to adjusting positions to more optimal levels than flipping IPO shares to avoid losses. The evidence of sizable interdealer trading also implies that the extent of flipping by initial buyers is overestimated.

Carter and Dark (1993) report that first-week trading volume is lower when IPOs are managed by high-tier underwriters. First-month and first-year returns are both inversely related to first-week trading, which implies that flipping has negative consequences for investor returns. Thus, top underwriters are more likely to serve investor clienteles with less propensity to flipping.

Bookbuilding and Allocation

The rationale of the bookbuilding method suggests that bids revealing more information about the prospective price of the issue are favored with greater allocations. In one of the few available studies, Cornelli and Goldreich (2001) provide evidence by analyzing the bids recorded in books run for international IPOs and find that the type and quantity of bids as well as the type of bidder influence the allocation of shares. These findings can be summarized as follows:

- More shares are allocated to investors who submit large bids and bids with limit prices.
- Allocations are greater to investors who submit revised bids.
- Frequent bidders (those participating in multiple offerings) receive greater allocations, especially of oversubscribed IPOs. This way they are compensated for their participation in cold offerings.
- The book-running investment bank appears to favor bids submitted to its own firm, thus earning greater fraction of the underwriting fees.

In a similar study of European IPOs, Jenkinson and Jones (2004) do not find much support for the view that more informative bids (such as limit or step bids) are favored with greater allocations. However, they do find that larger allocations go to frequent bidders and those submitting large bids. They also find that long-term investors are preferred over perceived flippers in the allocation of hot issues.

In a survey of investors who had participated in European IPOs, Jenkinson and Jones (2009) find that allocations are driven less by the investors' contribution to price discovery and more by the potential of reciprocal business deals between the investment bank and the investors. Contrary to the tenets of the bookbuilding hypothesis, only about one-half of the participating investors produce their own valuation models and the submitted bids fall short of being value revealing in the majority of IPO issues. Nor do investors appear to fully share their information with the underwriter.

The evidence from studies of US offerings is more in line with the workings of the bookbuilding method. Gondat-Larralde and James (2008) find that greater allocations go to investors whom underwriters trust to participate in both cold and hot issues as long as they can earn an acceptable return over the long run. Investor characteristics are less important for allocations contrary to the quid pro quo model of Jenkinson and Jones (2009) above.

Chemmanur, Hu, and Huang (2010) also report evidence that institutional investors who participate in bookbuilding appear to possess superior information about the new issues. For example, they earn superior trading profits in the aftermarket by selling back the stocks of younger more speculative issues and earn higher returns from long-term holdings of IPO shares. Consistent with the bookbuilding method, these investors are rewarded with greater allocations of promising issues, especially when they have a record of holding colder issues longer. They also receive smaller allocations when pre-IPO demand is high. On average, institutions participate and receive allocations more in hot as opposed to cold IPOs.

Irregularities in the Allocation of New Issues

The burst of the dot-com bubble in 2000 exposed underwriters to criticism related to the allocation of new securities because of the ethical concerns such practices raised. These practices were also held responsible for the excessive underpricing of new issues around that time. The alleged irregularities in the allocation of IPO shares culminated in the landmark Global Analyst Research Settlement between the SEC and 12 of the biggest investment banks in April 2003.

Laddering

Laddering is the practice of allocating more securities to clients on the condition they will place buy orders in the aftermarket with the purpose to boost price and create a positive buzz about the new issue. A prospective buyer can signal the intent for laddering by submitting expression of interest with notes like "will buy 2x" or "buy 3x" meaning the multiples of allotted shares the buyer intends to buy in the aftermarket (Hao, 2007). Laddering is prohibited by the Securities and Exchange Act of 1934. Underwriters benefit from laddering because strong buying in the aftermarket keeps the price of a new issue high enough so that there is less need for the underwriter to support the market price. The effect of laddering on offer prices can be ambiguous. An underwriter may choose to underprice more in order to extract more benefits from laddering as a payback to the allocation of underpriced issues. Or, anticipating a stronger aftermarket, an underwriter may choose a higher than otherwise offer price. Griffin, Harris, and Topaloglu (2007) analyze the net buying pattern of IPO shares conducted by institutional investors through their accounts with the lead underwriter and find excessive trading activity in the aftermarket which they interpret as evidence of laddering. Further, net buying by the underwriter's clients contributes positively to the first-day price. These buys do not appear to be driven by investment strategies or better execution of orders by the underwriter's firm. Evidence of a "tie-in" of underwriting and brokerage business is also reported in Nimalendran, Ritter, and Zhang (2007). They find evidence of excessive trading, especially in the internet bubble period of 1999–2000, when the hot IPOs of internet firms were highly coveted by investors. Reuter (2006) also reports unusual brokerage business between mutual funds and lead underwriters from whom they had received IPO allocations. The extent of business appeared to increase with the degree of underpricing.

Spinning

This is the practice of allocating hot new issues in the brokerage accounts of top corporate executives (i.e., CEO, CFO, directors) kept with the underwriting firm for the purpose of influencing the decision of choosing an investment bank for underwriting and other related deals. Liu and Ritter (2010) report excess underpricing of 23% over the normal rate in IPOs of firms whose top executives were given preferential allocations of other firms' new issues in the years 1996–2000, which coincided with the internet bubble period. Spinning was estimated to have produced an average gain of $1.3 million per executive. Spinning was formally banned by NASD (now FINRA) in 2002.

Nepotism

This is the practice of investment banks to favor their mutual fund affiliates with allocations of good-quality issues in order to boost the funds' performance. The opposite (the dumping down hypothesis) is the practice to allocate cold issues to affiliated mutual funds in order to avoid canceling a weak issue or in order to leave more of hot issues available for allocation to buyers who can generate "payback" income for the investment bank. While Reuter (2006) finds no evidence of nepotism, Ritter and Zhang (2007) find some evidence of nepotism but no evidence of "dumping down."

Distribution of the New Issue

The formal sale starts with the "opening of the book" of preliminary orders submitted to the syndicate during the preoffer period. Syndicate and selling-group members start contacting their customers who have expressed interest in buying the new issue and try to finalize their orders. If the issue is priced correctly, meaning the opening market price is above the offer price, the securities are sold fairly quickly, and the syndicate is dissolved. If, on the contrary, the opening market price turns out to be close or below the offer price, the sale will more likely proceed slowly, and it may even fail. If the syndicate has difficulty pushing the issue out, then the lead manager may decide to dissolve the syndicate. In this case, the syndicated underwriters have to carry the unsold securities in their portfolios and absorb the resultant losses.

Investors who have placed preliminary orders are under no legal obligation to follow through. They can renege if the current market conditions do not justify the offer price. Reneging is possible even after an investor has placed a formal order but before the settlement of the transaction. Reneging has the effect of increasing the uncertainty the underwriter has concerning the full distribution of the issue even despite a promising book of orders.

The Close of the Offering Process

The final steps in the offering process include delivery of the final prospectus, delivery of the new securities to the accounts of the buyers, and the payment of the net proceeds to the issuing firm. If the new issue has a secondary offering (that is, shareholders sell their own shares), they receive the net proceeds that correspond to their shares.

The net payment to the issuer and selling shareholders consists of the gross proceeds estimated at the offer price minus the underwriter (gross) spread and any other out-of-pocket expenses agreed to be paid by the issuer. The net proceeds are usually paid within 3 to 7 days after the offer day.

Initial buyers who buy the new security from the syndicate or in the immediate aftermarket must be furnished with the final prospectus which includes the final offer price. If after the preparation of the final prospectus, there are material new developments, the final prospectus must be amended. This is now easily done since the prospectus is available in digital form on the EDGAR system run by the SEC.

The Withdrawal Option

The underwriting agreement gives the issuer and the underwriting syndicate the option to withdraw the issue from the issuance process prior to its formal offering. This option is utilized when the issuer believes the offer price is below its reservation (minimum acceptable) price, or the underwriter fears the new issue will not be successfully placed at an acceptable offer price.

Conditions leading to the withdrawal of new issues include sharp market declines or release of unfavorable issuer-specific news. Benveniste, Ljungqvist and Wihelm (2003) find firms are more likely to complete IPOs if market conditions are strong, and concurrent IPOs perform well. The likelihood of completion decreases with more unstable conditions in the IPO market and greater incidence of withdrawn issues. Clarke, Dunbar, and Kahle (2001) find that SEOs have a lower probability to be canceled when insiders sell relatively more of their shares in the period around filing. This implies that when insiders believe their firm's stock is overvalued, they proceed with the flotation but dispose more of their holdings. The likelihood of cancelation also increases for smaller firms and for those whose value depends more on growth opportunities and when prices fall after filing. Venture capital (VC) backing and strong market conditions reduce the likelihood of withdrawal in IPOs (Busaba, Benveniste, and Guo, 2001).

The right to withdraw the issue is a valuable option to issuers. When investors have positive information, but are concerned an IPO may be withdrawn, they are more motivated to reveal their private information truthfully, thus improving the offer price (Busaba, Benveniste, and Guo, 2001).

Withdrawal of an offering is though costly to the issuer for at least three reasons. First, the issuer has to pay part of the underwriter's compensation for services associated with the offering and to forfeit the registration costs. Second, the issuer will be forced to seek more onerous financing of operations or abandon new investments. Third, returning to the market with a new offering can impose a lower valuation on the issuer. Lian and Wang (2009) find that second-try issuers have significantly lower valuation multiples, and switching underwriters helps reduce but does not eliminate the valuation discount. Nonetheless, second-try issuing firms realize long-run stock price and operating performance which is comparable to that of successful first-try issuers.

Dunbar and Foerster (2008) report that withdrawn issuers are more likely to credibly return for a second IPO attempt if their initial offering is managed by a reputable underwriter and has VC backing. Issuers are also more likely to withdraw if they believe a second offering will be successful. Otherwise, issuers are willing to accept a lower offer price and move on with the offering. The same authors report that 75% of successful reissues are conducted by a different underwriter, and the first-day returns are better than those realized by reissuers who retain the original investment bank.

Appendix A—Typical Timeline of Floating an IPO*

Week 1:

- Conduct organizational meetings (structure and timing of issue, tasks, and responsibilities of parties)

Weeks 2 to 5:

- Conduct due diligence (investigation of issuer's business and products, management, financial position, competition, future prospects)
- Draft the registration statement (include business information, financial information, recent performance and prospects, management and governance, board structure)
- Preparation of legal documents and agreements (underwriting agreement, comfort letter, etc.)
- Take steps for issuing firm to become a public company
- Determine eligibility of firm for listing on a US securities exchange

Weeks 6 to 8:

- Complete the registration statement
- File the listing application with an exchange

Weeks 9 to 16:

- Receive SEC preliminary approval of the registration statement/prospectus
- Receive stock exchange approval for listing
- Firm up the valuation of the issue (analyze market and investor sentiment)
- Set up marketing strategy (action plan for promotion of issue)
- Prepare for roadshow presentation and prep salesforce

Weeks 17 to 19:

- Salesforce calls to investors
- Launch the roadshow
- Start building the book of orders
- Execute pricing, allocation, and closing
- Print the final prospectus

Week 20:

- Closing (exchange new securities for funds—usually within 3 days)
- Remit net proceeds to issuer

---

* Adapted from Nasdaq publication: "Going Public: A guide for North American companies to listing on the US securities markets" published by Globe Business Publishing in association with The Nasdaq Stock Market (2011).

Appendix B—Example on Syndicate Compensation and Allocation Prices

We assume that the following terms apply to a new issue, say an IPO:

- shares to be placed: 1,000,000
- offer price: $20; bid price: $18
- underwriter compensation (gross spread): $20 − $18 = $2

The allocation of the underwriter compensation (on per share basis) is as follows:

- Management fee: $0.40 (20%)
- Underwriting fee: $0.40 (20%)
- Selling concession: $1.20 (60%)

The structure of the syndicate is:

- Lead manager
- Underwriting syndicate members
- Selling group

The allocation of the issue and the responsibilities of each group appear in Exhibit A-1 below.

Exhibit A-1

Syndicate Group	Origination	Underwriting	Distribution
Lead manager	1,000,000 shares	400,000 shares	500,000 shares
Underwriting syndicate (excluding the lead manager)		600,000 shares	400,000 shares
Selling group			100,000 shares

Given the above allocation of the issue, the compensation of the parties will be as follows:

Compensation of lead manager:

- For origination: 1,000,000 shares x $0.40 = $400,000
- For underwriting: 400,000 shares x $0.40 = $160,000
- For placement: 500,000 shares x $1.20 = $600,000

Total compensation of lead manager: $1,160,000

Compensation of underwriting syndicate members (excluding the lead manager):

- For underwriting: 600,000 shares x $0.40 = $240,000
- For placement: 400,000 shares x $1.20 = $480,000

Total compensation of underwriting syndicate members: $720,000

Compensation of selling-group members:

- For placement: 100,000 shares x $1.20 = $120,000

The total underwriter compensation or total gross spread can be also determined as:
Total compensation by member:

- Compensation of lead manager: $1,160,000
- Compensation of other syndicated underwriters: $720,000
- Compensation of selling group: $120,000

Total compensation: $2,000,000 (1,000,000 shares times the $2 spread)
Total compensation by service:

- Management (origination) fee: 1,000,000 shares x $0.40 = $400,000
- Underwriting fee: 1,000,000 shares x $0.40 = $400,000
- Selling concession: 1,000,000 shares x $1.20 = $1,200,000

Total compensation: $2,000,000
Intrasyndicate member transactions toward placement:
The lead manager:

- Buys 1,000,000 shares from the issuer at $18 per share.
- Sells 600,000 shares to other syndicate members at $18.40 per share [$18 plus the management fee or $20 (the offer price) minus the underwriting fee and selling concession].
- Sells 100,000 shares to dealers at $18.80 ($18 plus management and underwriting fee or $20 minus the selling concession).
- Sells directly 500,000 shares to public at $20.

The other syndicated underwriters:

- Buy 600,000 shares from the lead manager at $18.40 (i.e., $20 minus the underwriting management fee and placement fee).
- Sell 400,000 shares directly to public at the offer price of $20.

The dealers in the selling group (other than underwriting group):

- Buy 100,000 shares from the syndicated underwriters at $18.80 (i.e., $20 minus the selling concession).
- Sell 200,000 shares directly to public at $20.

If the lead manager allocates 20,000 shares out of the 500,000, the lead manager has to distribute, to outside broker/dealers at a reallowance fee of $0.40 per share, the reallowed dealers buy these shares at $19.60 and place them at $20. In this case, the lead manager gives up $8,000 of selling fees that could be made on the 20,000 shares.

Aftermarket Underwriting Activities

This chapter completes the description of the issuance process initiated in the previous chapter. It covers the activities that take place in the aftermarket in order to support and facilitate the successful completion of new issues and their emergence in the secondary markets.

Secondary Market Activities

The Opening of the Secondary Market

The most critical test relating to the success of a new issue is the opening market price of the new security in the secondary market, the New York Stock Exchange (NYSE) or Nasdaq. Public trading of the new securities in the secondary market starts on the offer day. In the case of initial public offerings (IPOs), which have no prior price history, the opening price is established through a call market that is run in the preopening period, that precedes the formal trading of the new securities. During the preopening period, investors and securities firms acting as market makers submit quotes, that is, prices at which they are willing to buy or sell quantities of the new securities. It is the lead manager, and less so the comanagers, who takes the leading role in submitting quotes. Wholesale securities firms, who are very active in market making, are also heavy participants by supplying quotes during the preopening period (Aggarwal and Conroy, 2000).

The purpose of the preopening period is to allow the market to "discover" the actual market price of the new securities. The first quote of the lead manager is usually indicative of the first trading price. For hot issues, the preopening period quotes are above the offer price, whereas for cold issues, they are at or below the offer price. When demand for the new issue is weak, the lead manager sets the opening bid at the offer price in order to provide price support. The impact of the opening price is such that most of the initial return of an IPO (i.e., the percentage change from the offer to the closing price on the first day) is determined by the first transaction price (Barry and Jennings, 1993).

> **Example:** Google, whose offer price was $85 per share, opened at a price of $100.00 and closed at $100.33. On the other hand, Facebook, whose offer price was $38 per share, opened at $42.05 and closed at $38.23. In this case, the opening price did not accurately predict the closing price and, hence, the first-day return.

Once public trading starts, it usually proceeds at a rapid rate. Falconieri, Murphy, and Weaver (2009) report that almost 20% of IPO shares are traded in the first 4 minutes of the opening. Chan (2010) finds that positive retail investor sentiment contributes to higher early aftermarket prices, especially in hot markets. In cold markets, it is large (mostly institutional) investors that influence the open-to-close first-day returns with some evidence that they provide support to keep prices above the offer price. Corwin, Harris, and Lipson (2004) find that NYSE-traded IPOs attract large number of limit orders at low bid-ask spreads on their first day of trading with sell orders exceeding buy orders for hot IPOs (those with a price pop of more than 15% over the offer price) and the reverse for cold IPOs. The quantities to buy at various prices (i.e., market depth) are higher for issues with larger syndicates and higher ranked underwriters. According to this study, IPOs with high imbalances in favor of buy orders in the preopening period predict higher first-day returns as well as better long run (1- and 3-year period) returns. Lewellen (2006) also finds that underwriters build large inventories of cold IPOs on the first-day by buying at or just below the offer price.

Price Stabilization

The placement effort of the syndicate can become difficult and costly if the offering runs into a climate of low market receptivity that depresses the market price of the new security. To remedy this problem, underwriters take steps to support the market price of the issue for a period of about up to 2 weeks after the offer day. The need for price stabilization reflects the investment bankers' belief that the supply of new issues creates a temporary excess supply which causes a "price pressure" on the new issue. The underwriter's problem is exacerbated by the "Rules of Fair Practice" of FINRA (Financial Industry Regulatory Authority) that restrict the syndicate to sell the new securities at the offer price while the formal offering is under way and the syndicate is in force.

Although price support is a form of price manipulation and thus prohibited, the SEC allows it under certain conditions in order to facilitate the distribution of new issues. The intention to undertake price stabilization activities must be disclosed in the prospectus and be approved by the SEC. The disclosure is intended to make investors aware that some form of price support may be undertaken so that they can judge whether the observed market price is the result of stabilization activities or a reflection of the intrinsic value of the security.

Methods of Price Stabilization

Price stabilization can be pursued by three different methods: stabilizing bids, short covering, and penalty bids.

Stabilizing Bids

This approach—also called pure stabilization—is the only form of price stabilization that is directly regulated by the SEC. As soon as trading starts in the secondary market, the lead manager submits bids to buy back shares in the open market. The stabilizing bid cannot exceed the offer price of the security or begin at a price exceeding the last independent transaction price for the security. Further, such bids must be disclosed to the specialist or other market makers as being "stabilizing bids." Stabilizing bids are not permitted following the breakup of the syndicate. Price stabilization through buying bids exposes the underwriter to losses from purchasing shares at higher prices than the market justifies. This risk along with the tight regulation of stabilizing bids and the attendant information disclosure costs explains why stabilizing bids are rarely utilized by underwriters (Aggarwal, 2000).

Example: Let us assume an offer price of $20 and because of weak demand the lead manager submits a stabilizing bid at $20 per share.

> *Scenario 1:* The market price starts to decline below $20, and the underwriter buys back, for example, 100,000 shares at $20 per share. If the market price of the new issue does not recover to $20 or better, the underwriter stands to suffer a loss.
> *Scenario 2:* The market price rises to $22. The stabilizing bid remains idle. No loss is incurred.

Short Covering

The lead manager can also engage in price stabilization by overselling the new issue, thus creating a short position. The short position is established when the lead manager commits to sell investors new securities at the offer price in excess of those issued by the issuing firm. To deliver the shorted securities, the lead manager borrows them from customer accounts with his/her firm or other syndicate members. Aggarwal (2000) finds that underwriters cover their short positions 14 to 19 days, on average, after the offer and that short positions last longer for underperforming issues. Since the oversold shares must be covered (i.e., returned to their owners), the lead manager maintains bid quotes to buy back shares at or slightly below the offer price of the security. If the market price of the issue falls below its offer price, the underwriter's bid provides price support and the bought shares are used to cover the short position. If the market price moves above the offer price, the short position is covered by buying at the (higher) market price, thus generating a loss.

Example: Let us assume an IPO in which 1 million shares are offered at an offer price of $20. The syndicate oversells the issue by 10% or by 100,000 shares at the offer price of $20 per share. To cover the short position, the lead manager maintains a stabilizing bid of $20 to buy up to 100,000 shares.

> *Scenario 1:* The market price falls to $18. The syndicate buys 100,000 shares at $20 for price stabilization purposes and covers the short position, thus breaking even (because they sold at $20 and bought at the bid of $20). If the lead manager opts to buy at the bid of $20 more than the shorted 100,000 shares in order to provide more price support, this will create a long position on the stock equal to the number of shares in excess of the short position of 100,000 shares. Unless the price recovers above $20, the lead manager will carry the long position at a loss.
> *Scenario 2:* The market price rises to $22. The syndicate buys back the 100,000 shares at $22 to cover its short. This generates a loss of $200,000 (i.e., 100,000 shares times the difference between the market price paid and the offer price received by the lead manager).

To avoid the risk exemplified in Scenario 2 of the above example, the underwriter can use the overallotment option (OAO) which gives the underwriter the right to buy from the issuer additional shares at the bid price and place them at the offer price as specified in the prospectus. The costs, if any, of the stabilization activities are shared proportionately by the syndicated underwriters, as part of their underwriting responsibilities, and come out of their underwriting fees.

Penalty Bids

When demand for a new issue is weak and investors sell their securities back to the selling dealers, the latter may attempt to sell these securities to the syndicate. To mitigate this problem, FINRA rules recognize the right of the lead manager to reclaim the selling concession from a selling-group member if securities allocated to such member are sold back to the syndicate. The provision for penalty bids and related information must be disclosed to FINRA, though no public disclosure is required.

The purpose of penalty bids is to discourage flipping and avoid a surge in selling orders which can depress the price of the new security. Indeed, Aggarwal (2000) finds that penalty bids—when exercised—restrain flipping. Penalty bids can be most beneficial to the underwriter in cold markets during which price pressure from flipping, while the placement has not been completed, can make distribution more difficult and costly. Even if the placement is over, putting pressure on price may trigger the need for price stabilization and potentially increase the overall cost of underwriting.

> **Example:** The prospectus of a new issue specifies a bid price to the issuer equal to $18, an offer price of $20, and a selling concession of $1.20. Let us assume that to support the price the underwriter submits bids to buy at the offer price. Let us also assume that once trading starts, the price declines to $19 and selling dealers flip 100,000 shares back to the lead manager. At the stabilizing bid of $20, the lead manager incurs a paper loss of $100,000 (100,000 shares times $1 per share). By reclaiming the selling concession of $1.20 per share, the underwriter manages to recoup the cost of stabilization and compel the selling dealers of the syndicate to place securities with investors who commit to hold the new securities.

Economic Rationale of Price Stabilization

The price stabilization methods provide price support by either expanding the demand or restricting the supply of the new issue. Stabilizing bids and short covering aim at stimulating demand; penalty bids aim at restricting supply. Price stabilization serves various purposes:

- *It reduces reneging.* Investors who expressed interest in the new issue during the preoffer period retain the option to cancel or reduce their orders if they are not confident the market price will remain above the offer price. Canceling preliminary orders is called reneging. Price stabilization provides investors with additional assurance that there will be aftermarket price support in the case of an unforeseen temporary worsening of market conditions that may depress the price. This assurance can, therefore, reduce the amount of orders that are reneged. Price stabilization as a way of countering order reneging is more effective if investors perceive the price stabilization will help keep the price above the offer price well into the aftermarket, that is, the stabilization has a permanent price effect (Schultz and Zaman, 1994; Aggarwal, 2000).

- *It protects the underwriter's reputation with investors.* According to Lewellen (2006), underwriters with strong retail securities business provide greater price support than underwriters who rely on institutional investor clienteles. There is no evidence though that price stabilization is concentrated in IPOs with greater uncertainty as a remedy to the adverse selection problem. Instead, price support is directed toward IPOs which are less risky, and IPOs underwritten by larger and higher ranked investment banks.
- *It reduces liquidity costs.* By setting a price floor, underwriters can protect dealers, who wish to make a market on the new issue, from realizing inventory losses due to a drop in the market price of the issue. For example, dealers who buy shares of the new IPO, say, at an offer price of $20 and hold them to satisfy buy orders of their customers, run an inventory risk associated with the possibility the price drops below $20. Protecting dealers against inventory losses can help narrow the bid-ask spread and, thus, lower the cost of liquidity to investors (Hanley, Kumar, and Seguin, 1993).
- *It protects underwriters against litigation risk.* Finally, price stabilization provides protection against the risk that the parties associated with the flotation (issuer, underwriter, and auditors) are sued for not properly discharging their due diligence obligation in connection to information disclosure in the case investors suffer losses due to a price drop. By stabilizing the price close to the offer price, this litigation risk is significantly curtailed.

Impact of Price Stabilization on Offer Price and Flipping

Stabilization Costs and Offer Price

The intent to provide price stabilization has two conflicting implications with respect to offer price. On the one hand, it provides assurance to investors and dealers that they will be protected against adverse price movements. This helps stimulate greater interest in the new issue than otherwise and thus can support a higher offer price. On the other hand, underwriters have an interest in setting a lower offer price in order to lessen the likelihood of price stabilization and its associated cost.

Offering price support through explicit stabilizing bids or by creating a short position is equivalent to giving the initial buyers a cost-free put option. The implicit value of this option is a cost to the underwriting syndicate and, hence, it reduces its net profit. Underwriters can lower the value of this put by choosing a lower than otherwise offer price (which serves as the exercise price of the put). For example, an offer price of $18 versus an offer price of $20 makes it less likely the price will drop below the offer price and investors will exercise their option to put the securities back to the syndicate.

Price Stabilization and Flipping

Benveniste, Busaba, and Wilhelm (1996) argue that the underwriter can use price stabilization to encourage informed investors to show more interest in the new issue since the intent to support the price signals the issue will not be overpriced. Since attracting informed investors to engage in price discovery may help to better price the issue, this view would offer more price protection to such investors by relaxing penalty bids and allowing more flipping in the case the issue turns out to be weak.

On the other hand, Chowdhry and Nanda (1996) argue that price stabilization is a more efficient method to protect uninformed investors against overpricing and thus mitigate their adverse selection problem (i.e., being allocated more of overpriced issues). Therefore, this view would favor relaxing flipping for retail investors. Both views explain price support as a substitute of underpricing, that is, the underwriter can choose a higher offer price and provide more price support, or choose a lower offer price and provide less price support.

From a different perspective, Schultz and Zaman (1994) and Lewellen (2006) argue that if price stabilization has a permanent positive effect on the value of the new securities, the benefit accrues to both informed and uninformed investors and thus discriminatory treatment with respect to flipping becomes irrelevant.

Size of Stabilization Costs

Short covering as a price stabilization method can be potentially very costly for the syndicate. However, underwriters can use the OAO to reduce their exposure to losses from buying at market prices above the offer price. The right of the underwriter to buy additional securities at the bid price specified in the prospectus protects the underwriter from the potential losses on the short position. Indeed, both Ellis, Michaely, and O'Hara (2000) and Aggarwal (2000) report that the stabilization costs consume a very small fraction of the underwriter's compensation.

The Overallotment Option

The OAO also called "Green Shoe" option (named after the issuing firm that first used it) gives the lead manager the right to buy a predetermined percentage up to 15% of the new issue in excess of the quantity initially offered to the public. The OAO usually expires 30 days after the offer day. Under the provisions of the OAO, the lead manager can purchase the additional quantity of the new issue at the bid price and sell it to the public at the offer price as agreed in the underwriting agreement. The provision for an OAO must be disclosed in the prospectus.

The OAO has the features of a call option. If the underwriter needs to cover a short position, the OAO will be exercised if the market price is equal to or above the bid price. If the market price is below the bid price, the underwriter would rather cover the short by buying at the lower market price. From a market-demand perspective, the exercise of the OAO is more likely when the market price is equal to or above the offer price of the new issue. Empirical evidence shows that indeed the OAO is exercised mostly in the case of issues with a market price above the offer price and to a much lesser extent in the case of cold IPOs, when the market price is below the offer price (Muscarella, Peavy, and Vetsuypens, 1992; Ellis, Michaely, and O'Hara, 2000).

Lee, Lochhead, Ritter, and Zhao (1996) report that the OAO provision is very common in new issues. They find that 99% of their sample of IPOs had an OAO provision and it was exercised in 54% of these IPOs. The OAO was found in 98% of their sample of SEOs and was exercised in 65% of those with an OAO. In the sample of convertible bond offering, the OAO was found in 90% of them and was exercised in 38% of these issues. The least occurrence of the OAO was found in straight debt issues. Only 48 straight bond issues out of 1,092 had the OAO provision.

Logue, Rogalski, Seward, and Foster-Johnson (2002) report that in a sample of 1,475 IPOs completed in the period 1988 to 1995, the average (median) size of the OAO was 4.95% (10%) of the initial size of the offer for issues priced below the filing price range, 8.44% (13%) for issues priced within the range, and 11.76% (15%) for issues priced above the price range. Thus, issues promising to sell better have a greater percentage of the OAO exercised.

Benefits of the OAO to Underwriters

The OAO serves the underwriter in several respects. First, it is an indirect way to increase the compensation of the underwriting syndicate by placing more securities if market conditions stimulate strong demand in the aftermarket.

Second, the underwriter can use the additional securities of the OAO to satisfy demand from investors who would be otherwise rationed out of strong issues. This helps the underwriter to strengthen relationships with institutional and retail investors by placing more securities that are well received.

Third, the OAO makes price stabilization less costly for the syndicate in cases the short position has to be covered at a market price above the offer price. By reducing losses from stabilization, the OAO can possibly lead to more aggressive pricing of new issues.

Fourth, the OAO protects the underwriters when they oversell the issue in order to offset orders that may be reneged. When the oversold amount exceeds the reneged amount, the excess creates a short position that must be covered in the open market. The OAO allows the underwriter to buy the excess short position at the bid price from the issuer instead at a possibly higher market price.

Benefits of the OAO to Issuers

The OAO provision is also valuable to issuers. Issuers might grant, for example, the OAO in exchange of a lower gross spread or higher offer price. Weak issuers can also trade the OAO for greater marketing effort by the underwriter. Issuers with strong funding needs can use the OAO to raise more funds without conducting a follow-on offering. The OAO, however, may be costly to the issuer if it motivates the underwriter to underprice the issue more heavily than needed in order to raise the likelihood the OAO will be exercised or in order to recoup the cost of additional marketing effort needed to place the additional securities of the

OAO. Issuers also bear the risk that the additional funds raised remain underutilized or the additional shares issued in the case of equity offers will exacerbate the dilution of equity.

Impact on Offer Price and Issuance Costs

By promising additional compensation to the underwriter, the OAO may enable the issuer to ask for a lower gross spread or a better pricing of the issue (the substitution hypothesis). An alternative hypothesis suggests that the underwriter uses the OAO-generated compensation to recoup costs of increased marketing and placement efforts which are not covered in the gross spread or are offset by the expected degree of underpricing of the offering (the complementarity hypothesis).

Impact on Offer Price

The expected impact of the OAO on the level of the offer price is ambiguous. Smith (1986) argues that the OAO gives underwriters a motive to choose a lower offer price and, hence, underprice more new issues so that they can profit from the exercise of the OAO. On the other hand, Ritter (1987) theorizes that the OAO can help reduce underpricing because more shares of strong IPOs are available for allocation to informed investors who, thus, become more incentivized to share positive information that improves the offer price. Evidence consistent with an inverse relationship between degree of underpricing and the OAO size is reported in Welch (1991). Hanley (1993) reports that in 85% of a sample of IPOs whose offer price was set above the price range the underwriters exercised the OAO and thus were able to allocate more of underpriced shares to investors. Since IPOs priced above their price range tend to be more underpriced, this finding supports Smith's (1986) view that the OAO is associated with underpricing. Nonetheless, it can also imply that responding to strong demand, underwriters exercise the OAO and are in a position to increase allocations to preferred investor clienteles.

Impact on Underwriter Compensation

Hansen, Fuller, and Janjigian (1987) find no evidence of the cost substitution hypothesis in a sample of seasoned equity offerings. They report no meaningful differences in gross spreads (or degree of underpricing) between issues with or without an OAO even after adjusting for differences in risk. This implies that OAO users did not enjoy any savings in issuance costs. More frequent use of the OAO is reported in the case of smaller issuers, larger offers (relative to issuer size), and issuers with higher share price volatility. Carter and Dark (1990) also find that the OAO size is independent of the underwriter fees, and, hence, the OAO is additional compensation for difficult to place issues, which could also have a higher incidence of reneged orders. Kim, Palia, and Saunders (2003) also find evidence against cost substitution; IPOs with an overallotment option are found to pay higher gross spreads. However, Welch (1991) reports evidence in favor of cost substitution supported by the negative relationship of the OAO to the underwriter's total compensation (gross spread plus rebates of other expenses) in a sample of IPOs.

The Interdependence of Price Stabilization and OAO

Underwriters can use the OAO to adjust the supply of a new issue in accordance with market conditions and thus affect the market price. If the issue is cold, the underwriter may not exercise the OAO and instead cover the short position through open market buys, thus restricting the total supply to 100% of the initial offering. If the new issue is hot, the short position is covered through the exercise of the OAO, and the supply potentially increases up to 115% of the initial offering. Thus, the OAO is closely related to the price stabilization effort. In its most important contribution to price stabilization, the OAO reduces the underwriter's exposure to the risk of having to cover the short position at a higher market price should the issue be well received in the market. It is not uncommon though for the underwriter to provide price support to weak issues and also exercise the OAO (Aggarwal, 2000). This study also finds that the average short position is 17.08% of the original size of the issue, that is, above the OAO limit of 15%. This implies that syndicates assume some "naked" exposure as part of price stabilization. Thus, hot IPOs with a short position over 15% can generate considerable losses to the syndicate. (Appendix provides an extensive example on how price stabilization and the OAO work.)

Providing Liquidity in the Aftermarket

An important aftermarket service, offered by underwriters, is to provide liquidity to the new issue and help it establish an active secondary market. This is particularly important in the case of IPOs and new bond issues. Many IPO firms are not well known, and different market makers (dealers) may hold divergent views about the fair value of the issue (the case of asymmetric information). This discourages dealers not affiliated with the syndicate from making a market on the issue for fear that their buy and sell quotes may be out of line with the true market value of the issue. Reluctance to offer liquidity services can cause the security to have a high bid-ask spread, thus increasing trading costs and depriving the security of a liquid market. In turn, high-trading costs increase the liquidity premium on the issuer's cost of capital. High aftermarket liquidity is also in the interest of the underwriter because more trading and investor participation can support a higher price.

The price stabilization activities establish the lead underwriter as the main source of liquidity to selling investors. The extensive information acquired during the underwriting investigation and the price discovery the lead underwriter has conducted give the lead manager greater confidence about the value of the issue and thus the ability to market the stock at a narrower spread than other dealers. Empirical research has shown that indeed lead managers transact heavily on new issues and at lower spreads than other competing dealers. Schultz and Zaman (1994) report that over the first 3 days, lead underwriters are more likely to submit quotes to buy at higher bid prices and are less likely to submit quotes to sell at lower asking prices than other dealers who are not serving as lead underwriters. Underwriters also hold greater long positions than those held by other securities firms. This pattern is more prevalent for cold IPOs which need more price support. Ellis, Michaely, and

O'Hara (2000) find that comanagers also act as market makers in the overwhelming majority of IPOs though lead managers maintain their dominant role in both cold and hot IPOs. As expected, underwriters accumulate a lot more of cold than hot IPO shares. Very importantly, this study finds that trading and inventory profits contribute up to 23% of the total underwriter's profits (comprised of the gross spread and market-making profits). The OAO makes a crucial contribution in protecting the underwriter's profitability from market making and price stabilization.

There is a possibility that once the stabilization period is over and restrictions against flipping are removed the bid-ask spread may widen because of reduced participation of the underwriter in the trading of the issue. Li, McInish, and Wongchoti (2005) find that indeed bid-ask spreads widen after the restrictions on flipping are relaxed. However, more heavily underpriced issues are traded at smaller bid-ask spreads. Underpricing attracts more investor attention to the new issue, including analysts; and with more information produced about the issue, information asymmetry declines causing the bid-ask spread to drop.

The End of the Quiet Period and Start of Analyst Coverage

The end of the quiet period marks the time that forward-looking statements can be made by the issuer and analysts of the managing group can issue earnings forecasts and recommendations about the new issue. Nonmanaging underwriters are allowed to initiate coverage sooner. Analyst research is important in developing the secondary market for IPOs and first-time bond offerings. The release of earnings forecasts and buy or sell recommendations is particularly important to retail investors who lack the means or expertise to engage in information production. Consequently, an important service lead underwriters provide is initiation of analyst coverage as soon as the "quiet period" ends. The rules regarding the expiration of the quiet period have been revised over the years. Currently (as of December 2016), analysts associated with underwriters and dealers involved in the offering can start coverage 10 days after the IPO effective date or 3 days after the SEO effective date.

The Role of Analysts

The role of analysts in new issues is important on two levels. First, analyst coverage is important to issuers who can benefit from strong trading activity for their new securities. Second, while issuers prefer more aggressive coverage, the analysts have to weigh their interest in maintaining objectivity against the interests of their underwriting firms in attracting clients through more optimistic valuations. Therefore, the questions of interest are as follows:

- How extensive the analyst coverage is and what factors affect coverage?
- How accurate analyst forecasts are and whether analysts affiliated with underwriters are biased in their recommendations?
- How the market perceives recommendations by affiliated analysts?

Analyst Coverage

In their study of 1,611 IPOs over the period 1996 to 2000, Bradley, Jordan, and Ritter (2003) report analyst coverage was initiated for 76% of the issues. In more recent years, coverage initiation had increased to about 96% of new issues. They find that almost all analysts issue "buy" or "strong buy" recommendations. The market seems to predict these positive recommendations because the issues in the study experience a price run-up leading up to the expiration of the quiet period. In contrast, issues without immediate analyst coverage do not realize price advances prior to the end of the quiet period. The number of managing underwriters is positively related to coverage initiation and price gains around the end of the quiet period. This and other studies (e.g., Rajan and Servaes, 1997; James and Karceski, 2006) find that the extent of analyst coverage is positively related to the degree of underpricing in the case of IPOs. This can be explained by analyst aversion to cover weak stocks for which they have to issue negative recommendations (Das, Guo, and Zhang, 2006). Stocks with good prospects attract more analysts and realize better stock returns and operating performance over the 3-year period following the IPO.

Quality of Coverage

Rajan and Servaes (1997) find that analysts overestimate the level and future growth of earnings of IPO stocks but eventually they adjust their estimates. Stocks with more (less) optimistic growth projections underperform (overperform) various benchmarks. Their evidence attributes the forecast errors to universal optimism and not to endemic bias by affiliated analysts. But Michaely and Womack (1999) find that analysts affiliated with underwriters issue 50% more "buy" recommendations than independent analysts, who are less reluctant to issue "sell" recommendations. This bias is confirmed by James and Karceski (2006) who also report that analysts display higher target price ratios (target price relative to stock price prior to the analyst report) for stocks managed by their underwriting firms.

Houston, James, and Karceski (2006) find that during the dot-com bubble years 1999–2000, underwriters set offer prices below the prices of comparable firms, whereas analysts set 1-year target prices above those of comparable firms. These deviations were significantly higher for the bubble period compared to earlier years. These findings support the Loughran and Ritter (2004) view that issuing firms were willing to accept lower valuations (i.e., offer prices) in exchange for bullish analyst forecasts in the aftermarket. An alternative explanation offered by Houston, James, and Karceski (2006) is that underwriters are more exposed to litigation risk in case of overvaluation than analysts.

The Market's View

An indirect way to assess the quality of analyst coverage is to look at how the market responds to forecasts and recommendations by affiliated and independent analysts. Michaely and Womack (1999) find evidence that investors react more strongly to recommendations if they are issued by independent (unaffiliated) rather than affiliated analysts. Stocks receiving positive recommendations by unaffiliated analysts also perform better in the long run. Weaker market response to "buy" recommendations made by affiliated analysts is also reported in James and Karceski (2006) and Barber, Lehavy and Trueman (2007). The latter study also finds that "hold" and "sell" recommendations by affiliated analysts outperformed those made by independent research firms. That is, given the reluctance of affiliated analysts to make negative recommendations, such recommendations are perceived as more credible than if they are made by unaffiliated analysts.

Following the Global Analyst Research Settlement of 2003, which established "fire walls" between analyst research and underwriting, recommendations have been classified into "buy," "hold/neutral," and "sell" categories. Kadan, Madureira, Wang, and Zach (2009) find that, in the post-Settlement period, "buy" recommendations have become less frequent, even by analysts that could potentially benefit from biased recommendations while "hold" and "sell" recommendations have become more frequent. As a result, price reaction to "buy" recommendations is more positive in the post-Settlement period because of the enhanced credibility of the "buy" recommendations. On the other hand, price reaction is less negative to "hold" and "sell" recommendations than before, since they are not as surprising as they used to be prior to the reforms. Overall, the evidence supports the view that retail (hence, less sophisticated) investors have been the primary beneficiaries of the reforms ushered in by the Global Analyst Research Settlement of 2003.

Finally, Bradley, Jordan, and Ritter (2008) report that at the end of the quiet period, the market disregards reports by lead underwriter-affiliated analysts but it displays stronger reaction in later upgrades and downgrades by affiliated analysts relative to unaffiliated analysts. This suggests the market recognizes that the conflicts of interest dissipate past the end of the quiet period.

The Closing

The lead manager declares the end of the offering deal (i.e., closes the books) when all of the new issue has been sold (including the portion that corresponds to the OAO) and the price stabilization has come to an end. If the placement of the issue is unsuccessful, the lead manager will decide, usually within 30 days, whether the placement is possible at the fixed offer price and if not will declare the effort over.

Expiration of the Lockup Period

Underwriting agreements restrict certain insiders of the issuing firm from selling their shares in the secondary market for a period of 180 days after the offer day. This time interval is known as the lockup period. The restriction applies to the officers and directors of the issuing firm and shareholders who hold over 5% of the stock as well as those shareholders who are a selling party in the secondary portion of the offering. If the new issue has a liquid market and the market price is sustained well above the offer price, underwriters may release the affected shareholders from the lockup restriction. Insiders and other shareholders subject to the lockup period who have acquired shares privately in the preoffer period are not permitted to resell prior to the expiration of the lockup period even if the holding requirement of Rule 144 has been met.

The Rationale for Lockup Periods

The lockup period provision serves as another price stabilization mechanism by restricting the supply of sell orders which can depress the market price and interfere with the placement of the issue and raise the cost of price stabilization. As such, the resale restriction imposed by the lockup period can be viewed as an indirect rent (compensation) the issuing shareholders surrender to the underwriter. Through restricting sales by insiders, the lockup agreement can also serve as a mechanism that aligns the interests of inside and outside investors. Insiders are motivated to commit to efficient management so that the value of their holdings does not decline by the time the lockup period expires and they are allowed to liquidate their shares (the commitment hypothesis). From a different perspective, by accepting stricter lockup restrictions, the insiders signal their confidence in the fundamentals of their firm, thus mitigating the adverse selection problem caused by information asymmetry (the signaling hypothesis).

The empirical evidence on these hypotheses is rather mixed. Brav and Gompers (2003) find evidence in support of the commitment hypothesis. Lockup restrictions are more severe for firms that are deemed to be more exposed to moral hazard problems, i.e., the possibility managers will prefer to advance their interests at the expense of firm value maximization. If insiders appear to be less committed to value maximization, the market should react negatively at the lockup period expiration day. Indeed, Field and Hanka (2001) find that the prices of stocks decline around the expiration of the lockup period. They interpret this to be a sign of the market's perception that, after reducing their holdings, insiders are less committed to value maximization. Consistent with this interpretation, Chen, Chen, and Huang (2012) find that excessive sale by CEOs and top executives in the postlockup expiration period are associated with negative long-run stock performance. However, Brav and Gompers (2003) attribute the price decline at the expiration of the lockup period to price pressure as more securities are offered for sale.

Evidence in favor of the signaling hypothesis is offered in Brau, Lambson, and McQueen (2005) who find that lockup restrictions are associated with issuing firms surrounded by greater information asymmetry. Since the bid-ask spread at which stocks are traded is affected by the degree of information asymmetry, it can be used to test the signaling value of lockup periods. Cao, Field, and Hanka (2004) find that insider selling following lockup expirations does not increase the bid-ask spreads of the affected stocks. Instead, liquidity costs decline after the lockup expiration. Hence, the expiration of the lockup period does not negate the positive signal it conveyed in the first place.

From a different perspective, Aggarwal, Krigman, and Womack (2002) link the lockup agreement to the degree of underpricing of new issues. According to this view, issuers use underpricing strategically to attract greater investor and analyst interest to the new issue in order to generate stronger price momentum toward the expiration of the lockup period.

Insiders are found to retain more shares in IPOs which are more heavily underpriced, attract more analysts, and enjoy higher prices at the lockup expiration.

Appendix—Examples of Price Stabilization With and Without the OAO

The examples below demonstrate how prize stabilization and OAO work and their cost consequences for the underwriter. For simplicity, the examples are based on stylized facts and transactions that refer to a hypothetical initial public offering.

We assume the following data:

- Shares to be issued: 1,000,000
- OAO: 15% of the original issue or 150,000 shares
- The prospectus shows that the offer price is $20, the bid price is $18, and the gross spread is $2

Scenario 1: The underwriter oversells the issue (i.e., goes short) by 15% or 150,000 shares. After the offer, the market price advances to $22. Under this scenario, there is no need for price support since the market price is above the offer price. We assume the underwriter exercises the OAO and places an additional 150,000 shares. Hence, we observe the following:

- Shares to be delivered to investors: 1,150,000 (the original 1,000,000 plus the 150,000 of the OAO)
- Exercise of the OAO at the bid price of $18 for 150,000 shares
- Delivery of 150,000 shares to cover the short position
- Total new shares issued: 1,150,000 (1,000,000 + 150,000)
- Net gain (loss) of stabilization through short covering: $0; no need for direct stabilization since the market price exceeds the offer price
- Net gain (loss) of placing 150,000 additional shares: $300,000 (the $2 spread times 150,000 shares)
- Combined net gain (loss): $0 from stabilization plus $300,000 from exercise of OAO

Scenario 2: The underwriter oversells the 150,000 shares of the OAO at $20. On offer day, price weakness causes investors to renege on 50,000 shares of preliminary orders. The market price drops to $19 per share. The underwriter decides to support the price through bids at $20 and not to use the OAO. We observe the following under this scenario:

- Shares to be delivered to investors: 1,000,000 (original) + 150,000 (OAO) − 50,000 (reneged) = 1,100,000
- The underwriter's short position is only 100,000 shares (150,000 from the OAO minus the 50,000 reneged shares)
- The underwriter buys 100,000 shares in open market at the placed bid of $20 per share and covers short position
- Total new shares issued: 1,000,000 (no exercise of OAO)

- Net gain (loss) of price support: − $100,000 (a loss of $19 − $20 on 100,000 shares)
- Net gain (loss) from short selling 100,000 shares: $0 (the 100,000 net oversold shares placed at $20 are bought in the open market at $20)
- Combined net gain (loss): − $100,000 + $0 = −$100,000

Scenario 3: The underwriter decides to engage in more aggressive price stabilization. The issue is oversold by 250,000 shares. Due to market weakness, preliminary orders for 50,000 shares are reneged. The net short position is 200,000 (the short of 250,000 minus the 50,000 reneged shares). The net short position will be covered with the exercise of the OAO for 150,000 shares and buy bids at $20 per share for the remaining 50,000 shares. The market price drops to $19 per share. We observe the following under this scenario:

- Total shares to be delivered: 1,000,000 (original) + 150,000 (OAO) + 50,000 (naked short) = 1,200,000 shares
- The underwriter's short position is: 200,000 (250,000 oversold shares minus 50,000 shares of reneged orders)
- The underwriter exercises the OAO: buys 150,000 shares at $18 from issuer to cover the short position
- The underwriter also buys 50,000 shares at $20 to support the price
- Total new shares issued: 1,000,000 (original) plus 150,000 (OAO) = 1,150,000
- Net gain (loss) from stabilization: − $50,000 (a loss of $19 − $20 on 50,000 shares bought in open market at buy bid of $20)
- Net gain (loss) from placing 150,000 additional shares through the OAO: $300,000 (a gain of $20 − $18 on 150,000 shares bought at $18 through the OAO)
- Combined net gain (loss): − $50,000 + $300,000 = $250,000

The losses from price stabilization in these examples are actually paper losses. Whether the syndicate incurs an actual loss depends at what price the syndicate eventually disposes the accumulated shares. If the price never recovers, the underwriter incurs an actual loss. If the price recovers and reaches the offer price or goes even higher, the syndicate breaks even or makes a profit. While the underwriters hold the unsold shares, they do incur though a carrying cost (i.e., interest) on the tied-up funds.

6

Underwriting Costs
and Compensation

This chapter describes the costs issuers incur under a firm commitment contract that provides for all the underwriting services. The chapter discusses the risks associated with the gross proceeds and the rationale for transferring some of these risks to the underwriter. The chapter describes and evaluates the underwriter's risks and costs and how these are factored into the underwriter's compensation.

Issuance Costs

The flotation of a new issue of securities imposes on the issuer several types of costs. These costs include out-of-pocket expenses, indirect costs, the underwriter's compensation, and the implicit cost arising from the possible underpricing of the new issue.

Out-of-Pocket Expenses

These expenses include the cost for the preparation of the registration statement and the various filing fees.

Printing costs: These include the expenses for printing the registration statement and also the electronic filing of documents through the SEC's Electronic Data Gathering and Retrieval system (EDGAR). Revisions to the documents and special printing features contribute to the printing costs.

Accounting fees: They are paid to the auditing firm that audits and certifies the financial statements, advises on questions from the Securities Exchange Commission (SEC) staff, and prepares the comfort letter. They are higher for issuing firms with weak history of accounting records. The more a firm needs to clean up its accounts and adjust them to comply with the Generally Accepted Accounting Principles (GAAP), the higher the accounting expenses are. The accounting fees are higher when the issuer retains a higher quality auditor.

Legal fees: These are fees paid to the legal counsel that advises on issue preparation, especially in relation to describing risks and legal matters in the prospectus. Retaining a law firm that specializes in filings with the SEC helps reduce the incidence of SEC staff comments and follow up revisions of the registration documents. Legal fees also rise with the stature of the law firm retained.

Filing fees: These fees include SEC registration filing fees; Financial Industry Regulatory Authority (FINRA) filing fees; indemnity insurance fee (to protect the underwriter); state filing fees; and registrar as well as transfer agent fees (paid to the organization that will keep records of stock ownership and transfers due to trading).

Listing fees: Firms executing initial public offerings (IPOs) must list their shares on an exchange. Therefore, they have to pay the initial listing fees charged by the marketplace that will list the new securities.

Indirect Costs

Issuing firms sometimes have to sweeten the underwriter's compensation with warrants. Warrants are call options that give the underwriter the right to buy a fixed number of shares of the issuing firm's stock at very low strike (exercise) price within a fixed time period (usually a few years) from the offer date. Should the new issue prove to be valuable and rise in price, the underwriter will earn an extra compensation. Underwriters are likely to demand warrants when the risky nature of the flotation of a new issue requires a gross spread considerably above the range suggested by the FINRA guidelines. Warrants are more often used in the cases of relatively small size offerings, offerings with a low offer price, and issues with greater risk.

Other indirect costs include the time and the value of the effort devoted by the issuer to the preparation of documents, negotiations, consultations, and meetings necessary to bring the issue to the market. These activities consume considerable time of the top officers and the staff of the issuing firm and may divert management's attention from other important business of the firm.

The Underwriting (Gross or Explicit) Spread

The underwriting spread, also called gross or explicit spread, represents the direct compensation of the underwriting syndicate for the cost of its services associated with placing the new issue in the market.

The gross spread is the difference between the proceeds of the new issue and the proceeds to the issuer. On a per unit basis, it is the difference between the offer price the investors pay to buy the security from the underwriting group and the bid price the underwriter pays to buy the security from the issuing firm.

The Implicit Spread

The implicit spread is the difference between the first market price of the new security in the secondary market and the offer price. When this difference is positive, i.e., the market price exceeds the offer price, it represents the underpricing of the issue. A positive implicit spread captures what is often called the "money left on the table," since the issuer sells the new issue at a price below its starting market price. This is an indirect cost to the issuer incurred in the form of foregone proceeds. Conversely, if the market price turns out to be lower than the offer price, the new issue is considered to have been overpriced. A negative implicit spread represents a gain to the issuer and, thus, helps reduce the flotation costs.

The Underwriter's Problem

In the typical underwriting arrangement, the underwriter buys the new issue from the issuer at a fixed bid price, P_b, and then sells it into an uncertain market at a fixed offer price, P_o. The difference between the offer and bid price ideally should cover the expected underwriting cost, and the bid price should satisfy the issuer's objective to maximize the proceeds from the sale of the issue.

Below we follow a four-step approach that encompasses the tasks the underwriter must execute to arrive at the offer and bid price of the new issue. This approach also helps highlight the factors that determine the underwriting costs that must be covered by the underwriting spread. Specifically, the underwriter is expected to:

1. Estimate the expected market price the new issue will command at the time of offer;
2. Set the offer price given the estimated market price;
3. Estimate the expected underwriting costs, given the estimated market price and the chosen offer price;
4. Set the bid price so that the gross spread (i.e., underwriter compensation) equals the expected underwriter cost and the bid price meets the issuer's objective.

Step 1—Estimating the Expected Market Price of the New Issue

The underwriter arrives at an estimate of the expected market value of the new issue by relying on the following sets of information:

- Information about the issuer and the issue the underwriter collects during the prefiling period by conducting a financial, accounting, legal, engineering, management, and industry-related investigation. The analysis of this information provides the underwriter with a first estimate of the likely value of the new issue.
- Private information collected from well-informed investors during the roadshows of the new issue. The book of preliminary indications of interest is particularly important to the underwriter in as far as it reveals the market's opinion and likely demand for the new issue.
- Public information relevant to the overall market as well as to the new issue in the period preceding the pricing of the new securities.

The estimation of the expected price depends on the reliability and completeness of the information gathered and the valuation skills of the underwriter. How much information is gleaned from the underwriting investigation, how extensive the participation of investors in the roadshows is, and how truthful the investors' price signals are impact the quality of the estimation. The degree of uncertainty with which the underwriter estimates the value of the new issue is affected by ex ante risk and information asymmetry. Ex ante risk is best described by the presence of factors that increase the likely outcomes with respect to the expected value of the new issue. For example, more uses of proceeds, more business lines operated by the issuing firm, and greater market volatility increase the number of likely factors that can affect the value of the new issue. Information asymmetry describes the gap of relevant information among the different parties involved in the placement of the issue: the issuer, the underwriter, and the investors. The greater the asymmetry, especially with regard to the information sets possessed, respectively, by underwriters and investors, the less reliable the estimated expected value is.

Information gathering and expertise in valuation become increasingly important as the level of ex ante risk and information asymmetry rise. Issues with higher ex ante risk and information asymmetry have higher costs for valuation.

Step 2—Setting the Offer Price

Once the underwriter has arrived at the best estimate of the value of the new issue, the next step is to select the offer price. Obviously, the estimated market price of the new issue is the upper bound for the offer price. The underwriter cannot expect to place the new issue at an offer price that exceeds the market price of the issue. Beyond this basic consideration, the underwriter must balance the interests of issuers and investors. Thus, the following two options are possible.

Option 1—Full Pricing of the Issue

Under this option, the offer price is set equal to the estimated market price of the new issue. This leaves the possibility open that the offer price turns out to be over the actual price of the issue if the latter falls short of the estimated market price. The underwriter who accepts this risk under option 1 must factor it in the estimation of the underwriting costs. As in the case of insurance services, the underwriter would expect to breakeven over a large number of underwriting deals. Full pricing though is not compatible with the bookbuilding method of rewarding informed investors with underpriced issues. Nor is it compatible with the case of information asymmetry under which less informed investors face an adverse selection problem, i.e., the possibility that they will overpay to buy a security of lesser value. In general, full pricing is incompatible with strategic pricing of new issues to satisfy various underwriter and issuer objectives.

Option 2—Underpricing of the New Issue

Under this option, the offer price is set below the estimated expected value of the issue. This implies that the probability of observing a market price below the offer price is less than in the case of full pricing. Thus, the underwriter bears less underwriting risk than in the case of full pricing. Although option 2 can lead to lower net proceeds to the issuer, issuers may have strategic reasons to go along with underpricing. Such reasons include the goal to create "buzz" about the issue in order to attract attention to the issuing firm; the goal to attract trading and analyst interest; and the goal to leave a "good taste" in the mouth of investors so that valuation of the issuer's securities becomes more favorable. On their part, underwriters also have interests in underpricing new issues. They can use underpricing to attract informed investors to roadshows in order to ease the price discovery effort or use underpricing to extract rents from issuers and investors. Consistent with these arguments, the empirical evidence confirms that new issues are on average underpriced.

Step 3—Estimating the Expected Underwriting Costs

The Origination Service Costs

Originating underwriters maintain relationships with issuers and develop the various skills that make them successful in the placement of new issues. Therefore, they must be compensated for their investment in these resources. In addition, the lead manager and the comanagers incur costs in structuring and preparing the new issue and organizing the syndicate and the selling force. Thus, the cost of the origination service is affected by the complexity and amount of effort required. Factors that contribute to the origination service costs include:

The size and type of issue: Larger, more complex issues (e.g., bonds with special terms) require more attention and effort.

The method and type of offering: Origination costs may differ for general cash offers versus rights offerings, for IPOs versus seasoned offerings, and for domestic versus international offerings.

Issuer characteristics: These refer to issuer size, complexity, and type of business (e.g., manufacturing versus information technology firms).

The Pricing Service Cost

The pricing service refers to the price discovery activities the underwriter performs to ensure the new issue will be placed in the market. The underwriter collects information and applies valuation analysis to arrive at an estimate of the market value of the issue. In addition, the underwriter organizes the gathering of information from investors through roadshows and other communications.

Marketing a new issue, especially an IPO, with retail investors can also influence the estimate of the market value of the new security. High publicity can generate interest in the issue and feed positive anticipation among retail investors most of which are rationed out of the allocation and expect to buy in the immediate aftermarket. Cook, Kieschnick, and Ness (2006) find that promotional efforts result in higher offer prices and underwriters are rewarded with higher fees.

Factors Contributing to the Pricing Cost

The factors contributing to the pricing cost include the degree of information asymmetry driven by investor disagreement about the issue's value, and various ex ante risk factors surrounding the offering. The greater the degree of asymmetric information and the higher the level of ex ante risk, the more expensive the price discovery effort is. Issue and issuer characteristics, as well as market conditions contribute to pricing difficulties and costs. In addition, the type of the offering method (e.g., bookbuilding versus auction) and the diversity of investor clienteles targeted for distribution of the issue also impact the marketing and pricing cost. In general, the more complicated the issuer's operations are, the greater the inherent volatility of the issue is and the more volatile the market is, the higher the pricing cost is. A final factor is the experience and skills of the underwriter. The more active an underwriter is in placing new issues and conducting other capital market operations (like trading and managing investments), the more likely it is the pricing tasks will be executed with greater cost efficiency.

The Underwriting Service Cost

The underwriting service refers to the underwriter's commitment to absorb any unsold portion of the new issue if full placement fails. This commitment generates the risk of an incomplete offer if the market price turns out to be very close to or below the offer price. This is what we call underwriting or placement risk which must be priced into the cost of the underwriting service. Two conditions affect this risk. The first is the requirement under the FINRA "Rules of Fair Practice" that the new securities be placed at the offer price which deprives the underwriter the opportunity to unload the securities at prices closer to the market price while the offer lasts. The second is the time that lapses from the point the offer price is set to the point the formal offer (sale) begins. Regulatory and procedural arrangements contribute to the length of this time interval.

To better understand the placement risk, we consider both the issuer's and the underwriter's perspective and identify the specific risk the issuers transfer to underwriters.

Issuer Risks

The main objective of the issuer is to raise capital by selling securities at the highest possible price. The interval that lapses between the point of time the issuer decides to issue and the time of the actual sale exposes the issuer to both waiting and pricing risks. These risks are borne over different time segments of the issuance process.

The Risk of Selling at an Inferior Price

The issuer will fail to maximize the proceeds from the offering if the new issue bears an offer price which is below the offer price that could be supported by the market conditions at the time of sale.

Waiting to price risk: The interval between the issuer decides to issue a new security and the time the offer price is set is the waiting to price interval. During this interval, the issuer is exposed to timing risk, that is the possibility the security's price will fall by the time the issue is priced. Specifically, waiting to price risk is the likelihood that the offer price, P_o, supported by a market state M_{DT} at the time the decision to offer was made, or $P_o|M_{DT}$, is higher than the offer price chosen given a market state M_{PT} at the time of the pricing of the issue, or $P_o|M_{PT}$. M stands for market valuation conditions (which affect the offer price), DT stands for the time the decision to issue is made and PT stands for the time the pricing takes place (i.e., the offer price is set). For example, let us assume that when the firm decided to proceed with the new issue, the market conditions could support an offer price of $20; however, by the time the issue was priced the market conditions would only support a price of $18. Ideally, the issuer would prefer to have the issue priced as close to the time of the decision to offer as possible. This, however, is not possible since preparation and pricing take time. Shelf registered issues avoid this risk because they can be sold at current prices into an ongoing market. Hence, Rule 415 issuers bear insignificant waiting to price risk for the issuer.

Waiting to place risk: If there is substantial lag between the time the new issue is priced and the time it is offered, the issuer bears the risk that the offer price turns out to be lower than the price that could have been set under the market conditions prevailing close to the time of the offering. This risk can be expressed as the likelihood that $P_o|M_{PT} < P_o|M_{OT}$, where M_{OT} is the market state at the offer time. The source of this risk is the possibility that the market may improve during the time that lapses from pricing to sale. Although the issuer could withdraw the offering in order to reset the offer price, two possibilities make this option costly and/or risky. First, the rescheduling imposes time delays and additional expenses. Second, there is no guarantee that by the time the rescheduled offering is ready to go to the market at the new price the market conditions have not adversely changed. For example, let us assume that the issue is priced at $20 per share but when the offer is ready to start market conditions support a price of $22 per share. Had the issuer been allowed to cancel the issue, there is no guarantee the price would remain above $20 by the new offer time.

This type of risk may vary depending on the procedural arrangements and regulation-related delays that apply in various countries and across offering methods. For example, in the United States new issues are priced very close to the time of offer. On the other hand, issues offered through the subscription method in foreign markets are priced well in advance of their actual offering.

The Risk of Overpricing or Placement Risk

This risk is also associated with the waiting to place risk but it refers to outcomes opposite to those of the previous section. It is the risk associated with overpricing the issue. Namely, the offer price set at the time the issue is priced turns out to be higher than the offer price that would be acceptable given the market conditions when the issue is sold. It refers to the possibility that $P_o|M_{PT} > P_o|M_{OT}$. For example, given the market conditions prevailing at the time the issue is priced, the offer price is set at $20 per share. When the issue is offered the price is $18 per share. In this case, the issuer is unable to place the whole issue and raise all the planned capital. This may cause delays in the financing and implementation of profitable investments or other corporate restructurings. It is this type of risk that issuers are able to shift to underwriters for a fee. Regulatory provisions and offering methods that allow pricing close to the offer time mitigate waiting to place risk that results in overpricing.

Pricing Risk

In addition to waiting risk, the issuer (and, as shown below, the underwriter) bears pricing risk. Pricing risk is associated with the likelihood the issuer will fail to estimate accurately the fair value of the new issue that is expected to be observed at the time of the offer. Pricing risk can arise due to poor valuation skills and limited experience or because of insufficient or wrong information.

Using an Underwriter

What types of risk can the issuer unload to the underwriter? Underwriting the issue cannot protect the issuer from the risk associated with the waiting to price risk. This risk arises from market movements and time delays prior to setting the offer price.

The issuer can, however, unload the risk of overpricing the issue to an underwriter. That is, the issuer can transfer the placement risk to the underwriter. Underwriting protects the issuer against waiting to offer risk and pricing risk. Let us assume that a firm plans a public offering to raise an amount of capital K with the issuance of N units of a security at an offer price of P_o, such that $K = N \times P_o$. The issuer faces the following probable outcomes in the respective cases of a nonunderwritten and an underwritten offering.

Nonunderwritten Offering

In the absence of underwriting, the proceeds to the issuer are:

$$\text{Proceeds without underwriter} = \begin{cases} N \times P_o = K, \text{if } P_o \leq P_m \\ N_a \times P_o < K, \text{if } P_o > P_m \end{cases},$$

where N_a is the actual number of units sold (in this case $N_a < N$), and P_m is the market value of the security at the offer time. If, at the offer time, the actual market price falls short of the offer price, part or all of the issue will not be sold. Hence, without an underwriter, the issuer bears the risk of failing to raise the planned amount of K.

Underwritten Offering

The issuer can use an underwriter who assumes the placement risk at a fee, F. The issuer's proceeds are now:

$$\text{Proceeds with underwriter} = \begin{cases} K - F = N \times P_o - F, \text{if } P_o \leq P_m \\ K - F = N \times P_o - F, \text{if } P_o > P_m \end{cases}.$$

These proceeds will be realized with full certainty whether P_o is less, equal to, or greater than P_m.

The issuer has two options: to go through with the new issue without an underwriter and be uncertain about the amount of the proceeds or use an underwriter and secure a certain amount given by $K - F$. This is the familiar problem of choosing between the expected value of the random proceeds and the certainty equivalent of the random proceeds which is below the expected value in the case of risk-averse issuers.

Underwriter Risks

The above analysis shows that the role of the underwriter is to protect the issuer against the possibility of overpricing the issue relative to its market price at the offer time. Thus, the waiting to offer risk and the pricing risk are transferred to the underwriter.

Factors Contributing to Waiting Risk

Waiting risk increases with the time it takes to bring an already priced issue to the market. The volatility of the market during the waiting interval also contributes to waiting risk. The more volatile the market is, the greater the likelihood the market price of the issue that will prevail at the offer time may deviate from the price estimated when the offer price was set. Different securities are affected more or less severely by market volatility depending on their sensitivity to market movements, exemplified by their beta or systematic risk. Also, different securities are more or less sensitive to risks specific to the firm. In general, stocks are more volatile than bonds as a result of market or firm volatility and, hence, expose underwriters to more waiting risk.

Factors Contributing to Pricing Risk

The following factors contribute to pricing risk:

Degree of asymmetric information: The underwriter and the investors may have different views about the quality of the issuer and the new security. The underwriter may fail to recognize the true strength of demand by investors while the latter may have incomplete information about the issuer. The less known the issuer is and the less the issuer has been subjected to the scrutiny of markets or lenders, the greater the degree of informational asymmetry can be. Thus, IPOs, are more likely to have greater informational asymmetry than seasoned equity offerings. Or firms that have ongoing borrowing relationships with banks may have less informational asymmetry compared to firms without such relationships.

Level of ex ante risk: Prior to observing the actual market price, the underwriter must estimate the likely factors that can contribute to different price outcomes for the new issue. The more dispersed these outcomes are relative to each other the greater the average deviation of probable prices from the expected price. Thus, ex ante risk can be understood as the standard deviation of likely market prices at the offer. From this perspective, stocks have greater ex ante risk than bonds, and lower quality bonds have more risk than higher quality bonds. Issuers with more complex operations may also have greater risk than firms with simpler business structures.

Market conditions: Volatile markets introduce more noise in the interpretation of the true state of the market and make price estimates become less reliable.

Quality of information: The degree to which the information gathered during the prepricing period is reliable and complete can impact pricing risk. For example, as explained in Chapter 4: The Mechanics of the Issuance Process, limit, and step bids are more informative than strike bids. The more uncertain the underwriter is about the demand schedule that emerges from the book the greater the risk of mispricing.

Underwriter expertise and experience: More experienced underwriters and those who engage in repeat underwriting deals develop superior skills in the valuation of securities.

Pricing the Underwriting Service

Below we present two approaches regarding the pricing of the underwriting service. The first approach prices the underwriting service as an insurance policy and the second as an option. The conceptual premise is the same for both approaches. The issuer buys an insurance from the underwriter because in firm commitment contracts proceeds to the issuer are guaranteed to be fixed. Similarly, under the contingent claims approach, the issuer buys a put option from the underwriter which sets the lower bound for the proceeds the issuer expects to receive when the market price of the issue falls below the price the underwriter committed to pay to the issuer. Under both approaches, the insurance premium or the put option's price (premium) is the cost the issuer pays for the firm commitment guarantee and represents the underwriter's compensation for the risk borne.

The Underwriting Service Priced as an Insurance Policy

Mandelker and Raviv (1977) price the underwriting service as an insurance policy. According to this approach, the issuer pays the underwriter a risk premium to receive a fixed amount of proceeds. The premium is a reward to the underwriter for the risk associated with the purchase of the securities at a fixed price, P_b, from the issuer and their sale at a fixed offer price, P_o, into an uncertain market where P_m may be less than P_o.

Given the variability of market price outcomes at the offer time, a risk-averse issuer determines the amount K_{ic}, as the certainty equivalent amount the issuer is willing to accept in lieu of giving up the right to collect the uncertain proceeds from the sale of the new issue. (We recall that the issuer faces two outcomes: $N \times P_o$ or $N_a \times P_o$.) The underwriter also determines the amount K_{uc}, as the certainty equivalent amount the underwriter is willing to pay the issuer. (The underwriter commits to pay a fixed sum whether he/she receives $N \times P_o$ or $N_a \times P_o$ from the sale of the issue.) K_{ic} is the minimum amount acceptable to the issuer, and K_{uc} is the maximum amount the underwriter is willing to pay. The issuer and the underwriter arrive at their respective certainty equivalent amounts by deducting their respective risk premium from the expected proceeds, $E(K)$, of the issue. The risk premium represents the discount one has to take in trading uncertain payoffs for a certain amount so that the utility of the certainty equivalent is equal to the expected utility of the uncertain payoffs.

Assuming underwriters are less risk averse than issuers, the underwriter's risk premium will be less than the issuer's risk premium and, hence, the underwriter's certainty equivalent will be greater than the certainty equivalent acceptable to the issuer, that is,

$K_{uc} > K_{ic}$. Therefore, the underwriter's reward, F, for the guarantee given to the issuer will be such that

$$E(K) - K_{uc} < F < E(K) - K_{ic}.$$

This means that the underwriter's reward, F, is lower than the risk premium (cost) of the issuer. Under this condition, the underwriting contract is acceptable to the issuer and the underwriter.

The Underwriting Service Priced as an Option

The underwriter's guarantee can be also analyzed within the contingent claims framework. This approach was first applied by Smith (1977) to price the underwriting service under a firm commitment contract. Smith (1977) views the firm commitment contract as a call option sold by the issuer to the underwriter. Within the same framework, Bae and Levy (1990) show that the underwriting service can be viewed and priced accordingly as a put option purchased by the issuer from the underwriter. Although both approaches arrive at the same conclusion in valuing the underwriting service, considering the underwriting service contract as a put option purchased by the issuer is directly analogous to the underwriting service construed as an insurance policy.

Smith (1977) postulates that under a firm commitment arrangement, the underwriter commits to buy from the issuer the new securities at a fixed sum of money, B. The underwriter then sells the securities at the offer price (if the latter is equal or less than the market price) or at the market price (if the offer price exceeds the market price). Smith (1977) shows that within a contingent claims framework, the underwriting service fee is equivalent to the value of (1) a long position on the new securities; (2) a cash payment B; and (3) a call written on the new securities.

These three transactions are equivalent to a synthetic put (Bae and Levy, 1990). Therefore, under a firm commitment contract, the value of the underwriting service can be expressed as

$$U = -e^{rT}p + X - B,$$

where U is the value of the underwriting service; p is the value of the put; X is the offer price; and B is the bid price (where all are on a per unit, e.g., share, basis).

Unless the underwriter systematically overprices or underprices the underwriting service, in a competitive equilibrium the expected value of the underwriting service, U, must equal zero. Ignoring the discounting factor for p, fair pricing of the contract implies $p = X - B$, that is, the value of the underwriting contract, p, is equal to the offer price minus the bid price. (Appendix provides a more detailed explanation of the option-based approach to valuing the underwriting service contract.)

Modeling the underwriting service contract as a put allows to identify several effects on the cost of the underwriting service. The cost of the underwriting service (i.e., value of the put) increases with the volatility of the underlying asset, the time to expiration, and the difference between the offer price and the bid price. Therefore, the underwriting risk premium is higher for more volatile issues and the longer the time lag is between pricing the issue (i.e., agreeing on the terms of the contract) and the actual offer date.

The above model prices only the underwriting service and not the other component costs of the underwriting contract. Hence, to arrive at the total expected underwriting fee or gross spread, these costs must be added to the underwriting service cost.

The Distribution Service Costs

The distribution costs include the expenses for the activities the underwriter has to undertake to place the new issue in the market. These costs are associated with the salesforce effort as well as the other resources (infrastructure in sales outlets, technology, etc.) required to execute the sale of the issue.

Factors Contributing to the Placement Cost of a New Issue

Uncertainty about the expected price of the issue: Greater uncertainty about the "true" price of the new issue makes it more likely the new issue may not be well received by the market because of a relatively high offer price. In this case, the distribution effort may last longer and the cost will be higher.

The average order size: The distribution cost is also affected by the average order size per buyer. Bond issues, usually placed in bulk with institutional investors, are less costly to distribute than stock issues which are sold to relatively more individual investors and in smaller amounts in order to secure widespread ownership.

The distribution terms: Some offerings require that a certain portion of the new securities is placed internationally. Terms that expand the scope and geography of the distribution of the securities can impose additional placement costs on the investment banker.

The carrying cost: If part of the issue is not sold, the underwriter will be forced to hold the new issue much longer than expected. During this time the underwriter will bear the cost of financing the unsold position as well as the risk the security's price will permanently decline below the price paid to the issuer.

Expected Underwriting Cost and Underwriting Spread

Once the underwriter has estimated the expected costs for all the underwriting services included in the contract, the total expected underwriting cost is the sum of the component costs,

$$E(UC) = E(OC) + E(PC) + E(USC) + E(DC),$$

where $E(UC)$ is the total expected underwriting cost; $E(OC)$ is the expected origination cost; $E(PC)$ is the expected pricing and marketing cost; $E(USC)$ is the expected underwriting service cost; and $E(DC)$ is the expected distribution cost. Given the estimated expected cost for underwriting the issue, the underwriter's compensation, i.e., the underwriting fee or gross spread, GS, should equal the expected underwriting cost, that is

$$GS = E(UC).$$

The level of the offer price chosen in relation to the estimated market value of the new issue can affect the various components of the underwriting cost and thus influence the level of the underwriter's compensation. There can be also trade-offs between components of the underwriting cost. These relationships and trade-offs are discussed below.

Interdependence of the Costs for Pricing and Underwriting Services

In executing the price discovery task, the underwriter has to predict the likely demand schedules that in conjunction with the fixed supply of the offered securities will determine the possible clearing prices. In practice, it is unlikely that the underwriter will acquire all the relevant information that is necessary to determine the full distribution of clearing prices. Hence, the underwriter has to rely on incomplete information that yields only a sample of the total population of probable clearing prices. Probability theory suggests that using a sample (rather than the population) to estimate the mean leads to estimation errors, that is, the sample mean deviates from the true mean of the population of likely clearing prices.

If the underwriter's sample estimate of expected market price is above the true mean, the underwriter runs the risk of overpricing the new issue; if it is below, the underwriter runs the risk of hurting the issuer by leaving too much money on the table. Therefore, the quality of the pricing service depends on the reliability of the underwriter's expected value as an estimate of the true mean of the likely clearing prices. Moreover, the more confident the underwriter is about the reliability of the estimated value of the security the more accurate the estimation of the underwriting service costs is. If confidence on the reliability of the estimated price is low, the underwriter has to charge more for the underwriting service to ensure recovery of the actual cost of these services. More resources and effort spent on price discovery can improve the reliability of the underwriter's estimate; but they also increase the cost of price discovery in terms of roadshows, information gathering, and valuation analysis.

While more thorough price discovery can reduce the cost of the underwriting service, it also raises the pricing service cost. Thus, there is a trade-off between pricing service costs and underwriting service costs. The optimal strategy is to expand the price discovery effort

Illustration 6.1 Interdependence of Pricing and Underwriting Service Costs

Type of Cost	Low Pricing Effort	Moderate Pricing Effort	High Pricing Effort	Very High Pricing Effort
Pricing service cost ($)	3.0	3.5	3.8	4.0
Underwriting service cost ($)	4.0	3.2	3.0	2.9
Sum of costs ($)	7.0	6.7	6.8	6.9

up to the point that the sum of the pricing service cost and the underwriting service cost is minimized. The trade-off of the pricing and underwriting service costs for a hypothetical case is given in Illustration 6.1.

In the above illustration, the optimal level of pricing effort is at the moderate level because it minimizes the sum of the two component costs.

Impact of Offer Price on Expected Underwriting and Distribution Costs

Given an expected market price estimate, the expected underwriting service and placement costs are decreasing with lower offer prices. In other words, the lower the offer price set relative to the expected market value of the issue, the lower the risk the offer price will turn out to exceed the actual market price and the faster the issue will be bought by investors. Therefore, both the cost of the underwriting service and the cost of the distribution service should drop as the offer price falls.

The trade-off between offer price and costs for underwriting and distribution services implies there is a range of underwriting service and placement service costs that correspond to different offer prices for a given estimate of the expected market price. This is illustrated for a hypothetical case in Illustration 6.2.

Illustration 6.2 is constructed by assuming the estimated expected market price of the new issue is $20. The illustration shows that as the offer price is set at a lower level relative to the expected market price, both the cost for underwriting service and the cost for distribution drop.

Illustration 6.2   Impact of Offer Price on Underwriting and Placement Service Costs

$E(P_m)$ ($)	P_o ($)	Underwriting Service Cost ($)	Placement Service Cost ($)
20	20	2.00	4.0
20	18	1.00	3.0
20	16	0.50	2.0

Relationship of Offer Price to Expected Implicit Spread

The expected implicit spread is the difference between the expected market price of the issue and its offer price. The nature of the underwriter's risk implies that the offer price should not exceed the expected market price. Accordingly, for a given estimate of the expected market price, as the offer price declines, the expected implicit spread rises.

The Relationship of Expected Implicit and Expected Explicit (Gross) Spread

The positive impact of offer price on the expected costs of the underwriting and distribution services implies that the offer price is also directly (positively) related to the expected total underwriting cost and, hence, to the explicit or gross spread. Given the direct relationship of the offer price to the expected implicit spread, it follows that the expected implicit spread is inversely related to the expected explicit (gross) spread of the new issue.

Choosing a lower offer price (given an estimate of the market price of the issue) increases the expected implicit spread [i.e., the difference $E(P_m) - P_o$] but at the same time it decreases the expected total cost of underwriting, and, hence, the explicit (gross) spread.

The direct relationship of the offer price to the expected underwriting cost has an important implication. The underwriter can use the offer price to adjust the expected total underwriter cost to the level of compensation, i.e., gross spread, negotiated with the issuer.

Step 4—Setting the Bid Price

Following the estimation of the total expected underwriting cost implied by the estimated expected market price and the chosen offer price, the underwriter is ready to set the bid price. The bid price must produce a spread relative to the offer price that covers the expected underwriting cost. Consequently, the bid price is the difference of the offer price minus the expected underwriting costs subject to the condition that the gross spread is equal to the expected underwriting cost.

The Issuer's Objective

The underwriter's decision regarding the choice of the offer price should also take into consideration the issuer's objective. From a value maximization viewpoint, the issuer's objective ought to be the maximization of the net proceeds from the offering. Since for a given expected market price, different offer prices result in different gross spreads, the issuer should choose the option with the bid price that maximizes the net issue proceeds.

Issuers might have various motives for not choosing the highest bid price possible if it comes with a higher than otherwise offer price. Issuers may prefer a lower offer price in order to achieve strategic objectives, like a promotional buzz, a positive valuation signal, or widespread distribution of the new issue (especially in IPOs). Issuers who plan to return soon to the market to sell more securities may also be concerned about investor sentiment relating to their experience from the previous issue.

Yeoman (2001) sets up an analytical approach that aims to maximize the net proceeds to the issuer by determining simultaneously the optimal offer price and gross spread subject to the constraint that the spread covers the competitive price of the underwriting risk as in Smith (1977). Yeoman shows that the optimal solution requires that the offer price be set below the expected market price of the issue. In this model, therefore, underpricing is consistent with the objective of maximizing the net proceeds.

Practical Issues

In practice, the issuer and the underwriter first negotiate the spread as a percent of the offer price and then the underwriter sets the offer price. Furthermore, the FINRA guidelines and industry practices relating to underwriting compensation add to the complications surrounding the determination of spreads and offer prices. The FINRA guidelines, for example, compel underwriters to keep the spread within a certain range whether the risks and costs of individual offers dictate a spread above the implied range. Also for competitive reasons, underwriting spreads tend to narrowly cluster around some percentage, especially in the case of IPOs. For example, IPOs with proceeds over $20 million are known to be underwritten at a gross spread of 7%—a practice that has been dubbed the "7 percent solution" (Chen and Ritter, 2000).

Whether constrained by FINRA guidelines or industry norms, such predetermined spreads may result in a mismatch between the gross spread and the expected costs the underwriter faces in the flotation of a new issue. In such cases, the underwriter can use the relationship between offer price and expected underwriting costs to bring about a parity between the compensation imposed by regulatory or industry constraints and the expected underwriting costs. In offerings whose overall riskiness and complexity suggests an underwriting cost that cannot be recouped by charging, say, the customary 7%, the underwriter can lower the offer price. Given the estimated expected market price of the issue, there is an offer price at which the negotiated gross spread equals the implied expected costs of the underwriting services.

The above conditions—agreeing first on the spread and then on the offer price along with the constraints on the gross spread—suggest that neither Yeoman's simultaneous determination of the optimal gross spread and offer price nor the four-step approach followed above describe accurately how the underwriting terms are negotiated. Furthermore, Yeoman (2001) shows that developing exact analytical formulas to derive the optimal offer price and gross spread that maximize net proceeds is not possible when agreeing on the spread precedes the setting of the offer price. Instead, in this case, the underwriter has to resort to an iteration process until the offer price and gross spread that maximize the net proceeds are identified.

The Net Gain to the Underwriter

Whether the gross spread achieves its goal to fully cover the actual underwriting costs becomes known only when the formal offer begins and the underwriter observes the actual market price. At this point, the underwriter can estimate the actual costs of the underwriting effort. Depending on the level of the actual market price relative to the underwriter's estimation, it is likely the underwriter incurs a net underwriter gain or loss. A net underwriter gain is realized when the difference between the gross spread charged and the actual (ex post) underwriting cost is positive. Conversely, a negative difference results in a net underwriter loss. Accordingly, the net underwriter gain (loss) is represented by the following equation:

$$\text{Net Underwriter Gain(Loss)} = \begin{cases} \text{Gain, if Actual Gross Spread} > \text{Actual Underwriting Costs} \\ \text{Loss, if Actual Gross Spread} < \text{Actual Underwriting Costs} \end{cases},$$

where the Actual Underwriter Cost $= OC + USC + PC + DC$; and OC, PC, USC, and DC are, respectively, the actual costs for origination service, pricing and marketing service, underwriting service, and distribution service.

The net underwriter gain can result either because of unanticipated events or deliberate overcharging by the underwriter. For example, it may turn out that the actual implicit spread (i.e., $P_m - P_o$) is much higher than its expected value that was used to set the gross spread. This wider than expected implicit spread implies that the underwriting service cost charged is higher than what is justified by the risk actually borne by the underwriter. In addition, the distribution fee may prove to be higher than what the actual conditions of placing the issue warrant. Hence, the actual ex post total underwriting cost is lower than what it was expected to be and, thus, lower than the gross spread earned as compensation. In this case, the underwriter has earned a net underwriter gain. The converse is also true. If market receptivity is not as strong as expected, the initial market price might turn out to be lower than what was anticipated by the underwriter. Hence, from an ex post perspective, the underwriter has not charged the commensurate underwriting premium and the implied placement costs. In this case, the underwriter incurs a net loss.

We can illustrate the underwriter's gain or loss based on ex post realization of market prices using the following example: Assume the underwriter sets the offer price at $15 and estimates the expected underwriting costs to be $1 based on the belief that prices are drawn from a random distribution with a mean value (expected price) of $15 and a standard deviation of $3. Thus, the underwriter applies full pricing. At the offer time, though, the prices of the new issue behave as if drawn from a distribution with a mean value of $20 and a standard deviation of $2. That is, the price distribution has shifted to the right of the distribution expected by the underwriter, and, hence, the issue comes out underpriced. Therefore, the actual underwriting costs turn out to be less than their expected level for a fully priced issue. Had the original price distribution materialized at the offer time, observing actual market prices exceeding the offer price of $15 should not be interpreted as evidence of a net gain or underpricing. The possibility of actual prices above or below the mean of the ex ante price distribution has been already incorporated in the estimation of the expected underwriting costs.

Although individual offerings may produce positive or negative net underwriter gains, over the long-run the net gains and losses should even out so that underwriters earn their fair competitive return on the services they provide to issuers.

Appendix—Derivation of the Option-Based Value of the Underwriting Service Contract

Following Smith (1977), under the firm commitment contract underwriter pledges to pay B dollars, on the offer date, to the issuer and receive shares of stock representing fraction γ of the total shares (or value V) of the firm. The fraction γ is the ratio of shares sold through the offering to the total number of shares outstanding, i.e., $\gamma = \frac{Q_R}{Q_S + Q_R}$. Q_R is the number of shares sold through the offering and Q_S is the existing number of shares, therefore $B = Q_R \times P_b$ which is the fixed sum to be paid to the issuer. The underwriter can sell the securities at the offer price and receive a total payment of $\Omega = Q_R \times P_o$, if the share price is above the offer price, or at the market price and receive $\gamma(V^* + B)$, if the share price is below the offer price, where V^* is the value of the firm's assets on the actual offer date (i.e., the expiration date of the call option underwriter holds). Thus, the value of the underwriting contract is given by:

$$\text{Value of underwriting contract} = \begin{cases} \Omega - B, \text{ if } P_o \leq P_m \\ [\gamma(V^* + B)] - B, \text{ if } P_o > P_m \end{cases}.$$

Using the contingent claims formulation, Smith (1977) shows that the value of the underwriting contract, U, can be written as follows:

$$U = e^{rT}\gamma V - (1 - \gamma)B - e^{rT}C(\gamma V; \Omega - \gamma B),$$

where $C(\gamma V; \Omega - \gamma B)$ represents the value of a European style call option with exercise price of $(\Omega - \gamma B)$ written on the underlying asset γV, where $\gamma V \approx S$, i.e., the stock price, and $(\Omega - \gamma B) \approx X$, i.e., the exercise price within the standard Black–Scholes–Merton option pricing formulation. According to Smith, the value of the underlying contract, U, to the issuer is equivalent to a portfolio consisting of a long position in the firm, a cash payment, and writing a call on γ of the firm with an exercise price equal to $(\Omega - \gamma B)$.

Smith (1977) develops the above model for the firm value and total payment by the underwriter to the issuer, i.e., total bid value, whereas Bae and Levy (1990) develop an equivalent model on a per share basis for both the offering as well as the bid price. The put-call-parity relationship for European style options within the standard Black–Scholes–Merton option pricing framework, i.e.,

$$P + S = C + e^{-rT}X,$$

can be applied to Smith's formulation to derive the equivalent contingent claims model representation of the underwriting contract presented by Bae and Levy (1990). Based on the put-call-parity relationship with $S = \gamma V$ and $X = (\Omega - \gamma B)$, the value of the call option can be written as:

$$C = P + \gamma V - e^{-rT}(\Omega - \gamma B).$$

Substituting this call value into the equation derived by Smith (1977) yields the following:

$$U = - e^{rT}P + \Omega - B,$$

which can be shown to be equivalent to the value of the underwriting contract derived on a per share basis by Bae and Levy (1990):

$$U = - e^{rT}p + X - B,$$

where p is the per share value of a put option written on newly issued shares, X is the offering price and B is the price per share to be paid to the issuing firm. Bae and Levy (1990) refer to the put option in the portfolio that represents the value of the underwriting contract as a "synthetic put" which is sold by the underwriter to the issuing firm. The put-call-parity relationship for European style options shows that a put option can be replicated, or synthetically created, by holding positions in the underlying security, cash and a call option.

Alternative Offering Methods in New Issues Markets

The previous chapters have described the issuance process under the practice that is referred to as the bookbuilding method. This chapter describes variations of this practice as well as other offering methods. The chapter also offers a review of theoretical arguments and empirical observations that pertain to the pros and cons of alternative offering methods.

Accelerated Seasoned Equity Offers

The relaxation of regulatory constraints in the offering of seasoned issues around the world has given rise to accelerated underwriting arrangements. For example, Rule 415 allows US issuers to sell seasoned equity at any time during a 3-year period, once the registration statement has become effective. The automatic effectiveness of the registration statement filed by "well-known seasoned issuers" has further accelerated the issuance of securities by such qualified issuers.

Accelerated offerings can have both a primary component that raises capital for the firm and a secondary component that allows current shareholders to liquidate part of their shareholdings. By 2004, accelerated offers had grown to more than 50% of global seasoned equity offerings in US dollars (Bortolotti, Megginson, and Smart, 2008).

There are two general forms of accelerated seasoned equity placements: (1) the block trade and "bought deal"; (2) the accelerated bookbuilt offering.

Block Trades and "Bought Deals"

Under this type of accelerated offer, the issuer or selling shareholders invite investment banks to bid for the shares offered. The offering method resembles an auction, in which the winning underwriter buys the new issue unconditionally and is responsible for its resale at a spread over the bid price. The typical first-time buyers are institutional investors. This issuance process does not allow the bidding underwriters to apply full due diligence or build a book of preliminary orders to gauge the demand for the new issue.

Accelerated Bookbuilt Offerings

In this type of offering, the issuer invites investment banks to bid for the new issue. In this case, however, the bidding underwriters do not buy the new issue outright at the submitted bid. Instead, the underwriters first submit a backstop (minimum) price guarantee with the final offer and bid price set after the winning underwriter has built the order book with the

Underwriting Services and the New Issues Market. DOI: http://dx.doi.org/10.1016/B978-0-12-803282-4.00007-9

help of syndicated underwriters. In addition to offering a competitive bid price, winning the underwriting deal also depends on other terms, such as the underwriting spread charged and the placement capabilities of the underwriter. The winning investment bank forms a small syndicate, markets the issue, and builds a book of preliminary orders. The underwriting is completed, usually within 48 hours, when the final offer price as well as the bid price are set. The underwriter is also responsible for price stabilization in the aftermarket.

The above types of accelerated offerings have different implications for the risks borne, respectively, by the issuer and underwriter. In block trades and "bought deals," the issuer is not exposed to waiting risk till the issue is priced for sale; this risk is transferred to the underwriter. In accelerated bookbuilt offerings, the issuer shares the waiting risk with the underwriter until the latter sets the final offer (and bid) price. Nonetheless, the backstop price guarantee still offers issuers some protection against adverse market movements.

Comparison of Accelerated and Traditional Offers

The much shorter time interval between the decision to offer and the pricing of the new issue affords accelerated offerings a clear advantage over traditional offerings with respect to reducing the waiting risk of the issuer. On the other hand, accelerated offerings do not have the advantage of the more intensive price discovery and marketing of traditional bookbuilt offers.

A recent study by Bortolotti, Megginson, and Smart (2008) has reported the following comparative findings for accelerated and traditional offers completed in the United States between 1991 and 2004:

- Accelerated offers are larger in gross proceeds and are executed by larger issuers.
- Accelerated offers have smaller syndicates.
- The stock price of issuers reacts similarly upon announcement of an accelerated or traditional equity offer.

Controlling for various factors, accelerated offers, in general, carry lower gross spreads and are less underpriced than traditional offerings. Accelerated bookbuilt offers are also found to have smaller underwriting spreads as well as underpricing than block trades and "bought deals." The lower underwriting spread for accelerated bookbuilt offers can be attributed to the lower underwriting risk borne by the underwriter (due to bookbuilding); while the lower underpricing is due to the presale information gathered by the underwriter that helps set offer prices closer to market prices. The benefits of accelerated offers in regards to underwriting cost and underpricing are less pronounced in the case of European and global (non-US) offers. Distinguishing between accelerated seasoned equity issues that use bookbuilding and those that are taken "off the shelf" (under Rule 415), Huang and Zhang (2011) find that accelerated bookbuilt offers carry higher average and median gross spreads because of the higher marketing and price discovery costs.

According to Gao and Ritter (2010) issuers who raise more capital or offer more shares relative to the preoffer number of shares outstanding prefer a fully marketed bookbuilt offering to an accelerated offering because the former method enables underwriters to expand the demand for the offered shares. Fully marketed issues display a more elastic demand after the issue (which adds to their liquidity) but suffer greater underpricing than accelerated issues (3.4% versus 1.6%).

The Subscription Method

The Pure Subscription Method

Until the early 1990s, the most common offering procedure used in new issues markets outside the United States was the subscription method—also known as the fixed-price method. In the typical case, the issuer gives an investment bank a mandate to act as the underwriter of the issue. It is not uncommon for the issuer to retain another investment bank to act as issue adviser. The task of the issue adviser is to advise and assist the issuer in relation to the structure of the offering, the pricing, and the regulatory as well as underwriting arrangements (e.g., audits, registration filings, choosing an underwriter and syndicate members). In the absence of an issue adviser, these services are carried out by the lead underwriter.

The lead underwriter's main tasks include: forming the offering syndicate, marketing the issue, setting the final price, organizing the subscription of investors to the new issue, and underwriting the risk associated with an incomplete subscription.

Once the issuer and the underwriter have agreed on the offer price and the other terms of the offering, they announce the subscription period, usually lasting up to a week, during which investors are invited to subscribe to the new issue at the fixed offer price. Among other things, the announcement includes the terms of allocation in the case of oversubscription. Depending on market receptivity, new issues may be subscribed many times their size. In these cases, the allocation rules give every investor a chance to receive part of the new issue in proportion to the investor's subscription. Hence, underwriters have no control over the allocation of the issue, unlike in a bookbuilt offering.

If the issue is fully subscribed, the underwriters have no risk exposure. They pay the issuer the offering proceeds minus their underwriting fee. If the issue is not, however, fully subscribed, the underwriters are obliged by the underwriting contract to absorb the unplaced amount of the issue at the offer price minus the underwriting fee. Thus, the subscription method is a fixed-price firm commitment offer but without presale marketing through bookbuilding.

The commission made on subscribed offerings is split among the syndicate participants according to their contribution to the management, underwriting, and subscription of the issue. Syndicate members with extensive branch networks (e.g., banks) are favored in generating greater subscriptions than members with limited retail and wholesale capacity. Sometimes, syndicate members may subunderwrite part of their allotment to other institutions for a fraction of the underwriting fee.

At least in the past, and more particularly in the case of initial public offerings (IPOs), there was a time gap between the end of the subscription period (placement) of the new issue and the start of trading in the secondary market. In these cases, interim trades could be executed in the gray market.

There are significant differences between the subscription and the bookbuilding methods:

- In subscription offerings, the offer price is set without the advantage of preoffering communications with informed investors regarding the value of the issue. This deprives the underwriter of the opportunity to garner information about the demand for the issue.
- The lack of control over allocation of the issue also prevents the underwriter from incentivizing informed investors to reveal positive information by promising preferential allocation of the new issue.
- There is a longer time lag between the time the offer price is set and the time the subscription period expires. Hence, the underwriter is exposed to greater underwriting (i.e., waiting and pricing) risk.
- Secondary market trading usually starts several days—even weeks—after the issue has been sold to investors. Greater investor uncertainty about the ultimate market price of the issue can contribute to lower bids by subscribing investors.

Hybrid Offerings (Subscription with Bookbuilding)

The growing involvement of US investment banks in international securities offerings, mostly driven by privatization of state-owned enterprises, led to greater acceptance of the book-building method, often in conjunction with traditional methods, thus giving birth to the hybrid offering.

A hybrid-offering method includes presale marketing and bookbuilding which is used to arrive at the fixed offer price at which investors are invited to submit subscription bids. In such hybrid deals, the lead manager organizes a roadshow to promote the new issue among institutional investors, after which other investment banks are invited to show their interest by submitting quantities and prices for the new issue. Interested underwriters do that after they have collected preliminary indications of interest (with respect to price and quantity) from their own institutional clients. The lead manager utilizes the information from the book to set the final subscription price for all—institutional and retail—investors. This usually is done the day before the subscription period starts. There is usually an ex ante indication how the new issue will be allocated with institutional and retail investors, with the bulk going typically to the former group.

In hybrid offerings, bookbuilding and subscription can be organized to take place either sequentially or simultaneously.

Simultaneous Hybrid Underwriting

In simultaneous hybrid offerings, the subscription period runs parallel with the bookbuilding phase. While the underwriter markets the issue, investors are invited to subscribe to the new issue by submitting quantity-specific orders. The preliminary prospectus circulated to interested investors contains an indicative price range which serves to guide subscribers in determining their order size. Moreover, the underwriter indicates that the final offer price will not exceed the upper bound of the price range. This gives subscribing investors a guarantee as to what the highest offer price might be. The final offer price is then set at the clearing price suggested by the book allowing for a price discount to guarantee complete subscription. Simultaneous hybrid offerings afford the underwriter the advantage to continue to gauge the demand for the new securities throughout the subscription period and set the offer price at the end of this period.

Sequential Hybrid Underwriting

In sequential hybrid offerings, the subscription period starts after the bookbuilding phase has been completed, and the final offer price has been set. The advantage of sequential hybrid offerings to investors is that they know the offer price of the issue. Therefore, they are better guided in setting the size of their orders. Compared to simultaneous hybrid offerings, underwriters are at a disadvantage with respect to waiting risk. In sequential offerings, there is more time that lapses between determining the offer price (at the end of the bookbuilding period) and the completion of the subscription period. Therefore, the underwriter bears more waiting risk, i.e., the possibility that price-related conditions may change before the issue is fully subscribed. Still, sequential hybrid offerings are more informative to the underwriter than the standard subscription method since the former approach allows underwriters to set the fixed offer price with the help of the order book.

The Auction-Offering Method

Auction methods to issue securities differ from the bookbuilding and the subscription methods because they have no predetermined offer price. The offer price is established at the time of the actual sale of the new securities, and it is set at the intersection of demand and supply. There are two auction methods that are usually followed in securities offerings.

Uniform Price Dutch Auction

In a uniform price Dutch auction, the issuer and underwriter usually set a reservation price, and investors are invited to submit price and quantity bids. The clearing price is the minimum price that allows full placement of the issue provided the clearing price is at least equal to the reservation price. The advantage of the uniform price auction is that investors who bid above the clearing price pay the common offer price which reflects the influence of more conservative bidders. Thus, uniform price auctions alleviate the adverse selection problem of less sophisticated investors who may bid too high in order to secure allocations of new securities. The main problem of uniform price auctions is that some investors may free ride by submitting high bids and thus receive large allocations at the expense of sophisticated investors who have submitted more conservative bids. To mitigate this problem, some markets impose limits on the quantity of the bids per investor.

Discriminatory Auctions

In a discriminatory auction, first the clearing price is determined as the maximum price at which the new issue is fully placed. Next, all bids above this price receive allocations until the issue is sold with each bidder paying the price submitted. Thus, discriminatory auctions result in multiple offer prices and do not protect unsophisticated bidders from the adverse selection problem.

As with the subscription method, auctions specify the rules that govern allocation in cases of oversubscribed issues.

Internet-Based New Issue Offerings

Offering Arrangements

Spring Street Brewing, Inc. was the first firm to offer a self-managed or direct IPO via the internet in March 1996. A year later, the firm's owner, Andrew Klein, went on to establish Wit Capital as the first online underwriting firm for the pricing and allocation of new issues through the internet.

Wit Capital was followed by the founding of W.R. Hambrecht & Co. as an all-internet underwriting firm. Other traditional underwriting firms moved to establish internet-based platforms to conduct securities offerings. In January 2000, the World Bank was the first to conduct a $3 billion bond offering over the internet with assistance from Goldman Sachs and Lehman Brothers.

In internet-based offerings, the roadshows, the building of the order book, and the distribution are executed online. Although these tasks can imitate the traditional offering model, early providers of online underwriting, like W.R. Hambrecht, innovated with respect to both the pricing and allocation of the new securities. Thus, the bookbuilding approach to pricing a new issue was replaced by a uniform price Dutch auction method. To lessen the free riding of investors submitting excessive bids, W.R. Hambrecht imposed limits on the quantity of bids. In some cases, though the offer price was set below the clearing price, resulting in a "dirty" auction. In contrast to the discretionary allocation of the bookbuilding approach, internet-based offers allocate the new issue by lottery or by favoring investors who place relatively larger or earlier orders. This fairer allocation scheme was assumed to appeal to issuers who advocate a more democratic distribution system that is friendlier to retail investors. Google, for example, adopted this approach in its 2004 initial public offering. A further appeal of internet-based underwritings was the much lower underwriting spreads charged, which ranged from 4% to 5% versus spreads in excess of 7% for traditionally offered IPOs. By fortuitous coincidence, the availability of the cheaper online offerings emerged as the SEC reforms of Regulation A and Regulation D in the early 1990s further eased the raising of capital by small issuers (Hass, 1998).

Notwithstanding their technological and investor appeal, internet-based offerings have not seen widespread adoption and acceptance by issuers and the underwriting industry. Internet-run offerings share some of the same problems with auctions. Small and relatively less-well known issuers may gain in cost savings but they risk leaving too much money on the table. Without the full price discovery effort of the underwriter, internet-based issues by small issuers may end up to be heavily underpriced. A case in point is Andover.net IPO, managed by W.R. Hambrecht, which was issued at a price below the clearing price (a "dirty" auction) and suffered an underpricing of 252%. Despite the ease of repeating the online bidding process, Andover.net chose not to delay the offering by refiling at a higher price range to accommodate the higher demand. Even the Google IPO, which was executed over the internet, was underpriced by almost 18%.

From an investor standpoint, the concern is that not all retail investors are savvy or informed enough to participate in internet-based offerings. If internet-based offerings attract predominantly retail investors, there is a risk that issues may be overpriced and, thus, expose uninform investors to the winner's curse problem. Conversely, if submitted bids fall below the issuer's reservation price the issue will have to be withdrawn.

Internet auctions also lack the aftermarket services of price stabilization, market making and analyst coverage of traditional offerings. To address one aftermarket issue, that of flipping, Wit Capital did impose a requirement that securities be held for 60 days (Wilhelm, 1999). Although nothing precludes the provision of aftermarket services, this would require that the manager is a full-service securities firm, as in the case of Google, which was managed by Goldman Sachs and Morgan Stanley.

The Empirical Evidence on Online Offerings

Degeorge, Derrien, and Womack (2010) study the performance of the total population of the 19 IPOs auctioned through the OpenIPO system of W.R. Hambrecht in 1999−2007. They find strong institutional participation amounting to 84% of the total demand. In 7 of the 19 deals, the offer price was set below the clearing price, thus compromising the auction process. The online offerings were found to experience similar rate of flipping whether the issues were cold or hot. Retail investors received more of the worst performing issues, apparently due to high bids which were not balanced by more conservative bids from sophisticated investors.

Chen, Morrison, and Wilhelm (2014) report that between 1998, the founding year of W.R. Hambrecht's OpenIPO platform, and the Google IPO in August 2004, W.R. Hambrecht had managed only 10 IPOs. In the following 10 years, it managed 10 more issues and comanaged two others. Even Google chose Goldman Sachs and Morgan Stanley as lead managers and W.R. Hambrecht only as comanager. Therefore, internet auctions have not caught up with issuers or underwriters. Their study of all 19 online IPOs executed in the United States (all managed by W.R. Hambrecht) in 1999−2007 reveals several interesting findings. First, online IPOs were smaller in proceeds than regular IPOs. Second, online IPOs had less aftermarket liquidity (measured by share turnover) than bookbuilt IPOs but were less underpriced than bookbuilt IPOs—the average initial return was 13.8% for online versus 38.2% for regular IPOs. Third, the online issues were offered at a mean discount of 4.5% from the clearing price—thus further contributing to their underpricing. Interestingly, the participation rate was lower for retail than institutional investors—a finding that stands opposite to the frequent claim that the bookbuilding method discourages retail investor participation compared to more direct offering systems. Finally, the online IPOs realized a market (Nasdaq)—adjusted return of −2.7% over the first 12 months.

Appraisal of Offering Methods

The principal methods of offering new securities are the bookbuilding method, the fixed offer price subscription method, and the auction method. Each method implies a different role for the underwriter and the way the price and allocation of the new issue are determined.

In bookbuilt offerings, the underwriter sets a preliminary price range, invites investors to produce and share information about the value of the issue, and then adjusts the final offer price to reflect the collected information. The underwriter also uses discretion in allotting securities to investors in order to induce truthful disclosure of information. In fixed offer price subscriptions, the underwriter sets the offer price without the benefit of information sharing by investors and investors respond to the price by subscribing to the issue. Allocations are made on a pro rata basis depending on the relative subscriptions of investors, thus depriving the underwriter of any influential role. In auctions the issue price is determined by demand and supply without the underwriter exerting any control over the price or allocation of the issue.

The differences with respect to price and allocation can have important implications with respect to the efficacy of each method in meeting the needs of issuers, underwriters and investors. A number of academic studies investigate the pros and cons of offering methods from a theoretical and empirical standpoint.

Size of Expected Proceeds

Issuers can raise more proceeds from new issues if either the offer price is set higher or the offering method allows adjustment to the offer size. Benveniste and Wilhelm (1990) compare offering methods with respect to regulatory restrictions placed on the offer price and/or allocation of new issues and show that freedom to discriminate in price and allocation increases the expected net proceeds to issuers. Although FINRA's "Rules of Fair Practice" do not allow offering of new issues at different prices, underwriters can combine underpricing and discretionary allocation to compensate informed investors for revealing positive information while offering retail investors just enough return to overcome their adverse selection problem. In the absence of discriminatory allocation, underpricing is the only way to induce investors to produce information and show interest in the issue. Thus, the overall underpricing is less in bookbuilt offerings than in offerings that restrict allocation discrimination.

Benveniste and Busaba (1997) compare a fixed-price subscription method with sequential selling to the bookbuilding method. Their theoretical model shows that the degree of underpricing is less under bookbuilding than under a fixed-price method. However, bookbuilding is also possible to result in a lower offer price, compared to the subscription method, if the revealed information about the value of the issue is negative. When preoffer demand is strong, the bookbuilding method, unlike the fixed-price method, offers the flexibility to raise the offer size by either amending the prospectus or exercising the overallotment option when the revealed information is positive. Benveniste and Busaba (1997) conclude that bookbuilding can produce higher proceeds but with higher uncertainty. Thus, issuers whose value is less certain will prefer the fixed-price offer method over the bookbuilding method.

The Case for Hybrid Offerings

In bookbuilt offerings, uninformed investors are allocated underpriced issues as compensation for the adverse selection problem they face. Informed investors, on the other hand, are allocated underpriced issues to compensate them for producing information that can improve the offer price. Hence, allocation of new securities to uninformed investors reduces the share of total underpricing that is left to compensate the more valuable informed investors. Sherman (2000) argues the underwriter can reduce the compensation of uninformed investors in the form of underpricing over the long run by forcing them to participate in all or most deals (including cold ones) the underwriter expects to manage over time. In auction-based offers, the underwriter has no such enforcement tool. Therefore, bookbuilding can produce less underpricing than open market auctions or fixed-price subscriptions. This makes the hybrid method (bookbuilding with fixed-price subscription) more efficient than the pure-auction method.

Jagannathan and Sherman (2005) note that IPOs conducted by the bookbuilding method in 1980−2001 raised almost $500 billion but issuing companies left on the table over $100 billion (at an average underpricing of 22%). Why don't issuers then use auctions to raise capital? And, why have uniform-price auctions not caught up in popularity with the bookbuilding method? They attribute the relative dearth of auctioned issues to issuer uncertainty about the proceeds, inaccurate pricing of new issues (especially when uninformed investors dominate as bidders), and uncertainty about the number of investors attracted to auctioned issues. Their proposed solution is the simultaneous hybrid system that combines bookbuilding to inform the offer price and the fixed-price subscription method to allow retail investor participation.

Pros and Cons of Discriminatory Allocation

The discretionary allocation of a new issue allowed in the bookbuilding method is often criticized for engendering practices that may benefit the underwriters and investors but hurt the interests of issuers. For example, underwriters may underprice more than necessary in order to reduce their actual underwriting costs, or because they expect preferential business deals with buying investors. But on the positive side, discretionary allocation may produce higher offer prices. Ljungqvist and Wilhelm (2002) investigate how the degree of allocation discretion observed across national markets affects the price efficiency of new issues. Their study of IPOs completed in the 15-member European Union countries in 1990−2000 reveals that institutional allocations exceeded 80% of the offer size versus 66% in the United States. They also find that constraints on allocation discretion are associated with smaller price updates from the initial price range. That means greater use of discriminatory allocation, which incentivizes investors to share their information, contributes to offer price improvement relative to the initial price range resulting in lower underpricing. They conclude that alloca-tion discretion (as applied in bookbuilding) contributes to greater price efficiency.

Wilhelm (2005) defends the discretionary allocation inherent in the bookbuilding method as an efficient method used by underwriters to resolve asymmetric information problems that can negatively affect the capital raising process. By maintaining ongoing relationships with investors, underwriters use allocation control to encourage information production and establish better prices for new issues. In addition to concerns related to SEC rules, underwri-ters also restrict retail investor participation in the roadshows because of the possibility they will free-ride on information produced (at a cost) by sophisticated investors. This possibility could discourage informed investors from sharing their information. Wilhelm argues that the importance and perishability of reputational capital restraints the rent seeking behavior of underwriters that is possible in bookbuilding arrangements.

Investor Participation

In order to ensure efficient price discovery, the bookbuilding method appears to favor sophisticated and regular investors over retail investors. Although the participation of retail investors may pose litigation risks for the issuance-related parties, Sherman and Titman (2002) present a more nuanced explanation. In particular, inviting a limited class of (informed) investors to the preoffer presentations is driven by the costs of information collec-tion and the need to produce accurate prices for new issues. Accurate pricing is important for secondary market liquidity and for correct investment decisions by issuers. Since alloca-tion is constrained by issue size, the pool of invited investors should be just large enough to yield truthful disclosure of information without excessive underpricing. If too many investors are invited underpricing must rise. Therefore, the size of the issue and the acceptable level of underpricing establish the optimal number of participating investors. The less challenging price discovery is and the less important price accuracy is, the smaller the investor pool and the lower the underpricing have to be. Methods that place greater restrictions on allocation impede underwriters from calibrating the investor pool thus leading to greater underpricing.

Sherman (2005) argues that investor participation in sealed-bid auction offers is depen-dent on whether investors expect to recover their information production costs. Uncertainty about the number of bidders contributes to their uncertainty about their payoff from partici-pating in the auction. If too few investors participate, the offer may fail. If too many investors participate, the profit for producing information may be driven down to zero. Thus, auctions can discourage investor entry, especially when the cost of information about the issue is high. Bookbuilding, on the other hand, allows underwriters to control the number of bidders to allow a fair compensation for their information production costs. Of all three methods, bookbuilding, fixed-price subscriptions and auctions, bookbuilding produces superior pricing efficiency because it allows issuers and underwriters to control offer price and allocation. The fixed-price system is, in turn, superior to auctions because it allows the underwriter to control the offer price which may encourage information production by investors in anticipa-tion of deliberate underpricing by the underwriter. In contrast, auctions are the least efficient price-wise because they allow control of neither the offer price nor the allocation of the issue by the underwriter.

Amihud, Hauser, and Kirsh (2003) analyze the pricing of IPOs sold in sealed bid auctions and in fixed-price subscriptions in the Tel Aviv Stock Exchange in 1989–1993. They find that underpricing is higher for subscribed than auctioned offers. Furthermore, the allocation size in subscribed IPOs varies inversely with underpricing. Hence, large subscribers end up with higher priced (even possibly overpriced) issues as predicted by Rock's (1986) adverse selection model. Consistent with Sherman (2000), the study finds that the number of orders is directly related to underpricing, and greater expected underpricing is associated with greater information production by sophisticated investors. Early signs of strong demand precipitate additional subscriptions, as predicted by Welch's (1992) cascades theory.

An empirical study of 84 Taiwanese IPOs offered under the hybrid (auction plus fixed-price) method confirms that unexpected entry of institutional investors and high bids by them are related to higher expected returns (Chiang, Qian, and Sherman, 2010). On the contrary, bids by retail investors do not appear to be conditioned by postoffer returns. Because the auctions studied were of the discriminatory type (i.e., bidders pay what they bid for) informed investors were able to earn higher returns by bidding below the average bid. This confirms that informed investors are more skilled than retail investors in identifying and participating in profitable new issues and calibrating their participation to ensure recovery of their information production costs.

Variability of Underpricing

Derrien and Womack (2003) examine how different offering methods control the variability of initial returns in cold and hot markets in samples of French IPOs offered through auctions, bookbuilding, and fixed-price subscriptions. They find that auctions produce less underpricing and less variability of underpricing across issues offered, respectively, in hot and cold markets. Issue prices set in auctioned offers appear to incorporate more fully market information than offer prices set in bookbuilt offers and fixed-price subscriptions. This inefficiency is found to be more pronounced in bookbuilt offers during hot markets. No evidence is presented though as to whether less underpricing in auctions also produces higher offer prices than those produced in bookbuilt or fixed-price offers.

Lowry, Officer, and Schwert (2010) notice unusual month-to-month variability in the initial returns of US IPOs executed over the period 1965–2000. Only a very small fraction (5%) of IPOs is underpriced close to the average initial return of 22% during this period, and nearly one third of IPOs are overpriced—i.e., have negative initial returns. They find that underpricing and variability of initial returns are significantly correlated, consistent with the notion that underpricing is driven by uncertainty about initial market prices, a condition more akin to young, small and technology-intensive (hence, difficult-to-value) firms. Therefore, the authors question the efficacy of the bookbuilding method in reducing the underwriter's uncertainty about the new issue's aggregate demand in the aftermarket. Interestingly, IPOs with the greatest price adjustment from the original price to the final offer price (that is with the most additional information gathered during the preoffer marketing period) exhibit the greatest volatility of initial returns. In contrast, a limited sample of IPOs offered with the auction method displayed lower average level and variability of initial returns.

Issuance Costs

Ljungqvist, Jenkinson, and Wilhelm (2003) estimate that by 1999, 80% of the IPOs from 65 countries in their sample were marketed as bookbuilt offers. They find that bookbuilding is associated with spreads twice as large as those of fixed-price offers. Controlling for various factors, US underwriters charge 48 basis points (i.e., 0.48%) more than non-US underwriters for issues listed and marketed abroad. Spreads are also higher by 41 basis points for domestic US issues managed by US underwriters. They find that both bookbuilt and fixed-price methods produce similar underpricing (around 20%), but issues offered with bookbuilding in Europe are more underpriced than those in the United States. Results indicate that bookbuilding on its own does not lead to lower underpricing. But when bookbuilding is used by US underwriters who market to US investors, it can reduce underpricing relative to fixed-price or bookbuilt offers conducted by foreign domestic underwriters. The lower underpricing of US bookbuilt offers is attributed to the more extensive investor networks of US underwriters that enable them to generate more information sharing and thus more accurate pricing. The greater savings realized in the form of lower underpricing exceed the excess spread paid to US underwriters. Switching to a cheaper offering method would have cost issuers an average of $11.7 million in money left on the table.

Kutsuna and Smith (2004) note that, shortly after its introduction in 1997, the bookbuilding method had effectively replaced the auction method in Japan. Bookbuilding is found to be less costly for large and well-known firms whereas auctions are less costly for small and young firms. Weighting total issue costs by issue size shows that both methods are equally cost-efficient. Despite this cost parity, bookbuilding is still the superior method for two reasons. First, by discouraging information production by investors and depriving issuers of the certification value of underwriter, auctions hinder good quality but less well-known firms to raise capital and pursue new investments. Second, bookbuilding can produce more accurate prices which can result in greater market liquidity and more reliable signals to issuers regarding investment decisions.

8

Assessing the Price Performance of New Issues

The performance of new issues can be assessed from several standpoints. The most important is their initial price performance which can result in the underpricing or overpricing of a new issue. New issues are also evaluated from the standpoint of long-run price performance. This chapter presents the measures and methods used to measure and assess the initial as well as long-run price performance of new issues.

Initial and Short-Term Price Performance

Initial price performance refers to the first market price a new issue obtains once secondary market trading starts. The initial price is the first indication of the value the market assigns to the new issue and reveals how close the offer price was set in relation to the issue's price in the open market. The interest in the valuation of a new issue can be also extended to include a look at the short-term price behavior of the issue after the offer time.

The Explicit, Implicit, and Combined Spread

Although the primary interest is in the relationship of the offer price to the initial market price, a more complete assessment of the performance of a new issue is obtained by also estimating the relationship of the bid price to the offer price and the market price, respectively. Define P_o as the offer price, P_b as the bid price (price paid to the issuer), and P_1 as the closing market price of the new issue on the first day of trading. For US issues, the first day coincides with the offer day, unless the security is thinly traded. We use these prices to calculate the following three spreads:

Explicit (gross) spread estimated as $P_o - P_b$.
Implicit spread estimated as $P_1 - P_o$.
Combined spread estimated as $P_1 - P_b$.

The explicit spread measures the compensation of the underwriter or the underwriting cost to the issuer. The implicit spread, if positive, measures the underpricing and, if negative, measures the overpricing of the issue relative to the initial market price of the issue in the secondary market. The implicit spread represents the gain or loss the initial investors realize on the new issue. When the implicit spread is positive, it represents the money left on the table by the issuer, and it is an additional issuance costs over and above the gross spread. The combined spread measures the total cost to the issuer.

Underwriting Services and the New Issues Market. DOI: http://dx.doi.org/10.1016/B978-0-12-803282-4.00008-0

For the purpose of comparing spreads across different issues, we calculate percentage spreads. To this end, the explicit, implicit, and combined spread is divided by the offer price, P_o. The implicit spread in percentage form is equal to the return an investor realizes by buying a new issue at the offer price and holding it until the first trading day and it is also referred to as the initial return (IR) of the new issue.

The estimation of the three types of spreads in the case of initial public offers (IPOs), seasoned equity offers (SEOs) and bond offers is explained below.

Initial Public Offerings

The explicit, implicit, and combined spreads of IPOs are estimated as shown above.

Seasoned Stock Offerings

The explicit spread of SEOs is calculated as defined above by comparing the offer price to the bid price of the issue. Unlike IPOs though, stocks associated with a SEOs have a record of prior market prices. This has given rise to two different ways of assessing the initial price performance of SEOs. The first is in terms of the relationship of the offer price to the last market price prior to the offer, referred to as the price discount or premium. The second is in terms of the relationship of the offer price to the first available market price, i.e., the IR. We can also estimate the total return that reflects the effects of both the discount (premium) and the IR.

The Price Discount or Premium

Offer prices in SEOs are set in relation to the closing market price of the stock on the day prior to the offer, i.e., day -1. If the offer price is below the last closing price the issue is offered at a discount; if the reverse is true, the issue is offered at a premium. The discount (premium) is often used as an alternative measure of underpricing (overpricing). Three different expressions of the discount (premium) appear in the literature. The first expression calculates the discount (premium) as the percentage difference of $P_{-1} - P_o$ relative to the offer price, P_o, as $D = (P_{-1} - P_o)/P_o$. The second expression calculates the discount (premium) as the percentage difference of $P_o - P_{-1}$ relative to P_o, as $D = (P_o - P_{-1})/P_o$. A positive (negative) value of D in the former expression signifies a discount (premium) whereas a positive (negative) value of D in the latter expression signifies a premium (discount).

Example: A new issue closed at a price of $14 the day before its offering. The underwriter sets the offer price at $13.5. Applying the first expression, the discount (premium) is

($14 $-$ $13.5)/$13.5 = 3.70%; that is, the issue was offered at a discount. The second expression yields ($13.5 $-$ $14)/$13.5 = -3.70%, which also represents a discount relative to the last market price.

The Initial Return

The IR is estimated using the expression for the implicit spread, that is,

$IR = (P_1 - P_o)/P_o$. If the first day of trading does not coincide with the offer day, then we use the closing market price of the first available day of trading. Continuing with the above example, if the first day market price of the security is \$15, the IR is:

$$(P_1 - P_o)/P_o = (\$15 - \$13.5)/\$13.5 = 11.11\%.$$

The Total Return

The total return around the time of a SEO measures the return realized by an investor who buys the stock at the last trading price prior to the offer and holds it until the first trading day. It is easy to show that the total return is comprised of two parts: the first part reflects the discounting of the new issue and the second part reflects the underpricing. Specifically, the total return from day -1 to the closing of the first trading day, 1, is estimated as follows:

$$\text{Total Return} = (P_1/P_{-1}) - 1 = \{(P_o/P_{-1}) \times (P_1/P_o)\} - 1$$
$$= (\text{Discount} + 1) \times (\text{Initial Return} + 1),$$

where the expression P_o/P_{-1} is an alternative measure of the discount (or premium) of the new issue[1].

Using the above example, the total return is:

$$\text{Total return} = \$15/\$14 - 1 = 7.14\% = \{(\$13.5/\$14) \times (\$15/\$13.5)\} - 1 = 7.14\%.$$

Bond Offerings

If we use B_o for the offer bond price, B_b for the bid price paid to the issuer, and B_m for the first market price of the bond in the aftermarket, the explicit, implicit and combined spreads of a bond issue expressed in price spreads are, respectively:

Explicit spread = Bond offer price − Bond bid price = $B_o - B_b$.
Implicit spread = Bond market price − Bond offer price = $B_m - B_o$.
Combined spread = Bond market price − Bond bid price = $B_m - B_b$.

Conventionally, the pricing of bonds is better understood in terms of their associated yields to maturity (i.e., market interest rates). Therefore, it is more appropriate to estimate yield spreads. Yield spreads are calculated from the bid yield, the offering (or reoffering) yield and the market yield. The bid yield, Y_b, is the yield to maturity estimated on the bid

---

[1] The ratio P_1/P_{-1} is the return relative from the last preoffer price to the first postoffer price. Multiplying this by P_o/P_o yields $(P_o/P_{-1}) \times (P_1/P_o)$. The first term is the discount plus 1 and the second term is the initial return plus 1.

price received by the issuer (i.e., the bond offer price net of the underwriter spread)[2].This is the effective interest rate or cost of capital to the issuer. The offering yield, Y_o, is the yield to maturity estimated on the bond's offer price paid by investors. This is the yield the initial investors expect to make on the bond. The market yield, Y_m, is the yield to maturity estimated on the market price of the bond at the close of the first day of trading. The market yield is the interest rate expected by the investors who buy the new bond at its first market price when trading starts. Since bond prices are inversely related to their yields, it follows that the bid yield is higher than the offering yield (since offer price exceeds the bid price), and the market yield is higher (lower) than the offering yield if the bond is overpriced (underpriced).

Expressed as yield spreads the explicit, implicit and combined spreads are, respectively:

Explicit yield spread = Yield at the bid price − Yield at the offer price = $Y_b − Y_o$.
Implicit yield spread = Yield at the offer price − Yield at the market price = $Y_o − Y_m$.
Combined yield spread = Yield at the bid price − Yield at the market price = $Y_b − Y_m$.

The calculation of the yields and the spreads for a new bond issue are illustrated in the following example.

Example: A new bond was offered at an offer price of $980 and a gross spread of 1% on the offer price or $9.80. This results in a bid price of $980 − $9.80 = $971.2. Let us assume the bond started trading at a market price of $995. In dollar terms, the spreads for this issue are:

Explicit spread = Offer price − Bid price = $980 − $970.2 = $9.8.
Implicit spread = Market price − Offer price = $995 − $980 = $15.
Combined spread = Market price − Bid price = $995 − $970.2 = $24.8.

If we assume this bond has a maturity value of $1,000, a coupon interest rate of 5%, pays interest semiannually, and matures in 10 years, the bid, the offering and the market yield are, respectively, $Y_b = 5.389\%$, $Y_o = 5.260\%$, and $Y_m = 5.064\%$. Therefore, the yield spreads are:

Explicit yield spread = $Y_b − Y_o = 5.389\% − 5.260\% = 0.129\%$.
Implicit yield spread = $Y_o − Y_m = 5.260\% − 5.064\% = 0.196\%$.
Combined yield spread = $Y_b − Y_m = 5.389\% − 5.064\% = 0.325\%$.

This bond was offered 12.9 basis points below its bid yield whereas investors who bought at the first market price earned a yield 19.6 basis points below the yield earned by the initial buyers who paid the offer price. The combined yield spread of 32.5 basis points indicates that the issuer's effective cost of capital was 32.5 basis points above the yield to maturity the bond realized at its market price. The higher cost was the result of both the underwriting fee and the underpricing of the bond.

---

[2] The yield to maturity is estimated as the discount rate at which the bond's payoffs (periodical interest payments and maturity value) have a present value equal to the price of the bond. From the perspective of the issuer, the initial buyers, and those who buy at the first market price, the bond prices to be used in the above calculation are, respectively, the bid price, the offer price and the first market price of the new bond.

Market-Adjusted Measures of Underpricing and Overpricing

When a market price on the offer day is available, calculating the implicit spread or IR as a raw return is appropriate. When, however, the first available market price of a new issue is several days after the offer, it is advisable that we account for market movements that affect the values of securities that share similarities with the new issue. Accordingly, a more accurate assessment of the degree of underpricing (overpricing) of the issue requires that we remove the market-related effect by estimating market-adjusted returns (MARs).

For stock offers, the benchmark portfolio (to be referred to hereafter as the market benchmark) ought to be a comprehensive market index, like the S&P 500, or any other equally-weighted or value-weighted index comprised of traded stocks. Sometimes, an index associated with a specific marketplace, like the New York Stock Exchange (NYSE) or Nasdaq, may be also used to assess the performance of new issues listed in the respective market. Empirical research has shown that a more reliable benchmark of the price performance of a new issue, often used to assess long-run price performance, can be comprised of portfolios of nonissuing firms that share similar characteristics with the issuing firm, such as market capitalization or book-to-market ratio. For new bonds, the market benchmark can be a portfolio of bonds of similar rating and maturity.

Estimation of MARs

For an interval comprised of T days, where day 1 is the offer day, the return of issue i relative to the offer price is $R_{i,T} = (P_{i,T}/P_{i,o}) - 1$. The same applies for any interest payments in the case of bond issues). Over the same period of T daily intervals, the market benchmark (say, a market index) return is calculated as $R_{I,T} = (I_T/I_{-1}) - 1$. The value of the market benchmark used is its closing value on the day prior to the offer day of the issue, i.e., I_{-1}. The MAR of issue i from the offer price to the market price T days after the offer day is as follows:

$$MAR_i(T) = R_{i,T} - R_{I,T}{}^3.$$

If for a given interval of T days, the MAR exceeds 0, there is evidence of underpricing. If, on the other hand, the MAR is below 0, there is evidence of overpricing.

Example: Suppose a new equity issue was offered at a price of $20 and its market price observed three days later was $24. Assume also that a stock index (e.g., S&P 500) was at 2,000 on the day before the offer day and at 2,040 three days later. The 3-day return relative of the issue is $R_{i,3} = ($20/$24) - 1 = 0.20$, whereas that of the market benchmark it is $R_{I,3} = (2,040/2,000) - 1 = 0.02$. Therefore, the new issue realized a MAR equal to $MAR_i(3) = 0.20 - 0.02 = 0.18$ or 18%. That is, the percentage change of the price of the new stock exceeded that of the market

(Continued)

---

[3] The MAR can be also estimated as the difference of the return relatives of the new issue and the market benchmark, respectively. The return relative is the simple return *plus* 1.

> **(CONTINUED)**
>
> benchmark by 18%. In this example, we find that the stock price advanced faster than the market over the 3-day interval. This can be interpreted to mean that the offer price of the stock was set lower than the level justified by the market.

It is possible, however, that, after the offer, the price of a new issue changes at a different rate than the value of the market benchmark because of positive or negative news specific to the issue. It is worth recalling that the underwriter prices a new issue based on the information available at the time of pricing. Hence, new information after the sale begins is not supposed to be reflected in the offer price. Consequently, caution must be exercised in the interpretation of aftermarket returns as indicators of under- or over-pricing when these returns are estimated over intervals going beyond the close of the offer day.

The Market-Adjusted Yield Spread for Bond Offerings

The underpricing and overpricing of bond issues can be also assessed in terms of market-adjusted yield spreads (MAYSs). In an interval of T days, the MAYS of a bond issue j is estimated as

$$\text{MAYS}_j(T) = \left(Y_{j,T} - Y_{j,o}\right) - \left(Y_{I,T} - Y_{I,-1}\right),$$

where $Y_{j,T}$ is the yield to maturity based on the market price of bond j on day T, $Y_{j,o}$ is the yield to maturity based on the offer price, and $Y_{I,T}$ and $Y_{I,-1}$, are, respectively, the values of an index of similar bonds on day T and the day before the offer, i.e., day -1.

If the $\text{MAYS}_j(T)$ is less than 0, this is evidence of underpricing; if the $\text{MAYS}_j(T)$ is greater than 0, this is evidence of overpricing.

> **Example**: Assume that $Y_{j,o} = 0.10$; $Y_{j,3} = 0.12$; $Y_{I,-1} = 0.10$; $Y_{I,3} = 0.11$. The MAYS is:
>
> $$\text{MAYS}_j(3) = (0.12 - 0.10) - (0.11 - 0.10) = 0.01 \text{ or } 1\%$$
>
> and indicates the new bond was overpriced. We arrive at this conclusion because the bond can have a market yield higher than its offer yield only if the bond's price declined below the offer price, and moreover this decline is greater relative to the price decline experienced by the bonds of the benchmark portfolio.

The degree of under- and over-pricing can also be assessed in terms of market-adjusted yield ratios. For a bond j whose first market price is observed T days after the offer day, the MAYR ratio is as follows:

$$\text{MAYR}(T) = \left(Y_{j,T}/Y_{j,o}\right)/\left(Y_{I,T}/Y_{I,-1}\right).$$

If the MAYR(T) is less than 1, this is evidence of underpricing; if the MAYR(T) is greater than 1, this is evidence of overpricing.

Example: Assume that $Y_{j,o} = 0.10$; $Y_{j,3} = 0.12$; $Y_{I,-1} = 0.10$; $Y_{I,3} = 0.11$. The market-adjusted yield ratio of the bond is as follows:

$$MAYR(3) = (0.12/0.10)/(0.11/0.10) = 1.2/1.1 = 1.0909 > 1.$$

Since MAYR exceeds 1, the bond issue has been overpriced. This conclusion is reached by realizing that for the yield of the new bond to be higher on day T than on the offer day its market price must have declined below the offer price. Moreover, the price drop realized by the new bond is more severe than the price drop of the average bond in the market benchmark. These two facts taken together, and in the absence of any issue- or issuer-related new information, suggest that the bond was issued at a price higher than the average yield of similar bonds warranted and as a result the market price of the bond underwent a downward adjustment.

Using yields to draw inferences about the relative movement of bond prices across bonds requires caution. Specifically, the new bond and the bonds in the market benchmark must have similar maturities and coupon interest rates. Otherwise, the comparison of yield changes cannot provide reliable interpretations about the relative movement of prices.

Measuring Return Volatility

Most of the models that purport to explain the behavior of the explicit and implicit spread (IR) use the volatility of returns as a measure of the ex ante risk or uncertainty of the new issue. High volatility is more likely to compel the underwriter to charge a higher underwriting spread and/or impose a higher degree of underpricing.

Seasoned Stock Offerings

The volatility of SEOs is estimated using returns estimated from prices in the preoffer period. Thus, we first calculate daily returns of the new issue i over an appropriate period before the offer day. The daily returns are estimated as $R_{i,t} = (P_{i,t}/P_{i,t-1}) - 1$, where P_t is the market price of day t. If any dividend has been paid in the $t-1$ to t day interval, it should be included to $P_{i,t}$ in the above expression.

The volatility of the new issue can then be calculated by using the formula of the standard deviation of daily returns:

$$\sigma_i = \left(\frac{\sum_{t=1}^{N} \left[R_{i,t} - E(R) \right]^2}{N-1} \right)^{1/2},$$

where $E(R)$ is the average return, and N is the number of daily returns in the preoffer period.

Initial Public Offerings

In the case of IPOs, the volatility is estimated from the aftermarket returns and is used as a proxy of the preoffer riskiness faced by the underwriter and investors. The above formula of standard deviation is also used to calculate the return volatility of IPOs.

Bonds Offerings

Bond volatility can be measured either in terms of returns or yields to maturity. Since new bond issues, like IPOs, have no preoffering price data, their volatility is calculated from returns or yields to maturity estimated from aftermarket bond prices. Whether yields or returns are used, the above standard deviation formula can be used to calculate the bond's return or yield volatility.

Long-Run Price Performance

The assessment of the long-run price behavior of new issues refers to the analysis of the returns realized by the investors who buy at the first available market price and sell at a later point of time. The long-run price behavior of new issues can be assessed in terms of cumulative returns as well as of buy-and-hold returns. Cumulative and buy-and-hold returns (BHRs) have been applied mostly to assess the price performance of stock offers but can also be applied in the case of bond offers.

Cumulative Returns

The cumulative return (CR) is the sum of the simple returns of a security over T periods:

$$CR_i(1, T) = R_{i,1} + R_{i,2} + \ldots + R_{i,T}$$

Because cumulative returns are estimated over long periods of time it is appropriate that they account for market movements that affect the values of the securities in the market benchmark; hence, they are estimated as cumulative abnormal returns (CARs).

To estimate the CAR over a period of T intervals (days, weeks, or months), we first estimate the abnormal return (AR) in each interval t. The AR of an interval t is the raw return of the new issue minus the raw return of a market benchmark appropriate for the type of the security offered in interval t. We can also calculate the new security and the market benchmark returns as return relatives, that is, the percentage price change plus 1. The AR of the new issue i on day t in the aftermarket is given by:

$$AR_{i,t} = R_{i,t} - R_{I,t},$$

where $R_{i,t}$ is the return of the security, i.e., $(P_{i,t}/P_{i,t-1}) - 1$, and $R_{I,t} = (I_t/I_{t-1}) - 1$ is the market benchmark return, where I is the value of the market benchmark. Conventionally, the return of the first interval is estimated from the closing market price of the offer day to the closing market price of day $+1$ relative to the offer day. This convention assumes that the long-run return performance is not affected by the IR that reflects the underpricing or overpricing of the issue. Hence, the long-run return performance captures the gain or loss realized by investors who buy at the first available aftermarket price of the new securities. The AR indicates the net advance or decline of the security's price (percentage-wise) after accounting for the advance or decline of the market benchmark during interval t.

The CAR of the new issue i over a period of T intervals is estimated by summing up the ARs:

$$\text{CAR}_i(1, T) = \text{AR}_{i,1} + \text{AR}_{i,2} + \text{AR}_{i,3} + \ldots + \text{AR}_{i,T},$$

where 1 is the first trading interval available, and T is the last interval of the investment period.

In an efficient market, whether the new security is underpriced or overpriced relative to the first market price, its price should quickly adjust toward its fair level. Hence, nonzero CARs in the postoffering period have been interpreted as evidence of both, possible underpricing (overpricing) as well as market inefficiency. However, ARs over a relatively long postoffer period can be caused by the release or arrival of new unanticipated information about the security. Therefore, as the estimation period of aftermarket cumulative returns grows longer, it is less likely the ARs and CARs are associated with underpricing (overpricing) or even market inefficiency.

The analysis of the price behavior of seasoned equity issues often includes calculation of CARs from preoffer prices. A positive preoffer CAR is indicative of a price run-up which can justify more aggressive pricing of the security. A negative CAR is indicative of a downward trend in the price of the stock relative to the market as the offer day approaches and it can lead to a more conservative pricing.

Buy-and-Hold Returns

A buy-and-hold return (BHR) is the return realized by an investor who purchases the security at the beginning of an interval (day, week, or month) and sells it at the end of the interval. It is estimated as follows:

$$\text{BHR}_{i,t} = R_{i,t},$$

where $R_{i,t}$ is the raw (simple) return of security i in interval t, estimated as $R_{i,t} = (P_{i,t} - P_{i,t-1})/ P_{i,t-1}$, where $P_{i,t}$ is the closing market price of the security at the end of interval t and $P_{i,t-1}$ is the closing price of the security at the end of interval $t - 1$.

Over a long period comprised of T shorter intervals t, the long-run buy-and-hold return $\text{BHR}_i(T)$ is the compounded return of the short interval returns and is given by the following expression:

$$\text{BHR}_i(T) = \left[(R_{i,1} + 1) \times (R_{i,2} + 1) \times \cdots \times (R_{i,T} + 1) \right] - 1,$$

which is also equal to $(P_{i,T}/P_{i,o}) - 1$, i.e. the total return relative minus 1.

If $\text{BHR}_I(T)$ denotes the buy-and-hold return of the market benchmark I, the buy-and-hold abnormal return (BHAR) over T intervals is given by:

$$\text{BHAR}_i(T) = \text{BHR}_i(T) - \text{BHR}_I(T).$$

A positive $\text{BHAR}_i(T)$ indicates the issue has overperformed relative to the market benchmark during the period of T intervals. Conversely, a negative $\text{BHAR}_i(T)$ indicates the new issue has underperformed. We can also form the ratio of the BHR of the security to the BHR of the market benchmark to calculate the wealth relative (WR) of the security, $\text{WR}_i(T)$, over an investment horizon of T intervals:

$$\text{WR}_i(T) = [\text{BHR}_i(T) + 1]/[\text{BHR}_I(T) + 1].$$

The WR estimates the value of a $1 investment made on the new issue as a percent of the value of a $1 investment made on the market benchmark at the end of the investment horizon. When the new issue has outperformed the market benchmark, the WR, as defined above, is greater than 1; if the issue has underperformed, it is less than 1. (Appendix presents an illustration on the calculation of BHARs and the WRs in the case of the Facebook IPO.)

> **Example**: Suppose we have estimated the 3-year $\text{BHR}_i(3)$ of a SEO and a market benchmark to be 0.25 and 0.40, respectively. Therefore, the buy-and-hold abnormal return of the issue is $\text{BHAR}_i(3) = 0.25 - 0.40 = -0.15$ or -15%. This means the offering has advanced in value 15% less than the market benchmark. The WR of this issue is $\text{WR}_i = (0.25 + 1)/(0.40 + 1) = 0.892$. It means the end-of-period value of $1 invested in the new issue is only 89.2% of the end-of-period value of $1 invested in the market benchmark. By both measures, the issue has underperformed the market benchmark. Investors would have been better off had they invested in the market benchmark.

Problems in Assessing Long-Run Price Performance

Assessing the long-run price performance of securities in general and new issues in particular is fraught with several problems that can compromise the validity of the conclusions. These problems are related to (1) the estimation of abnormal return performance; (2) the choice of the market benchmark; (3) possible measurement errors in estimating long-run return performance; and (4) erroneous inferences about the true return performance.

Estimation of Abnormal Returns

Ideally, the returns of a security should be compared to the "normal" returns that securities with similar characteristics (especially in riskiness) ought to generate over a period of time. The difference between the actual return of the security and the normal return measures the abnormal return performance of the security. Since there is no compelling evidence in favor of a model that generates "normal" returns, analysts have used several alternative models:

1. *The Market-Adjusted Model:* The AR in each interval t is estimated as follows:

$$\text{AR}_{i,t} = R_{i,t} - R_{m,t},$$

where $R_{i,t}$ is the return of security i in interval t and $R_{m,t}$ is the return of a market benchmark in t.

2. **The Market Model:** The AR is estimated as follows:

$$\text{AR}_{i,t} = R_{i,t} - (\alpha_i + \beta_i \times R_{m,t}),$$

where α_i and β_i are, respectively, the estimated intercept and the slope coefficient of the regression of the security returns against the returns of the market benchmark over T intervals.

3. **The Capital Asset Pricing Model (CAPM):** The AR is estimated as

$$\text{AR}_{i,t} = R_{i,t} - (R_{f,t} + \beta_i \times [R_{m,t} - R_{f,t}]),$$

where $R_{f,t}$ is the risk-free rate and $(R_{f,t} + \beta_i \times [R_{m,t} - R_{f,t}])$ is the theoretical (expected) return of security i. The coefficient β_i is estimated from the regression:

$$\left(R_{i,t} - R_{f,t}\right) = \alpha_i + \beta_i \times (R_{m,t} - R_{f,t}).$$

The difference $(R_{i,t} - R_{f,t})$ captures the risk premium of security i and should be equal to the theoretical risk premium given by $\beta_i \times (R_{m,t} - R_{f,t})$. Accordingly, the intercept coefficient, *alpha*, ought to be insignificantly different from zero. When *alpha* is statistically significantly different from zero, it represents the abnormal return (positive or negative) earned on the security per interval t over and above the level justified by the riskiness of the security.

4. **The Fama-French Three-Factor Model:** In this model, the AR is estimated as

$$\text{AR}_{i,t} = R_{i,t} - (R_{f,t} + \beta_{i,1} \times [R_{m,t} - R_{f,t}] + \beta_{i,2} \times \text{HML}_t + \beta_{i,3} \times \text{SMB}_t),$$

where the factor HML_t is the return of a portfolio of high book-to-market value ratio stocks minus the return of a portfolio of low book-to-market ratio stocks, and SMB_t is the return of a portfolio of small capitalization minus the return of a portfolio of big capitalization stocks (Fama and French, 1993). The slope coefficients β are estimated by regressing (usually) monthly excess returns of each security $(R_{i,t} - R_{f,t})$ against monthly values of the three factors:

$$\left(R_{i,t} - R_{f,t}\right) = \alpha_i + \beta_{i,1} \times [R_{m,t} - R_{f,t}] + \beta_{i,2} \times \text{HML}_t + \beta_{i,3} \times \text{SMB}_t.$$

The intercept of the regression, *alpha*, if nonzero, estimates the excess return earned on the security per interval t over and above the return warranted by the three risk factors. When models 3 and 4 are used to assess return performance, the analysis centers on the value and statistical significance of the estimated *alpha* coefficients.

5. **The Matched Control Firm Model:** The AR is estimated as

$$\text{AR}_{i,t} = R_{i,t} - R_{c,t},$$

where $R_{c,t}$ is the return of the matched control firm for the i new issue. The usual matching criteria include industry classification, equity capitalization, and the book-to-market value of equity ratio.

The Choice of Market Benchmark

The above return-generating models utilize either a market index or a portfolio of securities with characteristics similar to those of the analyzed security. Market indexes can be constructed so that the securities included are equally or value-weighted. In equally-weighted indexes, each security is equally-weighted, so the index is simply the arithmetic average of the security returns. In value-weighted indexes the return of each security is weighted by the security's relative market value in the index. As a result, equally-weighted indexes are influenced more by the return performance of small size securities.

Barber and Lyon (1997) show that market indexes also introduce a listing bias because market indexes include newly issued securities which generally underperform relative to the seasoned securities in the index. Comparing the returns of new issues to an underperforming index generates inflated ARs for new issues. Barber and Lyon (1997) show that the listing bias mostly affects the CARs. The same authors also show that equally-weighted indexes assume rebalancing over successive intervals in favor of better performing securities. The rebalancing bias in equally-weighted indexes mostly affects BHARs causing them to be negatively biased, i.e., to show that new issues underperform the market benchmark. In addition, BHARs suffer from severe positive skewness, that is, higher than normal frequency of very high positive values. To avoid these biases, both Barber and Lyon (1997) and Kothari and Warner (1997) recommend that the market benchmark be constructed by matching each (new) security with control firms of similar characteristics, especially in regard to equity market capitalization and market-to-book value of equity ratio.

Statistical Inference

When we infer that securities returns are positive or negative over the long run, we must have sufficient confidence that any deviation from zero is not due to random error. In statistical parlance, this means the measure of performance must have statistical properties that enable us to confidently reject the null hypothesis of no over- or under-performance when indeed the alternative hypothesis (of over- or under-performance) is true. Kothari and Warner (1997) find that when CARs or BHARs are estimated according to the above models, the rejection rates of the zero return (null) hypothesis (though higher than expected) are about the same whether one uses CARs or BHARs. The one exception is when BHARs are estimated according to the market model. In that case, rejection of the null hypothesis is dramatically higher than if one had used CARs. Barber and Lyon (1997) also confirm that CARs and BHARs generate test statistics which are generally biased. Both these studies conclude that market benchmarks comprised of matched control firms produce more reliable inferences, that is, inferences with less bias in favor of either return under- or over performance.

Appendix—The Facebook IPO

Price Performance Relative to Offer Price

Facebook placed its IPO shares on May 18, 2012 at an offer price of $38 per share. Table 8.A.1 reports the return relatives realized by investors who bought at the offer price and held the stock until the third-year anniversary of the IPO. Table 8.A.1 also reports the return relatives of the S&P 500 Index and the MARs for the Facebook stock. The return relatives for Facebook and S&P 500 are calculated by dividing, respectively, the closing price or index value of each day by the offer price or the index value on day −1. The MAR is estimated by subtracting the market index return relative from the Facebook return relative in each interval reported.

With an offer price of $38 and an offer day closing price of $38.23, the Facebook IPO had an IR of ($38.23 − $38)/$38 = 0.6%, which is equal to the return relative of 1.006 − 1. The positive IR indicates the Facebook IPO was slightly underpriced. Adjusting the return relative of the Facebook stock on the offer day by the return relative of the market index yields a MAR value of 1.3% (1.006 − 0.993 = 0.013) which also indicates underpricing. However, further inspection of the Facebook prices up to day 5 reveals that, excluding the offer day, the Facebook shares were traded at prices below the offer price yielding return relatives below 1. This is evidence of overpricing. The MARs are also negative up to day 5.

The Facebook stock price was also below the offer price around the lockup expiration time, that is, 180 days from the offer day, yielding a return relative of 0.588 or −0.450 on a market-adjusted basis. Thus, during the first 6 months, the original investors had lost (relative to the market) 45.0% of their investment in the Facebook IPO. Part of the loss was due to the erosion of Facebook's stock price by about 41% (i.e., 0.588 − 1) and part was due to the advance of the market by 3.9% (i.e., 1.039 − 1). However, 3 years from its IPO the Facebook stock was worth $78.99, yielding a return relative of 2.079, that translates to an appreciation of 107.9% (2.079 − 1 = 1.079; i.e., 107.9%) from the offer price. On a market-adjusted basis, the investors who bought at the offer price have earned a MAR of 0.463, which represents a net gain of 46.3% over the market benchmark return.

Table 8.A.1 Facebook IPO: Price Performance Relative to Offer Price

| | Market-Adjusted Returns (MARs) | | | | |
| | Facebook | | S&P 500 Index | | Facebook |
Day	Price	Return Relatives	Value	Return Relatives	MAR
Day −1			1,304.86		
Offer price	38.00				
Day 0	38.23	1.006	1,295.22	0.993	0.013
Day 1	34.03	0.896	1,315.99	1.009	− 0.113
Day 2	31.00	0.816	1,316.63	1.009	− 0.193
Day 3	32.00	0.842	1,318.86	1.011	− 0.169
Day 4	33.03	0.869	1,320.68	1.012	− 0.143
Day 5	31.91	0.840	1,317.82	1.010	− 0.170
Day 30	30.01	0.790	1,342.84	1.029	− 0.239
Day 180	22.36	0.588	1,355.49	1.039	− 0.450
Day 3-years	78.99	2.079	2,108.29	1.616	0.463

Day 0 stands for the offer day. For Day 1 to Day 5, the count is in trading days. For Day 30, to Day 3-years the count is in calendar days. If they do not coincide with a trading day, the price of the closest preceding trading day is used. The Return Relative is market price on Day *t* over offer price.

We use the S&P 500 index value on day −1 to estimate the market index return relative on day 0.

Facebook prices and S&P 500 values are taken from Bloomberg Professional terminal.

Price Performance Relative to First Market Price

The long-run price performance of the Facebook IPO is assessed by calculating BHARs and WRs realized over periods that extend from one month after the offer to about 3 years later.

Table 8.A.2   Facebook IPO: Price Performance Relative to First Day Market Price

		Buy-and-Hold Abnormal Returns (BHARs) and Wealth Relatives (WRs)						
		Facebook			S&P 500 Index			
Day	Price	Monthly Return Relative	End-of-Period BHR + 1	Value	Monthly Return Relative	End-of-Period BHR + 1	Facebook BHAR	Facebook Wealth Relative
Day 0	38.23			1,295.22				
Day 30	30.01	0.785	0.785	1,342.84	1.037	1.037	− 0.252	0.757
Day 60	28.09	0.936	0.735	1,363.67	1.016	1.053	− 0.318	0.698
Day 90	19.87	0.707	0.520	1,415.51	1.038	1.093	− 0.573	0.476
Day 120	22.00	1.107	0.575	1,465.77	1.036	1.132	− 0.556	0.509
Day 150	19.52	0.887	0.511	1,440.13	0.983	1.112	− 0.601	0.459
Day 180	22.36	1.145	0.585	1,355.49	0.941	1.047	− 0.462	0.559
Day 210	26.81	1.199	0.701	1,413.58	1.043	1.091	− 0.390	0.643
Day 240	31.72	1.183	0.830	1,472.05	1.041	1.137	− 0.307	0.730
Day 270	27.37	0.863	0.716	1,519.43	1.032	1.173	− 0.457	0.610
Day 300	27.04	0.988	0.707	1,563.23	1.029	1.207	− 0.500	0.586
Day 330	27.40	1.013	0.717	1,588.85	1.016	1.227	− 0.510	0.584
Day 360	26.82	0.979	0.702	1,633.77	1.028	1.261	− 0.560	0.556
Day 390	23.77	0.886	0.622	1,612.52	0.987	1.245	− 0.623	0.499
Day 420	25.91	1.090	0.678	1,680.19	1.042	1.297	− 0.619	0.522
Day 450	38.50	1.486	1.007	1,691.42	1.007	1.306	− 0.299	0.771
Day 480	43.60	1.132	1.140	1,683.99	0.996	1.300	− 0.160	0.877
Day 510	49.05	1.125	1.283	1,692.56	1.005	1.307	− 0.024	0.982
Day 540	47.53	0.969	1.243	1,770.61	1.046	1.367	− 0.124	0.909
Day 570	48.84	1.028	1.278	1,808.37	1.021	1.396	− 0.119	0.915
Day 600	58.23	1.192	1.523	1,837.49	1.016	1.419	0.104	1.074
Day 630	64.32	1.105	1.682	1,797.02	0.978	1.387	0.295	1.213
Day 660	69.80	1.085	1.826	1,878.04	1.045	1.450	0.376	1.259
Day 690	58.19	0.834	1.522	1,851.96	0.986	1.430	0.092	1.065
Day 720	56.76	0.975	1.485	1,875.63	1.013	1.448	0.037	1.025
Day 750	62.50	1.101	1.635	1,949.44	1.039	1.505	0.130	1.086
Day 780	65.29	1.045	1.708	1,977.65	1.014	1.527	0.181	1.119
Day 810	72.47	1.110	1.896	1,920.24	0.971	1.483	0.413	1.279
Day 840	77.26	1.066	2.021	2,007.71	1.046	1.550	0.471	1.304
Day 870	77.44	1.002	2.026	1,967.90	0.980	1.519	0.506	1.333
Day 900	75.76	0.978	1.982	2,012.10	1.022	1.553	0.428	1.276
Day 930	75.24	0.993	1.968	2,071.92	1.030	1.600	0.368	1.230
Day 960	78.45	1.043	2.052	2,058.20	0.993	1.589	0.463	1.291
Day 990	74.99	0.956	1.962	2,020.85	0.982	1.560	0.401	1.257
Day 1,020	80.90	1.079	2.116	2,098.53	1.038	1.620	0.496	1.306
Day 1,050	81.56	1.008	2.133	2,066.96	0.985	1.596	0.538	1.337
Day 1,080	78.99	0.968	2.066	2,108.29	1.020	1.628	0.438	1.269

Day 0 is the offer day (also the first trading day). Day 30, 60, and up to 1,080 indicate calendar days from Day 0. If they do not coincide with a trading day, the price of the closest preceding trading day is used. Return relative is the simple return of each month, R_t, plus 1. BHR means buy-and-hold return. Facebook prices and S&P 500 values are taken from Bloomberg Professional terminal.

Table 8.A.2 reports the monthly return relatives for each month and the values of BHR + 1 at the end of each period for the Facebook stock and the S&P 500 Index. The table also reports the WRs at the end of each holding period. The monthly return relative is the return calculated from the beginning and closing prices of each month as P_t/P_{t-1}. The "End of Period BHR + 1" column reports the values of BHR + 1 realized from the first market price to the closing price T months later. Thus, they represent the total buy-and-hold return (plus one) over a period of T months. They are calculated as the product of the monthly return relative of month t times the BHR + 1 at the end of the preceding month. For example, the BHR + 1 of day 60 is equal to $0.936 \times 0.785 = 0.735$. The WRs are calculated by dividing the BHR + 1 of Facebook say, 360 days after the offer day, by the BHR + 1 of the S&P 500 Index on the same day.

Table 8.A.2 shows that the investors who bought Facebook IPO shares at the closing market price of the offer day, that is, at $38.23, and held these shares for 420 days had realized a BHR + 1 and a WR that were below 1. This implies these investors had lost money on the stock itself as well as relative to what they could have earned if they had instead invested in the S&P 500 Index portfolio. On Day 450 after the offer day, Facebook was trading at $38.5, that is above its first (offer) day market price of $38.23 and generated a BHR + 1 of 1.007. But adjusted for the movement of the S&P500 Index, the WR was still below 1 (i.e., 0.771). The WR rose above 1 on day 600 (i.e., 1.074) and remained above 1 for the remainder of the 3-year period.

9

Theories of New Issue Pricing

Before we present the empirical evidence on the price performance of new issues in the following chapters, it is helpful to review the theories that have been advanced to explain the initial price behavior of new issues, that is, the relationship between offer price and initial market price.

The Underpricing Phenomenon

Casual observation and extensive empirical research in the United States and other countries has produced strong evidence that new issues are underpriced. By that we mean the average as well as median values of the initial returns measured from the offer price to the closing price of the first trading day are positive and statistically significantly different from zero. The question then is: why are new issues, in general, underpriced? If underwriters set offer prices to match the estimated expected market prices, we should observe new issues to be priced below or above the observed market price about evenly, that is, with a 50% chance. Within this paradigm, widespread underpricing would occur if the underwriters' estimates of expected market prices systematically underestimated the actual market prices. In the absence of such a systematic estimation bias, underpricing ought to be the result of underlying factors that compel underwriters to set offer prices below the expected, and eventually actual, market prices of new issues. The theories that follow attempt to identify these factors. Although these theories have been developed to explain underpricing in initial public offerings (IPOs), they can also apply to seasoned equity offerings (SEOs) and bond offerings.

Pricing Under Homogeneous Information

Homogeneous information describes a state where all parties involved in the new issues market, the issuer, the underwriter, and the investors, share a common set of information and beliefs about the true value of the new security. In such a state, and in the absence of institutional frictions, full pricing of the issue, that is, setting the offer price equal to the expected market value, is the rational policy. Setting the offer price above the commonly held expected market price is irrational because no investor will buy the issue. Setting the offer price below the expected market price is also suboptimal from the issuer's point of view. Although in the latter case, the gross spread should be lower the further the offer price is set below the expected market price, the net proceeds to the issuer would, in general, decline, and this is counter to the issuer's objective to maximize proceeds from the issue.

However, there may be conditions that can cause underpricing even when all parties share a common information set.

Underwriting Services and the New Issues Market. DOI: http://dx.doi.org/10.1016/B978-0-12-803282-4.00009-2

Underpricing as an Indirect Form of Underwriter Compensation

We have explained that for a given expected market price, lower offer prices should be associated with lower underwriter compensation as the expected underwriting cost declines. In underwriting markets without constraints on the choice of the offer price or the underwriter compensation, the underwriter charges the gross spread that fully compensates for the expected underwriting cost implied by the choice of the offer price.

It is possible though that the underwriting cost commensurate with a fully priced issue exceeds the level of underwriter compensation permitted by statutory provisions or regulatory constraints (e.g., the FINRA guidelines on underwriter compensation). In such cases the gross spread may not be sufficient to cover the expected underwriting costs for a fully priced new issue. Reilly and Hatfield (1969), Logue (1973b), and Ibbotson, Sindelar, and Ritter (1988) have advanced the argument that by selecting a lower offer price the underwriter can lower the underwriting costs and thus bring them to parity with the underwriting compensation. This is especially relevant to small issues given the practice to set the gross spread as a percentage of gross proceeds. When issue proceeds are low, the dollar spread may fall short of the expected costs of underwriting. Hence, underwriters increase the underpricing to reduce placement risk and distribution costs (Affleck-Graves and Miller, 1989).

Underpricing as a Form of Implicit Insurance Premium

Ibbotson (1975), Tiniç (1988), and Hughes and Thakor (1992) view underpricing as a means to mitigate the underwriter's exposure to litigation risk. If the market price declines below the offer price shortly after the sale of the new issue, disgruntled investors who have lost money may sue for misleading information or other violations of the due diligence rules of Section 11 of the Securities Act of 1933. If the litigation risk faced by the underwriter were insurable, its cost would be explicitly priced in the underwriter compensation. Due to various limitations, this does not appear to be the accepted practice. According to this argument, underpricing would seem to be a more efficient way to reduce the probability of litigation as well as its attendant costs.

Tiniç (1988) examined the initial returns of IPOs floated before and after the enactment of the Securities Act of 1933. Consistent with the litigation risk hypothesis, initial returns are higher in the post-1933 Act period. He also found that reputable underwriters, who, therefore, have a greater reputation capital to protect, have tended to avoid the underwriting of small and speculative IPOs in the post-1933 Act period.

Drake and Vetsuypens (1993) present, however, more direct evidence that does not support the implicit insurance hypothesis. They find no significant difference between the initial returns of litigated and nonlitigated IPOs. Further, most lawsuits relate to severe price drops later in the aftermarket that could not have been predicted at the pricing time. More supportive evidence in favor of the implicit insurance hypothesis is reported in Lowry and Shu (2002) who propose that litigation risk and underpricing are cause and effect of one another. Underpricing should be higher when risk is high; but higher underpricing reduces the probability of litigation. Accounting for this two-way interaction, the study finds that firms with higher exposure to litigation accept a higher degree of underpricing as a form of insurance against litigation. On its part, greater underpricing reduces the expected litigation costs and reduces the probability of a lawsuit. Zhu (2009) studies the effect of the Private Securities Litigation Reform Act of 1995 on the relationship between underpricing and the likelihood of litigation and finds mixed evidence on the efficacy of underpricing as a tool to mitigate litigation risk associated with initial public offerings.

The widespread underpricing of IPOs in countries outside the United States where there is much weaker protection of new issue buyers suggests that underpricing as insurance against litigation risk is not a sufficient explanation of underpricing.

Underpricing Due to Offer Price Constraints

The third reason new issues may be underpriced under conditions of homogeneous information is when by convention or regulatory constraint stocks are priced near their book or par value. Since the book or par value of a stock is normally lower than the market price, the new issues are almost certain to be underpriced. This pricing method, followed, at least in the past, in countries like South Korea (Kim and Lee, 1990) and Japan (Kunimura and Iihara, 1985), has been associated with severely underpriced IPOs.

Underpricing Due to Monopsony

According to this hypothesis, the underwriting market is not perfectly competitive and, therefore, underwriters can extract economic rents in the form of underpricing. However, monopsony rents are difficult to impose given FINRA's regulations about fair underwriting compensation. In addition, as Logue (1973b) has observed underpricing is often lower for issues managed by prestigious than nonranked underwriters, despite the former group's greater market power.

Underpricing as Reward for Reciprocal Business

Logue (1973b) was among the first to point out that by underpricing new issues investment banks could benefit from the reciprocal business directed to them from regular investors that received preferential allocations of underpriced new issues. This argument received increased attention and empirical scrutiny following the very high initial returns realized on IPOs executed in the dot-com period of the late 1990s and early 2000s (Loughran and Ritter, 2002).

Pricing Under Heterogeneous Information

Most theories of underpricing assume that issuers, underwriters, and investors hold different information sets or beliefs about the value of a new issue. These heterogeneous beliefs produce pricing outcomes in which the offer price is set below the expected market value. The assumption of heterogeneous information has spawned two different strands of theories: signaling theories and asymmetric information theories. The difference between the two theories is in the nature of the motive for underpricing.

In signaling theories, the underpricing is a deliberate decision to signal the true value of the firm so that in subsequent valuations investors revalue the security to align its price to its true market value. As such, underpricing is another signaling mechanism, similar to more traditional methods, like dividend policy and capital structure. In asymmetric information theories, the underpricing is an optimal solution in resolving informational advantages the respective parties may hold relative to each other.

Signaling Theories

Signaling theories of underpricing assume that the issuing firms' managers know more about the quality of their firms than outside investors. With imperfect information, investors cannot distinguish between high-quality firms and low-quality firms. Hence, high-quality firms choose to underprice their new issues in order to signal their true value. A critical condition of these models is that the true quality of the firm is revealed before the firm undertakes actions that trigger a fresh valuation subsequent to the issuance event. If the true state (or quality) of the firm is revealed before the firm has, say a follow-on seasoned equity offering, poor-quality firms cannot benefit from underpricing since investors learn of these firms' poor quality prior to the follow-on offering.

In Allen and Faulhaber (1989), high-quality firms trade off the loss from underpricing for better valuation by the market when they subsequently reveal their quality through earnings and dividend announcements. Investors respond favorably to these announcements by positively revaluing the firm's equity. In Grinblatt and Hwang (1989), the value of the firm's cash flows (in terms of mean and variance) is signaled through a combination of retention of shares by insiders as well as underpricing. Greater retention is a credible signal because only the insiders of high-quality firms can benefit from sacrificing the diversification of their wealth.

Welch (1989) conditions underpricing on the expectation that high-quality firms seek to achieve better valuation in future seasoned offerings. He predicts that high-quality firms underprice so that they can obtain a better value when they return to the public market. He finds that firms which underprice their IPOs are more likely to follow up with a seasoned offering and manage to raise more proceeds than other firms.

Jegadeesh, Weinstein, and Welch (1993) perform further tests of Welch's (1989) signaling hypothesis, and although they find a relationship between IPO underpricing and seasoned offering activity, they also detect that IPO underpricing per se does not have a unique role in explaining the behavior of follow-on seasoned offerings. Instead, the price behavior of IPOs in the aftermarket better explains the predictions about subsequent seasoned offerings. Garfinkel (1993) also finds that underpricing is not significantly associated with the likelihood the issuing firms will conduct subsequent seasoned offerings.

Michaely and Shaw (1994) perform extensive tests of the implications of signaling theories of Allen and Faulhaber (1989), Grinblatt and Hwang (1989), and Welch (1989) but find no supportive evidence. Instead, they find evidence in favor of Rock's (1986) winner's curse theory and the underwriter certification hypothesis (see below).

Asymmetric Information Theories

Depending on how the information sets differ across the different parties involved, asymmetric information theories can be classified with respect to whether the information divergence exists (1) between the issuer and the underwriter; (2) among investors; (3) between the issuer and the investors; and (4) between the underwriter and the investors.

Asymmetric Information Between Issuer and Underwriter

Baron (1982) develops a model in which the underwriter is more informed about the true value of the IPO than the issuer. It is also assumed that issuers cannot observe the distribution effort of the underwriters who may misrepresent the extent of their effort and overcharge the issuer. Hence, the issuer chooses to control the underwriting fees and yields the underwriter discretion over the pricing of the issue. The model predicts that offerings with greater uncertainty (and hence higher underwriting costs) are underpriced more as the underwriter tries to align the underwriting compensation to the expected costs.

A relatively direct test of Baron's hypothesis is possible when investment banking firms issue their own IPOs. In this case, there is no differential information between issuer and underwriter. Muscarella and Vetsuypens (1989) use a sample of self-managed issues by underwriting firms and find no difference in initial returns compared to regular IPOs. This evidence casts doubt on the validity of Baron's hypothesis.

Asymmetric Information Among Investors

The divergence of opinion hypothesis: Heterogeneous beliefs among investors can lead them to form divergent opinions about the value of a new issue. If short-sale restrictions in the immediate aftermarket prevent pessimistic investors to participate through short selling, the value of the new issue will reflect the opinions of the optimistic investors. Under this condition, Miller (1977) predicts that early aftermarket prices will be inflated due to the influence of optimistic investors and new issues will appear underpriced. Over time, as short-sale restrictions ease and more information becomes available about the security, the divergence of opinion subsides and prices move closer to their fair value.

Houge, Loughran, Suchanek, and Yan (2001) use proxies for the divergence of opinion (like, percentage of opening bid-ask spread, time to first trade, and flipping ratio) and confirm that all three proxies are associated with poor (market-adjusted) price performance 1 year after the IPO day. That is, high values of the proxies, which imply high degree of opinion divergence, result in inflated aftermarket prices which decline over time as they converge toward their long-run level as more pessimistic investors enter the market.

The winner's curse hypothesis: Rock (1986) also explains the underpricing of new issues as the result of asymmetric information between, what Rock calls, informed and uninformed investors. Informed investors have better information about the value of the new issue than uninformed investors, and, hence, can identify which firms will perform well in the aftermarket. Consequently, informed investors tend to oversubscribe to issues that turn out to be underpriced and subscribe less to issues that turn out to be overpriced. Uninformed investors, who cannot discriminate between good and poor quality issues, end up spreading their participation more evenly across overpriced and underpriced issues. Since by regulation the supply of the offered security is fixed, the rationing of new issues results in greater allocations of overpriced issues to uninformed investors and greater allocations of underpriced issues to informed investors (who refrain from bidding for poor quality issues). Thus, when uninformed investors receive greater allocations (of overpriced issues), they fall victims of the winner's curse.

If this pattern lasts, uninformed investors realize, on average, negative initial returns on their portfolio of new issues and eventually withdraw from the new issues market. To avoid this drainage of capital, underwriters entice uninformed investors to participate by underpricing all new issues up to the point that allows uninformed investors to earn a riskless rate on their investments. For Rock's model to hold there must be evidence of greater rationing of underpriced issues, especially with respect to uninformed investors, and the latter must realize nonzero initial returns. A frequent criticism of Rock's theory is that the issuance process practiced in the United States gives the underwriter discretion over the price and the allocation of the new issue. Therefore, the US new issues market does not avail itself for a valid test of Rock's theory.

A more appropriate setting to test this theory is a market where allocations are dictated by the subscription bids of the investors. Koh and Walter (1989) test Rock's hypothesis in such a market, specifically the Singapore Stock Exchange, where investors subscribe to IPOs and receive allocations according to a publicly announced formula. Koh and Walter find evidence that supports Rock's hypothesis. Uninformed investors seem to earn a return close to the riskless rate and they are allocated greater portions of overpriced issues.

Hanley and Wilhelm (1995) present evidence on IPO allocations in the 1980s which, contrary to Rock's model, shows that institutional investors participate extensively in cold (overpriced) and hot (underpriced) issues. Using discretionary allocations, which are possible under the bookbuilding method, underwriters award greater portions of underpriced issues to investors who reveal positive information and are committed to participate more steadily in the underwriter's managed issues (including cold issues). Therefore, whether a class of investors possesses an information advantage or not does not afford them the opportunity to refrain from bidding for less promising new issues. This makes Rock's model less relevant in explaining the pricing of new issues in the United States.

In an earlier study, Miller and Reilly (1987) estimate that in a sample of 510 IPOs, the underpriced issues generated an average initial return of 15.39%, whereas the 154 overpriced issues realized an average initial return of -2.88%. This implies that if uninformed investors were entirely rationed out of underpriced issues they would have earned a negative initial return, which is not consistent with the winner's curse hypothesis.

The cascades hypothesis: Welch (1992) also considers investors who are differentially informed about the true value of the new issue. Early investors who subscribe to the new issue cause other investors to adapt their own beliefs and submit subscriptions as well. The underwriter realizes that for an issue to be fully subscribed early subscribers must demonstrate a favorable reception of the issue. In the opposite event, the issue will not be fully sold. Therefore, the underwriter has reasons to underprice the issue in order to attract strong early subscriptions. Under the cascades hypothesis, the objective of underpricing is not to eliminate the winner's curse but rather to ensure the full subscription of the issue.

Asymmetric Information Between Issuers and Investors

The reputation effect hypothesis: Beatty and Ritter (1986) assume that the issuing firm has superior information about the value of its IPO than investors. This creates an adverse selection problem for investors who cannot discriminate between fairly priced and overpriced IPOs. Hence, new issues must be underpriced in accordance with the level of their ex ante uncertainty. In this model, underwriting firms can lend credibility to the proposed offer price because, unlike issuers, they must return to the market repeatedly for the flotation of future issues, and hence, they need to protect their reputational capital. This theory predicts that (1) deviations from the equilibrium level of underpricing cause underwriters to lose market share in the IPO market and (2) IPOs with higher ex ante uncertainty are more likely to create conditions of adverse selection and thus be underpriced more heavily relative to IPOs with less ex ante uncertainty.

Beatty and Ritter (1986) test these two predictions and find supportive evidence. The degree of underpricing is found to be directly related to proxies of ex ante uncertainty for their IPO sample, and underwriters who fall out of line with respect to the degree of underpricing experience losses in market share in subsequent years. Nanda and Yun (1997) also find that the stocks of underwriting firms that place overpriced IPOs suffer a negative market reaction at the offer day of the issues. In the case of moderately underpriced issues, however, the underwriter's stock value increases. Importantly, it is the party mostly responsible for pricing (i.e., the lead underwriter) whose stock suffers these valuation effects. The negative market reaction is evidence that overpricing is perceived as damaging to the investment bank's reputation capital and hence to its future revenue.

The certification hypothesis: Booth and Smith (1986) also assume asymmetry of information between issuers and investors, whereby the issuer is the party that enjoys an information advantage. Because of the adverse selection problem and the inability of the issuer to credibly reveal the value of the IPO an intermediary (i.e., underwriter) is used to certify the offer price. In effect, the underwriting firm leases its name to the issuer. The underwriter charges for both the certification benefit and the cost for acquiring information about the quality of the issue. Since issuers have an incentive to issue new securities when they are overvalued, certification is more valuable when investors stand to lose more due to asymmetric information. The certification hypothesis predicts that underwriter compensation and underpricing are positively related to proxies of asymmetric information. Booth and Smith (1986) provide evidence in favor of a positive relationship between gross spreads and underpricing on the one hand and proxies of uncertainty on the other.

The underwriter prestige hypothesis: Carter and Manaster (1990) build on the certification and reputation hypotheses to advance the proposition that the need to protect the prestige of an underwriter affects the selection of IPOs and their pricing. Prestigious underwriters are able to distinguish between high-quality and low-quality issuers and protect their reputation by avoiding the latter. High-quality issuers also have an interest to attract high reputation underwriters in order to separate themselves from low-quality issuers and, thus, avoid the greater underpricing associated with low-quality issuers. The Carter and Manaster hypothesis predicts that prestigious underwriters are mostly associated with (1) low-risk issuers and (2) less underpriced IPOs. Their tests provide evidence in favor of both these predictions.

Investor dispersion and aftermarket price and liquidity: Chemmanur (1993) models underpricing as reward for the production of information by investors willing to discover the true value of the new issue. In this case, the issuer's motive is to improve the aftermarket value of the security so that it can be priced higher in follow-on offers. High-quality firms benefit the most from more information production and dissemination, thus have an incentive to underprice their issues though the degree of underpricing varies inversely with the probability an issuer is recognized as a high-quality firm. The degree of underpricing varies directly with the cost of price discovery.

Booth and Chua (1996) assume that in a state of information asymmetry between issuers and investors the former have an interest to attract a broad investor base who will spend resources to learn more about the new issue and support a liquid secondary market. To achieve this, issuers are willing to accept underpricing. The equilibrium degree of underpricing is that which meets the issuer's expectations for ownership dispersion and liquidity and adequately compensates investors for information production costs so that they remain in the new issues market. The role of the underwriter is to lend credibility and, thus, attract more investors. Greater investor interest results in greater oversubscription which has a positive effect on offer price and helps issuers maximize issue proceeds. When new issues are clustered together, information production spillovers help reduce the information production costs for individual investors, and this results in lower underpricing. Their empirical findings are broadly supportive of their hypothesis.

Underpricing and corporate governance: Brennan and Franks (1997) propose that underpricing is used by insiders in order to reduce outside monitoring and increase the value of their control rights. Greater underpricing encourages more investors to subscribe to the new issue which intensifies the degree of rationing against investors who wish to buy large blocks. This prevents the emergence of outside investors with large enough blockholdings to justify active monitoring. Using a sample of IPOs completed in the United Kingdom, they find that greater underpricing is associated with more discriminatory allocations against large applicants.

Stoughton and Zechner (1998) take the opposite view and propose that issuing firms use underpricing in order to attract large investors who will engage in active monitoring which in turn will improve the stock's value. Thus, issuers trade off a lower offer price (and, hence, greater underpricing) for the benefit of attaining higher market value. The role of the underwriter is to identify investors who are potentially effective monitors of firm management and set the offer price at a level that attracts such investors.

Boulton, Smart, and Zutter (2010) relate the underpricing to the managers' interest in reducing the likelihood of takeover attempts after the firm becomes public. They find that when activity in the takeover market intensifies subsequent IPOs are underpriced relatively more and the dispersion of stock ownership after the IPO is negatively related to the likelihood of a takeover. The presence of a dual-class share structure (which protects against losing control) makes pre-IPO M&A activity less impactful on underpricing.

Asymmetric Information Between Underwriter and Investors

Underpricing as reward to private information: Benveniste and Spindt (1989) assume that investors possess private information that can help the underwriter price the issue closer to its true market value and successfully complete the offering. In the United States, the bookbuilding method allows underwriters to determine the range of possible offer prices of a new issue and then try to presell the issue by eliciting expressions of interest from investors. Furthermore, the underwriter has discretion over the allocation of the issue. The preselling activity is valuable because it enables the underwriter to collect additional information about the value of the issue before the offer price is fixed. The underwriter then uses the offer price and the allocation to reward those investors who reveal positive information and, thus, help to set the offer price close to its fair level. Well-informed investors will refrain from withholding positive information or revealing false information, because the underwriter can exclude them from the allocation of future IPOs. In return for the information they receive, underwriters commit to discount the offer price so that informed investors will realize a gain. The underwriter underprices the issue and allocates enough IPO shares to these investors so that they realize a positive return on their IPO investment over the long run.

The predictions of this model are (1) underpricing directly relates to the ex ante value of investors' information—the more valuable to price discovery the information is, the greater is the underpricing the underwriter must promise; (2) underpricing is directly related to the level of interest in the premarket period; and (3) underwriters prefer to allocate new issues to regular informed investors because rewarding such investors over the long run reduces the overall level of underpricing and forces informed investors to also participate in cold issues. Given the fixed supply of a new issue for sale, extracting positive information can be rewarded mostly through underpricing than through greater allocations. By increasing the available supply, the overallotment option is a useful tool in reducing underpricing under the bookbuilding method. The Benveniste and Spindt's (1989) theory is also known as the information extraction hypothesis.

An interesting implication of this theory is that issues priced close to or above the upper bound of the price range (an indication of strong preoffer interest) are likely to experience greater actual underpricing than issues priced close to or below the lower bound of the range. Indeed, Hanley (1993) finds that IPOs priced above the price range have average initial returns of 20%, whereas IPOs priced below the range have average initial returns of only 0.6%.

10

The Price and Operating Performance of Initial Public Offerings

This chapter presents the empirical evidence in relation to three important topics: the initial pricing of initial public offerings (IPOs); their long-run price performance; and the operating performance of firms conducting IPOs. The chapter also reviews empirical studies that analyze the performance of IPO stocks and issuing firms from a variety of perspectives that highlight the influence of uncertainty and certification effects.

The Initial Pricing of IPOs

The initial pricing of new issues refers to how the offer price relates to the first postoffer market price and is assessed by the sign and magnitude of the initial returns of the new issues in the aftermarket. A positive initial return is an indication of underpricing, i.e., the new security has been placed at a price below what the market is willing to bear. Conversely, a negative initial return is an indication of overpricing.

The empirical evidence on the initial price behavior of IPOs provides insights to the following questions: (1) Do the initial returns provide evidence of underpricing or overpricing? (2) What factors explain the variation of initial returns across IPOs? (3) What explains periods of severe underpricing or so-called "hot issue" markets? and (4) Are IPOs efficiently priced?

General Findings

Table 10.1 presents average and median initial returns from studies of IPOs completed in the United States from the 1960s to the 2000s. During that long period, average initial returns ranged from 12.74% in the 1980s to 28.89% in the 2000s. The median initial returns ranged from 5.07% in the 1980s to 12.38% in the 2000s. One reason average initial returns appear to be unusually high (17.76%) in samples from the 1960s is that some studies report initial returns over long intervals, e.g., a week or even a month after the issue day, without adjusting for market movement.

During the dot-com bubble years 1999 and 2000, average and median initial returns shot up sharply to 77% and 44.5%, respectively, as reported by at least two studies. Table 10.1 shows that over long periods of time that encompass several decades, average (median) returns ranged from 8.34% (2.88%) in the sample period 1986–2000 to 31.21% (8.33%) in the sample period 1970–2000.

Table 10.1 Initial Returns of US IPOs by Sample Period—Various Studies

Study	Sample Period	Initial Return		Return Interval
		Mean	Median	
1960s				
Reilly and Hatfield (1969)	1964–1965	9.90	0.90	1, MA
McDonald and Fisher (1972)	1969–1970	28.50	n.a.	2
Ibbotson (1975)	1960–1965	11.40	n.a.	3
Ibbotson, Sindelar, and Ritter (1994)	1960–1969	21.25	n.a.	
	Average	**17.76**	**0.90**	
1970s				
Reilly (1977)	1972–1975	10.80	3.30	2, MA
Ibbotson, Sindelar, and Ritter (1994)	1970–1979	8.95	n.a.	
Affleck-Graves, Hegde, and Miller (1996)	1975–1991	9.96	n.a.	
Ritter (1984)	1977–1982	26.30	n.a.	
Carter and Manaster (1990)	1979–1983	16.18	6.34	4, MA
	Average	**14.44**	**4.82**	
1980s				
Booth and Chua (1996)	1977–1988	13.10	3.13	
Gompers (1996)	1978–1987	13.60	6.70	
Carter, Dark, and Singh (1998)	1979–1991	8.08	2.38	MA
Ibbotson, Sindelar, and Ritter (1994)	1980–1989	15.18	n.a.	
Lowry, Officer, and Schwert (2010)	1981–1990	9.20	8.50	5
Loughran and Ritter (2004)	1980–1989	7.30	1.90	
Hoberg (2007)	1984–1990	22.70	7.80	
	Average	**12.74**	**5.07**	
1990s				
Krigman, Shaw, and Womack (1999)	1988–1995	12.30	6.20	
Lowry and Schwert (2004)	1985–1997	12.32	n.a.	
Ibbotson, Sindelar, and Ritter (1994)	1990–1992	10.85	n.a.	
Habib and Ljungqvist (2000)	1991–1995	13.80	7.10	
Falconieri, Murphy, and Weaver (2009)	1993–1998	16.30	8.90	
Chemmanur and Paeglis (2005)	1993–1996	14.35	9.40	
Lee, Lochhead, Ritter, and Zhao (1996)	1990–1994	12.05	n.a.	
Loughran and Ritter (2004)	1990–1998	14.80	7.80	
Ljungqvist and Wilhelm (2005)	1993–2000	28.10	n.a.	
Lowry, Officer, and Schwert (2010)	1991–2005	25.80	18.40	5
Chemmanur, Hu, and Huang (2010)	1990–2003	54.85	23.29	
	Average	**19.59**	**11.58**	
Dot-com Years				
Ljungqvist and Wilhelm (2003)	1999–2000	89.00	57.00	
Loughran and Ritter (2004)	1999–2000	65.00	32.00	
	Average	**77.00**	**44.50**	

(Continued)

Table 10.1   (Continued)

Study	Sample Period	Initial Return		Return Interval
		Mean	Median	
2000s				
Loughran and Ritter (2004)	2001–2003	11.70	8.80	
Arnold, Fishe, and North (2010)	1998–2005	40.16	15.05	
Loughran and McDonald (2013)	1997–2010	34.80	13.30	
	Average	**28.89**	**12.38**	
Long Periods				
Lowry, Officer, and Schwert (2010)	1965–1980	12.10	5.30	5
Lowry, Officer, and Schwert (2010)	1965–2005	16.60	11.90	5
Kim, Palia, and Saunders (2003)	1970–2000	31.21	8.33	
Boulton, Smart, and Zutter (2010)	1980–2001	18.50	6.30	
Gao, Mao, and Zhong (2006)	1980–2000	18.85	n.a.	
Loughran and Ritter (2004)	1980–2003	18.70	6.30	
Ritter (2015)	1980–2012	17.90	n.a.	
Benveniste, Ljungqvist, Wilhelm, and Yu (2003)	1985–2000	20.22	7.50	
Ghosh, Petrova, Feng, and Pattanapanchai (2012)	1985–2009	18.00	6.00	
Edelen and Kadlec (2005)	1985–2000	23.20	8.70	
Cai, Ramchand, and Warga (2004)	1986–2000	8.34	2.88	
	Average	**18.51**	**7.02**	

Studies are classified in a decade if most of the years in the sample period are from that decade. MA means market-adjusted, i.e., the initial return has been adjusted by the change in the value of a market index. Initial returns are calculated from the offer price to first day's closing price. Studies which use different initial return intervals are identified as: (1) Offer price to first Friday's closing price; (2) Offer price to market price of first Wednesday; (3) Offer price to market price 1 month later; (4) Offer price to market price 2 weeks later; (5) Offer price to market price 21 days later. n.a.: not available.

The evidence reported in Table 10.1 shows that the magnitude of initial returns does vary over time. It also shows that in some periods it rises significantly above the average level recorded over long-run periods. From a practical standpoint, these findings suggest two obvious conclusions: (1) on average, issuers leave significant amounts of money on the table and (2) on average, initial investors earn positive returns by buying at the offer price and selling at the first aftermarket price.

Determinants of the Initial Returns

The statistical information reported in Table 10.1 indicates that IPOs are on average underpriced. Nonetheless, the magnitude of underpricing varies not only across periods, it can also vary across the IPOs of different firms. What then explains this cross-sectional variation?

The pricing theories reviewed in Chapter 9: Theories of New Issue Pricing have established a number of explanations for the underpricing of new issues. Three factors that appear to be important in most of these theories are: (1) ex ante risk; (2) asymmetric information; and (3) certification of issue quality. These factors and the conditions that affect waiting and pricing risk, identified in Chapter 6: Underwriting Costs and Compensation, provide the main explanatory framework of initial returns in the various cross-sectional studies.

Empirical studies that analyze initial returns utilize various proxies to capture the effects of the above factors on the initial pricing of new issues. The most widely used empirical proxies are described below.

Issuer-Related Proxies

Age: Older firms are more well-known and well-established in their fields; hence, it is easier to assess the quality and risk of older firms. Age is used as a proxy of ex ante risk and asymmetric information.

Size of sales or assets: Larger size issuers are associated with more successful operations and, hence, with less risk and greater investor interest. Larger issuer size is associated with less uncertainty about the value of the issue and, hence, less underpricing.

Issue-Related Proxies

Gross proceeds: Gross proceeds are related to the issuer's size so, if large, they can signal less value-related uncertainty. However, a high ratio of gross proceeds to issuer's capital base may signify financing problems and add to the level of uncertainty. Attempting to sell too many shares may also put price pressure on the issue.

Overhang: In equity issues, overhang is the ratio of shares retained to the new shares placed. Lower overhang signifies lower participation of existing shareholders in the ongoing operations of the firm—an indicator of low confidence in the quality of the issuer.

Fraction of secondary offering: This is the ratio of shares offered on behalf of selling shareholders to the total number of shares offered. A lower ratio signals greater confidence on part of insiders in the future of the firm and reduces the level of uncertainty and, hence, underpricing. However, a sizable secondary offering makes selling shareholders sensitive to underpricing (money left on the table) and, hence, more eager to negotiate a more aggressive pricing of the issue.

Price range: A wider price range in the preliminary prospectus indicates less confidence on part of the underwriter about the exact location of the expected market value of the issue. It signifies greater ex ante risk and asymmetric information.

Offer price relative to price range: When the offer price is set close to or above the upper bound of the price range, underpricing is, on average, greater. The positive relationship is a direct implication of the partial price adjustment hypothesis in the case of bookbuilt offers.

Underwriting spread: A greater underwriting spread implies greater underwriting and placement risk due to higher uncertainty. Thus, as a proxy of risk, the underwriting spread would be positively associated with underpricing. It is also possible to observe an inverse relationship between the gross spread and degree of underpricing since greater underpricing reduces the underwriting costs.

Number of uses of proceeds: The greater the number of the uses of the funds enumerated in the prospectus the more difficult it is to estimate their net value contribution to the value of the issuer. Thus, the level of pricing risk is higher and this can contribute to greater underpricing.

Standard deviation of returns: The volatility of returns is a direct proxy of ex ante risk.

Bid-ask spread: The bid-ask spread at which a new security is traded in the aftermarket serves as a proxy of information asymmetry with respect to the true value of the security. Wider spreads indicate greater market uncertainty about the true value of a security.

Marketplace of listing: Listing venues such as the New York Stock Exchange (NYSE) or Nasdaq are viewed differently with respect to their ability to certify the quality of securities. The stricter the listing criteria and the greater the visibility of the trading venue the greater the perceived certification power of the marketplace is. Thus, the marketplace the new issue is listed serves as proxy of ex ante risk and asymmetry of information.

Market-Related Proxies

Market volatility: Market volatility in the prepricing period contributes directly to the overall uncertainty regarding the estimated market price of the issue and, hence, affects the level of pricing risk.

Volume of new issues: A greater volume of new issues indicates that investors are receptive to new offers. This can motivate underwriters to set the offer price more aggressively (i.e., closer to the expected market price). Greater volume of new issues may also coincide with investor overoptimism which can result in aggressive buying in the aftermarket, which can contribute to heavier underpricing.

Underpricing of recent new issues: Greater underpricing of recent issues is more likely to be followed by greater underpricing of current issues, given the documented serial correlation of initial returns.

The initial pricing of new issues can be also impacted by differences in underwriting arrangements (e.g., negotiated versus competitive offerings), the scope of offering (general cash offer versus rights offer), the contract type, and other offering features, as for example, the underwriter and syndicate choice. The impact of these factors is discussed in Chapters 15 and 16.

Empirical Studies in Initial Returns

The pricing of new issues, especially IPOs, has been analyzed in a large number of studies over the last 40 years. A number of these studies that purport to test the predictions of the major theories of new issue pricing were presented in Chapter 9: Theories of New Issue Pricing. Below we review the main findings of additional studies that have analyzed the initial returns of IPOs in the context of various market and firm related factors.

Mispricing in the Aftermarket

Measuring underpricing by comparing offer price to the immediate aftermarket price relies on the premise that aftermarket prices are fair representations of the values of the new securities. Although this can be a reasonable assumption in the case of seasoned stocks, it may not necessarily hold in the case of unlisted securities that have no prior history of market prices. Aggarwal and Rivoli (1990) postulate that underpricing can be the result of "fads," that is, speculative behavior that pushes the market prices of newly listed stocks, above their fair level. They find that (after adjusting for market movement) market prices of a sample of IPO stocks are on average below the level of offer prices one year after the issue. This finding suggests that new issues may be overpriced relative to their long-run value notwithstanding their initial underpricing. In a related study, Hunt-McCool, Koh, and Francis (1996) find that the excessive underpricing found in "hot issue" markets (see below) can be explained by both deliberate underpricing and mispricing in aftermarket trading.

Mauer and Senbet (1992) propose that the primary market, where new issues are priced, and the secondary market, where market prices are set, are segmented and populated by different classes of investors. While primary markets are influenced by the behavior of informed investors, secondary markets are influenced by retail investor behavior. This can cause a disconnect between the offer price and the secondary price of a new issue. They compare initial returns of IPOs of firms from industries populated by many comparable firms (which, therefore, share common valuation characteristics) and find that their initial returns are lower than the initial returns of IPOs conducted by firms with more unique characteristics and from industries with less homogeneous firms. This implies that initial pricing is closer to market prices when more valuation-related information is available.

Short-Sale Restrictions

Aftermarket pricing can be affected by short-selling restrictions. Selling new issues short in the aftermarket is restricted by the relatively small public float of shares and by restrictions on insider sales during the lockup period. These conditions prevent investors with pessimistic assessment of IPO stocks to enter the market and exert downward pressure on price. Ofek and Richardson (2003) find evidence that short-sale restrictions were relatively high during the internet bubble years leading to 2000. In addition, institutional holdings in internet stocks were significantly lower than in the stocks of other comparable firms. If institutions represent the more "rational" segment of the market an important countereffect to the over-optimism of retail investors was lacking. Indeed, IPOs with lower institutional trading were much more underpriced than IPOs with higher institutional trading.

Edwards and Hanley (2010) report that short selling is observed in 99.5% of IPOs immediately after trading starts and is of the same average magnitude as that observed for nonissuing stocks. They find little evidence that short selling is impeded by various market conditions. Interestingly, they do not find support for the view that short selling contributes to more efficient aftermarket prices and, hence, lower underpricing. Instead short selling activity correlates with underpricing.

Information Spillover Effects

Firms that share common valuation factors can reduce the cost of price discovery by tapping the IPO market around the same time (Benveniste, Busaba, and Wilhelm, 2002). However, the firm that moves first incurs the initial higher cost of price discovery whereas later IPO issuers free-ride on the already produced information. Underwriters can reduce the first-mover's disadvantage by bundling the IPOs of similar firms and thus reduce underpricing across all firms (Benveniste, Ljungqvist, Wilhelm, and Yu, 2003). This pattern of IPO production can also explain the negative correlation between initial returns and volume of IPOs.

Offer Price Effects

Bradley, Cooney, Jordan, and Singh (2004) find that IPOs with integer offer prices had average initial returns that were significantly higher than those with noninteger offer prices—24.5% versus 8.1%—in the period 1981–2000. They also report that the difference in initial returns between IPOs with integer and noninteger offer prices had increased over the years, with the bubble period of 1999–2000 displaying the largest difference—a whopping 64.2% between integer and noninteger priced IPOs. Issuers and underwriters are found to adopt coarser (i.e., integer) prices when they encounter offerings with greater degree of valuation uncertainty or when the offer price is relatively high. Adopting an integer offer price is less costly than attempting to refine the offer price by adopting a noninteger price.

Ex Ante Risk and Information Asymmetry

Muscarella and Vetsuypens (1989) find that initial returns are lower when firms, previously taken private, execute a "second" IPO to return to the public market. Since the market already knows more about these issuers, information asymmetry is less resulting in less underpricing. The level of asymmetric information and degree of underpricing is also lower for firms that have completed private placements of equity (Cai, Lee, and Sharma, 2011) or public debt offers (Cai, Ramchand, and Warga, 2004). Chemmanur and Paeglis (2005) find that management quality can also reduce ex ante uncertainty and result in lower underpricing. High quality managers are able to attract more prestigious underwriters and provide stronger certification of their firm's value. Falconieri, Murphy, and Weaver (2009) find that accounting for ex post (i.e., postoffer) risk proxies, like the bid-ask spread, in addition to ex ante risk factors, can better explain cross-sectional differences in the degree of underpricing. Arnold, Fishe, and North (2010) find that the language used to articulate risk factors in the prospectus affects investor perceptions about uncertainty. Their measure of relative ambiguity, i.e., the ratio of soft (more ambiguous) to hard references to risk factors, is positively related with the degree of underpricing.

Gonzalez and James (2007) find evidence that establishing bank relationships prior to the IPO has a certification effect that reduces the asymmetric information surrounding the firm's value. Compared to firms with no bank relationships prior to their IPO, firms with bank relationships completed IPOs which were less underpriced and realized better operating improvement after the IPO.

Firms concerned about the release of vital business information that can harm their competitive advantage request and often are granted permission from the SEC to redact sensitive content from their public filing. Boone, Floros, and Johnson (2016) report that 40% of their sample of firms that completed IPOs in 1996–2011 withheld full disclosure. The price of reduced information transparency is greater underpricing for redacting firms compared to nonredacting firms. To blunt the negative pricing effect, redacting firms employ, on average, more reputable underwriters. Such firms also sell less of the firm's equity at the IPO and more in follow-on SEOs compared to nonredacting firms. Interestingly, redacting firms display superior operating performance relative to nonredacting firms in the 3 years past the IPO.

Marketing and Promotion Effects

Issuers can reduce the degree of underpricing by committing resources to activities and parties that can credibly promote the value of the issue. These include bookbuilding, choosing a reputable underwriter, a full-service contract (i.e., firm commitment contract), a high-quality auditor and legal counsel or a more visible marketplace, like the NYSE. Habib and Ljungqvist (2001) find that underpricing decreases as promotion costs increase. Demers and Lewellen (2003), however, come to the opposite conclusion about the link between underpricing and publicity. Issuers may use underpricing to buy publicity (i.e., create a "buzz") about their issue. Demers and Lewellen (2003) find a direct association between degree of underpricing and postissue web traffic (i.e., website visits). The positive relationship between "buzz" about an IPO and underpricing is also confirmed in Cook, Kieschnick, and Van Ness (2006). IPO firms exposed to greater publicity and promotion during the prepricing period have higher valuations compared to same industry firms. However, high publicity IPOs are also underpriced more due to stronger aftermarket prices. This implies that despite the strong prepricing visibility and publicity, underwriters do not fully revise the offer price to reflect the greater investor attention and interest.

Venture Capital-Backed IPOs

Firms going public are often backed by venture capital (VC) funds. The presence of these specialized investors can add credibility to valuation and enhance the monitoring of the underwriting group. The certification value of VC funds in IPOs is enhanced by the fact that normally VC shareholders retain relatively more shares after the firm goes public and VC-backed IPOs are also brought to market by higher reputation underwriters. Overall, however, the evidence on the impact of VC funds on underpricing is mixed.

Consistent with the certification and monitoring hypotheses, Barry, Muscarella, Peavy, and Vetsuypens (1990) and Megginson and Weiss (1991) find that VC-backed IPOs have lower underpricing. Lerner (1994) finds that VC-backed firms time their IPOs to coincide with market peaks and these IPOs realize lower underpricing. However, Bradley and Jordan (2002) report no significant difference in initial returns between VC-backed IPOs and non-VC-backed IPOs after accounting for other factors that influence initial returns.

On the opposite end, Gompers (1996) advances the "grandstanding" hypothesis according to which VC funds, especially new ones, establish reputation by succeeding in taking firms they have funded public. Early success attracts more capital to the VC firm for follow-on investments. The eagerness of these young VC funds to have successful IPO deals coupled with the usually young age of the issuing firms results in greater underpricing. Lee and Wahal (2004) find that, correcting for the selectivity bias in the VC funds' choice of firms they back, VC-backed IPOs are underpriced by 5% to 10.3% more than "matched" non-VC-backed IPOs. Consistent with the grandstanding theory, they find that the degree of underpricing varies directly with the number of IPOs and the future capital flows to the VC firms involved.

Ritter (2015) reports that growth capital-backed IPOs realize lower underpricing compared to other IPOs. Growth capital funds invest in firms rich in tangible assets and committed to acquisition-based growth (e.g., restaurants, retail operations, dental and medical offices). Hence, these IPOs are less exposed to information asymmetry.

The "Hot Issue" Markets

The term "hot issue" describes a new offer whose immediate aftermarket price exceeds the offer price by an unusually high premium. Ibbotson and Jaffe (1975) define a "hot issue" as an issue with an initial return above the median initial return of new issues completed over a long period of time. Clusters of hot issues, during different time periods, are called "hot issue" markets. The opposite of hot issues are cold issues, that is issues whose underpricing is below the long-run average degree of underpricing. Time periods with clusters of cold issues are called "cold issue" markets.

Ibbotson and Jaffe (1975) were the first to perform a thorough analysis of "hot issue" markets in the period from 1960 to 1970. Their main findings can be summarized as follows:

- Initial returns are serially autocorrelated. Months with IPOs that have high (low) initial returns of IPOs are highly likely to be followed by months with IPOs that have high (low) initial returns. This means hot (cold) issue markets are predictable. The autocorrelation dissipates as the time period between initial returns grows.
- Positive (negative) initial returns predict positive (negative) abnormal returns in postissue intervals but this correlation fades quickly. Thus, investing in underpriced issues yields, on average, above normal returns in the short-term period following the offer.
- There is no evidence that the volume of IPOs in one interval (e.g., month) can be predicted by the magnitude of initial returns of IPOs in past time intervals. Furthermore, the time series of IPO volume and IPO initial returns do not seem to correlate to each other.
- Issuers benefit if they execute IPOs in cold issue periods during which underpricing is low.

Ritter (1984) studies hot market periods in a sample of IPOs conducted in 1960−1982 and adds the following findings:

- Monthly volumes of new IPOs are serially correlated across months.
- High volume periods are followed by periods of high initial returns.
- Although initial returns seem to vary with the level of ex ante risk and information asymmetry, the hot issue markets are not necessarily caused by the clustering of IPOs of unusually risky firms.

Ibbotson, Sindelar, and Ritter (1994) using a large sample of 10,626 IPOs in the 1960–1992 period confirm the above findings and offer some additional explanations for the phenomenon of "hot issue" markets. Specifically, they note that:

- A positive feedback or momentum motivates investors to bid excessively in the aftermarket after having observed high initial returns in past issues.
- The market goes through windows of opportunity during which excessively high valuation multiples are applied to new issues. Despite very ebullient market conditions, issuers accept severe underpricing because offer prices are still high by historical standards. For example, let us assume that the average market price–earnings (P/E) ratio is 50 and earnings per share for an issuing firm are $3. Also, let us assume that the historical P/E ratio of the industry of that firm is 20. At the historical multiple, the offer price could be set at around $60 (20 × $3) per share. At the current P/E ratio the price could be set at $150 (50 × $3). A proposed offer price of, say, $80 is higher than the price of $60 but it still falls short of the market price that is likely to be realized in the aftermarket as a result of the temporary excessive valuation climate.

Helwege and Liang (2004) confirm Ritter's finding that IPO firms do not come from distinct industries in hot and cold markets. Instead, hot issue markets tend to occur about the same time across industries; hence, the "hot issue" market phenomenon is mainly triggered by economy-wide conditions.

Loughran and Ritter (2002) and Edelen and Kadlec (2005) attribute the correlation of initial returns to the clustering of IPO filings within similar time periods. As a result, IPOs of different firms share overlapping waiting periods and are affected by the same market conditions. If the common market factor is only partially incorporated in the offer prices but more fully in the market prices, initial returns appear to be cross-sectionally and serially correlated.

Yung, Çolak, and Wang (2008) report that the big waves of IPOs are triggered by broader surges of firm values that drive both good and poor quality firms to tap the IPO market. Faced with greater uncertainty about the true quality of issuers, underwriters and investors impose higher underpricing than they would in normal volume markets.

Khanna, Noe, and Sonti (2008) argue that the positive relationship between volume of new issues (especially IPOs) and underpricing may be explained by the fact that underwriters have inelastic supply of screening skills that limits their capacity to thoroughly process new issuers. Thus, in high-volume periods, screening standards decline and firms of lower quality decide to raise capital. Faced with less certainty about issuer quality, underwriters increase underpricing to protect themselves against hidden underwriting risks and the prospect of placing overpriced issues.

Are IPOs Efficiently Priced?

Pricing theories of new issues predict that costly information production and asymmetric information can result in deliberate underpricing as a means to incentivize investors to acquire and share information with the underwriter. In such cases, offer prices reflect only part of the private information revealed during the prepricing period. However, offer prices should reflect all other information that is available to the underwriter through his/her own investigation or is available to all investors in the form of market information. Consequently, a question of interest is: Do offer prices reflect the appropriate set of information?

The Impact of Public and Private Information

Since public information is available to all, it should be fully reflected in the offer price. The same is true of information that becomes available to the underwriter through the underwriting investigation. On the other hand, private information revealed by investors may not be reflected in the offer price in order to reward information sharing.

To better understand the interaction between information and new issue pricing, we need to identify the four stages new issues go through from the very first price indication to the eventual market price formation in the aftermarket. These stages coincide with distinct periods in the offering process: the prefiling period; the prepricing period (from filing to fixing the offer price); and the postissue period.

Initial pricing: It refers to the initial price range filed with the prospectus following the underwriter's investigation. The midpoint of the range is considered as the first estimate of the expected market price of the new issue by the underwriter.

Price update: It refers to the update of the price range following the roadshows and the building of the book of informal orders. In many cases, there is no formal resetting of the price range through an amendment of the prospectus. In this case, the price update refers to the selection of the final offer price. It is measured by the percentage change from the midpoint to the offer price.

Final pricing: It refers to the setting of the final offer price once bookbuilding is over.

Market pricing: It refers to the first available market price when trading of the new issue starts in the postoffer market.

If pricing proceeds in an efficient way, the initial price range ought to fully incorporate firm- and market-related information the underwriter acquires in the prefiling period. The price update (toward the final offer price) should fully incorporate firm- and market-related information that becomes available to the underwriter in the postfiling period. It should also reflect, but only partially, any private information gleaned from the roadshows and the book of preliminary orders. The price update (or offer price) should not, however, reflect information acquired prior to setting the initial price range as this information should have been already incorporated in the initial price range of the issue. Finally, the first market price, and by implication the initial return, should reflect only information (public and private) that becomes available to investors in the interval between setting the final offer price (the evening before offer day in the United States) and the start of the secondary trading. The first market price should not be related to information available in the period prior to the final pricing since this information should be reflected in the offer price. If the price updates or the initial returns are impacted by information available in, say, the prefiling period or the prepricing period, respectively, that would imply that this information was not fully incorporated in the price update. According to the market efficiency hypothesis, this information is considered "old news" and should not impact later prices.

In general therefore, the pricing of new issues is affected by (1) how information up to the final pricing is incorporated in the offer price and (2) how postpricing information is incorporated in the first market price of the issue. The first condition relates to the efficiency of the pricing function of the underwriter. The second relates to the pricing efficiency of the postoffer secondary market.

The Empirical Evidence

Several studies provide evidence that the pricing of IPOs is not entirely consistent with the influence of relevant issue and market related information. Instead other behavioral or strategic factors appear to influence the degree of underpricing.

Loughran and Ritter (2002) were the first to challenge the view that offer prices fully reflect public information. For example, they estimate that issuers left $27 billion on the table for IPOs executed in the period 1990–1998. It appears that instead of maximizing the level of their wealth, issuers behave as if they are satisfied to maximize the changes to their wealth in accordance with a behavioral characteristic predicted by the "prospect" theory. Applying this theory, issuers form expectations about the value of their retained shares on the basis of the midpoint of the initial price range. When public information indicates that the prospective market value of the retained shares will be considerably higher, issuers do not mind the opportunity loss they suffer if the offer price does not match the market price the shares are worth. Although issuers sell their equity at a discount from fair prices, they pay more attention to the positive wealth gain realized on their remaining shareholdings in the firm.

Loughran and Ritter (2002) conjecture that the prospect theory applies mostly in strong market periods. By imposing excess underpricing, underwriters are able to derive other benefits. For example, lower offer prices result in lower placement costs. Second, by selling heavily underpriced IPO shares to favored investors, underwriters can extract revenue through follow-up business dealings (e.g., trading commissions, brokerage fees, price support for cold new issues, etc.). These additional gains more than cover the loss in gross spread which is set as percentage of (the lower than otherwise) offer price. Ljungqvist and Wilhelm (2005) find evidence supporting the behavioral model of Loughran and Ritter (2002). They find that top officers of issuing firms are less likely to switch to another underwriter if they have been satisfied according to the prospect theory paradigm. However, the explanatory power of this paradigm seems to have waned in the post-dot-com bubble years and it is weaker in the case of skilled and experienced CEOs and VC-backed IPOs.

Bradley and Jordan (2002) also find evidence that offer prices are not fully adjusted to publicly available information. When firms sell a smaller number of shares relative to shares retained, the cost of underpricing is relatively smaller and this may induce insiders to be less demanding of higher offer prices. They find that initial returns of IPOs are not fully adjusted to market information about the initial price performance of past IPOs. Edelen and Kadlec (2005) find evidence of excessive underpricing when the issuing firm is expected to earn a large value surplus from going public in relation to the firm's value as private entity. Underpricing serves the "strategic" goal of increasing the probability of a successful placement and capturing a positive net surplus. If, on the other hand, the surplus is relatively small, the marginal cost of failing to complete the offer is low and issuers push for more aggressive pricing.

Lowry and Schwert (2004) provide more direct evidence on the price efficiency of IPOs. They find that price updates reflect market information from the prefiling (preinitial pricing) period which is inconsistent with efficiency, as well as market information from the postfiling period as they should. Initial returns appear to be related to information generated after the final pricing of the issue as they should, but also to information from the prepricing period which is inconsistent with efficiency. They stress though that the influence of stale information is statistically weak. They draw more attention to the finding that initial returns are found to be positively and significantly related to price updates which is evidence that offer prices partially reflect the private information revealed during the prepricing period, in line with the premise of the bookbuilding model of Benveniste and Spindt (1989).

Ghosh, Petrova, Feng, and Pattanapanchai (2012) examine the pricing efficiency of new issues in a sample of IPOs executed as part of equity carve-outs (ECOs). ECOs offer the information advantage that the underwriter and the investors have information about the parent's value. Therefore, underwriters should be better placed to align the new issue offer price with its market price. The study finds though that initial returns are related to the parent stock returns during the preinitial pricing period as well as to parent stock returns in the preoffer period. Both these findings are inconsistent with price efficiency (i.e., postoffer prices reflect information that should have already been reflected in previous phases of the pricing process).

The Influence of *Quid Pro Quo* Arrangements

If new issues are priced efficiently, why have initial returns varied so dramatically over time? Loughran and Ritter (2004) report that average initial returns were 7% in the 1980s, 15% for most of the 1990s, and 65% in the dot-com years 1999−2000 before declining to 12% in the post-dot-com period. Noting the same variability, Ljungqvist and Wilhelm (2003) document dramatic declines in the number of shares sold by insiders through secondary offerings in more recent periods. When these insiders sell less of their equity stakes they may become less concerned with the level of offer price and, hence, less motivated to demand that underwriters maximize the gross proceeds from new issues. At the same time, this study finds, insiders were offered new shares at below market prices, thus further diluting their incentive to exercise effective monitoring over the issuance process.

Loughran and Ritter (2004) extend this reduced monitoring hypothesis to propose that the excessive underpricing around the closing of the past century is reflective of a change in the objective function of the issuers. Instead of maximizing issue proceeds, insiders sought to maximize the total proceeds of the following three components:

$$a_1[\text{IPO proceeds}] + a_2[\text{Proceeds from future equity offers}] + a_3[\text{Side payments}],$$

where a_1, a_2, and a_3 are the weights an issuer places on each of the three components. The more weight insiders place on the last two components (by increasing a_2 and a_3) the less emphasis is placed on maximizing proceeds from the current issue. If the emphasis placed on the three weights shifts over time, this can explain the variability in the degree of under-pricing. When insiders are concerned with maximizing proceeds from future equity sales they prefer to choose underwriting firms with star analysts (the "analyst lust" hypothesis) to enhance the promotion of the stock. Insiders may also seek to extract side payments from underwriters as, for example, in the form of preferential allocations of hot issues by the underwriters they choose. Underwriters recoup the cost of these favors to insiders through higher underpricing which gives them two advantages. First, higher underpricing helps reduce their overall underwriting costs and second it empowers the underwriter to extract rents from regular investors (the main beneficiaries of underpricing) in the form of reciprocal business deals as, for example, brokerage and trading.

Using a large sample of IPOs completed in the period 1980−2003, Loughran and Ritter (2004) find support for the changing issuer objective function hypothesis. First, the average number of managing underwriters (a proxy for analyst coverage) had increased from 1.5 in the 1980s to 4.4 in 2001−2003. Second, prestigious underwriters, who were best positioned to gain from *quid pro quo* arrangements, were associated with much more severe underpri-cing than less prestigious underwriters—72% (37.5%) versus 35% (12.2%) measured by aver-age (median) initial returns. They find no evidence for the realignment or reduced monitoring hypothesis of Ljungqvist and Wilhlem (2003) or the changing risk hypothesis, namely, the hypothesis that the degree of underpricing varies because of dramatic changes in the ex ante risk of IPOs offered in different periods. However, a more recent study by Lowry, Officer, and Schwert (2010) finds evidence that variability in the degree of informa-tion asymmetry across time may have partly accounted for the variability of initial returns.

The issuers' preference for analyst quality and support is also documented in Liu and Ritter (2011), who note that the shift to choosing underwriters on nonprice factors is mostly a relatively recent phenomenon observed after the mid-1990s.

The Long-Run Price Performance of Firms Conducting IPOs

Investors who are rationed out of new issues can buy new IPO shares in the aftermarket. The question of interest then is whether these investors earn normal rates of return by holding these shares over relatively long periods of time. Normal returns are those realized by stocks that share similar risk and other characteristics with the IPO stocks.

If new issues are priced efficiently at the opening of their secondary market, their prices should be unbiased estimates of the values the market assigns based on the information available at that time. If, however, the immediate aftermarket prices are systematically set over or below their fair level, that is, if investors systematically overpay or underpay, then long-run returns will be negative or positive, respectively, as prices eventually incorporate all available information and any optimistic or pessimistic bias subsides over time.

General Findings

As explained in Chapter 8: Assessing the Price Performance of New Issues, the long-run return performance of new issues is assessed by estimating buy-and-hold returns (BHRs) and cumulative returns (CRs). Adjusted by the return realized by a market benchmark, these returns are referred to as the buy-and-hold abnormal returns (BHARs) and cumulative abnormal returns (CARs), respectively.

Table 10.2 presents the evidence on the long-run stock price performance of samples of IPOs completed in the United States and reported in various studies. The table reports the mean and median of raw (unadjusted) returns and the mean and median of adjusted returns. Not all studies report all four measures. These return measures are estimated over investment horizons of 2, 3, 5, or 6 years from the issue time. The returns are grouped by the benchmark used: a market index or a portfolio of matched control firms.

All studies find that long-run unadjusted returns measured as BHRs or CRs are positive. The lowest BHR is 15.7% for IPOs completed in the period 1970–1990 while the highest BHR is 52.6% for IPOs completed in 1975–1992. With few exceptions, the market benchmarks generate considerably higher long-run returns. As a result, on an adjusted basis, long-run returns given by BHARs and CARs are negative implying that IPO stocks underperform over long horizon periods. For example, an investor who had bought the portfolio of IPOs completed in the period 1975–1992 would have realized a negative mean BHAR of −44.2% compared to a portfolio that had mimicked the S&P 500 index (over a 5-year horizon). Similarly, an investment in the IPOs completed in 1970–1990 would have yielded a negative mean BHAR of −50.7% compared to a portfolio of nonissuing firms matched by equity market capitalization (over a 5-year horizon). The worst relative performance, measured by CARs, is realized by IPOs completed in 1980–2000 when compared to the CRSP index of stocks traded on NYSE, AMEX, and Nasdaq. These IPOs generated a negative mean CAR of −80.81%. The few exceptions of positive adjusted long-run returns are produced when the market benchmark is comprised of control firms matched by market capitalization and book-to-market ratio.

Long-run returns, whether measured as BHARs or CARs, vary by the benchmark used, that is, type of market index or matching criteria utilized. Long-run returns also differ depending on whether the IPO returns are equally or value-weighted. Checking same-study results reveals a general tendency for equally-weighted IPO returns to be lower (more negative) than value-weighted IPO returns when the benchmark is a market index. This pattern is not as clear when the benchmark is a portfolio of matched control firms. The impression from Table 10.2 is that IPO portfolios perform better when they are stacked against similar firms than against market indexes.

The variation in long-run price performance across benchmarks and weighting methods highlights the challenges and problems in assessing the long-run performance of securities in general which was discussed in Chapter 8: Assessing the Price Performance of New Issues.

The Market Benchmark Specification Debate

Table 10.2 shows evidence that measured by BHARs or CARs, IPO stocks underperform various proxies. How valid is, however, this conclusion? Academic studies appear to disagree on this important question.

Loughran and Ritter (2000) argue that because many IPOs are executed by small young firms, the market indexes and other matching criteria must be appropriate for capturing the

Table 10.2 Long-Run Stock Return Performance of US IPOs by Benchmark—Various Studies

Study	Sample Period	IPO Return Mean	IPO Return Median	Adjusted Return Mean	Adjusted Return Median	Benchmark Return	Benchmark Portfolio	Weight of Returns	Horizon (years)
Panel A: Buy and Hold Returns (BHRs)									
Benchmark: Market Index									
Loughran and Ritter (1995)	1970–1990	15.70		−22.60		38.30	S&P 500	EW	5
Brav, Geczy, and Gompers (2000)	1975–1992	33.10		−44.20		77.30	S&P 500	EW	5
Brav, Geczy, and Gompers (2000)	1975–1992	52.60		−25.70		78.30	S&P 500	VW	5
Loughran (1993)	1973–1991	17.29		−58.94		76.23	Nasdaq	EW	6
Brav, Geczy, and Gompers (2000)	1975–1992	33.10		−31.10		64.20	Nasdaq	EW	5
Brav, Geczy, and Gompers (2000)	1975–1992	52.60		−15.60		68.20	Nasdaq	VW	5
Carter, Dark, and Singh (1998)	1979–1991			−19.92	−50.72		Market VW	EW	3
Carter, Dark, Floros, and Sapp (2011)	1981–2005			−16.88			CRSP VW	EW	3
Carter, Dark, Floros, and Sapp (2011)	1981–1997			−20.87			CRSP VW	EW	3
Dong, Michel, and Pandes (2011)	1980–2006			−14.01	−56.46		CRSP EW	EW	3
Houge, Loughran, Suchanek, and Yan (2001)	1993–1996	34.60		−42.70		77.30	CRSP VW	EW	3
Carter, Dark, Floros, and Sapp (2011)	1998–2005			−4.66			CRSP VW	EW	3
Benchmark: Matched Control Firms									
Ritter (1991)	1975–1984	34.47		−27.39		61.86	MV, IND	EW	3
Loughran and Ritter (1995)	1970–1990	8.40		−26.90		35.30	MV	EW	3
Loughran and Ritter (1995)	1970–1990	15.70		−50.70		66.40	MV	EW	5
Brav, Geczy, and Gompers (2000)	1975–1992	35.80		6.60		29.20	MV, BM	EW	5
Brav, Geczy, and Gompers (2000)	1975–1992	56.60		1.40		55.20	MV, BM	VW	5
Eckbo and Norli (2005)	1972–1998	36.70		−28.70		65.40	MV	EW	5
Eckbo and Norli (2005)	1972–1998	53.70		−19.10		72.80	MV	VW	5
Carter, Dark, Floros, and Sapp (2011)	1981–2005	28.60		−10.00		38.60	MV, BM	EW	3
Carter, Dark, Floros, and Sapp (2011)	1981–1997			−7.24			MV,BM	EW	3
Carter, Dark, Floros, and Sapp (2011)	1998–2005			−18.15			MV, BM	EW	3
Dong, Michel, and Pandes (2011)	1980–2006			−12.77			MV, BM	EW	3
Dong, Michel, and Pandes (2011)	1980–2006			−16.05			MV, BM	VW	3

Panel B: Cumulative Returns (CRs)

Benchmark: Market Index

	Period				Index	Weight	Years
Brav, Geczy, and Gompers (2000)	1975–1992	35.90		−38.30	S&P 500	EW	5
Brav, Geczy, and Gompers (2000)	1975–1992	40.70		−20.80	S&P 500	VW	5
Brav, Geczy, and Gompers (2000)	1975–1992	35.90		−32.00	Nasdaq	EW	5
Brav, Geczy, and Gompers (2000)	1975–1992	40.70		−16.80	Nasdaq	VW	5
Schultz (2003)	1973–1997		74.20	−29.40	CRSP VW	EW	5
Schultz (2003)	1973–1997		61.50	−11.40	CRSP EW	EW	5
Gao, Mao, and Zhong (2006)	1980–2000		67.90	−38.48	Nasdaq	EW	3
Gao, Mao, and Zhong (2006)	1980–2000		57.50	−35.00	CRSP VW	EW	3
Gao, Mao, and Zhong (2006)	1980–2000			−80.81	CRSP EW	EW	3

Benchmark: Matched Control Firms

	Period				Index	Weight	Years
Ritter (1991)	1975–1984			−29.13	MV, IND	EW	3
Brav, Geczy, and Gompers (2000)	1975–1992	42.30	32.60	9.70	MV, BM	EW	5
Brav, Geczy, and Gompers (2000)	1975–1992	53.00	49.70	3.30	MV, BM	VW	5
Affleck-Graves, Hegde, and Miller (1996)	1975–1991			−7.56	MV	EW	2

MV is market value of equity; BM is the book-to-market value of equity ratio; MB is the market-to-book value of equity ratio. IND means that IPO returns are industry-adjusted. EW and VW in the column "Weight of Returns" mean the new issue returns of IPO stocks are, respectively, equally or value-weighted. EW and VW next to a market index means the returns are equally or value-weighted, respectively. CRSP Index is an index of returns of stocks in the data base of the Center of Research in Security Prices of the University of Chicago.

risk—return relationship of such issuing firms. They also propose that the market benchmarks should not contain any firms that had conducted equity issues before the start of the investment horizon under investigation. This purging should also apply to the factors for small versus large stocks and high versus low book-to-market (HML) ratio in the Fama—French model. After making their recommended adjustments to benchmarks, Loughran and Ritter conclude that IPO stock return underperformance is concentrated among firms that execute IPOs in high-volume years.

Brav, Geczy, and Gompers (2000) apply the three-factor Fama—French model and find IPO underperformance is mostly detected in portfolios of equally-weighted IPO returns. Adding a momentum factor (a measure of past return performance) to the Fama—French model removes all evidence of underperformance. Excluding NYSE listed stocks (usually larger than Nasdaq and AMEX listed stocks) from the HML factor of the Fama—French model also removes the evidence of underperformance. Brav, Geczy, and Gompers argue that the performance of IPO firms is impacted by investor sentiment as well as factors that affect the valuation of firms with similar characteristics whether they execute equity issues or not. Accordingly, compared to appropriately constructed benchmarks, IPO stocks neither under- or over-perform in the long-run.

Eckbo and Norli (2005) introduce leverage and share turnover (a liquidity proxy) to the factors that impact the performance of IPOs. By virtue of issuing equity, IPO firms become less levered. Stocks of issuing firms are also found to have greater trading liquidity. Both these attributes justify lower expected required returns (i.e., cost of capital) for IPO firms relative to their nonissuing peers. As a result, the lower returns of IPO firms may be due to their stock returns adjusting to the lower level of expected returns. (In equilibrium, actual and expected returns ought to be equal.) Adjusting for these two factors, Eckbo and Norli find Fama—French alphas (a measure of excess return) that are insignificantly different from zero.

Lyandres, Sun, and Zhang (2008) propose that the IPO underperformance is the result of IPO firms investing more than similar nonissuing firms in the postissue years. As firms expand their investments they usually adopt projects with lower marginal returns and this causes the overall return on the firm's equity to decline. Adding an investment factor to the Fama—French model, Lyandres, Sun, and Zhang find IPOs have insignificant alphas. When IPO firms are matched with control firms by size, book-to-market ratio and the investment factor, the 4-year average BHAR is also insignificant.

Explanations of the Long-Run Price Performance of IPOs

With the caveat that long-run stock return performance still presents unsettled measurement challenges, below we present empirical explanations of the long-run price performance of IPO stocks.

The Windows of Opportunity Hypothesis

Ritter (1991) proposes that the evidence of underperformance is more consistent with the presence of fads and overoptimism based on the preissue strong performance of issuing firms. By placing disproportionate weight on the usually strong recent performance of firms that conduct IPOs, investors form overoptimistic expectations about future growth and earnings that lead them to bid up the aftermarket prices of new issues. Overoptimism is observed more in relation to relatively young growth firms and in years with high volume of IPOs. This implies that issuers exploit windows of opportunity to go public. Loughran (1993) also finds that the negative return performance of firms going public on Nasdaq extends to six calendar years when compared to the performance of the Nasdaq index. Nasdaq listed IPO stocks tend to be smaller and more growth intensive than seasoned firms, and hence more susceptible to investor overoptimism.

Xiao and Yung (2014) find that high-growth firms underperform in the long-run. This is consistent with the view that investors extrapolate recent high growth rates into the future only to be later disappointed. The underperformance of high-growth firms holds independently of underwriter reputation, size or VC-backing. Even analysts most often fail to correctly forecast the postoffer growth of high preoffer growth firms.

Issuers can also contribute to investor euphoria by managing their earnings. Teoh, Welch, and Wong (1998) find that IPO firms that aggressively manage their earnings by manipulating discretionary accruals underperform worse than less aggressive firms over a 3-year postissue horizon. These differences are more pronounced for smaller IPOs and those with low book-to-market ratio (higher growth firms). As the true size of earnings is eventually revealed in the postissue period, aggressive firms lose value and are hindered from raising more capital through follow-on offerings. Chan, Cooney, Kim, and Singh (2008) also find that growth firms that report high discretionary accruals underperform, whereas firms that report low discretionary accruals overperform in the long run despite their early lackluster profitability.

Schultz (2003) argues that firms go public when they sense prices are high because of the strong market fundamentals of firms similar to issuer and not because of temporary overoptimism by managers. Schultz calls this "pseudo timing." When the high valuations are eventually reversed, IPOs underperform in the long-run.

The windows of opportunity hypothesis is often referred to as the managerial opportunism hypothesis to denote that issuing firm managers are more inclined to issue securities when they believe the valuation of their firms will decline as investor sentiment subsidies or the firm fundamentals deteriorate.

Time Variability of Long-run Performance

As with initial returns, an interesting question is whether long-run return performance varies for IPOs completed in different time periods. Carter, Dark, Floros, and Sapp (2011) find that IPOs underperformed compared to matching firms if they were completed in 1981−1997 and the bubble years of 1999−2000 but not if they were completed in 2001−2005. They conclude that the evidence of underperformance reported in earlier studies is due to the lack of data from the more recent years. Gompers and Lerner (2003) also find evidence of underperformance for IPOs completed in the pre-Nasdaq period 1935−1972, but it is mostly concentrated among small firms.

The Influence of Initial Returns

Affleck-Graves, Hegde, and Miller (1996) report that underpriced IPOs generate slightly higher long-run returns than overpriced IPOs, though both groups underperform matching firms.

Dong, Michel, and Pandes (2011) also find a positive relationship between initial returns and long-run return performance. Carter, Dark, Floros, and Sapp (2011) find this relationship to vary by period.

Monitoring and Certification Effects

Third parties, like VC firms and prestigious underwriters, have an interest to associate themselves with better-quality issues or ensure that IPO firms are efficiently managed. The monitoring theory of Brav and Gompers (1997) suggests that VC funds choose better-quality firms to back and protect their investments through active oversight of managers. As a result, VC-backed IPOs are found to generally overperform non-VC-backed IPOs. When matched with similar firms by market capitalization and book-to-market ratio, even small non-VC-backed and VC-backed IPOs overperform their matches. Brav and Gompers conclude that the long-run return underperformance is not uniquely related to firms conducting IPOs but rather to their characteristics, namely, small capitalization and low book-to-market ratio.

In addition to venture capitalists, the presence of prestigious underwriters has also been found to improve the long-run price performance of IPOs (Carter, Dark, and Singh, 1998). Similarly, Dong, Michel, and Pandes (2011) find IPOs with high quality indicators (like greater number of managing underwriters and higher underwriter reputation) overperform their market and matched control firm benchmarks, whereas IPOs with low quality markers underperform. The impact of these quality factors is more important in the case of high uncertainty IPO firms. This confirms the beneficial function that high-quality lead and managing underwriters perform in providing superior marketing, certification and information production services.

Flipping and Secondary Market Sales

If there is disagreement about the value of a new issue among investors in the early aftermarket, those who seem to be better informed will sell in order to avoid long-term losses. Krigman, Shaw, and Womack (1999) find that the magnitude of flipping varies with the degree of underpricing and both, flipping and initial returns, are negatively related to the future price performance of IPO stocks. One-year returns (relative to the first-day price) are positive for hot IPOs, negative for cold IPOs, and worst for extra-hot IPOs (those with initial returns over 60%). The negative implication of early flipping by institutional investors on postissue returns is also reported in Boehmer, Boehmer, and Fishe (2006) and Houge, Loughran, Suchanek, and Yan (2001). In addition, Gao, Mao, and Zhong (2006) and Houge, Loughran, Suchanek, and Yan (2001) document a negative relationship between the degree investors diverge in their value estimates and future price performance of IPOs.

Pukthuanthong-Le and Varaiya (2007) report a negative relationship between block sales (by institutions, market makers and other block holders) in the first 2 days after the offer and the 3-year returns of IPOs. The size of block sell trades appears to be associated with measures indicating overvaluation of the IPO stock. The findings imply an informational advantage for the class of informed investors who unload bought IPO shares in the aftermarket.

The Influence of Subsequent Financing Activity

Billett, Flannery, and Garfinkel (2011) examine the long-run return performance of IPOs by taking into consideration subsequent financing events like SEOs, private equity placements and public debt offerings. When they isolate the effect of subsequent financing activities, Billett, Flannery, and Garfinkel find no evidence of underperformance as a result of the first offering, in this case, the IPO. Therefore, the postissue underperformance is not related to the issuance per se but rather to the negative signal associated with the persistent need of issuing firms for external funding.

However, Bhabra and Pettway (2003) find no evidence of underperformance in the case of IPO firms that execute subsequent SEOs or are acquired after going public.

The Long-Run Operating Performance of Firms Conducting IPOs

The stock price underperformance of new issues implies that the expectations about the firm's future performance that investors hold at the opening of the secondary market fail to materialize. One way to investigate this is to analyze changes in the operating performance of the firms that conduct new issues.

As in the case of measuring long-run price performance, it is critical that the operating performance of issuing firms is judged in relation to an appropriate benchmark portfolio of firms. Barber and Lyon (1996) recommend that the benchmark firms operate in the same industry as the issuing firm and are similar in asset size and operating profitability (i.e., return on assets) prior to the issue. Matching by preissue performance neutralizes the documented tendency of accounting metrics to revert to their long-run mean. For example, a firm cannot keep realizing high operating returns for too long without eventually experiencing a decline either due to competition or managerial complacency.

General Findings

Jain and Kini (1994) conduct one of the earliest thorough studies of the operating performance of firms that executed IPOs in 1976–1988. The benchmark portfolio consists of seasoned firms matched by industry. Their main findings are:

- IPO firms experience declines in operating returns (income plus depreciation divided by assets) before and after adjusting for the performance of control firms in the 3-year postissue period. Postissue decline is also observed when performance is measured by a cash flow metric, that is, income plus depreciation minus capital expenditures over assets.
- Industry-adjusted sales and capital expenditures improve but asset utilization rate (turnover) declines.
- Industry-adjusted operating returns and sales decline more for firms with low equity retention rates by insiders.
- The degree of underpricing has no impact on operating returns.

- Valuation metrics, like market-to-book value of equity and P/E ratios, decline in the postissue years in line with the decline of postissue stock returns.
- Operating performance is positive (relative to the benchmark portfolio) in the years leading to the IPO, consistent with the hypothesis that new issues are timed to coincide with strong firm performance.

Mikkelson, Megan Partch, and Shah (1997) apply the matching criteria recommended by Barber and Lyon (1996) and find the following:

- Operating returns decline from year -1 to $+1$ but not from year $+2$ to year $+10$.
- Declining operating performance is detected mostly within groups of small to medium size firms and younger firms.
- VC-backed IPO firms perform better than non-VC-backed firms during the first postissue year but not afterwards.
- Operating return performance is positive in the years leading to the IPO.
- The relationship between the fraction of the secondary offering and operating performance is unclear over different postissue years.
- Changes in ownership of equity by top executives and officers from the years before to the years after the IPO are not related to post-IPO performance.

Explanations of the Long-Run Operating Performance of IPOs

The Windows of Opportunity Explanation

The bulk of the evidence on operating performance appears to mirror the long-run price performance of IPOs. In general, issuing firms underperform their peers in the postissue years despite a superior operating performance in the preissue years. This underperformance seems to be concentrated more among smaller, younger and more growth-intensive issuers. These findings reinforce the arguments of the windows of opportunity and managerial opportunistic hypotheses according to which firms go public after periods of strong operating performance which are not expected to last.

Pástor, Taylor, and Veronesi (2009) propose that when firm profitability is high managers infer that expected profitability is also high and thus decide to take the firm public. However, postissue performance fails to match these optimistic expectations. In this case, the timing of the IPO is not related to a window of opportunity or opportunistic behavior but rather to managerial beliefs about the value of the firm as a public concern.

A special case is that of previously public firms that had been taken private but decide to return to public ownership through an IPO in a reverse leveraged buyout (LBO) transaction. Degeorge and Zeckhauser (1993) find that firms execute reverse LBOs after a year of strong operating performance relative to peer firms which declines in the postissue years. Nonetheless, postissue stock return performance is similar to that realized by nonissuing peers. This finding implies that even in the case of firms about which more is known, managers seem to time the IPO decision, but the market is not surprised by the inferior postissue operating performance.

Analyst Coverage and Long-Run Operating Performance

The overoptimism about IPO firm's performance extends beyond the IPO investors. Analysts who release earnings forecasts and "buy" and "sell" recommendations also seem to miss the subsequent postissue deterioration in the operating performance of IPO firms. Rajan and Servaes (1997) find that analysts form more optimistic expectations about IPO firms than other similar firms. Analyst optimism is stronger in high IPO volume markets and analysts temper their optimism as initial earnings growth rates fail to materialize. Although postissue operating performance is worse for IPO firms that receive the most optimistic forecasts, those firms that receive less optimistic forecasts outperform their peers. Analyst overoptimism usually coincides with overall market euphoria and the concomitant occurrence of high valuations which create windows of opportunities that attract IPO issuers.

Michaely and Womack (1999) also find evidence that analysts overestimate the postoffer performance of IPO firms. This pattern is more common among analysts affiliated with the underwriting firm. Analysts also seem to miss the exact impact of discretionary accruals on earnings and, hence, fail to make unbiased earnings forecasts (Teoh and Wong, 2002). Both independent and affiliated analysts seem to be prone to this bias. Analyst overoptimism leads to higher prices in the aftermarket and eventually to stock return underperformance in subsequent periods. The failure to detect overvaluation due to managed earnings can also contribute to managers taking their firms public when their firms are overvalued.

Chan, Cooney, Kim, and Singh (2008) report that higher discretionary accruals are associated with negative changes in postissue operating returns. For larger issuers, negative postissue operating performance is mitigated if the IPO is underwritten by a prestigious underwriter and is VC-backed.

Other Explanations

Field and Karpoff (2002) find that the post-IPO operating performance of IPO firms that employ antitakeover defenses is not significantly different from that of firms that do not. There is no evidence that antitakeover defenses are taken for the purpose to increase the takeover premium. Rather they serve managerial interests related to control and compensation.

Johnson, Kang, and Yi (2010) report that firms with large public corporate customers have higher postissue operating returns than same-industry peers. VC-backing and research-and-development expenditures have a positive impact on post issue operating returns but fraction of shares sold (secondary offering) and underwriter prestige have negative impact.

The Viability of IPO Firms

The "life expectancy" of IPO firms is another important metric of postissue performance. Hensler, Rutherford, and Springer (1997) report that the survival time of IPO firms is longer for IPOs that have higher initial returns and coincide with high IPO activity periods. The survival time is also longer for IPOs of larger and older firms and when insiders retain more stock. Survival time is shorter for IPOs of riskier firms and those IPOs occurring at times the market is at a high valuation level.

11

The Price and Operating Performance of Seasoned Equity Offers, Debt Offers and Other Offerings

This chapter presents the empirical evidence on the initial pricing and the long-run price performance of seasoned equity issues (SEOs), debt issues, and other special cases of issues, including dual-share offers and private investments in public equity (PIPE). The chapter also discusses the evidence concerning the operating performance of firms that conduct seasoned equity offerings and debt offerings.

The Initial Pricing of Seasoned Equity Offerings

The initial pricing of seasoned equity offerings is assessed in terms of the price discount or premium as well as the initial return from the offer price to the first market price in the secondary market. Many of the theories that purport to explain the initial pricing of initial public offerings (IPOs) can be also applied to explain the initial pricing of SEOs. Nonetheless, unlike initial public offerings, seasoned equity offerings have a trading history and, hence, available market prices. Therefore, informational asymmetry among issuers, underwriters, and investors ought to be comparatively lower. Accordingly, underwriters should have less need for the private information of informed investors; and the adverse selection problem of retail investors should be less severe.

In another difference from initial public offerings, the preoffer public trading of SEO stocks allows optimistic investors to buy shares prior to the offer as a hedge against the possibility of being excluded from the offering due to oversubscription. This can generate a pattern of discounted offer prices and positive initial returns (Parsons and Raviv, 1985). We can illustrate this by the following example. Let us assume the last preissue price was $20 and the offer price was discounted down to $19.5 while the first market price turned out to be $20.5. An initial investor who bought at the preissue price and sold at the aftermarket price would have earned $0.50 per share. An investor who bought though at the offer price and sold at the first market price would have earned $1. This is the true implicit spread of the issue. If the offer price had been set at the last trading price, the firm would have left only $0.50 per share on the table. Given the discounting of $0.50, the firm ended up leaving on the table $1 per share.

Underwriting Services and the New Issues Market. DOI: http://dx.doi.org/10.1016/B978-0-12-803282-4.00011-0

General Findings

The lower valuation uncertainty surrounding SEOs suggests that seasoned equity offerings should be underpriced less than IPOs. Although early research on SEOs found no or little evidence of nonzero discounts and initial returns, more recent evidence shows an increase in both.

Table 11.1 presents the average and median values of discounts (or premiums) and initial returns for samples of SEOs completed during the last three decades as reported in various studies. When the discount (premium) is estimated as the percentage difference of the offer minus the last trading price of the issue it is negative (positive), whereas when it is estimated as the percentage difference of the last available price minus the offer price, it is positive (negative). For an easier interpretation of the results, Table 11.1 reports all discount values with a positive sign and all premium values with a negative sign. The samples include SEOs executed with a firm commitment contract and refer to primary or combined primary and secondary offerings.

First, the findings reported in Table 11.1 show that SEOs are both offered at a discount from the last trading price and are underpriced relative to their first available market price. Therefore, firms that execute equity offerings leave money on the table in the form of a discount and underpricing. The second pattern the data reveal is a clear upward trend in average discounts and initial returns from the 1980s to the 2000s. Samples of SEOs completed in the 1980s have average (median) discounts of 1.11% (0.37%), which increase to 2.76% (1.49%) in the 1990s and increase further to 3.57% (n.a.) in the 2000s. Similarly, samples of SEOs have average (median) initial returns of 0.47% (0.02%) in the 1980s, 2.64% (1.37%) in the 1990s and 2.83% (n.a.) in the 2000s. Samples that include SEOs from long-periods of time (from the 1970s to the 2000s) show an average (median) discount of 2.65% (1.54%). Of these studies, only one reports initial returns, which average 2.63% and have a median value of 0.93%.

A third pattern observed in the data is that discounts and initial returns are lowest for stocks listed on the New York Stock Exchange (NYSE) and higher for those listed on the American Stock Exchange (AMEX) or Nasdaq. This reflects the influence of stricter listing standards maintained by the NYSE which serve to certify the quality of stocks listed on this exchange.

Determinants of the Discount and Initial Returns of SEOs

As with initial public offerings, the initial pricing of SEOs is affected by ex ante risk, asymmetric information, and certification effects. In addition, conditions and arrangements that affect the waiting and pricing risk exert further influence on the pricing of seasoned equity offerings.

Studies of the discount and underpricing of seasoned equity offerings have utilized many of the same empirical proxies used in IPO studies. Given the preissue record of market prices, the empirical proxies in SEO studies also include: the preissue-return performance of the SEO stocks (as a proxy of positive price momentum) and the stock's preissue price as proxy of issuer quality.

Table 11.1   Discounts and Initial Returns of US SEOs—Various Studies

Study	Sample Period	Discount		Initial Return		Exchange	Discount Calculations
		Mean	Median	Mean	Median		
1980s							
Loderer, Sheehan, and Kadlec (1991)	1980–1984	0.03	0	−0.07	0	NYSE	a
Loderer, Sheehan, and Kadlec (1991)	1980–1984	1.17	0	0.80	0	AMEX	a
Loderer, Sheehan, and Kadlec (1991)	1980–1984	2.96	2.13	−1.62	−1.05	Nasdaq	d
Safieddine and Wilhelm (1996)	1980–1988	0.55	0	0.52	0		a
Safieddine and Wilhelm (1996)	1988–1991	0.46	0	0.45	0		a
Mola and Loughran (2004)	1986–1989	1.20				NYSE/AMEX	b
Mola and Loughran (2004)	1986–1989	1.00				Nasdaq	b
Kim and Shin (2004)	1983–1988	1.20	0.00	0.96	0.00	NYSE/AMEX	a
Kim and Shin (2004)	1983–1988	1.45	0.45	2.25	1.19	Nasdaq	a
Average		**1.11**	**0.37**	**0.47**	**0.02**		
1990s							
Altınkılıç and Hansen (2003)	1990–1997	1.47	0.53	1.78	0.80	NYSE/AMEX	c
Altınkılıç and Hansen (2003)	1990–1997	3.01	2.13	3.01	1.72	Nasdaq	c
Corwin (2003)	1993–1998	1.52	0.63			NYSE	a
Corwin (2003)	1993–1998	3.51	2.38			Nasdaq	a
Mola and Loughran (2004)	1990–1995	2.00				NYSE/AMEX	b
Mola and Loughran (2004)	1990–1995	4.00				Nasdaq	b
Mola and Loughran (2004)	1996–1999	2.20				NYSE/AMEX	b
Mola and Loughran (2004)	1996–1999	4.50				Nasdaq	b
Kim and Shin (2004)	1988–1998	2.14	0.95	2.15	0.96	NYSE/AMEX	a
Kim and Shin (2004)	1988–1998	3.28	2.33	3.63	2.00	Nasdaq	a
Average		**2.76**	**1.49**	**2.64**	**1.37**		
2000s							
Henry and Koski (2010)	2005–2006	1.87		1.53		NYSE	a
Henry and Koski (2010)	2005–2006	6.06		2.83		AMEX	a
Henry and Koski (2010)	2005–2006	3.38		3.46		Nasdaq	a
Chemmanur, He, and Hu (2009)	1999–2004	2.97		3.50			c
Average		**3.57**		**2.83**			
Long Periods							
Kim, Palia, and Saunders (2003)	1970–1990			2.63	0.93		
Corwin (2003)	1980–1998	0.92	0			NYSE	a
Corwin (2003)	1980–1998	2.72	1.67			Nasdaq	a
Mola and Loughran (2004)	1986–1999	3.00	1.60				b
Huang and Zhang (2011)	1985–2004	3.18	2.16				b
Chan and Chan (2014)	1984–2007	2.58	1.43				b
Intintoli, Jategaonkar, and Kahle (2014)	1991–2011	3.51	2.37				a
Average		**2.65**	**1.54**	**2.63**	**0.93**		

Positive values of $(P_{-1}/P_o) - 1$ and negative values of $(P_o/P_{-1}) - 1$ indicate a price discount and are reported with a positive sign.

Negative values of $(P_{-1}/P_o) - 1$ and positive values of $(P_o/P_{-1}) - 1$ indicate a price premium and are reported with a negative sign.

(a) Discount is calculated as $(P_o/P_{-1}) - 1$, and reported as percentage.

(b) Discount is calculated as $(P_{-1}/P_o) - 1$, and reported as percentage.

(c) Discount is calculated as $\log(P_{-1}/P_o)$, and reported as percentage.

(d) Discount is calculated as $(P_o/Ask_{-1}) - 1$, and reported as percentage, where Ask_{-1} is the asking price.

Empirical Studies on Discounts and Initial Returns of SEOs

Altınkılıç and Hansen (2003) report that discounts are larger for issues with higher return volatility and low offer prices. Hence, discounts increase when the placement costs are estimated to be higher than anticipated. Discounts decline as gross proceeds rise but start to increase beyond a level of proceeds; thus, discounts are U-shaped in relation to proceeds. This is attributed to the disproportionate increase in placement costs for high gross proceeds. SEOs which are led-managed by prestigious underwriters have lower discounts as do stock issues listed on the NYSE. Finally, this study finds evidence that, as in IPOs, underwriters do not utilize all available market information in setting offer prices although they seem to incorporate private information they glean from the book of orders.

Corwin (2003) identifies underpricing with the price discount and reports a significant rise from an average of 1.15% in 1980−1989 to 3.72% in 1996. Discounts increase with return volatility, relative offer size (evidence of price pressure), negative preissue returns, and degree of underpricing of IPOs in the same month as the SEO. Discounts are negatively affected by preoffer price, and NYSE listing. The relative size of the issue exerts an upward pressure on discounts when the SEO firm has very small capitalization, high risk and the offer price is low. Because Nasdaq traded stocks are priced off the bid, SEOs listed on Nasdaq tend to have larger discounts all else equal[1].

Mola and Loughran (2004) document greater clustering of offer prices at integer numbers (a sign of greater ex ante risk) in SEOs completed in the 1990s, and this explains the upward trend of the discount. The upward trend in discounts is also attributed to the growing market power of high rank underwriters who employ top tier analysts. More frequent equity issuers appear to enjoy smaller discounts. Nasdaq listing, operating in the tech sector, gross spread, and analyst status positively impact discounts.

Chemmanur, He, and Hu (2009) find that greater preoffer institutional net buying and greater allocations to institutions reveal the confidence of informed investors and this results in lower average discounts. SEOs with lower discounts are also associated with greater post-offer net buying by institutions—a sign of the superior skills these investors possess in regards to identifying and trading in higher quality SEOs.

Huang and Zhang (2011) propose that greater marketing effort (including number of managers, roadshows and analyst involvement) by the underwriting syndicate can increase the price elasticity of new issues so that more quantity is demanded at the proposed offer price. Thus, greater number of underwriting managers is associated with lower discounts, especially in the case of issuers with greater return volatility and larger issue size. Discounts are also lower for stocks with higher institutional holdings. Discounts increase with the issuer's equity capitalization and return volatility, and for issues with integer offer prices. Issues by firms operating in technology sectors also have greater discounts.

---

[1] The bid is lower than the midpoint of the bid−ask spread which is more representative of a transaction price on an auction-type exchange like the NYSE.

Chan and Chan (2014) also find that discounts decrease as number of analysts increases and when SEO stock prices comove with the prices of other related stocks as price synchronicity helps reduce valuation uncertainty. Discounts increase with relative number of shares offered and preissue stock price run up, and for integer offer prices.

When informational asymmetry is high, it is in the interest of a private firm to first execute an IPO and follow-up with an SEO after the market learns more about the firm. Intintoli, Jategaonkar, and Kahle (2014) report that in 1991−2011 of 4,651 SEOs, 906 were follow-on SEOs. These SEOs had a median discount of 1.83% versus 2.5% for all other SEOs. The discount is positively impacted by preissue price run up, integer offer price, market capitalization of issuer, and return volatility. Discounts are negatively affected by preoffer day price, NYSE listing, fraction of secondary offering, number of managing underwriters, and analyst following. Duarte-Silva (2010) reports that firms with pre-SEO lending relationships with the underwriter realize higher abnormal returns at the announcement time and have smaller bid−ask spreads in the aftermarket, which is evidence of reduced information asymmetry.

These studies suggest that higher ex ante risk and asymmetric information contribute toward greater discounts and initial returns (i.e., underpricing).

Short Selling Effects on SEOs

Prior to 1988, it was possible to short-sell the stock of a firm planning to have an SEO and then cover the short by buying at the offer price. This raised the possibility that short selling could depress the market price and allow short sellers to cover the short position at the lower offer price. In 1988, the Securities and Exchange Commission (SEC) adopted Rule 10b-21 which prohibited shares shorted during the registration period to be covered with shares purchased at the SEO. The downside of restricting short sales is that the pre-issue stock prices may not reflect all adverse information and thus provide less reliable guidance in setting the offer price. A potential outcome of the prohibition then could be a widening of the discounts. Kim and Shin (2004) find the number of SEOs with discounts increased after the prohibition along with the magnitude of the discounts. Evidence in Corwin (2003) supports the view that discounts increased after adoption of Rule 12b-21. On the contrary, Safieddine and Wilhelm (1996) report that discounts fell after adoption of Rule 10b-21.

Rule 12b-21 was replaced in 1997 by Rule 105, which restricted covering a short sale at the offer price only if the short position had been established within 5 days prior to the offer day. Henry and Koski (2010) find the amount of short selling within the 5-day period is still considerable and the closer to the offer day short selling takes place the greater the discount is. Short selling before the restricted period is also found to contribute to discounting. New rules adopted by the SEC in 2007 prohibit those who short within the 5-day period to even purchase shares offered in a SEO.

The Long-Run Price Performance of Firms Conducting SEOs

As with IPOs, the long-run price performance of SEOs is of great interest to investors who buy newly issued shares in the aftermarket. It is also of interest from the standpoint of price efficiency. If new equity issues are priced efficiently in the aftermarket, investors should not be able to earn excess returns by buying at the first aftermarket price and holding the security into the postissue period. Systematic under- or over-performance of new issues signifies that investors overpay or underpay relative to fair value when they buy new shares in the aftermarket. This can be explained if investors fail to form unbiased expectations from the available information or because they have insufficient information about the true quality of the issuer.

The postissue return performance of SEOs is particularly interesting in light of the well-documented negative stock price reaction when firms announce their decision to have an SEO. The negative announcement reaction implies the market considers the stock to be overvalued. Therefore, one would expect that by the offer time the stock price would be fully adjusted to the new information and, hence, aftermarket prices should not show signs of over- or under-valuation. This in turn means that investors should not be able to realize nonzero returns in the postissue period.

General Findings

Table 11.2 presents the evidence on long-run stock returns of firms that conducted SEOs since the 1960s that has been reported in various studies. The table reports means and medians of raw (unadjusted) and adjusted buy-and-hold returns (BHRs) and cumulative returns (CRs) of new equity issues. It also reports the investment horizon and whether the means and medians of the new issues are equally or value-weighted.

First, new equity issues of seasoned firms realize positive returns over horizons of up to 5 years. However, on an adjusted basis, they underperform the various market benchmarks used. Second, new issues underperform whether their long-run returns are calculated as buy-and-hold abnormal returns (BHARs) or cumulative abnormal returns (CARs) and whether they are compared to market indexes or matched control firm portfolios. Third, adjusted return performance exhibits a wide variation across different benchmarks.

In general, the underperformance is worse when the mean and median returns of issuers are equally than value-weighted. This is the result of the presence of many relatively small issuing firms which tend to underperform. An equally-weighted approach accentuates the negative performance of these issuers.

The Market Benchmark Specification Debate

As with IPOs, the analysis of long-run returns of stocks that conduct SEOs is fraught with problems associated with the market benchmark and the model used to detect abnormal return performance.

Loughran and Ritter (1995) find that SEOs underperform whether return performance is measured by market-adjusted or matched-control firm adjusted BHRs or by the alpha

Table 11.2 Long-Run Stock Return Performance of US SEOs by Benchmark—Various Studies

Study	Sample Period	SEO Return Mean	SEO Return Median	Adjusted Return Mean	Adjusted Return Median	Benchmark Return	Benchmark Portfolio	Weight of Returns	Horizon (years)
Panel A: Buy-and-Hold Period Returns (BHRs)									
Benchmark: Market Index									
Loughran and Ritter (1995)	1970–1990	33.40		−9.60		43.00	S&P 500	EW	5
Loughran and Ritter (1995)	1970–1990	33.40		−34.30		67.70	CRSP AMEX-NYSE VW	EW	5
Loughran and Ritter (1995)	1970–1990	33.40		−32.90		66.30	CRSP AMEX-NYSE EW	n.a.	5
Loughran and Ritter (1995)	1970–1990	46.90		−28.30		75.20	CRSP Nasdaq EW	EW	5
Loughran and Ritter (1995)	1970–1990	46.90		−19.50		66.40	CRSP Nasdaq VW	n.a.	5
Brav, Geczy, and Gompers (2000)	1975–1992	57.50		−30.10		87.60	S&P 500	EW	5
Brav, Geczy, and Gompers (2000)	1975–1992	57.50		−19.40		76.90	Nasdaq	EW	5
Brav, Geczy, and Gompers (2000)	1975–1992	75.30		−19.00		94.30	S&P 500	VW	5
Brav, Geczy, and Gompers (2000)	1975–1992	75.30		−14.20		89.50	Nasdaq	VW	5
Benchmark: Matched Control Firms									
Eckbo, Masulis, and Norli (2000)	1964–1995	44.20		−26.90		71.10	MV	EW	5
Eckbo, Masulis, and Norli (2000)	1964–1995	50.60		−21.20		71.80	MV	VW	5
Eckbo, Masulis, and Norli (2000)	1964–1995	44.30		−23.20		67.50	MV, BM	EW	5
Eckbo, Masulis, and Norli (2000)	1964–1995	51.60		−10.60		62.20	MV, BM	VW	5
Loughran and Ritter (1995)	1970–1990	15.00		−33.00		48.00	MV	EW	3
Loughran and Ritter (1995)	1970–1990	33.40		−59.40		92.80	MV	EW	5
Jegadeesh (2000)	1970–1993			−34.30			MV, MB	EW	5
Jegadeesh (2000)	1970–1993			−33.50			MV, MB	VW	5
Spiess and Affleck-Graves (1995)	1975–1989	34.11		−22.84		56.95	MV, IND	EW	3
Spiess and Affleck-Graves (1995)	1975–1989	55.72		−42.39		98.11	MV, IND	EW	5
Brav, Geczy, and Gompers (2000)	1975–1992	57.60		−26.30		83.90	MV, BM	EW	5
Brav, Geczy, and Gompers (2000)	1975–1992	57.00		−27.30		84.30	MV, BM, MOM	EW	5
Brav, Geczy, and Gompers (2000)	1975–1992	72.50		−25.00		97.50	MV, BM	VW	5
Brav, Geczy, and Gompers (2000)	1975–1992	75.70		−23.80		99.50	MV, BM, MOM	VW	5
Lee (1997)	1976–1990	31.20	14.20	−18.90	−25.30	50.10	MV, IND	EW	3
Lee (1997)	1976–1990	31.20	14.20	−20.30	−30.60	51.50	MV, BM, MOM	EW	3

(Continued)

Table 11.2 (Continued)

Study	Sample Period	SEO Return		Adjusted Return		Benchmark Return	Benchmark Portfolio	Weight of Returns	Horizon (years)
		Mean	Median	Mean	Median				
Denis and Sarin (2001)	1977–1990	43.08	12.39	−29.14	−28.36		MV	EW	3
Denis and Sarin (2001)	1977–1990	73.79	21.04	−47.91	−42.28		MV	EW	5
Denis and Sarin (2001)	1977–1990	36.93	5.86	−12.36	−9.23		MV, MB, SIC	EW	3
Denis and Sarin (2001)	1977–1990	61.43	13.36	−21.36	−8.24		MV, MB, SIC	EW	5
McLaughlin, Safieddine, and Vasudevan (2000)	1980–1994			−6.80			MV, BM, MOM	EW	3
Clarke, Dunbar, and Kahle (2001)	1984–1996	28.00	8.40	−14.30	−31.40		MV, MB	EW	3
Eberhart and Siddique (2002)	1980–1992			−18.28	−16.21		MV, BM	EW	3
Eberhart and Siddique (2002)	1982–1990			−22.63	−20.14		MV, BM	EW	4
Eberhart and Siddique (2002)	1982–1990			−22.65	−25.96		MV, BM	EW	5
Panel B: Cumulative Returns (CRs)									
Benchmark: Market Index									
Brav, Geczy, and Gompers (2000)	1975–1992	51.50		−24.00		75.50	S&P 500	EW	5
Brav, Geczy, and Gompers (2000)	1975–1992	51.50		−19.20		70.70	Nasdaq	EW	5
Brav, Geczy, and Gompers (2000)	1975–1992	60.40		−9.80		70.20	S&P 500	VW	5
Brav, Geczy, and Gompers (2000)	1975–1992	60.40		−8.80		69.20	Nasdaq	VW	5
Schultz (2003)	1973–1997			−22.80			CRSP VW	EW	5
Schultz (2003)	1973–1997			−11.40			CRSP EW	EW	5
Benchmark: Matched Control Firms									
Spiess and Affleck-Graves (1995)	1975–1989			−39.36			MV	EW	5
Spiess and Affleck-Graves (1995)	1975–1989			−31.24			MV, IND	EW	5
Spiess and Affleck-Graves (1995)	1975–1989			−30.99			MV, BM	EW	5
Brav, Geczy, and Gompers (2000)	1975–1992	53.20		−15.40		68.60	MV, BM	VW	5
Brav, Geczy, and Gompers (2000)	1975–1992	52.40		−15.30		67.70	MV, BM, MO	EW	5
Brav, Geczy, and Gompers (2000)	1975–1992	56.00		−15.90		71.90	MV, BM	VW	5
Brav, Geczy, and Gompers (2000)	1975–1992	56.60		−17.20		73.80	MV, BM, MO	VW	5

MV is market value of equity; BM is the book-to-market value of equity ratio; MB is the market-to-book value of equity ratio. IND means that IPO returns are industry-adjusted; MO is momentum (preissue return performance). In the column "Weight of Returns," EW and VW mean the new issue returns are, respectively, equally or value-weighted. EW and VW next to a market index means the returns in the index are equally or value-weighted, respectively. CRSP Index is an index of returns of stocks in the data base of the Center of Research in Security Prices of the University of Chicago. n.a.: not available.

coefficient estimated from the three factor Fama−French model. Underperformance is larger for relatively small issuers and more pronounced when returns are equally-weighted. Spiess and Affleck-Graves (1995) also find a general pattern of underperformance (measured by BHARs) which is more severe for issuers with very low market capitalization and book-to-market ratios (growth firms) and stocks listed on the Nasdaq. They find no evidence of fads as the reason for the underperformance of SEOs.

Loughran and Ritter (2000) recommend that the Fama−French model be purged of issuing firms so that the factors can better mimic the performance of issuers. They still find evidence of underperformance indicated by the positive and significant alphas. Underperformance is more severe in high-volume SEO markets when greater numbers of small issuers are represented in the population of equity-issuing firms.

Brav, Geczy, and Gompers (2000) also find negative 5-year BHARs and CARs for SEO stocks. After they purge the HML (high capitalization minus small capitalization) factor of NYSE listed stocks and add a momentum factor to the three-factor Fama−French model, no evidence of underperformance is detected. These authors conclude that the SEO long-run price performance is no different from that of other firms with which issuers share common pricing factors.

Eckbo, Masulis, and Norli (2000) propose that lower postissue leverage and greater stock liquidity in the post-SEO period should drive expected equity returns down and, as a result, actual returns should fall. Regressions that include various leverage-related macroeconomic factors produce evidence of insignificant underperformance by SEO stocks.

Jegadeesh (2000) uses benchmarks of matched control firms without equity issues and sorts SEOs by market capitalization and market-to-book ratio. All subsamples of issuers exhibit underperformance measured by BHARs without a clear pattern in favor of larger issuers. Alpha coefficients estimated from the Fama−French model show evidence of underperformance for the small and medium size issuers but not for the larger issuers. However, excess returns of issuers minus those of nonissuers produce negative and significant alphas for all size groups. Therefore, Jegadeesh (2000) concludes that underperformance is not just a small-firm phenomenon.

As in the case of IPOs, Lyandres, Sun, and Zhang (2008) propose that the SEO underperformance is driven by overinvestment by issuing firms relative to similar nonissuing firms. Adding their investment factor to the three-factor Fama−French model, they find no significant excess returns (i.e., alphas). Buy-and-hold abnormal returns (BHARs) are also markedly less negative when the investment factor is added to the matching criteria.

Explanations of the Long-Run Price Performance of SEOs

The Windows of Opportunity Hypothesis

The generally documented patterns of preissue overperformance and postissue underperformance of SEOs imply that firms choose to issue new equity when (1) markets are in transient periods of high valuation; (2) investors extrapolate overoptimistic expectations from the recent strong performance of issuing firms; or (3) managers believe their firm's stock is over-valued based on the managers' private information.

Loughran and Ritter (1995) find that the SEOs in their sample had realized an average BHAR of 72% in the year before the offering. This implies that firms choose to issue more equity after periods of unusually high price performance which they fail to maintain in the postissue period. Although this reversal in stock performance could be due to a regression to the long-run mean return, their tests rule out this explanation.

If insiders (including top executives) have private information they should sell (buy) prior to SEOs they consider overvalued (undervalued) and the stocks should subsequently under-perform or overperform, respectively. Lee (1997) finds evidence of stock return underperfor-mance whether top executives buy or sell shares in the period leading up to the issuance. Although firms appear to be successful in timing new primary equity offers before valuation declines, insiders fail to time their own trades. This implies that managers may not be sure about the direction of their firms. On the other hand, top insider purchases (sales) more accurately predict the stocks' over- (under-)performance in secondary equity offers. But Clarke, Dunbar, and Kahle (2001) report that adjusted long-run returns are negatively related to insider abnormal sales in the quarter prior to issue date. Insiders sell more shares before and on the offer day if the SEO is to go through than if it is to be canceled. This is evidence of managers exploiting private information that their stock is overvalued. Alderson and Betker (2000) find that market reaction upon announcement of a SEO is negative whereas market reaction at the announcement of a withdrawal is positive. This is consistent with the notion that managers decide to issue equity when they believe it is overvalued. Further evi-dence suggests that overvaluation is greater within the group of small and less well-known (neglected) firms.

Eberhart and Siddique (2002) argue that the underperformance of SEO stocks may be caused by a transfer of wealth from equity-holders to debt-holders as new equity reduces the default risk of debt. If this is so, postissue total firm returns (calculated by combining stock and bond returns) ought to be close to zero. However, Eberhart and Siddique find combined returns to be negative, which signifies that the whole firm as an asset is overvalued at the issue time.

Manipulation of earnings through discretionary accruals is one way to pump up investor expectations about firm profitability prior to equity issuance. When discretionary accruals eventually adjust to their normal level, investors are negatively surprised with regard to earn-ings. Teoh, Welch, and Wong (1998) find that stocks of firms with aggressive discretionary accruals significantly underperform the stocks of firms with conservative discretionary accruals in the post-SEO period. Rangan (1998) also finds that larger discretionary accruals are negatively related with post-SEO return on assets (ROA) and market-adjusted stock returns.

If SEOs indeed disappoint investors with their postissue operating performance, then the market should react worse at earnings announcements by SEO firms in the postissue period. Jegadeesh (2000) finds that SEO firms perform worse than benchmark firms around the time of earnings announcements in the postissue period. This implies that investors are surprised more by the earnings announcements of issuing firms. Therefore, the return underperformance of issuers can be attributed to overoptimistic expectations investors hold when they buy SEO stocks in the aftermarket. However, the above evidence is challenged by Brous, Datar, and Kini (2001) who find that the market's negative reaction to earnings announcements extends to stocks of firms similar to those that conduct SEOs. This is evidence that investors are surprised by the earnings performance of issuers and nonissuers that share common characteristics. Denis and Sarin (2001) also examine market reaction to postissue announcements and find evidence that surprises are concentrated among the smallest size quartile of SEO firms.

Influence of Investor Recognition Factors

Gibson, Safieddine, and Sonti (2004) find that SEO stocks associated with higher institutional buying activity around the offer and more positive revisions by analysts exhibit stronger long-run performance. Institutional stock holdings also increase more than in similar nonissuing firm stocks. The results suggest that institutions are capable of identifying higher quality SEOs. Hao (2014) also finds that higher stock liquidity (a proxy of investor recognition) is positively associated with long-run postissue returns.

Influence of Subsequent Financing Activity

Billett, Flannery, and Garfinkel (2011) examine the long-run stock return performance of SEO firms by taking into consideration subsequent financing events, like follow-on SEOs, private equity placements and public debt offerings. No evidence of underperformance of SEO stocks is found when such financing events are taken into consideration.

The Long-Run Operating Performance of Firms Conducting SEOs

Most studies that analyze the long-run operating performance of firms that conduct SEOs show evidence of preissue superior and postissue inferior operating performance relative to various benchmarks of matched control firms. This evidence is consistent with the windows of opportunity hypothesis according to which managers time SEOs to coincide with a period of strong firm performance. Their decision to issue new equity should be stronger if they have private information of an impending deterioration of their firms' prospects in the near future.

To avoid drawing wrong inferences, empirical tests of operating performance should rectify the possibility of a reversion to the mean by matching issuing firms with nonissuing firms that have a similar preissue operating performance as suggested by Barber and Lyon (1996).

The Empirical Evidence

Loughran and Ritter (1997) compare various metrics of operating performance of firms conducting SEOs to those of control firms which by industry, asset size, and preissue operating ROA are similar to the issuing firms. Their findings are summarized below:

- Match-adjusted ROA is positive in the three preissue years and negative in years +2 to +4. Changes in match-adjusted ROA from year 0 to +4 are significantly negative. The same is true for operating income before depreciation to assets or sales, profit margin, capital expenditures plus R&D, and market-to-book ratio.
- The deterioration is widely spread encompassing both small and large equity market capitalization firms but predominates among the smallest asset-size firms.
- The pattern of underperformance is similar for pure primary and combination (primary and secondary) offerings.

McLaughlin, Safieddine, and Vasudevan (1996) confirm the above pattern of operating over- and under-performance in the pre- and postissue years, respectively. There is also evidence that firms that perform best in the preissue years experience more severe deterioration in performance. These authors find that the negative performance is concentrated among issuers with below median book value of assets and above median market-to-book value ratios, that is, within smaller and growth firms.

Fu (2010) posits the hypothesis that the operating underperformance of SEO firms is due to their overinvestment relative to similar firms, consistent with the free cash flow agency arguments. Indeed, most of the SEO firms in the sample invest more than their control firms and ROA is negatively related to the excess investment.

Finally, Hao (2014) attributes postoffer operating underperformance to lower outside monitoring of the firm, especially in firms with relatively low managerial equity stakes, that is, firms in which the interests of managers and shareholders are weakly aligned.

Debt Offers

Initial Pricing

In some respects, debt offerings resemble initial public offerings. Even when the issuing firm has bonds outstanding, new bonds most likely have different features, like maturity, coupon rate, callability or convertibility, and possibly different rating. Therefore, the prior price record of the outstanding bonds of the issuing firm may not be very informative about the expected market price of the new bond. The initial pricing of bond issues is assessed by comparing the offering (also called reoffering) yield of new bonds to their market yield or to the market yield of a portfolio of outstanding bonds that have similar characteristics. Under either method, underpricing is detected when the reoffering yields of the new bonds are higher than their market yields or the yields of the benchmark portfolio. This is so because a higher reoffering yield implies the new bond is offered at a lower price than the market price implied by its market yield or the yield of the benchmark portfolio. The initial pricing of bond issues can also be assessed in the form of initial returns estimated from the offer and market price of the new bond.

As in the case of IPOs and SEOs, the empirical studies of the pricing of new bonds utilize proxies for ex ante risk, asymmetric information and certification effects. Additional proxies that pertain to bond issues include bond-specific features like maturity and rating and market trends in interest rates.

The Empirical Evidence

In early research on the pricing of bond issues, researchers questioned whether the market yields of already outstanding bonds fairly represented the current valuation state of these bonds and, hence, whether these bonds could serve as a valid benchmark of newly issued bonds with similar characteristics. An often-made argument was that new bonds have undergone a fresh price discovery process and, hence, their prices may reflect current information more efficiently than seasoned outstanding bonds. It must be noted that the possibility of a misalignment between the values of outstanding and new bonds was more important in the past when bond trading was much thinner than now. Even under those conditions, the weak evidence for underpricing or overpricing made that argument less relevant.

Lindvall (1977), for example, finds no evidence of underpricing during periods of stable interest rates. Several other studies also find evidence that new bond issue underpricing is absent (e.g., Weinstein, 1978; Martin and Richards, 1981; Fung and Rudd, 1986) or very low (Sorensen, 1982). Marr and Thompson (1984) investigate whether gross spreads and reoffering yields of new bonds are mutually affected and find no evidence that reoffering yields are impacted by the gross spread. This suggests that underwriters do not use the pricing of new bonds to adjust the underwriting cost to their compensation. Instead, reoffering yields impact the gross spread so that bonds with lower reoffering yields have higher fees.

Kang and Lee (1996) analyze benchmark-adjusted initial returns of new convertible bonds from the offer price to the first available market price and find no evidence of underpricing. Datta, Iskandar-Datta, and Patel (1997) also find no evidence of underpricing in their overall sample of straight bond initial public offers (BIPOs). They attribute this to the dominance of the bond market by dealers who are less susceptible to the adverse selection problem that can cause underpricing according to the Rock (1986) model. Cross-sectional analysis reveals that underpricing (measured by initial returns) falls with higher underwriter reputation, higher bond rating, and is lower for firms listed on the NYSE or AMEX than firms listed on the Nasdaq market. Interestingly, high grade bonds appear to be offered overpriced whereas low grade bonds are offered underpriced. Contrary to previous evidence, greater underwriter compensation correlates with greater underpricing. This would suggest that underpricing helps complement the compensation received as gross spread. As in Kang and Lee (1996) above, there is no evidence of excess returns after the offer day, which implies that postissue bond prices are efficient.

In a later study, Datta, Iskandar-Datta, and Patel (1999) examine offer yields of BIPOs and find that issues of firms with a bank lending relationship have offer yields that average 68 basis points below the yields of issuers without lending relationships. The authors suggest that bank debt financing prior to the bond issue reduces information asymmetry and serves as certification of the quality of the issuing firm.

Cai, Helwege, and Warga (2007) report evidence of significant underpricing (measured in initial returns) for firms issuing bonds for the first time whether publicly or privately. By comparison, seasoned (i.e., non-first-time) bond offers are underpriced much less and, if privately offered, they have no sign of underpricing. Underpricing increases for non-NYSE listed issuers and with bond maturity and decreases with issue size. Underpricing is insignificant among investment grade bonds. Bond offers following a recent bond issue are also less underpriced but the opposite is true if the bond issue follows a recent IPO. The greater underpricing of first-time bond issuers and bond issues following IPOs is attributed to greater uncertainty because not enough information is available for such issuers.

The Long-Run Stock Returns of Firms Conducting Debt Offers

The long-run valuation effects of debt issues are studied with respect to the impact bond issues have on the postissue stock returns of the issuing firms.

Table 11.3 presents long-run stock returns following the issuance of straight and convertible bonds as reported in various studies. First, we notice that stocks underperform various benchmarks whether the firm issues straight or convertible debt. However, straight bond issuers realize less negative (especially on an adjusted basis) long-run postissue stock performance than convertible bond issuers. This can be explained by the higher quality of the straight bond issuers and by the equity-like features of convertible bonds. Due to the convertibility feature, the codependence between the value of convertible bonds and the value of equity is greater than that between straight debt and equity. Second, there is considerable variability of performance depending on the matching criteria used to form benchmark portfolios. In general, using more criteria to match issuing firms to nonissuing firms generates weaker evidence of underperformance.

Explanations of the Long-Run Stock Price Performance of Debt Issues

Compared to the long-run adjusted stock returns following SEOs (Table 11.2), the long-run adjusted returns following debt issues (Table 11.3) appear to be of lower magnitude. In general, firms issue equity when managers believe their firm's stock is overvalued and expect firm performance to decline subsequent to the issuance of equity. On the contrary, debt financing is assumed to signal a firm's positive assessment of future opportunities. The negative postissue stock returns reported in Table 11.3 suggest though that investors overpay when they buy the common equity shares of debt issuers right after the bond offering. This in turn implies that, as in the case of equity offers, investors overestimate the future value of equity of debt-issuing firms because of overoptimistic expectations which subsequently fail to be realized.

The studies reviewed below shed light on two issues. First, whether the stock return performance differs following the issuance of different types of bonds (e.g., straight versus convertible

Table 11.3 Long-Run Stock Return Performance Following Debt Issues—Various Studies

| Study | Sample Period | Raw BHR | | Adjusted BHAR | | Benchmark BHR | Benchmark Portfolio | Weight of Returns | Horizon (years) |
		Mean	Median	Mean	Median				
Panel A: Straight Bonds									
Spiess and Affleck-Graves (1999)	1975–1989	83.06		−14.31		97.37	MV, BM	EW	5
Eckbo, Masulis, and Norli (2000)	1964–1995	52.10		−3.00		55.10	MV	EW	5
Eckbo, Masulis, and Norli (2000)	1964–1995	51.70		−11.20		62.90	MV, BM	EW	5
Eckbo, Masulis, and Norli (2000)	1964–1995	29.20		−0.60		29.80	MV	VW	5
Eckbo, Masulis, and Norli (2000)	1964–1995	31.10		−1.20		32.30	MV, BM	VW	5
Bae, Jeong, Sun, and Tang (2002)	1985–1990			−18.00	9.00		MV, BM	EW	3
Bae, Jeong, Sun, and Tang (2002)	1985–1990			−8.00	26.00		MV, BM	EW	5
Lyandres, Sun, and Zhang (2008)	1970–2005			−11.40			MV, BM	EW	3
Lyandres, Sun, and Zhang (2008)	1970–2005			−6.20			MV, BM, INV	EW	3
Butler and Wan (2010)	1975–1999			−24.00	−13.00		MV, BM	EW	5
Butler and Wan (2010)	1975–1990			−3.00	−7.00		MV, BM, LIQU	EW	5
Panel B: Convertible Bonds									
McLaughlin, Safieddine, and Vasudevan (1998)	1980–1993	28.20	12.00	−11.40	−8.30		MV, BM	EW	3
Lee and Loughran (1998)	1975–1990	47.10		−30.40		77.50	MV, BM	EW	5
Spiess and Affleck-Graves (1999)	1975–1989	23.19		−36.95		60.14	MV, BM	EW	5
Eckbo, Masulis, and Norli (2000)	1964–1995	49.30		−29.50		78.80	MV	EW	5
Eckbo, Masulis, and Norli (2000)	1964–1995	51.70		−16.00		67.70	MV, BM	EW	5
Eckbo, Masulis, and Norli (2000)	1964–1995	45.00		−27.90		72.90	MV	VW	5
Eckbo, Masulis, Norli (2000)	1964–1995	45.20		−28.20		73.40	MV, BM	VW	5
Bae, Jeong, Sun, and Tang (2002)	1985–1990			−14.00	−18.00		MV, BM	EW	3
Bae, Jeong, Sun, and Tang (2002)	1985–1990			−8.00	−15.00		MV, BM	EW	5

(Continued)

Table 11.3   (Continued)

Study	Sample Period	Raw BHR		Adjusted BHAR		Benchmark BHR	Benchmark Portfolio	Weight of Returns	Horizon (years)
		Mean	Median	Mean	Median				
Lyandres, Sun, and Zhang (2008)	1970–2005			−15.80			MV, BM	EW	3
Lyandres, Sun, and Zhang (2008)	1970–2005			−20.00			MV, BM	EW	5
Lyandres, Sun, and Zhang (2008)	1970–2005			−9.40			MV, BM, INV	EW	3
Lyandres, Sun, and Zhang (2008)	1970–2005			−9.60			MV, BM, INV	EW	5
Butler and Wan (2010)	1975–1990			−24.00	−18.00		MV, BM	EW	5
Butler and Wan (2010)	1975–1990			−12.00	−12.00		MV, BM, LIQU	EW	5

MV is market value of equity; BM is the book-to-market value of equity ratio; INV is an investment factor used as matching criterion; LIQU is a stock liquidity factor used as a matching criterion. EW and VW in the column "Weight of Returns" means the new issue returns are equally or value-weighted, respectively.

or investment grade versus noninvestment grade bonds). Second, whether different market benchmarks generate different evidence in regards to stock performance following debt issues.

Lee and Loughran (1998) find that investment grade convertible bond issues produce higher BHARs than noninvestment grade bonds. Larger investment grade issues also perform better than smaller issues; but no such size effect is detected in noninvestment grade debt issues. Underperformance is worse when a convertible bond issue has been preceded by an IPO or SEO by the same firm in the prior 2 years.

Spiess and Affleck-Graves (1999) study straight and convertible bond offerings. Overall, debt issuers outperform matching firms in the 5 years prior to the offer. Following the debt offer, convertible (but not straight) debt issuers realize significant stock return underperformance relative to their matching firms. Assessed by the Fama–French model, only equally-weighted portfolios of alphas are significantly negative for both straight and convertible debt issuers, which is evidence of the general underperformance of small-size issuers. Assessed by matched-adjusted BHRs, straight and convertible debt issues generate significant stock return underperformance. Younger issuers and those listed on the AMEX or Nasdaq are those that perform worse. Nonrated and speculative debt offers are associated with negative stock return performance while investment grade debt offers are not. Convertible debt issues generate similar patterns with the exception that even issuers listed on the NYSE underperform with respect to stock returns in the postissue years.

If the firm's leverage rises after a debt issue, the cost of equity should also increase. Therefore, in the long run, debt-issuing firms should realize higher stock returns relative to the returns of benchmark portfolios. Eckbo, Masulis, and Norli (2000) show that after accounting for the leverage effect, there is little evidence of stock return underperformance following both straight and convertible debt issues. Underperformance appears to be more evident among utility firms issuing debt.

Lyandres, Sun, and Zhang (2008) argue that the level of investment can negatively impact postissue stock return performance. Their multivariate analysis, including an investment factor, produces significant and negative equally-weighted alphas but insignificant value-weighted alphas for straight and convertible bond issuers.

Butler and Wan (2010) propose that the degree of stock liquidity in the market can affect the expected and actual equity returns (e.g., lower liquidity stocks ought to have higher required returns). Therefore, lower liquidity firms have a reason to avoid equity financing. Indeed, the study finds that firms with lower stock liquidity are more likely to issue debt. Adding the liquidity factor to a multifactor model produces insignificant alphas whereas models without the liquidity factor still produce negative significant alphas. Adding the liquidity factor to the matching criteria, given by market capitalization and book-to-market ratio, eliminates the evidence of stock return underperformance measured by BHARs.

Billett, Flannery, and Garfinkel (2011) find that when subsequent financing events (e.g., SEO, private equity issues, and public debt offers) are incorporated in a multiple regression model there is no evidence of stock return underperformance for debt issuers.

The Operating Performance of Firms Conducting Debt Offers

The evidence from the stock price performance of debt issuers suggests that debt issuance, especially of straight debt, is not as consequential for postissue stock returns as the issuance of equity. Nonetheless, the empirical evidence shows that debt-issuing firms exhibit operating underperformance in the years following the new debt issuance.

McLaughlin, Safieddine, and Vasudevan (1998) find that nonconvertible debt issuers realize negative median changes in adjusted operating returns in several years after the issue. The negative performance is worse for smaller issuers (i.e., those with below median book value of assets). Debt issuers perform better than matching firms in the preissue years, but those who perform best experience worse postissue operating performance, a sign of timing. Operating underperformance is also realized by firms that issue convertible bonds (McLaughlin, Safieddine, and Vasudevan, 1998).

Lee and Loughran (1998) find that convertible debt issuers underperform matching firms of similar capitalization and book-to-market ratio with respect to profit margin and ROA in the postissue years. Bae, Jeong, Sun, and Tang (2002) report convertible (but not straight) bond issuers underperform control firms with respect to ROA in the postissue periods.

Other Special Case Offers

Preferred Stock Offerings

There is little empirical evidence on the pricing of preferred equity issues. Loderer, Sheehan, and Kadlec (1991) analyze preferred issues completed in the early 1980s and find no evidence of significant discounts or initial returns. However, there is evidence that

30-day postissue returns relative to offer price produce small negative excess returns, which would suggest overpricing.

Bajaj, Mazumdar, and Sarin (2002) analyze a larger sample of straight and convertible preferred issues with fixed-offer yields completed in 1980−1999. Spreads of straight preferred stock yields versus benchmark bonds are positive, an indication that these issues are offered at a discount relative to similar rating bonds. Convertible preferred stocks carry negative spreads, an indication they are offered at premiums relative to benchmark bonds. The lower yields of convertible preferred issues are attributed to the convertibility option embedded in the price of convertible preferred stock that makes convertible preferred attractive to investors.

Closed-End Fund Issues

Closed-end (investment) funds (CEFs) are capitalized through the issuance of shares. Like other corporate entities, CEF shares become publicly traded through an IPO. Since CEFs derive their value from the underlying stocks or bonds held in the name of the fund, CEFs are relatively easy to value. Therefore, the usual asymmetric information problems that afflict corporate IPOs should not be a significant factor in pricing new share issues by CEFs. Thus, they provide a good experimental context to test the impact of informational imperfections on underpricing.

Consistent with no or little underpricing, Weiss (1989) finds that IPOs of CEFs produce insignificant initial returns. CEFs of foreign stocks (which bear more uncertainty) have small significant initial returns of 3.22%. Also, consistent with the fact that CEFs trade at a discount from their net asset value (NAV), Weiss finds that, by the 120th day after the IPO, the CEFs lose on average 15% of their first day market price on a cumulative market-adjusted basis. These price declines are, however, concentrated in the domestic and foreign stock CEFs but not the bond CEFs. Bond funds trade at parity 24 weeks after issue. The most affected investors by the decline appear to be individual investors.

IPOs of CEFs are offered at a premium over their NAV in order to cover the underwriting expenses. Therefore, original buyers buy overpriced shares. When trading starts in the secondary market, the price should adjust to the NAV level which would imply a theoretical initial return close to the premium. However, Peavy (1990) reports that immediate aftermarket prices are on average only 0.62% below the offer price. This implies that the aftermarket investors also buy overpriced CEF shares at prices exceeding the NAV of the fund. As market prices gradually adjust to their NAV level, these investors realize a loss of 12.78% by the 100th day after purchase. Anderson, Born, and Beard (1991) confirm that IPO shares issued by bond CEFs are offered at a premium compared to the average prices of seasoned bond CEFs consistent with the 7% takedown that compensates the underwriters.

Hanley, Lee, and Seguin (1996) report that SEOs of CEFs are overpriced, i.e., are sold to initial investors at a premium relative to the funds' NAV. This results in excessive flipping by large buyers which underwriters counter with price stabilization in the aftermarket by using flipped and OAO shares to cover their short positions on the new shares. Marketing seems to be directed toward less sophisticated investors who buy overpriced shares and hold them over longer periods of time.

Akhigbe and Madura (2001) find that SEOs by CEFs are motivated by whether the fund is overvalued relative to its NAV or whether it has high market liquidity in terms of trading volume. SEO announcements by CEFs generate significant negative returns of −2.53% in the interval days −1 to +1 relative to the announcement day, which is evidence of overvaluation. The market reaction is more negative as expense ratio rises and size of fund gets bigger. CEFs that conduct SEOs realize negative 3-year BHARs of −37.91%.

Higgins, Howton, and Howton (2003) also report a negative return of −0.65% at the announcement of SEOs by CEFs. Over a 3-year period, the CEF shares realize on average a BHAR of −9.16%. Announcement returns are more negative for funds traded at a premium, that is, they are overvalued.

Master Limited Partnership Issues

Master Limited Partnerships (MLPs) are entities whose shares or units are listed and traded in an exchange. MLPs attract little interest from institutional investors because MLP income is taxable, while control rights are ceded to the MLP general manager and administrative costs are borne by institutional investors. The generally known information that institutions refrain from bidding for MLP IPO shares resolves the adverse selection problem of the uninformed retail investors. That is, retail investors do not have to be concerned they will be rationed out of good-quality issues by informed investors. The absence of informed investors also removes the need to reward them with underpriced shares for sharing information with the underwriter.

Muscarella (1988) finds that initial public offerings of MLPs produce statistically insignificant average initial returns. Michaely and Shaw (1994) also confirm the above findings. They find average initial returns of −0.04% for MLPs versus 8.5% for nonfinancial IPOs. Controlling for industry, offer size, and institutional-holdings MLPs have no underpricing compared to similar samples of IPOs by other firms.

Real Estate Investment Trust Issues

Real Estate Investment Trusts (REITs) are investment vehicles like CEFs, but the value of their underlying assets is more uncertain because real estate properties lack the continuous markets of stocks and bonds held by CEFs. There is also greater uncertainty about the use of offer proceeds in the case of REITs. Accordingly, the IPOs of REITs are expected to be underpriced more than the IPO shares of investment companies or even traditional industrial firms.

Wang, Chan, and Gau (1992) show that, contrary to this expectation, REITs in their sample were overpriced, i.e., they had negative initial returns of about −2.82%. In contrast, contemporaneous industrial firm IPOs were underpriced by 15.07%. However, REITs underwritten by top-ranked investment banks had initial returns indistinguishable from zero. Riskier REIT IPOs and those that used the "best efforts"[2] contract had less overpricing. Despite the overpricing, the prices of REIT stocks declined on the first trading day and

---

[2] As explained in Chapter 15: Structuring Securities Offerings, in "best efforts" contract the underwriter is not responsible for underwriting the full placement of the issue.

continued to do so over a period of 190 days after the offer. As a result, REITs underperformed a market benchmark of other seasoned REITs. The principal explanation of the overpricing is the limited interest and participation of informed institutional investors in the IPOs of REITs. The study finds that institutional holdings averaged less than 10%. It seems REIT shares are marketed mostly to retail (uninformed) investors who end up buying overpriced shares.

However, Ling and Ryngaert (1997) find evidence that contradicts that reported by Wang, Chan, and Gau (1992) above. In a sample of REIT IPOs in the 1990s, Ling and Ryngaert (1997) find evidence of valuation uncertainty and greater participation by institutional investors that reaches up to almost 50%. They report significant positive average initial returns of 3.6% for REIT-related IPOs, which is evidence of underpricing. Heavier institutional investor participation generates more underpricing—up to an average of 4.26% versus insignificant underpricing for holdings below 30%. Controlling for other factors, underwriter reputation has a negative impact on underpricing. BHARs up to 100 days are positive (negative) for higher (lower) institutional holdings and higher (lower) quality underwriters. This implies that when underwriters utilize information from informed investors they underprice more in order to compensate these investors.

Friday, Howton, and Howton (2000) examine the post-SEO operating performance of REITs. They find no underperformance in industry-adjusted cash flow to assets following the equity offer. REITs with greater preissue cash holdings display worse operating performance due to the possible suboptimal investment of the free cash flow that results from the equity offer.

Insurance Firm Issues

Wang and Ligon (2009) argue that insurance firms present an interesting case to test whether the motives of insiders affect underpricing. In stock insurance firms, insiders who participate in the secondary offerings have an interest to limit the degree of underpricing. In mutual insurance firms, on the other hand, insiders do not hold shares and may be less concerned with underpricing. The difference in underpricing between the samples of IPOs by the two types of insurance firms is found to be insignificant. This finding implies that insider participation in the sale of equity shares does not explain the degree of underpricing. Whether insiders liquidate shares, as in stock insurance firms, or not does not seem to bear on the relative degree of underpricing.

Dual Stock Issues

In addition to regular shares, firms may also issue a class of shares that give owners enhanced voting rights. Firms, with dual-class shares, prefer to issue regular shares to raise capital in order to avoid dilution of the control of those investors with the enhanced voting rights.

Smart and Zutter (2003) examine the initial returns of IPOs conducted by firms with dual and single-class share structures, respectively. Dual-class issuers are less motivated to achieve widespread distribution of shares (to protect their control) and, hence, underpricing is not as critical as a means to this end. Indeed, dual-class issuer IPOs are underpriced by 11.9% compared to single-class issuer IPOs which are underpriced by 13.7%. However, dual-class IPOs are associated with larger issuers, more reputable underwriters, greater offer size, and fewer uses of proceeds. Hence, the lower initial returns may be explained by lower ex ante risk. Controlling for these factors, dual-class IPOs are still underpriced less than single-class IPOs but the lower underpricing results in greater ownership concentration than it is observed for the more underpriced single-class IPOs. The lower underpricing of IPOs of dual-class issuers comes at the cost of lower valuation than for single-class IPOs. The lower underpricing of dual-class IPOs persists even after controlling for the impact of price stabilization (Smart and Zutter, 2008).

Penny Stock Issues

Bradley, Cooney, Dolvin, and Jordan (2006) examine the initial pricing and long-run price performance of penny stocks in 1990–1998. They find average underpricing of 22.4% versus 15.4% for nonpenny stock IPOs. The average lockup period is more than twice that of regular IPOs, with non-venture capital-backed penny stock IPOs having longer lockup periods than IPOs backed by venture capital firms. Penny stock IPOs also carry higher average underwriting spreads (9.7%) than regular IPOs (7.2%). The 3-year market-adjusted returns of penny stocks are −101.8% versus −39.9% of regular IPOs.

Private Investments in Public Equity

Issuance Structure and Mechanics

Private Investment in Public Equity (PIPE) is a method of capital raising by firms having difficulty raising equity through more traditional channels, like a seasoned equity offering. Such firms may also be in financial distress or urgent need of funds and need expeditious financing. PIPE shares are issued under the SEC rules governing private placements. Hence, speed of execution comes at the cost of restrictions on the resale of the new shares. Nonetheless, PIPE investors gain access to the secondary market much sooner than investors in typical private placements because the PIPE issuers are required to register the new shares with the SEC within 30 days of signing the purchase agreement.

   PIPE transactions are classified as "traditional" if they offer common stock and fixed-price convertibles and as "structured" if they offer common stock along with contingent securities, like floating price convertibles or convertible resets. The inclusion of contingent claims has the purpose to either condition the availability of funds on firm performance (as in the case of PIPEs with warrants) or to reduce losses to the PIPE investors because of miss-estimation of the risks of their investment (as in the case of PIPEs with resets of the warrants' exercise price or floating price convertible or convertible resets). The inclusion of these investor-friendly terms enables issuers to negotiate a higher offer price or a lower price discount.

   The issuer usually retains an underwriter who acts as a placement agent. In this capacity, the underwriter prepares the offering memorandum, organizes roadshows, and presentations to investors and markets the issue. The agent's fee may include sweeteners that grant the agent the right to execute future PIPEs or other financing activities. The value of the underwriter rises with the complexity of the special terms in the offer. The total flotation cost for PIPE transactions includes the agent's fees, the price discount from the current stock price, and the value of any warrants granted to investors. PIPEs are executed with a "best efforts" contract and, hence, the underwriter has no responsibility to take up any unsold securities.

Chaplinsky and Haushalter (2010) find that PIPEs with contingent claim contracts, like warrants and price resets, are associated with firms that burn a lot of cash, have mostly intangible assets and poor stock performance prior to the issue—that is, firms with greater moral hazard and adverse selection problems. Inclusion of the contingent claims shows that the price discount is not enough to compensate investors in the case of such financially constrained issuers. Dai, Jo, and Schatzberg (2010) report an average agent fee of 6.2%. They also find that the probability of retaining an agent is inversely related to financial distress, and reputable underwriters are preferred for the quality of their analysts.

PIPEs have grown considerably as a capital raising method from $4.1 billion in 1996 to $16.8 billion in 2005 (Dai, Jo, and Schatzberg, 2010). A more recent study (Bengtsson and Dai, 2014) reports that there were about 15,000 PIPE transactions from 1999 to 2012 that raised over $500 billion. The top five agents by gross proceeds raised were Goldman Sachs & Co., JP Morgan Chase & Co., Credit Suisse Securities (USA) LLC, UBS Investment Bank, and Citigroup Global Markets, Inc.

The Empirical Evidence

Dai, Jo, and Schatzberg (2010) find that greater postoffer analyst coverage is associated with less postissue volatility of returns and lower bid–ask spreads. Thus, reputable underwriters provide certification over and above the characteristics of the issue. The all-in-net discount[3] averages 24.4% for PIPEs retaining an underwriter versus 10% without. Net discounts are on average lower in PIPEs managed by reputable than less prestigious underwriters (18.7% versus 22.1%). The net discount increases with the presence of an agent and decreases with the fraction of PIPE shares bought by insiders.

Bengtsson and Dai (2014) find that PIPEs carry more investor-friendly terms and have smaller price discounts if managed by reputable agents. Similar to public equity offers, PIPE stocks realize negative long-run return performance, which is less negative if the PIPE has more investor-friendly terms and is managed by a reputable underwriter. Traditional PIPEs have a decreasing effect on the discount. PIPEs completed in recent years had an average discount of 9.5%.

Chaplinsky and Haushalter (2010) find that the probability of delisting of firms conducting PIPEs is higher for firms that grant contingent claims, and stock returns to the PIPE investors are similar to those realized by benchmarks for up to 24 months, except in the case of PIPEs with price resets, which underperform.

---

[3] The all-in-net discount is equal to $1 - (I/V)$, where I is the proceeds raised and V is the market value of stock and warrants received by investors.

12

The Empirical Evidence on Underwriting Spreads

This chapter presents the empirical evidence on the underwriting (gross) spreads of initial public offerings (IPOs), seasoned equity offerings (SEOs) and debt offers. This chapter complements the theoretical analysis of Chapter 6: Underwriting Costs and Compensation that discussed the risks and the compensation of underwriters.

Underwriting Cost Structure and Gross Spreads

The underwriting (gross) spread is the compensation of the underwriter for the services provided to the issuer. Under the most comprehensive underwriting contract, that is, the firm commitment contract, these services include origination, underwriting (insurance), marketing and pricing, and placement. The costs to deliver these services include both a fixed and a variable cost component.

The fixed costs include services which are common to all types of issues and are incurred irrespective of the size (i.e., proceeds) of the issue. They include costs underwriters incur for their engagement in the preparation and filing of the issue, holding roadshows, performing due diligence tasks, as well as price discovery and placement.

The variable costs include expenses over and above the fixed costs and vary with the difficulty of estimating the issue's value, the extent of the marketing effort, and the intensity and scope of the placement activities. Beyond a certain level, the size of proceeds adds to issuance costs as the effort to place larger issues becomes costlier.

If F is the total fixed cost of the overall underwriting effort, v is the variable cost per dollar of proceeds and K is the issue proceeds, the gross spread, S, expressed as a percent of proceeds is as follows:

$$S = F/K + v.$$

The above expression implies that as K increases, the average fixed cost, F/K, falls. If v is also constant irrespective of the size of proceeds, then S will fall as the proceeds rise. Thus, the underwriting service enjoys economies of scale which produce the often-observed inverse relationship between gross spreads (S) and proceeds.

However, the variable cost may not be constant as proceeds increase. First as the proceeds rise, the underwriter has to exert greater effort to market the issue and to certify its value. Thus, v may start to rise at an increasing rate as proceeds exceed a certain level. This means that beyond a level of proceeds the underwriter is faced with diseconomies of scale.

Underwriting Services and the New Issues Market. DOI: http://dx.doi.org/10.1016/B978-0-12-803282-4.00012-2

As the variable cost per dollar rises faster than the fixed cost per dollar of proceeds falls the percent gross spread will start to increase with proceeds. The emergence of diseconomies of scale suggests that the gross spread follows a U-shaped curve in relation to proceeds as illustrated in Fig. 12.1 (Altınkılıç & Hansen, 2000).

Altınkılıç and Hansen (2000) build on this structure of the gross spread to argue that firms of different quality produce a spectrum of spread-proceeds relationships or curves. Low quality (usually smaller) firms realize diseconomies of scale (i.e., rapidly increasing variable costs) at a lower scale of proceeds. Should such firms decide to raise greater proceeds the spread curve would rise steeply from its bottom point. This is so because to raise more funds requires proportionally greater effort and resources per dollar of capital to ensure successful completion of the deal. On the other hand, high quality (usually large) firms face diseconomies of scale at much higher levels of proceeds. Hence, each type of firm faces a different spread-proceeds curve. When spreads are averaged across all types of issues, we obtain the usual downward slopping spread curve which implies economies of scale. Altınkılıç and Hansen (2000) find that variable costs do rise faster beyond a level of proceeds and as a result gross spreads are found to display a U-shaped curve in relation to proceeds. Furthermore, marginal costs rise faster for smaller (lower quality) issues. These relationships

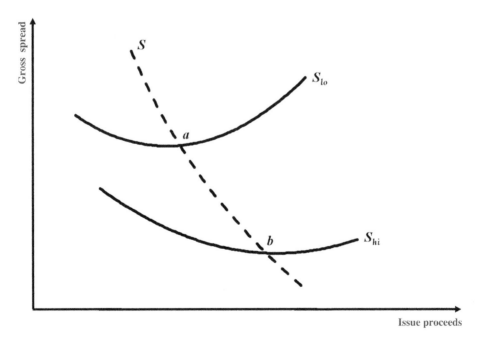

FIGURE 12.1 Relationship between Gross Spread and Issue Proceeds. Curves S_{lo} and S_{hi} depict the relationship of gross spread to issue proceeds for lower (higher) quality issuers requiring more (less) service, respectively. Curve S depicts the relationship of gross spread and issue proceeds derived from pooled groups of both smaller (lower quality) and larger (higher quality) issuers. Points a and b illustrate the levels of issue proceeds above which diseconomies of scale cause gross spreads to increase with issue size for each category of issues. *The figure is adopted from Altınkılıç, O. & Hansen, R.S. (2000). Are there economies of scale in underwriting fees? Evidence of rising external financing costs. Review of Financial Studies, 13(1), pp. 191–218.*

are shown to hold for seasoned equity as well as debt offers, but we can reasonably assume they apply to IPOs as well.

The Determinants of the Gross Spread

The factors that explain the magnitude and variation of gross spreads are associated with the determinants of the cost of the underwriting services offered. Some of these factors are related to characteristics that impact the resources dedicated to the underwriting effort. Other factors are related to the risks encountered by the underwriter in relation to placing new securities into an uncertain market environment. As in the case of new issue pricing, we can classify the factors affecting gross spreads into three categories: issue-specific factors, issuer-specific factors, market-specific factors.

The underwriting costs and, hence, the spreads can be also impacted by differences in underwriting arrangements (e.g., negotiated versus competitive offerings), type of offer (e.g., traditional versus shelf registration), the method of offering (e.g., general cash offer versus rights offer), and other offer factors, as for example, the underwriter and syndicate choice. The impact of these factors is discussed in Chapter 15: Structuring Securities Offerings and in Chapter 16: New Issue Decisions: The Underwriter, Syndicate, Auditor and Legal Counsel.

Issue-Specific Factors

Size: Because of fixed costs, the gross spread should decline as size of proceeds rises. A large offering also gives the issuer bargaining power to negotiate better terms with prospective underwriters. On the other hand, large offerings increase the overall risk exposure of the underwriter in the case of unforeseen adverse market conditions that make placement more challenging and costlier. This can cause the gross spread to rise beyond a certain level of proceeds.

Riskiness of offered security: Riskier securities require greater pricing and marketing effort. For example, price uncertainty is, in general, greater for stocks than bonds. Higher quality and shorter maturity bonds are also less costly to price than lower quality and longer maturity bonds.

Placement characteristics: Issues placed in large blocks involve lower direct costs of distribution than issues with more diffused placement. Thus, bonds which are placed mostly with institutional investors in large lots per buyer have lower distribution costs than stocks which, relative to bonds, require more intensive placement with retail investors. International offerings also contribute to the placement costs in comparison to purely domestic offerings. The presence of an overallotment option can also affect the spread, if the underwriter has to exert greater effort to place a larger issue in the market.

Issuer-Specific Factors

Operations: Firms with complex and diversified operations and lines of business require a more extensive underwriting investigation to ensure compliance with due diligence and thorough assessment of the underwriting risks involved. In general, issuers operating in more established and traditional sectors are easier to value than issuers operating in technology and innovation-driven sectors.

Size: Large issuers are more well-known and attract greater investor interest both of which can reduce the costs of price discovery. Large issuers can also negotiate better terms with underwriters. For example, the underwriter may accept a lower compensation because of the prospect of earning future business on other corporate deals (e.g., new issues, M&A, etc.) from the issuer.

Market-Specific Factors

Volatility: Volatility of market prices or interest rates makes it difficult to distinguish between genuine trends and "noise." An underwriter working in a volatile market must either spend more resources for price discovery, or charge a higher gross spread to cover the greater underwriting risk.

How Efficient is the Pricing of Underwriting Services?

If the underwriting services are priced efficiently, then we should observe gross spreads to be related to the costs of the services. More specifically, the gross spreads should vary according to the theoretical cost of the underwriting services.

Bae and Levy (1990) investigate whether the underwriting fee (i.e., the compensation for the underwriting risk) accurately reflects the risk the underwriter assumes for full placement of the issue. To this end, the authors price the underwriting risk as a put option written by the underwriter and sold to the issuer and compare the theoretical price (cost) of the put to the actual underwriting fee charged. Using a sample of SEOs, they find that the fees charged are on average higher than the theoretical value of the underwriting risk service, that is, they are higher than the value of the put. Hence, underwriters earn a net gain or premium (see also Chapter 6: Underwriting Costs and Compensation). The excess premium declines with issue size, volatility of returns (which raises the value of the put) and when the issue is shelf-registered. The excess premium increases with relative size of issue (i.e., new shares to total shares). When the authors factor the costs of carrying unsold securities into the overall cost of the underwriting risk service, they conclude that the excess underwriting premium becomes insignificant from an economic point of view.

Chen and Ritter (2000) note that over the 13-year period from 1985 to 1998, 91% of IPOs with proceeds in the $20 million to $80 million range carried gross spreads equal to 7%. Due to economies of scale, the average gross spread drops below 7% once proceeds exceed $80 million. In contrast, no such clustering of gross spreads is observed for SEOs. Chen and Ritter argue that the absence of variation of gross spreads across IPOs of different size of proceeds is evidence of inefficient pricing of the underwriting contract. Explanations they consider for the observed clustering include: avoidance of aggressive underwriter competition in terms of gross spreads; and reluctance to differentiate gross spreads according to the idiosyncratic features of each issue in preference for a less costly uniform compensation across issues. They also conjecture that other indirect issuance costs, like underpricing and market making may render issuers less sensitive to the lack of variation in gross spreads.

Hansen (2001) challenges the conclusions of the above study and proposes that underwriters can calibrate the cost of other ancillary services (pricing, market making, analyst coverage) so that the overall cost of their services is adequately compensated at a uniform 7% gross spread. In addition, by charging a uniform gross spread, the underwriter avoids disclosing the quality of an issue which could either adversely impact the valuation of weak issues or lead syndicate members to exert less marketing and placement effort on behalf of strong issues. Hansen finds that clustering at 7% is less prevalent for IPOs managed by top investment banks than less prestigious banks and clustering has increased in recent years despite increased competition due to the entry of commercial banks into underwriting. These developments are inconsistent with underwriter collusion. Gross spreads at 7% are also observed for many small IPOs which would cost more to the underwriter—a finding consistent with the view that the underwriter is indirectly compensated by offering fewer services in other areas. Hansen's estimates of predicted spreads fall above the 7% charge—a finding that does not support the presence of rents. Finally, Hansen finds that issues with a 7% gross spread are more difficult to value and place and are more heavily underpriced. Thus, by charging 7%, underwriters are still sufficiently compensated by reducing their costs through greater underpricing of the issue, as explained in Chapter 6: Underwriting Costs and Compensation. Kim, Palia, and Saunders (2010) confirm the complementarity of gross spreads and underpricing (or discount in the case of seasoned offerings) for large samples of IPOs and SEOs completed in the period 1980 to 2000.

Overall, the evidence shows that underwriting services are fairly priced and practices, like the 7% solution, are efficient compensation arrangements within a more complex set of services issuers receive from underwriting firms.

The Empirical Evidence on the Gross Spreads of IPOs

General Findings

Table 12.1 presents the average and median gross spreads of samples of IPOs reported in various studies. Median gross spreads exhibit less variability than average gross spreads and appear to vary within a narrow band around 7%. Same-study data on gross spreads reveal a downward trend in underwriting costs from the 1970s to the 2000s, which is more pronounced for average spreads. For example, Kim, Palia, and Saunders (2008) report that average (median) spreads were 8.24% (7.7%) in the 1975–1989 period but had declined to 6.60% (7%) in the years 1999–2004. This decline can be attributed to the entry of commercial banks into underwriting following various relaxations of the Glass–Steagall prohibitions.

Empirical Studies of Gross Spreads of IPOs

Several studies report gross spreads that exhibit economies of scale. In a comprehensive analysis of spreads, Lee, Lochhead, Ritter, and Zhang (1996) report an average gross spread

Table 12.1 Underwriting (Gross) Spreads of IPOs, SEOs and Debt Offers by Period—Various Studies

Study	Sample Period	IPOs Mean	IPOs Median	SEOs Mean	SEOs Median	Debt Offers Mean	Debt Offers Median	Notes
1960s								
Stoll (1976)	1967–1970			5.56				i
Stoll (1976)	1967–1970			6.17				ii
	Average			**5.87**				
1970s								
Kim, Palia, and Saunders (2003)	1970–1979	7.70	7.52	5.63	5.51	1.56	0.88	v
	Average	**7.70**	**7.52**	**5.63**	**5.51**	**1.56**	**0.88**	
1980s								
Kim, Palia, and Saunders (2008)	1975–1989	8.24	7.70	5.40	5.24			
Kim, Palia, and Saunders (2008)	1975–1988					1.18	0.88	v
Kim, Palia, and Saunders (2003)	1980–1989	7.91	7.27	5.52	5.24	1.75	0.88	v
Bae and Levy (1990)	1982–1985			4.76				
Denis (1993)	1982–1985			4.21	4.00			
Mola and Loughran (2004)	1986–1989			5.10				
	Average	**8.08**	**7.49**	**5.00**	**4.83**	**1.46**	**0.88**	
1990s								
Chen and Ritter (2000)	1995–1998	7.00						
Lee, Lochhead, Ritter, and Zhang (1996)	1990–1994	7.31		5.44		1.62		v
Lee, Lochhead, Ritter, and Zhang (1996)	1990–1994					2.92		vi
Altınkılıç and Hansen (2000)	1990–1997			5.38		1.09		v
Mola and Loughran (2004)	1990–1995			5.10				
Mola and Loughran (2004)	1996–1999			5.00				
Butler, Grullon, and Weston (2005)	1993–2000			4.80	5.00			
Kim, Palia, and Saunders (2003)	1990–1999	6.67	7.00	4.70	4.93	0.84	0.65	v
Kim, Palia, and Saunders (2008)	1990–1998	7.45	7.00	5.07	5.00			
Kim, Palia, and Saunders (2008)	1989–1998					0.94	0.65	v
Livingston and Miller (2000)	1990–1997	7.11				1.10		v
	Average	**7.11**	**7.00**	**5.07**	**4.98**	**1.42**	**0.65**	
2000s								
Kim, Palia, and Saunders (2008)	1999–2004	6.60	7.00	4.60	5.00	0.70	0.63	v
	Average	**6.60**	**7.00**	**4.60**	**5.00**	**0.70**	**0.63**	
Long periods								
Corwin (2003)	1980–1998			5.41				iv
Corwin (2003)	1980–1998			4.29				i
Corwin (2003)	1980–1998			5.86				Iii
Kim, Palia, and Saunders (2003)	1970–2000	7.83	7.00	5.74	5.48	1.29	0.75	v
Kim, Palia, and Saunders (2008)	1975–2004	7.62	7.00	5.08	5.00	0.88	0.65	v
Hansen (2001)	1980–1997	6.98						
Kim, Palia, and Saunders (2010)	1980–2000	7.43	7.00	5.46	5.26			
Huang and Zhang (2011)	1985–2004			5.29	5.25			
	Average	**7.47**	**7.00**	**5.30**	**5.25**	**1.09**	**0.70**	

Gross spread is calculated as a percentage of the offer price.

Notes: (i) NYSE, (ii) AMEX, (iii) Nasdaq, (iv) All, (v) Straight Bonds, (vi) Convertible Bonds.

of 9.05% for IPOs of less than $10 million of proceeds and a monotonic decline of gross spreads as proceeds rise. IPOs with proceeds in excess of $500 million had an average spread of 5.21%. Economies of scale are also present in the other direct costs (i.e., registration fee, printing, filing, legal and auditing fees). For small issues, and as percentage of proceeds, these expenses can be a substantial component of the total issuance costs. For example, they averaged 4.39% for issues that raised between $1 million and $20 million. There were no significant differences in gross spreads for various brackets of proceeds across industrial and utility firms.

Kim, Palia, and Saunders (2008) find that the gross spreads of IPOs (like those of SEOs and debt offers) are U-shaped, which is evidence of diseconomies of scale for very large issues, and are higher for issues with greater return volatility. Gross spreads decline with greater issuer profitability and size, higher underwriter reputation and the star power of the lead underwriter's analysts, and rise for issuers with higher preissue return volatility. Interestingly, IPO gross spreads are found to decline as the number of contemporaneous IPOs increases. Cook, Kieschnick, and Van Ness (2006) find that both total underwriter compensation and the selling fee increase with the amount of publicity (promotional effort) generated by the underwriting firm. Their IPO data show that the relationship of spreads and selling fees to size of proceeds exhibits evidence of significant economies of scale.

Evidence on the Components of Gross Spread of IPOs

As previously explained, the gross spread is comprised of the management fee (for the compensation of the managing group), the underwriting fee (for the compensation of the underwriting syndicate) and the selling fee (for the compensation of selling group). The customary split of the gross spread is 20% for management, 20% for underwriting, and 60% for selling.

Torstila (2001) finds that the actual distribution of the gross spread comes very close to this decomposition. In a large sample of IPOs completed in the 1990s, the average fees for management, underwriting, and selling are, respectively, 20.8%, 21.79% and 57.39%. Furthermore, these component fees display evidence of economies of scale, with the largest issues recording fees about 10% to 15% lower than those for very small issues. An interesting finding is the direct relationship of the selling fee to the gross spread which implies that as the total compensation rises the lead manager has more bargaining power to shift compensation dollars toward the component of which he/she captures the lion's share.

The Empirical Evidence on the Gross Spreads of SEOs

General Findings

Table 12.1 shows that there has been a downward trend in average and median gross spreads of SEOs over the past 40 years since the 1960s. Kim, Palia, and Saunders (2003) report that the average (median) gross spreads were 5.63% (5.51%) in the 1970s, 5.52% (5.24%) in the 1980s, and 4.7% (4.93%) in the 1990s. As in the case of IPOs, the declining gross spreads for SEOs can be explained by increased competition due to the entry of commercial banks.

Table 12.1 also shows that issues listed on the New York Stock Exchange (NYSE) enjoyed lower spreads than issues listed on the American Stock Exchange (AMEX) or Nasdaq (Stoll, 1976; Corwin, 2003).

Empirical Studies of Gross Spreads of SEOs

Like IPOs, SEO gross spreads also display evidence of economies of scale. Lee, Lochhead, Ritter, and Zhang (1996) report an average gross spread of 7.72% for SEOs that raised between $2 million and $10 million, and an average spread of 3.03% for SEOs that raised over $500 million. Similarly, other direct expenses ranged from 2.49% for issues that raised between $10 million and $20 million to 0.12% for issues that raised more than $500 million. Industrial firms were charged much higher gross spreads than utility firms. For example, to raise between $100 million and $200 million an industrial firm would pay, on average, a gross spread of 3.97% whereas a utility firm would pay 2.83%. Economies of scale for gross spreads of SEOs are also reported in Altınkılıç and Hansen (2000).

Kim, Palia, and Saunders (2008) find that gross spreads of SEOs increase with preissue return volatility and decline with greater issuing firm profitability and size, higher underwriter reputation, and analyst quality of the lead manager. Gross spreads have also been found to vary inversely with issuer size, share price, number of managers and vary positively with underwriter reputation (Butler, Grullon, and Weston, 2005). The same authors also document significant savings in gross spreads by firms with more liquid stocks. Liquidity reduces the trading costs of investors and market makers (including the lead manager) in the aftermarket, thus lowering the placement costs. Firms with very high stock liquidity pay on average 100 basis points less in fees than firms with very low liquidity. The liquidity effect on spreads is stronger for large issues which require greater placement effort. Lee and Masulis (2009) find evidence that issuers with poor-quality accruals pay higher underwriting spreads and have a higher probability of withdrawing the issue (which can also contribute to larger gross spreads).

The Empirical Evidence on the Gross Spreads of Debt Offerings

General Findings

Table 12.1 shows that issuers are charged much lower gross spreads for debt offers relative to IPOs and SEOs. The main reasons for the lower spreads are (1) the lower pricing risk of bond issues due to their overall lower price volatility and (2) the lower cost of placement because bond issues are mostly offered to institutional as opposed to many retail investors.

As with IPOs and SEOs, we notice a significant drop in gross spreads for debt offers over time. Kim, Palia, and Saunders (2003) report average (median) gross spreads of 1.56% (0.88%) in the 1970s and 0.84% (0.65%) in the 1990s. Gross spreads of debt issues have declined considerably following the entry of commercial banks into the debt underwriting business in 1989. Consistent with higher price volatility, convertible bond issuers are charged higher spreads than straight bond issuers.

Empirical Studies of Gross Spreads of Debt Offers

Debt offers also enjoy economies of scale with respect to gross spreads. Lee, Lochhead, Ritter, and Zhang (1996) report that in the years 1990–1994, the average gross spread ranged between 2.07% for straight debt offers raising between $2 million and $10 million and 1.39% for issues raising over $500 million. The corresponding values of average spread for convertible bond offers were 6.07% and 2%, respectively. Direct expenses also vary inversely with proceeds from over 2.3% to between 0.09% and 0.25% for straight and convertible bonds, respectively. There is also a clear pattern of rising average gross spreads as bond rating declines. Noninvestment grade bonds are charged significantly higher gross spreads than investment grade bonds with convertible noninvestment grade bond issuers paying gross spreads that approach those of SEOs.

Altınkılıç and Hansen (2000) find that gross spreads of straight bond issues vary inversely with bond quality (i.e., low rating bonds have greater spreads). The gross spreads are also found to exhibit economies of scale, but they tend to increase as issue proceeds rise relative to the issuer's equity value which is evidence of diseconomies of scale for relatively large issues. Livingston and Miller (2000) find that, after controlling for other factors, more prestigious underwriters charge lower gross spreads in nonconvertible bond offers. Kim, Palia, and Saunders (2008) find the gross spread of straight bond issues to vary directly with the preissue volatility of the issuer's stock return and bond maturity. The gross spread varies inversely, with underwriter reputation, issuer profitability, bond quality, issue size, analyst quality, and callability.

The Empirical Evidence on the Gross Spreads of Preferred Stock Issues

Bajaj, Mazumdar, and Sarin (2002) report that in the period 1980–1999, convertible preferred issues had an average gross spread of 4.76% versus 2.36% for straight preferred. Other flotation expenses averaged 2.22% and 0.44%, respectively. Gross spreads were found to be lower for utility firms than industrial firms. Gross spreads were inversely related to the firm's rating and the size of the issue (evidence of economies of scale). Investment grade straight preferred issues appeared to exhibit diseconomies of scale beyond a certain level of proceeds.

The International Evidence on Gross Spreads

Torstila (2003) reports average and median gross spreads of IPOs completed in various countries during the period 1986–1999. The average (median) spread is 2.5% (2.5%) in Southeast

Asia, 3.8% (4.0%) in Europe, 6.7% (6.5%) in Canada, and 7.5% (7.0%) in the United States. The lower gross spreads of IPOs executed in Asian and European countries can be explained by the less costly underwriting methods (i.e., subscription and auctions) used in those countries. There is also evidence that clustering, though not as pervasive as in the United States, is an international phenomenon. Clustering appears to be greater in Asian than European countries. IPO underwritings are also found to display economies of scale in gross spreads although the decline of spreads as size of proceeds rises is not as fast as in the United States. More extensive clustering is found in countries where spreads are lowest which casts doubt that clustering is the result of collusion among underwriters.

Ljungqvist, Jenkinson, and Wilhelm (2003) report statistics on gross spreads of IPOs completed in 65 countries during the period 1992−1999. For bookbuilt offers, the average gross spread is 4.43% in Europe, 4.10% in Asia-Pacific, 6.37% in Africa/Middle East, and 5.17% in North America (Canada, Mexico, and the United States). For fixed-price offers (subscription method), the average gross spread is 2.19% in Europe, 2.21% in Asia-Pacific, 2.19% in Africa/Middle East, and 5% in Canada. Gross spreads are, in general, higher if a US underwriter is in a top position of the syndicate than if not. US underwriters also charge higher gross spreads for US-listed IPOs than non-US-listed issues. If the IPO is not marketed to US investors, gross spreads are, in general, lower than those charged for IPOs marketed to US investors. Although bookbuilt issues have higher gross spreads than fixed-price offers, bookbuilt offerings are also less underpriced when managed by US underwriters and are marketed to US investors. Therefore, the higher gross spreads charged by US underwriters are justified by the superior marketing and placement effort of US underwriters due to their extensive investor networks.

Abrahamson, Jenkinson, and Jones (2011) use a more recent sample to compare the gross spreads of US and European bookbuilt IPOs completed in 1998−2007. During this period, the gross spread averaged 6.76% in the United States versus 3.76% in Europe. While clustering has trended up in the United States, relative to the earlier findings of Chen and Ritter (2000), it is quite rare in European IPOs. Both US and European IPOs show evidence of economies of scale in gross spreads. Adjusted for factors that affect gross spreads, European IPOs carry lower spreads than US IPOs. The discrepancy in gross spreads cannot be explained by differences in legal costs, fraction of retail placement, litigation risk, sell-side analysts, and underpricing. Thus, bookbuilt offers cost US issuers significantly more than what they cost European issuers. Part of the reason may be that underwriting competition in the United States has not been affected as much by the entry of European underwriters as competition has been affected in Europe by the entry of US underwriters.

13 ▦

International Offers: Mechanics and Performance

First, this chapter describes institutional features that are found in securities offerings in major foreign markets. This is followed by the review of empirical evidence on the price performance of new issues completed outside the United States. The chapter also presents evidence on foreign issues completed in the United States. Finally, the chapter concludes with an overview of equity offers conducted in privatization programs of state-owned enterprises.

New Issue Mechanics in Select Countries

Although placement methods, such as bookbuilding, fixed-price subscription, and auctions, are now commonly used in countries outside the United States, various features of these methods are different across national new issue markets.

European Offering Characteristics

Since the 1990s, European offerings have been adjusted to the bookbuilding method followed in the United States. The most notable features found in European offerings are listed below[1]:

- There is no quiet period and, hence, overt promotion during the preoffer period is commonly observed in European offerings.
- As a result, communications to investors start in the prefiling period. Both independent and affiliated analysts prepare valuation reports that they distribute to prospective investors.
- Communications take the form of exchanges of information through (1) one-on-one meetings of investors with the underwriter and the issuer; (2) roadshows; and (3) marketing efforts by the sales force of the underwriters directed towards investors.
- The price range is set after the underwriter has collected significant price-related information from informed investors, and it is followed by the circulation of a "pathfinder" prospectus. The price range is typically set at €2.
- Following the setting of the price range, a "when-issued" market usually emerges which helps the underwriters gauge market demand and adjust the final offer price accordingly.
- The final offer price is set after bookbuilding is over, and it is rarely set outside the price range—this happens only in 10% of offerings compared to 50% of offerings in the United States.

[1] The main sources of this information are Ritter (2003) and Jenkinson, Morrison, and Wilhelm (2006).

Underwriting Services and the New Issues Market. DOI: http://dx.doi.org/10.1016/B978-0-12-803282-4.00013-4

- Gross spreads are lower than in US offerings but offers placed through bookbuilding carry higher gross spreads.

Offering Methods in the United Kingdom

A firm can enter the public markets by simply listing its stock on the Main Market or the Alternative Investment Market of the London Stock Exchange. This is called "introduction." Following its introduction, the firm can execute a public offer, which is in essence an initial public offering. The advantage of this two-stage access to capital markets is that the stock establishes a record of market prices that provides a reliable basis for the stock's valuation when the public sale takes place (Derrien and Kecskés, 2007).

Following the introduction of general cash (in addition to rights) offerings in 1986, new issues can be executed in one of two offering methods. The first is a fixed-price subscription method. The second is "placing," which resembles a firm commitment contract in the United States but without the benefit of bookbuilding (Levis, 1993). In a placing, the underwriter purchases the new shares at a fixed-price, net of underwriting fees, and then offers them at an offer price to investors, usually financial institutions. The absence of presale marketing and investor-assisted price discovery implies that the value of the new issue is primarily certified by the underwriter. This has two important consequences. First, it is mostly large, known, and sound firms that can be matched with underwriters for the execution of an offering through placing. Second, the higher issuer quality and the stronger commitment as well as value certification by the underwriter serve as positive signals about the firm's prospects.

Offering Methods in France

Initial public offerings (IPOs) in France may be conducted as fixed-price subscription offerings; as auctions; or, after 1993, as bookbuilt offers. In fixed-price offerings, the offer price is negotiated between the underwriter and the issuer and set 1 week before trading starts. The day before the offer, investors place orders specifying the number of shares at the fixed-price. Allocation of new shares is done on a pro rata basis.

In auctions, a minimum (reservation) price is set by the underwriter and the issuer 1 week before the IPO date. The day before the offer, investors place sealed bids with the Society of French Exchanges (SBF). The underwriter and the issuer negotiate with the SBF in order to choose the offer price that is common to all bidders (uniform price auction). Also, a maximum price is chosen, and bids above this price are dropped. This is done to discourage investors from placing high and unrealistic bids to increase the likelihood of participation in the allocation. Bidders who place orders between the offer price and the maximum price receive shares on a pro rata basis. If demand is too high, the placement is postponed, and the offer is changed to a fixed-price offering.

In all offerings, a call market system is used to set the opening price in the aftermarket. If the market price exceeds (usually by 10%) the offer price, the call market procedure is repeated the next business day starting at the higher clearing price (Degeorge, Derrien, and Womack, 2007).

Offering Methods in Germany

Bookbuilding has become the dominant offering method in Germany since 1995. However, as in France, issuers also employ hybrid offerings that combine bookbuilding with a fixed-price subscription. In contrast to the bookbuilding process in the United States, underwriters can enter into communications with investors before setting the price range. Following European practice, the price range is almost never amended, and setting the final offer price outside the price range is rare. Prior to the formal offer, when-issued shares can be traded in a "gray market" (Aussenegg, Pichler, and Stomper, 2006).

Offering Methods in Japan

Before 1973, equity capital was raised almost exclusively through rights offerings with the exercise price set at the par value of the stock. Underwritten public offerings became popular after 1969 and were conducted under a fixed-price subscription method. However, due to the early pricing of the issue and the pricing formula applied, IPOs were heavily underpriced. For example, Pettway and Kaneko (1996) estimated the average underpricing to be 62% for IPOs placed under such pricing schemes.

A hybrid auction and fixed-price system was adopted in 1989. Under this arrangement, 50% of the issue is offered by auction, and the remainder 50% is offered at a fixed offer price through a subscription. The auction process starts with a minimum price determined as in the older regime. Next, a preliminary or "first revised" prospectus with firm- and issue-related details (but no price indication) is distributed to investors. This is followed by a "second revised" prospectus that includes the minimum price for acceptable bids. Shares are allocated starting with the highest bidder and continuing until the auction tranche of the auction has been allocated. Final prices to investors are set according to a discriminatory auction system, i.e., investors pay what they bid. The auction bids are limited to 5,000 shares; hence, the incentive to produce information in order to profit from possibly buying underpriced issues is severely curtailed. Once the auction is over, another prospectus is circulated with an offer price not higher than the average of the successful bids and not lower than the minimum permissible bid. A 5,000-share limit applies to the public offering segment as well. In addition, insiders are prevented from participating in the auction or public tranche of the offer.

The discriminatory auction system was discontinued after 1997 and was replaced by the bookbuilding method. Similar to the US practice, the underwriter has great discretion in pricing and allocating the new issue. The underwriter first circulates a preliminary prospectus with an indicative price set prior to any marketing efforts. This is followed by a "first revised" prospectus which includes a price range based on information gathered during the roadshow. The offer price is announced in a "second revised" prospectus (Kutsuna and Smith, 2004). There is no rule regarding the price range. However, the updated price range in the "first revised" prospectus is binding on the offer price, in the sense that the final price cannot exceed the upper bound of that range. To avoid having to sell at a minimum price that is too low relative to the eventual market value of the new issue, underwriters set very broad price ranges.

In Japanese offerings, the effective day is when the "second revised" prospectus is issued. Aftermarket trading begins only after all or most of the issue has been placed. Since 2002, Japanese offerings can have an overallotment option (Kutsuna, Smith, and Smith, 2009). Overall, the Japanese issuance process is more similar to the European version of the book-building arrangement than its US version.

Offering Methods in China

In China, the volume of new issues every year is set by a three-party authority (the State Council Securities Committee, the State Planning Commission, and the People's Bank of China). This constrains the supply of shares and leads to inflated prices. The determination of offer prices follows various regulatory guidelines and restrictions although more recent reforms have allowed pricing to be more in tune with market fundamentals. Still though, offer prices fall well below the fair market values of the new issues. In fixed-price issues, offer prices are set well in advance of the subscription period and listing takes place months after the offer. Therefore, the waiting and pricing risks are quite high. New issue auctions were introduced in early 2000s (Chan, Wang, and Wei, 2003) and bookbuilding in 2005 (Song, Tan, and Yi, 2014). The bookbuilding approach comprises two stages: the pre-liminary inquiry and the accumulated bidding inquiry. The preliminary inquiry serves to set the price range, whereas the accumulated bidding inquiry serves to set the final offer price. Since 2012, all firms can choose to conduct an accumulated bidding inquiry (Song, Tan, and Yi, 2014).

IPO pricing reforms in June 2009 further improved the bookbuilding approach. However, China's regulators have yet to thoroughly adopt the market-based IPO pricing approach used in developed markets and continue to control IPO pricing through "window guidance" (Song, Tan, and Yi, 2014). As of May 2012, "window guidance" implies the offer price be set so that "the IPO firm's P/E multiple may not exceed 25% of the average P/E multiple of the firm's industry peers."

Most participants in China's stock market are individual investors, who are often prone to applying speculative rather than value-driven investment criteria. As a result, stock prices in China are easily influenced by investor sentiment. The strong investor interest in new issues, fueled by the anticipation of high initial returns, results in very few placement failures. Therefore, the underpricing of Chinese offerings is not the result of deliberate undervaluation observed in developed markets in response to the adverse selection problem (Song, Tan, and Yi, 2014).

Offering Methods in India

Bookbuilding was introduced in India in 2003. Since 2006, the Indian IPO bookbuilding process has enjoyed extraordinary transparency as both the timing and subscription pattern for the different investor groups are observable and frequently updated on the stock exchange's website. At the close of each day during bookbuilding, the website shows the cumulative bids for all categories of investors at their respective prices. Furthermore, since May 2007, new issue regulations have required all IPOs be graded by at least one credit rating agency. Grades are intended to provide potential investors with an independent, reliable, and consistent assessment of the fundamentals of the IPO firm.

The allocation of shares to investor classes is predefined. Institutional investors (known as qualified institutional buyers or QIBs) are allocated no more than 50% of the offered shares. Noninstitutional investors, defined as individuals bidding for more than Indian Rupee (INR) 100,000, are allocated 15% of the offered shares. Retail investors, who can invest up to a maximum of INR 100,000, have to be allocated no less than 35% of the offered shares (Khurshed, Paleari, Pande, and Vismara, 2014).

The Initial Price Performance of Non-US IPOs

The underpricing phenomenon is widely observed in many national stock markets. Surveys of international studies in Loughran, Ritter, and Rydqvist (1994) and Ritter (2003) provide extensive evidence of IPO underpricing around the world. The underpricing phenomenon appears to hold across various offering methods and regulatory and legal systems. However, the degree of underpricing varies considerably across national markets. For example, in the more recent survey of Ritter (2003), a sample of Chinese IPOs completed in the 1990s had the highest average initial returns (256%) whereas a sample of Danish IPOs completed in the 1980s and 1990s had the lowest average initial return (5.4%).

Table 13.1 expands the international evidence on IPO underpricing by reporting findings from more recent studies. The table excludes new issues executed in the United States. We notice that IPOs executed in various European countries are, in general, less underpriced than IPOs executed in other regions of the world, especially in China. In all cases, underpricing appears to be more severe when the IPO initial returns are adjusted for the stock market movement between the offer day and the day of the first available market price of the IPO stock.

Below, we review studies from various national markets that highlight the implications of the institutional arrangements on the pricing of stocks sold in initial public offerings.

European Offers

Although European IPOs are underpriced relatively less than IPOs conducted in other parts of the world, we still observe significant differences in mean and median initial returns across European national markets (see Table 13.1). Crosscountry variation of underpricing is also reported in studies that analyze European IPO markets during the same period.

One such study is Jenkinson, Morrison, and Wilhelm (2006) that examines the initial price performance of IPOs completed in eight European countries during the 1990s. They report an overall average initial return of 22.3%, with German IPOs recording the highest average initial return (47.5%) and Swedish IPOs recording a negative average initial return (−2.2%),

Table 13.1   Initial Returns of IPOs Outside the US—Various Studies

Study	Country	Sample Period	Raw Returns		Market-Adjusted Returns	
			Mean	Median	Mean	Median
Europe						
Akyol, Cooper, Meoli, and Vismara (2014)	Europe (before EUGC)	1998–2012	18.70			
Akyol, Cooper, Meoli, and Vismara (2014)	Europe (after EUGC)					
Jakobsen and Sorensen (2001)	Denmark	1998–2013	14.30			
Vismara, Signori, and Paleari (2015)	France, Germany, and Italy	1984–1992	3.90			
Thomadakis, Nounis, and Gounopoulos (2012)	Greece	1999–2013	9.64	2.09		
Thomadakis, Gounopoulos, Nounis, and Merikas (2016)	Greece	1994–2002	52.48	22.51	38.94	14.14
Bertoni and Giudici (2014)	Italy	1990–2013	12.10	3.22	52.15	24.27
Hoque and Lasfer (2015)	United Kingdom	1997–2012	22.50	9.90		
Brennan and Franks (1997)	United Kingdom	1999–2006	25.73	4.76	9.52	10.01
Puri and Rocholl (2008)	Germany	1986–1989	22.27	2.80		
Kaustia and Knüpfer (2008)	Finland	1997–2004	24.70	12.40		
Derrien and Kecskés (2007)	United Kingdom	1995–2000	19.00	8.70		
Chambers and Dimson (2009)	United Kingdom	1995–2004				
Bouzouita, Gajewski, and Gresse (2015)	Euronext Paris	1987–2007			2.80	0.05
Lyn and Zychowicz (2003)	Hungary	1995–2008			15.12	13.62
Lyn and Zychowicz (2003)	Poland	1991–1998			54.45	28.28
Aussenegg, Pichler, and Stomper (2006)	Germany	1991–1998	46.98	19.46		
Kiymaz (2000)	Turkey	1999–2000			13.10	
Degeorge, Derrien, and Womack (2007)	France[a]	1990–1996	20.57	8.94		
Degeorge, Derrien, and Womack (2007)	France[b]	1993–1998	15.93	7.69		
		Average	**22.06**	**9.32**	**26.58**	**15.06**
China						
Chan, Wang, and Wei (2004)	China[c]	1993–1998	177.80		175.40	
Chan, Wang, and Wei (2004)	China[c]	1999–2001	107.50		104.70	
Chan, Wang, and Wei (2004)	China[d]	1993–1998	11.60		13.20	
Chan, Wang, and Wei (2004)	China[d]	1999–2001	32.60		38.50	
Su (2004)	China[c]	1994–1999	128.20			
Kao, Wu, and Yang (2009)	China	1996–1999	134.00	117.00		
Chi, Wang, and Young (2010)	China	1996–2002	131.86	128.16	131.69	119.36
Deng and Zhou (2015)	China	2009–2012	34.41	25.24		

Study	Country	Period				
Cao, Tang, and Yuan (2013)	China	2009–2010	50.17			
Chen, Shi, and Xu (2014)	China	2004–2012	61.30			
Hao, Shi, and Yang (2014)	China	2004–2011	74.85			
Güçbilmez (2014)	China	2009–2012	33.44	29.25		
Liu, Uchida, and Gao (2014)	China	1997–2009			123.02	103.80
Song, Tan, and Yi (2014)	China	2006–2011	66.30	40.50		
Chen, Wang, Li, Sun, and Tong (2015)	China	1999–2007			127.00	104.69
Wang, Cao, Liu, Tang, and Tian (2015)	China	2002–2010	79.30	52.41	78.84	51.67
		Average	**80.24**	**65.43**	**99.04**	**94.88**
Asia (excluding China)						
Chang, Chen, Kao, and Wu (2014)	Hong Kong	2006–2010	12.71	6.12		
Khurshed, Paleari, Pande, and Vismara (2014)	India	1999–2011			24.60	13.60
Brooks, Mathew, and Yang (2014)	India	2007–2012	85.51	16.23	82.37	16.58
Sun, Uchida, and Matsumoto (2013)	Japan	1998–2006	70.50	34.30		
Kutsuna, Smith, and Smith (2009)	Japan	1997–2003	25.50	13.40		
Kutsuna and Smith (2004)	Japan[a]	1995–1999	70.81	20.00		
Kutsuna and Smith (2004)	Japan[b]	1995–1999	7.12	3.77		
Beckman, Garner, Marshall, and Okamura (2001)	Japan	1980–1998	31.50	18.40		
Kaneko and Pettway (2003)	Japan[a]	1993–2001	48.00			
Kaneko and Pettway (2003)	Japan[b]	1993–2001	11.40			
Ahmad-Zaluki, Campbell, and Goodacre (2007)	Malaysia	1990–2000	95.20	76.50		
Mohd Rashid, Abdul-Rahim, and Yong (2014)	Malaysia	2000–2012	29.44	34.00		
Chang, Chen, Kao, and Wu (2014)	Taiwan	2006–2010	50.60			
Firth (1997)	New Zealand	1979–1987			25.87	21.93
Lee, Taylor, and Walter (1999)	Singapore	1973–1992	31.73	20.52		
da Silva Rosa, Velayuthen, and Walter (2003)	Australia	1991–1993	25.43	12.00		
Sullivan and Unite (2001)	Philippines	1987–1997	22.69			
		Average	**41.21**	**23.20**	**44.28**	**17.37**

EUGC: EU Governance Code.
[a] Sample of bookbuilt offers.
[b] Sample of auctioned offers.
[c] Sample of A shares.
[d] Sample of B shares.

which is evidence of overpricing. In contrast, during the same period, IPOs executed in the United States had realized average initial returns of 25.2%. The study finds that the price range of European IPOs is very informative of the value of the IPO as final offer prices are rarely set outside the price range. The reliability of the price range as an estimator of the fair value of the issue is also evinced by the preponderance of strike bids (only quantity indications) as the more price-informative limit and step bids are less necessary. However, another study of European IPOs (Jenkinson and Jones, 2004) presents evidence that the preponderance of the strike bids can be attributed to the reluctance of institutional investors to submit more informative types of bids.

A similar study of European IPOs executed between 1995 and 2002 finds an average underpricing of 21.48% across 12 European markets (Cornelli, Goldreich, and Ljungqvist, 2006). The highest underpricing (average initial return of 74.6%) is observed in the sample of Finnish IPOs, whereas samples from two countries (Austria and Greece) show evidence of overpricing.

Cornelli, Goldreich, and Ljungqvist (2006) also find evidence that investor sentiment— manifested in gray market prices—affects the degree of underpricing. When gray market prices reflect overoptimism, lead underwriters set offer prices higher. In contrast, when gray market prices are low, underwriters rely more on informed investor indications to set offer prices. Overoptimistic gray markets are found to be associated with negative long-run price reversals.

Evidence consistent with the influence of ex ante risk and information asymmetry on IPO pricing is provided in a study of UK IPOs by Derrien and Kecskés (2007). They find that firms which first introduce (list) their shares into the public market and later conduct an IPO experience average (median) price discounts (from last trading price) of 13.9% (10%) and average (median) initial returns of 11.9% (11.3%). Average (median) initial returns of issues with direct (no introduction first) IPOs are, in contrast, 24.7% (12.4%). Thus, the two-stage system affords first-time issuers the informational advantage observed in seasoned equity offerings (SEOs). Introduction is preferred during periods of cold markets, whereas the direct IPO method is preferred in hot markets because it avoids the delay imposed by listing the stock first through introduction.

Chambers and Dimson (2009) take a long view on the performance of UK IPOs by studying the period from World War I to 2007. They find that average underpricing (on an equally-weighted basis) was 8.04% between 1917 and 1945; 12.09% in 1946–1986; and 19% after the deregulation of 1986. They attribute the higher underpricing of more recent IPOs to higher litigation risk and the importance of underwriting reputation rather than to changes in the composition of issuing firms.

Degeorge, Derrien, and Womack (2007) report that during the 1990s, bookbuilding took hold in France and eventually prevailed over the auction method in spite of the auction method's potential to produce more efficient pricing and the evidence of greater underpricing in bookbuilt offers. They attribute the appeal of bookbuilding to the involvement of affiliated analysts who tend to provide favorable coverage to the issuing firms. The analysts of unaffiliated underwriters are "recruited" through favorable allocations of new issues by lead underwriters. The heavier concentration of favorable analyst recommendations in bookbuilt offers compared to auctioned offers cannot be explained by differences in issue quality or better long-run price performance. Bouzouita, Gajewski, and Gresse (2015) also find that the degree of underpricing in French IPOs is higher the greater the analyst coverage and the more liquid the IPO shares are in the aftermarket.

Aussenegg, Pichler, and Stomper (2006) examine German IPOs executed as hybrid (bookbuilt and fixed-price) offers to evaluate the impact of the preoffer when-issued (gray) markets in 1999–2000. They find that offer prices are strongly influenced by the when-issued market prices. Initial returns are much higher for constrained issues in which the offer price must equal the maximum price of the range or the last gray market price. There is no evidence of partial price adjustment since the gray market replaces bookbuilding as a source of preoffer information about the market demand for new issues.

Keloharju (1993) analyzes Finnish IPOs offered through the subscription method in the 1980s. Although IPOs are on average underpriced, Keloharju finds that investors who bid for and receive larger allocations earn negative returns consistent with the winner's curse hypothesis. Kaustia and Knüpfer (2008) find that investors in Finnish IPOs exhibit behavior consistent with reinforcement (or momentum) learning. That is, the higher the returns investors have earned on past IPOs the more likely it is they will participate in future IPOs.

Japanese Offers

As shown in Table 13.1, studies that analyze the initial returns of Japanese IPOs find that underpricing is higher under the bookbuilding method than a hybrid method comprising fixed-price subscription and auction (Kaneko and Pettway, 2003; Kutsuna and Smith, 2004). Kaneko and Pettway (2003), in particular, find an average initial return of 48% for bookbuilt IPOs and 11.4% for auction offers, respectively. The higher underpricing of bookbuilt IPOs is due to underwriters' setting the upper bound of the price range too low which amounts to low-balling the price range. However, Kutsuna and Smith (2004) find that bookbuilding allows good-quality firms to separate themselves and attain better valuation than if only auctions were allowed. Therefore, accounting for total issuance costs and firm characteristics, Kutsuna and Smith conclude that bookbuilding is a more efficient method to raise capital for larger and better established firms.

Kutsuna, Smith, and Smith (2009) find evidence that part of the underpricing in bookbuilt offers is the result of implicit agreements among issuers, underwriters, and investors to constrain the offer price within the initial filing range even when market information is positive. The constraint is particularly harmful to issuers when public (market) information is positive in the preoffer period and could have resulted in higher offer prices.

Chinese Offers

Table 13.1 reveals that Chinese IPOs are heavily underpriced. The studies included in Table 13.1 show an average (raw) initial return of 80.24% and an average (market-adjusted) initial return of 99.04%. A large part of this underpricing can be explained by the heavy participation of retail (individual) investors in the Chinese IPO market. As found in other national markets (e.g., the United States and Europe), retail investor sentiment is mostly responsible for pushing up the aftermarket prices of IPO stocks. Retail investor participation also explains the higher underpricing of IPOs of A-shares (predominantly owned and traded by Chinese nationals) compared to the lower underpricing of IPOs of B-shares (predominantly owned and traded by foreign nationals).

The difference in underpricing between IPOs of A-and B-shares, respectively, is well documented in Chan, Wang, and Wei (2004). They find that IPOs of A-shares issued in the Shanghai and Shenzhen stock exchanges during 1993–1998 realized average initial returns of 177.8% (raw) and 175.4% (after adjusting for market movement between offer and listing). IPOs of B-shares experienced average underpricing of 11.6% (in raw returns) and 13.2% (in market-adjusted returns). The lower underpricing of the B-share IPOs can be explained by the participation of more sophisticated foreign investors and the considerably shorter interval between offer and listing.

Su (2004) also documents high positive initial returns for A-share IPOs which, however, have declined from a high average initial return of 314.5% in 1994 to 56.4% in 1999. Underpricing is related to ex ante risk factors, and it is higher for firms that raise larger proceeds in follow-on SEOs. Interestingly, there is no relationship between time to trading and degree of underpricing. Follow-on SEOs are more likely when post-IPO market values rise (as predicted by the market-feedback hypothesis) than higher IPO underpricing (as predicted by signaling theories).

The Long-Run Price Performance of Non-US IPOs

As in the United States, stock issues placed through initial public offerings in national markets outside the United States are, in general, associated with negative long-run returns. Loughran, Ritter, and Rydqvist (1994) present evidence from eight non-US IPO markets that include sample periods between 1970 and 1990. In all but three of these samples, IPO stocks realized negative long-run buy-and-hold abnormal returns. Brazilian IPOs realized the worst performance (−47.0%) and Japanese IPOs the best (+9.0%).

Table 13.2 provides additional evidence on the long-run return performance of IPOs completed in different regions of the world. Inspection of the but-and-hold abnormal returns (BHARs) reported in Table 13.2 reveals wide variation of long-run performance across samples, even from within the same country. The worst (most negative) BHARs are reported for samples of IPOs from Brazil, China, and Denmark; whereas the highest BHARs are reported for samples from China and France.

Table 13.2 also reports evidence on long-run price performance measured by cumulative abnormal returns (CARs). Adjusted by local stock market indexes, the IPO long-run stock returns are mostly negative. The lowest mean (median) CAR of −58.05% (−57.45%) is reported for a sample of Chinese IPOs completed in 1999–2007. The highest CAR (with a mean of 9.60%) is also realized by a sample of Chinese IPOs conducted in 1996–2002. With

Table 13.2 Long-Run Stock Return Performance of International IPOs

Study	Country	Sample Period	Adjusted Return		Benchmark Portfolio	Horizon (years)	Weight of Returns
			Mean	Median			
PANEL A: Buy-and-Hold Abnormal Returns (BHARs)							
Benchmark: Market Index							
Thomadakis, Nounis, and Gounopoulos (2012)	Greece	1994–2002	−37.56	−22.69	ASE Index	3	VW
Jakobsen and Sorensen (2001)	Denmark	1984–1992	−13.40		CSE Index	3	VW
Jakobsen and Sorensen (2001)	Denmark	1984–1992	−26.60		CSE Index	5	VW
Vismara, Signori, Paleari (2015)	France, Germany, and Italy	1999–2013	−3.84	−18.23	Corresponding Indices	3	EW
Stehle, Ehrhardt, and Przyborowsky (2000)	Germany	1960–1992	1.54			3	VW
Chi, Wang, and Young (2010)	China	1996–2002	16.60		SSSE A-share Index	3	EW
Song, Tan, and Yi (2014)	China	2006–2011	4.10	−7.90	SSSE Index	3	EW
Chen, Shi, and Xu (2014)	China	2004–2012	−8.90		SSSE Index	1	EW
Kutsuna, Smith, and Smith (2009)	Japan	1997–2003	−34.40	−15.50	JASDAQ	1	EW
Ahmad-Zaluki, Campbell, and Goodacre (2007)	Malaysia	1990–2000	−14.23		KLSE Composite Index	3	EW
Aggarwal, Leal, and Hernandez (1993)	Brazil	1980–1990	−47.00	−76.60	BOVESPA	3	EW
Aggarwal, Leal, and Hernandez (1993)	Chile	1980–1990	−23.70	−31.80	IGPA	3	EW
Aggarwal, Leal, and Hernandez (1993)	Mexico	1980–1990	−19.60	−38.90	IPC	3	EW
Benchmark: Matched Control Firms							
Jakobsen and Sorensen (2001)	Denmark	1984–1992	−33.00		MV	3	VM
Jakobsen and Sorensen (2001)	Denmark	1984–1992	−12.30		MV	5	VM
Jeanneret (2005)	France	1993–2001	−4.44	−0.01	BM, Ind	3	EW
Jeanneret (2005)	France	2001–2010	6.43	−8.77	BM, Ind	3	EW
Hoque and Lasfer (2015)	United Kingdom	1999–2006	−18.30		MV, MB	3	EW
Chan, Wang, and Wei (2004)	China	1993–1998	−19.77		MV, MB	3	EW
Wang, Cao, Liu, Tang, and Tian (2015)	China	2002–2010	−25.42	−30.63	MV, Ind	3	EW
Sun, Uchida, and Matsumoto (2013)	Japan	1998–2006	−12.40	−28.20	MV, Ind	3	EW

(Continued)

Table 13.2 (Continued)

Study	Country	Sample Period	Adjusted Return		Benchmark Portfolio	Horizon (years)	Weight of Returns
			Mean	Median			
Ahmad-Zaluki, Campbell, and Goodacre (2007)	Malaysia	1990–2000	−2.01		MV	3	EW
Ahmad-Zaluki, Campbell, and Goodacre (2007)	Malaysia	1990–2000	−10.21		MV	3	VW
PANEL B: Cumulative Abnormal Returns (CARs)							
Benchmark: Market Index							
Thomadakis, Nounis, and Gounopoulos (2012)	Greece	1994–2002	−16.18		ASE Index	3	VW
Jakobsen and Sorensen (2001)	Denmark	1984–1992	−16.10		CSE Index	3	VW
Jakobsen and Sorensen (2001)	Denmark	1984–1992	−25.90		CSE Index	5	VW
Chi, Wang, and Young (2010)	China	1996–2002	9.60		SSSE A-share Index	3	EW
Chen, Wang, Li, Sun, and Tong (2015)	China	1999–2007	−58.05	−57.45	SSSE Index	3	EW
Ahmad-Zaluki, Campbell, and Goodacre (2007)	Malaysia	1990–2000	0.75		KLSE Composite Index	3	EW
Levis (1993)	United Kingdom	1980–1988	−22.96		All Share Index	3	EW
Keloharju (1993)	Finland	1984–1989	−26.40		HSE	3	EW
Benchmark: Matched Control Firms							
Jakobsen and Sorensen (2001)	Denmark	1984–1992	−32.80		MV	3	VM
Jakobsen and Sorensen (2001)	Denmark	1984–1992	−31.80		MV	5	VM
Hoque and Lasfer (2015)	United Kingdom	1999–2006	−26.10		MV, MB	3	EW
Kao, Wu, and Yang (2009)	China	1996–1999	−24.00		MV	3	EW
Wang, Cao, Liu, Tang, and Tian (2015)	China	2002–2010	−15.13	−18.42	MV, Ind	3	EW
Ahmad-Zaluki, Campbell, and Goodacre (2007)	Malaysia	1990–2000	0.43		MV	3	EW
Ahmad-Zaluki, Campbell, and Goodacre (2007)	Malaysia	1990–2000	−8.16		MV	3	EW

MV is market value of equity; BM is the book-to-market value of equity ratio; MB is the market-to-book value of equity ratio. EW: BHARs or CARs are equally-weighted; VW: BHARs or CARs are value-weighted.

a few exceptions, all matching firm-adjusted CARs are negative. By that benchmark, the worst performers are Danish IPOs completed in 1984−1992. The best performance (a mean CAR of 0.43%) is realized by a sample of Malaysian IPOs completed in 1990−2000.

International US Firm Offerings

Many large, especially multinational, US firms choose to tap the international markets to raise funds. In their study of international SEOs by US firms, Chaplinsky and Ramchand (2000) report that issuers benefit from expanded investor base and greater demand of shares that generate more favorable (albeit still negative) stock price reaction than in the case of domestic issues. The better announcement returns they find for US international issues are not offset by higher underwriter spreads and other expenses or by adverse price movements during the offering period. International issues are also found to coincide with strong US equity markets, which implies that going abroad is not motivated by poor domestic conditions.

Wu and Kwok (2002) argue that US firms raising equity internationally benefit from a risk premium reduction and expansion of investor base; reduced asymmetric information and adverse selection problems due to higher quality; and the exploitation of windows of opportunity. They also find less negative price reaction for international than domestic issues announced by US firms. International issues of US firms also generate less negative abnormal long-run returns than domestic issues. Both Chaplinsky and Ramchand (2000) and Wu and Kwok (2002) find that international offerings by US firms are charged lower gross spreads than domestic issues—around 4% compared to over 5% for domestic issues.

Foreign Firm Issues in the United States

Bruner, Chaplinsky, and Ramchand (2004) analyze foreign firm IPOs completed in the United States between 1991 and 1999 through an American Depository Receipt (ADR) or ordinary shares listing. IPOs by foreign firms are larger than domestic firm IPOs both in issuer asset size and relative issue size. Nonetheless because many foreign issuers come from high country risk markets, they need more certification. That explains why most of foreign issues list on the New York Stock Exchange (NYSE). The study finds that foreign firm issues are less underpriced than US domestic issues (irrespective of size) and carry slightly lower gross spreads; however, the differences become (statistically) insignificant once other factors are accounted. Issues of emerging market firms have higher initial returns, whereas the conduct of simultaneous offers in multiple markets reduces initial returns and gross spread for foreign as well as US issuers.

Chen, Fauver, and Yang (2009) study samples of IPOs and SEOs that were listed in the United States as ADRs between 1980 and 2004. The overwhelming majority of ADR IPOs and SEOs list on the NYSE. The study finds that both ADR IPOs and SEOs carry average and median gross spreads that are lower than those for comparable US offerings. Likewise, average and median initial returns are lower for ADR IPOs, whereas those of ADR SEOs are equivalent to the average and median returns of US domestic issues. Due to less asymmetric information, ADR IPOs with a prior listing have lower gross spreads and initial returns than those without.

Chaplinsky and Ramchand (2000) analyze the reoffering yield spreads of debt offers placed by foreign firms in the US public and private markets (Rule 144A) in 1991–1997. They find that the 144A market has become the market of choice for lower quality foreign issuers, many of them from developing countries. Unlike domestic US issuers in the 144A market, foreign issuers do not subsequently apply for registration with the Securities and Exchange Commission (SEC) because the reporting and disclosure costs are deemed too high. The study finds that whereas foreign investment grade debt placed in the private market carries higher reoffering yield spreads than if placed in the public market, the reverse is true in the case of foreign high-yield (high risk) debt. This signifies the greater efficiency of private markets in pricing riskier and more informationally challenged debt issues. Within the sample of investment grade bonds, foreign issues of lower bond rating and from emerging market countries carry higher yield spreads. Finally, the study finds that borrowing costs (i.e., yield spreads) have declined since the inception of the Rule 144A market in 1991.

Privatization Issues

The capital market liberalization in Western Europe in the mid-1980s, followed by the transition of the Soviet Block countries to free market economies as well as China's capital market liberalization in the early 1990s, triggered an unprecedented wave of privatizations of state-owned enterprises (SOEs) across the globe. One study reports that between 1977 and 2000 state governments had conducted 2,457 privatization issues worth $1.2 trillion (Megginson, Nash, Netter, and Poulsen, 2004).

Privatization of state-owned enterprises refers to the sale of whole or partial equity stakes in the capital markets or to strategic investors and turning the partial or total control of the firm to private owners. Share issue privatizations (SIPs) have been conducted through auctions, fixed-price sales, bookbuilding, and private placements. Governments are more likely to choose an SIP program when local capital markets are less developed, level of income equality is greater, there is greater investor protection, and the larger and more profitable the SOEs are. Also, governments prefer to execute SIPs in hot markets (Megginson, Nash, Netter, and Poulsen, 2004).

In structuring a SIP program, a government must decide (1) whether to sell the entire equity at once or in stages; (2) which offer method to use and how to set the offer price; and (3) how to allocate the shares among different classes of prospective investors. Closely related to these decisions are the political and economic objectives of the government that initiates the SIP program. Some of the most common stated objectives of privatization programs have been: (1) the development and spreading of share ownership; (2) the development of capital markets; (3) the improvement of the economic performance of the privatized enterprises; and (4) the raising of funds.

Early studies of privatization programs revealed two patterns: (1) the gradual sale of equity stakes and (2) severe underpricing that often exceeded the degree of underpricing observed in private firm IPOs. Perotti and Guney (1993) presented early evidence that many countries (including the United Kingdom, France, Spain, and Turkey) had adopted privatization-in-stages programs. Although auctions of public shares had produced little underpricing, most privatization programs were conducted through a fixed-price offering method that resulted in extensive underpricing. Interestingly, the degree of underpricing of privatization issues exceeded on average that of private firm offerings despite the fact that privatized state-owned enterprises were older, better known, and operated in the utility services sector that traditionally has more predictable cash flows. Therefore, the informational asymmetry arguments could not explain the pricing experience of privatization issues.

Perotti (1995) uses a confidence-building paradigm to explain these patterns. If a state chooses to sell the whole equity at once and transfer control to private owners, investors may be concerned that state policies, following the sale of public enterprises, could affect the payoffs to private owners. Therefore, investors would be reluctant to pay the full fair value of the shares. This concern is most relevant in industries like utilities, whose future cash flows can be affected by government policies (e.g., taxes, fees, regulation, etc.). Therefore, an investor must weigh the likelihood of state commitment to arms-length policies against the likelihood of populist policies. Given this investor conundrum, a state can maximize the proceeds from a privatization program by adopting a partial sales program. The government signals its commitment to arms-length policies by accepting deep price discounts (i.e., underpricing) in the early privatization stages. As investor confidence that the state will not engage in cash flow capturing from privatized enterprises rises, investors are willing to pay higher offer prices to buy equity stakes offered in later stages of the privatization program. Thus, the confidence-building hypothesis derives the following predictions:

- Committed governments prefer to privatize gradually.
- Committed governments underprice their privatization shares in the early stages of the SIP program.
- The greater the potential for redistributive policies, the lower the initial equity fraction sold or the greater the degree of underpricing.
- Sectors that are more competitive and, hence, less susceptible to government policies are more likely to follow a faster and more aggressive privatization program and offer lower price discounts.

The Empirical Evidence

Initial and Long-run Price Performance

Jones, Megginson, Nash, and Netter (1999) conduct a comprehensive study of 630 SIPs completed in 1981–1997 and report the following findings:

- Both firm and issue size are larger in privatization IPOs (PIPOs) than private firm IPOs.
- Governments use almost exclusively the fixed-price subscription method; auctions and bookbuilding are used mostly for tranches offered to institutional or foreign investors.
- Average (median) underpricing is 34.1% (12.4%) for privatization IPOs and 9.4% (3.3%) for follow-on privatizations of SOEs.
- In privatization, IPOs' direct flotation costs average 4.4% (with a median of 3.3%), which is lower than the cost of private firm IPOs; the lower spreads are apparently justified by the generous underpricing.
- Governments allocate substantial amounts of privatization shares to firm employees and retail investors in over 90% of the issues.
- Governments favor domestic investment banks to serve as lead or co-lead managers.
- About one-third of the shares are allocated to foreign investors.
- On average, 43.9% of the firms' equity is sold through the privatization IPO (i.e., governments follow a gradual sale).
- The initial returns of PIPOs are positively related to the equity fraction sold, indicating that investors demand higher underpricing for higher initial equity stakes offered as predicted by Perotti (1995). Underpricing also increases with the degree of income inequality.
- The degree of underpricing is related more to meeting political objectives than to overcoming informational asymmetry. And there is no evidence of populist behavior.

Dewenter and Malatesta (1997) also document higher underpricing for PIPOs than private firm IPOs. Underpricing is higher for PIPOs in regulated industries (due to fear of cash flow appropriation). Dewenter and Malatesta find that when PIPOs in United Kingdom are excluded, underpricing is about even across PIPOs and private firm IPOs.

Boutchkova and Megginson (2000) and D'Souza and Megginson (1999) report similar findings regarding the initial pricing of PIPOs. Specifically, Boutchkova and Megginson (2000) report average (median) initial return of 9.4% (3.3%) and find that 61% of the issues are executed through a fixed offer price subscription. A third of the new shares are allocated to foreign investors and the balance to employees. Choi, Lee, and Megginson (2010) report that the degree of underpricing has declined over time from 27.6% in the 1980s to 8% in 2000–2003.

PIPOs have been found to generate positive market-adjusted long-run returns. Megginson, Nash, Netter, and Schwartz (2000) report 1-, 3-, and 5-year average buy-and-hold returns of 25.1%, 81.1%, and 176.5%, respectively. These returns exceed those of various benchmark portfolios. Choi, Lee, and Megginson (2010) also report positive long-run returns for PIPOs up to 5 years when returns are match-adjusted by size and book-to-market. Excess returns (i.e., alphas) derived from the Fama–French three-factor model are also positive. The same authors cite numerous studies that show that PIPOs conducted in various countries realize positive average excess long-run returns.

Operating Performance

D'Souza and Megginson (1999) show that following SIPs, privatized firms' profitability, real sales, output per employee, and dividend payout increase, whereas leverage decreases.

Greater operating improvement is found in programs in which voting control is relinquished to private owners and in noncompetitive industries or if privatized firms are domiciled in industrialized countries. These findings collaborate the findings of Megginson, Nash, and Van Randenborgh (1994) and Boubakri and Cosset (1998) from earlier samples of SIPs. Wei, Varela, D'Souza, and Hassan (2003) report similar improvements of operating performance in a sample of Chinese share privatization programs. Improvements are stronger for privatized firms in which voting control is transferred to private owners. The evidence, concerning Chinese privatization programs, is corroborated by the findings of Sun and Tong (2003) who, in addition, find positive post-issue long-run stock returns up to 5 years.

The overall evidence on the long-run price as well as operating performance of privatized firms is consistent with the expectation that firms previously wholly owned by the state are more efficiently managed when they come under private management and the discipline of public markets.

14

The Decision to Issue Securities

This chapter describes the motives that drive firms to go public through an initial public offering (IPO). Next, the chapter presents an analytical method that allows the financial evaluation of the decision to proceed with an IPO. The chapter concludes with a discussion of the motives and valuation of the decision to execute seasoned equity offerings (SEOs) and debt offers.

The Decision to Go Public

The decision to have an IPO, that is, to "go public," is an important step in the life of a firm. The transformation from a privately owned to a publicly owned and traded company entails serious financial and organizational consequences for the firm's governance and shareholders. The going-public decision should weight the costs and benefits of public ownership and trading against those of private ownership. When the net benefits of operating as a public firm overtake the net benefits of continuing as a private concern, a firm should consider to go public.

The Motives for Going Public

The Wealth of Original Owners as a Constraint to Firm Growth

New firms are set up with equity capital contributed by the founders, family members, venture capital, and other financial backers called angels. After a period of incubation and development, the new firm reaches the point when it needs to scale up its operations to attain further growth. Often the capital required at that point may well exceed what its founders and backers can afford to contribute or what the firm's banks are willing to lend. Therefore, gaining access to capital sources, especially for financially constrained firms, is a strong motive for an IPO (Poulsen and Stegemoller, 2008).

Funding Investments and Growth

Successful new firms generate valuable growth opportunities that require prompt funding lest they are lost or competed away by rivals. Lowry (2003) finds evidence that the decision to go public is motivated by the need to finance growing product demand and when managers have optimistic expectations about future prospects. Kim and Weisbach (2008) analyze the uses of funds of a large sample of IPOs completed around the world and find that funding new investments and R&D is the main purpose for tapping the public markets. Pástor, Taylor, and Veronesi (2009) conclude that financing future growth and investment opportunities are factors that motivate firms to go public.

Underwriting Services and the New Issues Market. DOI: http://dx.doi.org/10.1016/B978-0-12-803282-4.00014-6

Need to Diversify the Owners' Wealth

When the owners of a new venture are heavily invested in it, their personal investment risk is mostly impacted by the idiosyncratic risk of the venture. This high-risk exposure may restrain the owners from pursuing risky projects. By going public and liquidating part of their investment, the owners can diversify their personal wealth and become less risk averse. The pursuit of riskier projects can in turn make the firm more competitive (Chod and Lyandres, 2011).

Investors' Need to Liquidate Their Equity Stakes

Related to the diversification motive is also the need of the original investors and especially venture capital firms to liquidate their equity stakes. Venture capital firms usually have an investment horizon of 5−7 years during which they expect to help the firm attain a mature enough state so that it can go public. Liquidation of their equity holdings allows venture capital firms to move on to new investments in pursuit of high yields.

Advantages of Publicly Traded Equity

Publicly traded stock can be used as a means of payment in acquisitions. Hovakimian and Hutton (2010) report that one-third of IPO firms execute an acquisition within 3 years of the IPO. Both the cash raised and the public equity provide the payment means to facilitate acquisition plans.

The availability of market prices for publicly traded stocks has additional benefits. Prices provide managers with credible signals about the value of their investment decisions. The availability of market prices also makes executive compensation plans easier to price and implement.

Prestige and Visibility

The IPO generates publicity for the firm and its products; thus, it provides cost-free advertising that can help the firm expand its customer base, raise the profile of top executives and increase their professional recognition and value. In addition, the on-going analyst coverage of the firm's stock adds to the visibility of the firm.

Timing Factors

Besides the above motives for going public, a firm must find itself in the right operational or market environment that will make the going-public decision more timely and compelling.

Favorable Operating and Product Market Conditions

Yung, Çolak, and Wang (2008) find that waves of IPOs begin with public issues of firms that achieve innovation gains followed by issues of lower quality firms which, however, have lower survival rates. Chemmanur, He, and Nandy (2010) also find that advances in firm productivity beyond that of industry peers are more likely to lead to the going-public decision. However, in hot market periods, firms may decide to go public even if they have not realized any productivity advantages—presumably, because of favorable valuations (Chemmanur and He, 2011). The above views stand opposite to the conclusions of Helwege and Liang (2004) that IPOs in hot and cold markets do not differ by the intensity of innovation in their industries or other operating quality metrics. New public firms are instead found to come from diverse industries. These researchers argue that the IPO waves are better explained by the confluence of broad economic conditions.

Favorable Information Environment

When the firm-specific or market-wide information environment is favorable to the firm, equity can be sold to the public market at higher prices. IPOs have been found to follow positive earnings releases (Korajczyk, Lucas, and McDonald, 1991), periods of high valuations and underpricing (Lowry and Schwert, 2002), and industry-wide overvaluation (Pagano, Panetta, and Zingales, 1998). IPOs can also be driven by analyst overoptimism which, however, is not borne out by subsequent earnings performance (Lewis and Tan, 2016).

Managerial Timing

The evidence shows that firms prefer to go public when they perform well and before their operating performance declines (Ritter, 1991; Jain and Kinni, 1994). Baker and Wurgler (2000) also show that equity issuance (IPOs and SEOs) precedes market declines. These patterns imply that either managers have information about the impeding decline of their firms' performance or they exploit windows of investor overoptimism that is fueled by the good performance of the firm. In this view, IPOs are more likely when the level of information asymmetry is relatively high.

Survey Findings

Surveys of Chief Financial Officers (CFOs) and Chief Executive Officers (CEOs) of firms that have executed IPOs confirm most of the above motives for the going-public decision. Brau and Fawcett (2006) and Brau, Ryan, and DeGraw (2006) find that:

- Executives give more consideration to the state and conditions of the IPO market than to the industry and overall market.
- Executives display strong preference for going public during bull market periods.
- Funding firm growth is ranked highly by executives as a motive.
- Executives also consider liquidity, that is, the ability to use stock as a means of payment in future acquisitions, to be a strong motive.

Executives are found to assign lower priority to the following motives for an IPO:

- Obtain an optimal capital structure by increasing equity.
- Increase opportunities for changing the control of the firm (as, e.g., via a merger or acquisition).

- Provide an exit for venture capitalists.
- Allow original owners to exit the firm.

Bharath and Dittmar (2010) report that greater liquidity, financial flexibility and greater investor recognition are important motives behind the decision to remain public versus private.

Financial and Organizational Consequences

Turning the firm into a public corporation has significant financial and organizational consequences.

Reporting responsibilities: The IPO turns the firm into a reporting company that must comply with financial disclosure requirements. It must also comply with securities laws and exchange regulations. Public trading on an exchange requires the firm to restructure its corporate governance, including the appointment of independent directors on the board and the adoption of formal compensation policies.

Creation of class of outside stockholders: Selling common stock to outside investors creates a class of owners who may not have the privilege or means to monitor the firm's operations and plans. This creates the potential that inside owners might engage in actions that disproportionately benefit them at the expense of outside owners. This gives rise to agency problems that can be rectified through costly monitoring and bonding[1].

Need to service shareholders and investors: As a public company, the firm needs to distribute certain materials to its shareholders, call shareholder meetings, and maintain regular contacts with analysts to present its current and future prospects.

Pressure to meet short-term performance expectations: Publicly held firms are exposed to the potential risk of "short-termism." Management may be too concerned about the reaction of analysts and investors to the announcement of adverse earnings news to the point that it risks becoming reluctant to undertake projects with long-term profitability lest they depress short-term earnings.

Financial Benefits and Costs

The financial and organizational consequences of the going-public decision translate into monetary benefits and costs that impact the value of the firm.

---

[1] Monitoring refers to mechanisms that allow outside stakeholders (stock- and debt-holders) to acquire timely information and oversee insiders. Some monitoring mechanisms include seats on the board, frequently audited reports, and meetings with insiders. Bonding refers to mechanisms that help align the interests of insiders with the interests of outside stakeholders. The most usual bonding tool is granting insiders stock and/or stock options in order to incentivize value-maximizing behavior.

Benefits

Public ownership and trading of equity can generate significant value-related benefits to the firm:

Avoiding the loss of valuable growth opportunities: Raising new capital enables the firm to finance valuable growth opportunities which could otherwise be lost if private financing is no longer feasible.

Lower cost of capital: Public trading of the stock can lower the cost of capital due to a lower liquidity premium and higher recognition factor that enlarges the firm's investor base and improves risk sharing.

Greater financial flexibility: As a public and reporting company, the firm increases its capacity to resort to financing sources outside those afforded to private firms. This improves the financial flexibility of the firm and can lower the firm's financing costs.

The potential takeover premium: The public trading of the stock makes easier the takeover of the firm or the purchase of large blocks of shares by strategic investors. This can enhance the firm's value by adding a potential takeover premium.

Public equity as means of payment: The public stock of the firm can become a sort of "currency" the firm can use in its acquisition and takeover pursuits. For example, internet firms that went public in the late 1990s used their public equity to execute acquisitions that would have been otherwise difficult to complete by cash or debt. A case in point is the takeover of Time-Warner by America Online (AOL). The availability of market prices also makes public stock a more reliable means of payment in executive compensation programs.

Costs

The above financial benefits come, however, at a cost.

Flotation costs: IPOs entail significant flotation costs, including the potential for underpricing.

Loss of value to competitors: The obligation to disclose information about the firm's business and management may benefit the firm's competitors and result in loss of revenue and growth or poaching of key employees by rivals.

Compliance expenses: The firm must periodically incur expenses to comply with regulatory reporting requirements.

Shareholder servicing costs: They include the cost of annual meetings and reports and materials that must be distributed to shareholders.

Listing costs: These are the fees paid to an organized exchange (e.g., New York Stock Exchange (NYSE) or Nasdaq) to initially list the stock for trading and keep it listed thereafter.

Agency (bonding and monitoring) costs: These are the direct and indirect costs to adopt and enact mechanisms that minimize the negative implications of agency problems associated with the presence of inside and outside stakeholders.

Financial Evaluation of the IPO Decision

Just like any other firm decision, the IPO decision must be evaluated from the perspective of the owners of the original equity of the firm at the time of the decision. Specifically, the net gain of the going-public decision is the difference between the value of the original (pre-IPO) equity of the firm with the IPO decision (i.e., the firm goes through with the IPO and all its consequences) and the value of the original equity without the IPO (i.e., the firm continues as a private concern). The evaluation of the IPO decision may arise as one of the advisory services an underwriter is assigned before the decision to go on with the offering is formally adopted.

If the net gain is equal to zero or positive, the IPO decision is, respectively, value neutral or value enhancing, and it should be accepted. If the net gain is negative, then the decision to execute an IPO is value-reducing for the original equity owners, and it should be canceled or postponed.

Below, we present two approaches to the estimation of the net gain of the going-public decision.

The Net Gain as the Change of the Value of Equity of Original Shareholders

This method follows the most direct approach to the estimation of the net gain of the IPO decision by calculating the net gain as the difference between the value of the pre-IPO original equity with the IPO and the value of the original equity without the IPO. Thus, the net gain to the original equity-holders of the private firm is:

$$\text{GAIN(IPO)} = E_o(\text{PUB}) - E(\text{PRI}) = [E(\text{PUB}) - E(\text{IPO})] - E(\text{PRI}). \tag{14.1}$$

GAIN(IPO) is the net value gain of the IPO decision. $E_o(\text{PUB})$ is the value of the original equity with the IPO when the firm operates as a public firm. $E_o(\text{PUB})$ is estimated as the difference between the total value of equity with the IPO decision, $E(\text{PUB})$, and the value of equity that belongs to the new equity-holders who bought the new shares offered through the primary portion of the IPO, $E(\text{IPO})$. The value represented by $E(\text{IPO})$ is the value of the IPO shares at their estimated market value. Finally, $E(\text{PRI})$ is the value of original equity without the IPO, that is, the value of equity the firm estimates to have if it continues to operate as a private concern[2]. The firm accepts the IPO decision if the net gain, GAIN(IPO) given in Eq. (14.1), is equal to or greater than 0.

The value of the equity with the IPO, $E_o(\text{PUB})$, is also equal to the total value of the firm with the IPO, $V(\text{PUB})$, minus the value of debt with the IPO, $D(\text{PUB})$, and the value of equity that belongs to the new shareholders, $E(\text{IPO})$. Thus, $E_o(\text{PUB})$ can be expressed as:

$$E_o(\text{PUB}) = V(\text{PUB}) - D(\text{PUB}) - E(\text{IPO}).$$

Similarly, the value of original equity, $E(\text{PRI})$, is the total value of the firm continuing as a private concern (i.e., without the IPO), $V(\text{PRI})$, minus the value of the debt without the IPO, $D(\text{PRI})$, that is,

$$E(\text{PRI}) = V(\text{PRI}) - D(\text{PRI}).$$

---

[2] As the evaluation of the IPO decision is conducted prior to the IPO, we should utilize estimated market values.

Therefore, the net gain of the IPO decision can be also calculated as:

$$\text{GAIN(IPO)} = [V(\text{PUB}) - D(\text{PUB}) - E(\text{IPO})] - [V(\text{PRI}) - D(\text{PRI})]. \tag{14.2}$$

The value of total debt of the firm with the IPO can be expressed as:

$$D(\text{PUB}) = D(\text{PRI}) + \Delta D(\text{PRI}) - \text{REPMT} + \text{NDEBT}.$$

Thus, the value of the firm's debt with the IPO, $D(\text{PUB})$, equals the original debt, $D(\text{PRI})$, plus the change in its value (if any), $\Delta D(\text{PRI})$, minus any repayment of old debt, REPMT, plus any new debt the firm takes on as a result of the IPO, NDEBT.

The change in the value of the pre-IPO debt, $\Delta D(\text{PRI})$, captures the possible revaluation of the old debt because of the issuance of public equity and any restructuring of the firm's liabilities. If these activities make the original debt safer (due, e.g., to the equity increase), the value of debt will rise. This, however, represents a transfer of wealth from the equity-holders to the debt-holders and reduces the value of their equity. The reverse effect occurs when the restructuring following the IPO makes the original debt less safe.

Incorporating these debt-related effects in Eq. (14.2), we can express the net gain as:

$$\text{GAIN(IPO)} = \left[V(\text{PUB}) - \left\{D(\text{PRI}) + \Delta D(\text{PRI}) - \text{REPMT} + \text{NDEBT}\right\} - E(\text{IPO})\right] - [V(\text{PRI}) - D(\text{PRI})]. \tag{14.3}$$

The Net Gain as the Sum of the Value Components of the IPO Decision

This approach decomposes the total value of the going-public decision into several components each of which captures the value of distinct value drivers associated with the consequences of the IPO decision. This allows the firm's decision makers to identify the relevant sources of value associated with the going-public decision and thus develop a more thorough understanding of the factors that can impact the value of this decision. The value components of the IPO decision are shown below[3].

The value of public ownership and trading: This value is estimated as the value of the financial benefits and costs associated with the public ownership and trading of the firm's equity. It is given by:

The value from:

- Lower cost of capital,
- The potential takeover premium,
- Lower cost of executing acquisitions.

minus

The value of:

- Regulatory compliance costs,
- Costs for public relations with analysts and investors,
- Adverse effects from increased information disclosure,

---

[3] This approach draws from Papaioannou (1996).

- Shareholder servicing costs,
- Initial and continued listing costs,
- Agency and monitoring costs associated with public ownership.

The value of the capital raising costs: This is the value of the flotation costs incurred in the process of issuing and placing shares in the public market. It is given by:

- The underwriting (gross) spread,
- Other out-of-pocket and indirect issuance costs,
- The underpricing or overpricing of the offered shares.

The value of new investments and growth opportunities: This value is estimated as the net present value (NPV) of new investments and growth opportunities the firm can undertake only as a result of its reorganization as a public firm. It is given by:

The value of:

- New investment opportunities made possible by the IPO,
- New growth opportunities due to the IPO.

The value of financial restructuring: This is the net value generated by the rearrangement of the firm's capital structure (i.e., equity and debt) as a result of the going-public decision. Apart from its impact on the firm's cost of capital, rearranging the capital structure of the firm can engender additional benefits in the form, for example, of enhanced financial flexibility, but it can also affect the agency problems associated with debt and equity. The firm may also attain a more efficient realignment of debt maturities that better match the timing and risk of its cash flows from operations. Therefore, the net value of capital structure changes is given by:

The value of:

- Enhanced financial flexibility,
- Changes in the maturity and riskiness of the firm's liabilities.

minus

The value of:

- Agency and monitoring costs associated with the restructuring of equity and debt.

The value of revaluation effects: This is the value associated with any revaluation the firm will undergo because of its decision to go public. For example, investors may revise their expectation about the future prospects of the firm, if they perceive the IPO as a signal the firm is financially stronger than previously thought. The firm should also account for any revaluation of its original, pre-IPO debt. Therefore, the revaluation effects are given by:

The value of:

- Any positive or negative revaluation of the firm's assets in place caused by the going-public decision,
- Any revaluation of the pre-IPO debt of the firm.

The Net Gain Calculation

The sum of the value components associated with the going-public decision is the net value gain of the IPO decision. This is also equal to the difference between the value of the pre-IPO equity with the IPO and the value of the pre-IPO equity without the IPO, or $E_o(\text{PUB}) - E(\text{PRI})$.

If we incorporate the effects of capital structure changes in the cost of capital and separate the value of the change of the cost of capital from the net value of public ownership, the net gain can be written as:

$$\text{GAIN(IPO)} = \text{NPV(POC)} + \text{NPV}(\Delta\text{WACC}) + \text{NPV(FC)} + \text{NPV(INV)} + \text{NPV(REV)} + \Delta D(\text{PRI}). \quad (14.4)$$

NPV(POC) is the net present value of the cost of the public ownership; NPV(ΔWACC) is the net present value due to the change of the weighted average cost of capital (WACC); NPV(FC) is the net present value of the flotation costs; NPV(INV) is the net present value of investments and other rearrangement of assets made possible because of the IPO; NPV(REV) is the value gain or loss that affects the value of assets in place, excluding the revaluation of old debt, $\Delta D(\text{PRI})$, which we include by itself for exposition purposes.

The value component due to the change of the weighted average cost of capital, NPV (ΔWACC), warrants further clarification. The value-related effect of a change in the cost of capital as a result of the IPO decision should be estimated only in relation to the cash flows the firm expects as a private concern. The cost of capital is likely to change due to two effects. The most direct effect of going public is the reduction of the liquidity premium embedded in the firm's cost of capital. The second effect is due to the possible change in the capital structure of the firm post-IPO. If we incorporate both effects (i.e., the liquidity and the capital structure effect) in the cost of capital, the incremental value of a change in the cost of capital is the value of the cash flows with the IPO discounted at the cost of capital the firm is expected to have as a public company minus the value of the same cash flows discounted at the cost of capital the firm is expected to have if it remains a private concern.

The firm accepts the going-public decision if the net value gain, given in Eq. (14.4), is equal to or greater than 0. (The Appendix presents an illustration of how the net value gain is calculated under the two approaches.)

The Value of the Decision to Have a Seasoned Equity Offering

Motives

The main motives for raising capital through a seasoned equity offering are as follows:

Funding of new investments: Although firms may have a preference for self-financing by utilizing internally generated cash flows, it is possible that either the firm does not have enough retained earnings in liquid balances to self-finance its growth, or the firm adheres to a target-dividend policy and profits are not enough to support both the funding of new investments as well as the distribution of dividends.

Maintaining a preferred capital structure: The firm may have exhausted its debt capacity and further indebtedness could imperil its financial soundness, or the firm may have veered away from the target—debt ratio considered appropriate by investors. By moving closer to its optimal capital structure or target—debt ratio, the firm can increase its overall value and, specifically, the market price of its stock.

Timing Factors

Lower issuance costs: Choe, Masulis, and Nanda (1993) find evidence that equity issuance increases with good economic conditions when the adverse selection costs (i.e., lower offer prices) are lower and investors are more receptive to equity issues. Bayless and Chaplinsky (1996) propose that SEOs are more likely when information asymmetry is low because this reduces the costs of information production and lowers the issuance costs in the form of underwriter compensation and underpricing. They find that SEOs completed in hot markets are associated with less negative stock price reaction than if executed in cold markets. Bayless and Chaplinsky (1996) attribute this to the less adverse effects of information asymmetry during hot markets.

Managerial timing: Brous (1992) reports downward adjustments of analysts' earnings forecasts following SEOs, whereas Loughran and Ritter (1995) and Spiess and Affleck-Graves (1995) note that firms execute SEOs following periods of strong operating and stock price performance which are followed by declining post-issue performance. DeAngelo, DeAngelo, and Stulz (2010) also find that SEOs typically follow periods of positive price advances due to the emergence of growth opportunities and more positive investor sentiment. However, they also find that there are firms with signs of strong growth and price run-ups that do not issue equity. Instead, according to these authors, the strongest motive for SEOs appears to be the need to raise cash, as many of these firms would face liquidity problems without fresh equity capital. Howe and Zhang (2010) also find evidence that SEOs are motivated by the need for capital but they are timed to coincide with favorable performance. Dittmar and Thakor (2007) qualify the timing hypothesis by showing evidence that firms prefer to raise equity capital when there is greater agreement between manager and investor expectations about the future cash flows of the firm. Times of such agreement tend to coincide with high equity prices.

Announcement Effects of Seasoned Equity Offerings

The empirical literature shows that when firms announce their decision to sell new equity their stock loses on average 3% of its market value. For example, based on a variety of studies, Smith (1986) calculates the average abnormal stock price reaction in a 2-day interval around the announcement time to be -3.14% for industrial stocks and -0.75% for utility stocks, both being statistically significant. In more recent SEOs, D'Mello and

Ferris (2000) find that the negative reaction is stronger if the issuing firm is relatively small, has higher growth opportunities, and is covered less by analysts. But the negative reaction is less for firms that have completed three or more SEOs in the past, due apparently to the lower asymmetric information for such firms (D'Mello, Tawatnuntachai, and Yaman, 2003).

The negative stock price reaction associated with equity issuance has been attributed to an unfavorable signaling effect. The market perceives the equity financing as evidence of the firm's inability to self-finance its growth due to an unexpected drop in current or future cash flows which leads to a downward revision of expected cash flows (Miller and Rock, 1985). The equity issuance may also signal that in the opinion of insiders (management), the firm is overvalued and shares can be sold at prices above their intrinsic value (Myers and Majluf, 1984). It is also possible that the negative stock price reaction upon announcement of an SEO anticipates the impact of issuance costs (gross spread, other expenses, and underpricing). Hull and Kerchner (1996) find that the issuance costs of new equity issues are reflected in the market reaction to equity issue announcements. The impact of issuance costs is found to be greater for Nasdaq-listed stocks.

Common stock is also issued for the purpose of retiring debt, in a so-called equity-for-debt exchange offer. Smith (1986) reports that such exchanges cause insignificant stock price reaction. The insignificant price reaction can be attributed to the market's belief that the firm is attempting to move back toward a more optimal capital structure. However, Cornett and Travlos (1989) find a significant negative stock price reaction in stock-for-debt exchange offers. They attribute the negative reaction to increased ownership diffusion that reduces the effectiveness of monitoring and increases agency costs.

The above evidence suggests that firms that plan to raise new equity should account the loss of value on the original shares as part of the overall cost of the decision to have an SEO. For example, if the current equity market value (without the SEO) is, say, $1 billion, the firm should expect to lose, on average, 3% or $30 million of equity value. This cost is borne directly by the existing shareholders. Thus, if the purpose of the equity issue is to finance new investments with an initial NPV of, say, $100 million, the net (with the issue) NPV of the new investment opportunity would be only $70 million.

The Net Gain of the SEO Decision

Firms that raise capital through an SEO are already public. Therefore, the impact of value changes related to the public ownership and trading are minimal. That means the firm is not expected to enjoy any significant gains in liquidity that will reduce its core cost of capital and is not expected to be burdened by significant incremental costs of compliance or servicing its shareholders. The main components of value change are: (1) the flotation costs (gross spread and underpricing); (2) the value of any capital structure changes; (3) the value of new investments and growth opportunities; and (4) any revaluation effects.

As in the case of an IPO, the SEO decision can be evaluated by estimating the net gain to the original, pre-SEO equity-holders, GAIN(SEO), by applying the following formulas:

$$\text{GAIN(SEO)} = E_o\left(w/\text{SEO}\right) - E_o\left(w/o\ \text{SEO}\right), \tag{14.5}$$

or

$$\text{GAIN(SEO)} = \left[V\left(w/\text{SEO}\right) - D\left(w/\text{SEO}\right) - E(\text{SEO})\right] - \left[V\left(w/o\ \text{SEO}\right) - D\left(w/o\ \text{SEO}\right)\right], \tag{14.6}$$

or

$$\text{GAIN(SEO)} = \text{NPV(FC)} + \text{NPV(INV)} + \text{NPV(REV)} + \Delta D_o(w/\ \text{SEO}). \tag{14.7}$$

$E_o(w/\text{SEO})$ and $E_o(w/o\ \text{SEO})$ are, respectively, the value of equity that belongs to the original shareholders with and without the SEO. $V(w/\text{SEO})$ and $V(w/o\ \text{SEO})$ are, respectively, the firm value with and without the SEO. $D(w/\text{SEO})$ and $D(w/o\ \text{SEO})$ are, respectively, the value of total debt with and without the SEO. $E(\text{SEO})$ is the value of the equity that belongs to the new shareholders given by the market value of the new shares. $NPV(\text{FC})$ is the net present value of the flotation costs, i.e., gross spread, other costs, and underpricing. NPV(INV) is the net present value of investments made possible by the SEO; therefore, it is the net present value of incremental cash flows over and above those expected from investments the firm is expected to undertake without the SEO. NPV(REV) is the change in the value of the assets in place due to revaluation caused by the SEO (e.g., the documented 3% decline in equity value upon announcement of a stock offering). $\Delta D_o(w/\text{SEO})$ is the change in the value of the original debt caused by the SEO, and it represents a gain or loss for the original shareholders.

If the net gain of the SEO decision, GAIN(SEO), is equal to or greater than 0, the firm should go ahead with the seasoned equity offering.

The Value of the Decision to Have a Debt Offering

Motives

Firms raise new capital through the issuance of debt securities for the purpose to (1) either finance new investments; (2) adjust their capital structure toward a more optimal debt ratio; or (3) buy back equity and effect a more drastic increase of their leverage.

Timing

As discussed in Chapter 11: The Price and Operating Performance of Seasoned Equity Offers, Debt Offers, and Other Offerings, debt offers are followed by declines in the operating performance of the issuing firms. Debt-issuing firms are also found to realize negative stock price performance in the long-run, which Spiess and Affleck-Graves (1995) interpret as evidence that managers time debt offers to coincide with unusually strong firm performance.

Announcement Effects of Debt Issues

The empirical evidence shows that debt issues cause a more subdued reaction in the stock price of the issuing firm. Smith (1986) reports a negative 2-day announcement abnormal return of -0.26% for straight bond issues and a more negative abnormal stock return of -2.07% for convertible bond issues in the case of industrial firms. More recent evidence also shows a significant negative stock price reaction to the announcement of straight bond issues (Datta, Iskandar-Datta, and Patel, 2000). When new debt is, however, issued to retire equity, the stock price reaction is positive and significant (Cornett and Travlos, 1989).

In general, the evidence of milder stock price reaction in the case of new debt issues (as opposed to new equity issues) and even of positive stock price reaction in the case of debt-for-equity exchanges can be explained by the weaker market perception that the firm is overvalued and the expectation of additional tax savings on the interest paid on the firm's debt.

The Net Gain of the Debt Offer Decision

Publicly traded firms that issue debt need not worry about incurring any material additional costs due to the public ownership and trading of their securities. Private firms which issue public debt for the first time must, however, register with the SEC and become reporting companies. Hence, these firms should take into account the costs and benefits of public ownership and trading.

Apart from these costs, the other value components are associated with (1) flotation costs; (2) capital structure rearrangement; (3) new investments and growth opportunities due to the new debt funds; and (4) any revaluation effects affecting the assets and the liabilities in place prior to the debt issuance.

The net value effect of a debt offer (DO) is also evaluated from the original shareholders' perspective and is calculated as the change in the value of equity owned by the original shareholders. The debt offering is accepted if the net gain of the debt offer decision, GAIN (DO), is positive or equal to 0.

The GAIN(DO) is calculated by one of the following formulas:

$$\text{GAIN(DO)} = E_o\left(w/\text{DO}\right) - E_o\left(w/o\ \text{DO}\right), \tag{14.8}$$

or

$$\text{GAIN(DO)} = \left[V\left(w/\text{DO}\right) - D\left(w/\text{DO}\right)\right] - \left[V\left(w/o\ \text{DO}\right) - D\left(w/o\,\text{DO}\right)\right], \tag{14.9}$$

or

$$\text{GAIN(DO)} = \text{NPV(FC)} + \text{NPV(INV)} + \text{NPV(REV)} + \Delta D_o\left(w/\text{DO}\right). \tag{14.10}$$

$E_o(w/DO)$ and $E_o(w/o$ DO) are, respectively, the values of original equity with and without the debt offer. $V(w/DO)$ and $V(w/o$ DO) are, respectively, the values of the firm with and without the debt offer. $D(w/DO)$ and $D(w/o$ DO) are, respectively, the values of debt with and without the debt offer. NPV(FC) is the net present value of the flotation costs (gross spread, other issuance expenses, underpricing). NPV(INV) is the net present value of new investments and asset restructuring the firm plans to have with the debt offer. NPV(REV) is the net present value of the revaluation of assets. $\Delta D_o(w/DO)$ is the revaluation of the original debt of the firm as a result of the debt offer.

Whether debt is issued without retirement of equity or for the purpose to buy back (treasury) stock, the original shareholders continue to hold all the shares. Thus, in both cases, we need not account for the part of equity held by new shareholders, as we did in the case of estimating the net gain of the IPO or SEO decision.

Appendix—Illustration of the Calculation of the Net Gain of the IPO Decision

Below, we illustrate how the net gain of the IPO decision can be calculated according to the valuation approaches presented in this chapter.

The Value of the IPO Decision for a Firm With Debt

The (fictitious) New Tech Company (NTC) is planning an initial public offering. An investment bank has been hired to advise the company on whether going ahead with the IPO is a value-added decision for the existing NTC shareholders.

Advisory Tasks

The advisory agreement with the investment bank has five parts. In particular, the investment bank has agreed to the following:

Part A: Calculate the Net Gain of the IPO decision following two different approaches:
   1. The difference of the equity values of NTC as a public and private firm, respectively.
   2. The sum of the value components associated with the decision to go public.
Part B: Estimate the total cost of turning NTC into a public company.
Part C: Estimate the expected price per share with the IPO.
Part D: Estimate the number of new shares NTC must issue to raise the $40 million of gross proceeds.
Part E: Show the allocation of equity between original and new shareholders following the IPO.

Data and Assumptions

The data and assumptions to be used by the investment banker are given below:

Projections if NTC Continues as a Private Firm	
Free cash flows to the firm from operations	$25,000,000 in perpetuity[a]
WACC applicable to NTC as private firm	20% per year
Estimated market value of debt	$45,000,000
Number of existing shares	8,000,000
Projections if NTC Undertakes the IPO	
Free cash flows to the firm from operations	$25,000,000 in perpetuity
Incremental free cash flows to the firm from new investments with the IPO	$9,600,000 in perpetuity[a]
WACC applicable to NTC as public firm	16% per year[b]
Projected value of debt with IPO	$46,000,000[c]
Underpricing cost (money left on the table)	$4,000,000
Underwriting costs (gross spread)	$2,000,000
Other out-of-pocket issuance costs	$400,000
Annual costs for SEC reporting and shareholder services	$500,000 in perpetuity[d]
Funds needed for new investments	$40,000,000[e]
Shares to be issued in IPO	to be estimated

Assumptions:

[a]All cash flows are assumed to start 1 year from now (time of decision) and to be realized at the end of each year. They represent the total free cash flow to the firm.

[b]The WACC (weighted average cost of capital) of NTC is assumed to decline to 16% because of the favorable consequences of higher liquidity due to public ownership and trading. To simplify calculations, we have assumed that the new WACC is also appropriate to discount the incremental cash flows from new investments with the IPO, i.e., NTC is expected to invest in new projects that have similar operating and financial risk as its existing operations.

[c]NTC will not assume any new debt; however, the value of its old debt of $45 million is projected to rise to $46 million due the strengthening of the firm's balance sheet and the resultant lower default premium.

[d]The annual compliance and shareholder-related costs are not included in the $9.6 million of incremental cash flows NTC expects from its new investments.

[e]NTC plans to raise net proceeds of $40 million, which the firm will use to fund the new investments.

We will illustrate the investment banker's execution of agreed tasks for two scenarios: (1) NTC and investment banker agree that the IPO will be underpriced; (2) they decide against underpricing the new issue.

Case of Underpricing

It is assumed that the expected underpricing will be 10% of the offer price. Execution of the agreed tasks and associated calculations undertaken by the investment banker to help NTC with its going-public decision are detailed below:

Part A: Find the Net Gain of the IPO Decision

The IPO Gain as the Change in the Equity Value of the Original Shareholders
We use Eq. (14.2) to measure the change in the value of equity as follows:

$$\text{GAIN(IPO)} = [V(\text{PUB}) - D(\text{PUB}) - E(\text{IPO})] - [V(\text{PRI}) - D(\text{PRI})].$$

The value of the firm as a public company, V(PUB), is the present value of the cash flows the firm projects as a public entity. These cash flows include the free cash flows from operations (those expected if firm continues as a private concern plus the incremental cash flow expected if the firm turns public), the flotation expenses (excluding the underpricing), and the expenses due to public ownership, e.g., various servicing costs. In the interest of clarity, we discount these classes of cash flows separately. We use the WACC the firm estimates to have as a public entity to discount the above cash flows.

$$V(\text{PUB}) = \text{PV}(\text{FCF}_{\text{Pri}}) + \text{PV}(\Delta\text{FCF}_{\text{Pub}}) + \text{PV}(\text{FC}) + \text{PV}(\text{POC})$$

$$V(\text{PUB}) = \frac{\text{FCF}_{\text{Pri}}}{\text{WACC}_{\text{Pub}}} + \frac{\Delta\text{FCF}_{\text{Pub}}}{\text{WACC}_{\text{Pub}}} + \text{FC} + \frac{\text{POC}}{\text{WACC}_{\text{Pub}}}$$

$$= \frac{\$25\text{m}}{0.16} + \frac{\$9.6\text{m}}{0.16} + (-\$2.4\text{m}) + \left(-\frac{\$0.5\text{m}}{0.16}\right)$$

$$= \$156.25\text{m} + \$60 - \$2.4\text{m} - \$3.125\text{m}$$

$$= \$210.725\text{m}.$$

The value of the debt when the firm turns public, D(PUB), is given to be $46 million, whereas its current pre-IPO value, D(PRI), is $45 million.

The market value of the IPO shares, E(IPO), is estimated to be $44 million and represents the equity that will belong to the shareholders who will buy the new shares of the IPO. As the net proceeds to NTC are planned to be $40 million and the underpricing (implicit spread) is expected to be 10%, the estimated market value of the IPO shares is $44 million, i.e., $44 = \$40 \times (1 + 0.10)$. The difference of $4 million is money the original shareholders anticipate leaving on the table. (Note that not all new shares are necessarily expected to be bought by new shareholders. It is possible, though less likely, that existing shareholders also buy new IPO shares. In this event, the loss to the buying original shareholders due to the underpricing will be less.)

The value of NTC as private concern, V(PRI), is the free cash flow of $25 million discounted at 20%, the WACC the firm has as a private firm. That is:

$$V(\text{PRI}) = \frac{\text{FCF}_{\text{Pri}}}{\text{WACC}_{\text{Pri}}} = \frac{\$25\text{m}}{0.2} = \$125\text{m}.$$

Therefore, the net gain of the IPO decision is:

$$\text{GAIN(IPO)} = [V(\text{PUB}) - D(\text{PUB}) - E(\text{IPO})] - [V(\text{PRI}) - D(\text{PRI})]$$

$$= [\$210.725\text{m} - \$46\text{m} - \$44\text{m}] - [\$125\text{m} - \$45\text{m}] = \$120.725\text{m} - \$80\text{m}$$

$$= \$40.725\text{m}.$$

We notice that $[V(\text{PUB}) - D(\text{PUB}) - E(\text{IPO})]$ is the value of original equity with the IPO, i.e., $E_o(\text{PUB})$, whereas $[V(\text{PRI}) - D(\text{PRI})]$ is the value of original equity without the IPO, i.e., $E(\text{PRI})$. Therefore, we can also estimate the net gain of the IPO decision as $\text{GAIN(IPO)} = E_o(\text{PUB}) - E(\text{PRI}) = \$120.725\text{m} - \$80\text{m} = \$40.725\text{m}$, which is the net gain estimated above.

The Net Gain as a Sum of the Value Components of the IPO Decision

We use Eq. (14.4) that calculates the net gain of the IPO as the sum of the value components that accrue to the original shareholders over and beyond the value of their equity should the firm remain a private entity:

$$\text{GAIN(IPO)} = \text{NPV(POC)} + \text{NPV}(\Delta\text{WACC}) + \text{NPV(FC)} + \text{NPV(INV)} + \text{NPV(REV)} + \Delta D(PRI),$$

which yields:

$$\text{GAIN(IPO)} = (-\$3.125\text{m}) + \$31.25\text{m} + (-\$6.4\text{m}) + \$20\text{m} + \$0\text{m} + (-\$1\text{m})$$

$$\text{GAIN(IPO)} = \$40.725\text{m}.$$

The value components in the above calculation are estimated as follows:

The NPV(POC) is equal to the net present value of the cost of the public ownership, i.e., the various compliance and shareholder-related costs estimated as $-\$0.50\text{m}/0.16 = -\$3.125\text{m}$.

The NPV(ΔWACC), the value component due the change of the weighted average cost of capital, is calculated as the value of the cash flows the firm expects to realize as private concern discounted at the public firm's WACC minus the value of the same cash flows discounted at the WACC of the firm as a private concern. This yields:

$$\text{NPV}(\Delta\text{WACC}) = \frac{\text{FCF}_{\text{Pri}}}{\text{WACC}_{\text{Pub}}} - \frac{\text{FCF}_{\text{Pri}}}{\text{WACC}_{\text{Pri}}} = \frac{\$25\text{m}}{0.16} - \frac{\$25\text{m}}{0.20} = \$156.25\text{m} - 125\text{m}$$

$$\text{NPV}(\Delta\text{WACC}) = \$31.25\text{m}.$$

The NPV(FC), which is the net present value of the flotation costs, is calculated as the sum of the gross spread ($2m), other issuance expenses ($0.4m) and the implicit spread, i.e., amount of underpricing ($4m). Thus,

$$\text{NPV(FC)} = (-\$2\text{m}) + (-\$0.4\text{m}) + (-\$4\text{m}) = -\$6.4\text{m}.$$

The NPV(INV), which is the net present value of investments and other rearrangement of assets made possible because of the IPO, is simply the net present value of the incremental cash flows discounted at the new WACC minus the investment outlay, i.e., $\text{NPV(INV)} = \frac{\$9.6\text{m}}{0.16} - \$40\text{m} = \$60\text{m} - \$40\text{m} = \$20\text{m}$.

The NPV(REV) is equal to zero, as there is no mention of any revaluation effects in the data of the case.

The $\Delta D(\text{PRI})$ is the change in the value of the original debt due to the revaluation of the original debt of the firm without the IPO, i.e.,

$$\Delta D(\text{PRI}) = D(\text{PRI}) - D_o(\text{PUB}) = \$45m - \$46m = -\$1m.$$

The minus sign implies that the $1m represents a loss of value to the original shareholders.

Part B: Estimate the Net Value of Public Ownership

The net value of public ownership and trading of NTC's stock is given by the value created from the reduction of the WACC minus the costs of public ownership. In this case, we have assumed that the drop in the WACC is entirely due to the reduction of the liquidity premium, as we have assumed that the restructuring of the assets and liabilities has not impacted the firm's cost of capital. In the general case, when the WACC is also affected by changes in the operating and financial risk of the firm, we need to estimate the reduction of WACC that is due only to the lower liquidity premium. The net value of public ownership is equal to

$$\text{NPV}(\Delta \text{WACC}) + \text{NPV}(\text{POC}) = \$31.25m + (-\$3.125m) = \$28.125m.$$

Part C: Estimate the Market Price Per Share With the IPO

The price per share with the IPO is the expected market price the NTC stock is projected to have once secondary trading starts in the aftermarket.

The price is estimated according to two different methods: (1) by using the number of original shares and (2) by using the total number of shares following the IPO.

Using the Original Number of Shares
The value of the original equity of the firm with the IPO is given by:

$$E_o(\text{PUB}) = V(\text{PUB}) - D(\text{PUB}) - E(\text{IPO}) = \$210.275m - \$46m - \$44m = \$120.725m.$$

Therefore, the new price is:

$$\text{Price(PUB)} = \frac{E_o(\text{PUB})}{\text{Old No. of Shares}} = \frac{\$120.725m}{8m} = \$15.091 \text{ per share.}$$

To estimate the stock price without the IPO, we first calculate the firm's value of equity without the IPO: $E(\text{PRI}) = V(\text{PRI}) - D(\text{PRI}) = \$125m - \$45m = \$80m$

Hence, the price without the IPO is:

$$\text{Price(PRI)} = \frac{E(\text{PRI})}{\text{Old No. of Shares}} = \frac{\$80m}{8m} = \$10 \text{ per share.}$$

If we are interested in the net gain of the IPO decision on a per share basis, we can write;
$\text{Price(PUB)} - \text{Price(PRI)} = \$15.091 - \$10 = \$5.091 \text{per share}$. Multiplying this gain by the 8 million original shares, we obtain: $\$5.091 \times 8m = \$40.725m$, which is equal to the total net gain estimated above.

Using Total Number of Shares With IPO

This approach to estimating the stock price with the IPO requires that we know the total number of the shares outstanding with the IPO. Hence, we need to estimate the number of new shares the firm plans to issue. To this end, we first estimate the new value of equity that belongs to all shareholders, old and new. The total value of equity with the IPO, that is, $E(\text{PUB})$ is given by:

$$E(\text{PUB}) = V(\text{PUB}) - D(\text{PUB}) = \$210.725\text{m} - \$46\text{m} = \$164.725\text{m}.$$

The value of the equity with the IPO, $E(\text{PUB})$, is also equal to the number of old shares times the new share price with the IPO plus the number of new shares times the new share price. Hence, we can write:

$$E(\text{PUB}) = [(8\text{m shares}) \times \text{Price}(\text{PUB})] + \left[\left(\frac{\$40\text{m}}{\text{Price}_{\text{offer}}}\right) \times \text{Price}(\text{PUB})\right],$$

where $[(8\text{m shares}) \times \text{Price}(\text{PUB})]$ is the value of the original shares at the projected public market price, and $\left[\left(\frac{\$40\text{m}}{\text{Price}_{\text{offer}}}\right) \times \text{Price}(\text{PUB})\right]$ is the market value of the new shares to be issued. The number of new shares is the gross proceeds of the IPO (\$40m) divided by the offer price ($\text{Price}_{\text{offer}}$), i.e., $\left(\frac{\$40\text{m}}{\text{Price}_{\text{offer}}}\right)$. As the anticipated underpricing is 10% of the offer price, the offer price as a function of Price(PUB) is: $\text{Price}_{\text{offer}} = \left(\frac{\text{Price(PUB)}}{1.1}\right)$. Substituting ($\text{Price}_{\text{offer}}$) into the $E(\text{PUB})$ equation to solve for Price(PUB), we get:

$$\$164.725\text{m} = [(8\text{m shares}) \times \text{Price}(\text{PUB})] + \left[\left(\frac{\$40\text{m}}{\text{Price}(\text{PUB})/1.1}\right) \times \text{Price}(\text{PUB})\right]$$

$$[(8\text{m shares}) \times \text{Price}(\text{PUB})] = \$164.725\text{m} - (\$40\text{m} \times 1.1)$$

$$\text{Price}(\text{PUB}) = \left(\frac{\$164.725\text{m} - \$44\text{m}}{8\text{m shares}}\right) = \left(\frac{\$120.725\text{m}}{8\text{m shares}}\right) = \$15.091 \text{ per share},$$

which is the same price we obtain based on approach (a) by using the original number of shares.

Part D: Estimate the Offer Price and the Number of New Shares

Given the anticipated 10% of underpricing of the IPO shares, the offer price is:

$$\text{Price}_{\text{offer}} = \frac{\text{Price}(\text{PUB})}{1.1} = \frac{\$15.091}{1.1} = \$13.719 \text{ per share}.$$

Thus, to raise the gross proceeds of \$40m, the firm needs to issue:

$$\frac{\$40,000,000}{\$13.719 \text{ per share}} = 2,915,644 \text{shares}[4].$$

---

[4] This number (2,915,644) is 54 shares less than the actual number (2,915,718) due to rounding of the offer price (\$15.091) to three decimal digits in our illustrative calculations.

Part E: Show the Allocation of Equity Between the Original and New Shareholders

The equity value of NTC will be divided as follows:

Original shareholders: 8,000,000 shares at $15.091 = $120,725,000[5]
New shareholders: 2,915,664 shares at $15.091 = $44,000,000[6]
Total equity: 10,915,664 shares at $15.091 = $164,725,000[7]

The old shareholders of the firm will own 73.29% (i.e., $120.725m/$164.725m) of the total equity, whereas the new shareholders will own 26.71% (i.e., $44m/$164.725m).

The original shareholders will sell the new shares for $40 million but they will surrender equity worth $44 million in market value terms. The difference of $4 million represents the underpricing, and it is a transfer of wealth from the original to the new shareholders.

The balance sheets below show the financial "transformation" of the firm from a private to a public firm in market value terms (Illustration 14A.1).

Illustration 14A.1   Effects of the IPO Decision on NTC's Balance Sheet

NTC's Balance Sheet as a Private and as a Public Firm

Panel A: NTC as a private firm				
Assets	$125.000m	D(PRI)		$45.000m
		E(PRI)		$80.000m
V(PRI)	**$125.000m**	**V(PRI)**		**$125.000m**
Panel B: NTC as a public firm				
V(PRI)	$125.000m	D(PUB)		$46.000m
ΔV(w/IPO)[a]	$85.725m	D(PRI)	$45.000m	
		ΔD(PRI)	$-$1.000m	
		E(PUB)		$164.725m
		E_o(PUB)	$120.725m	
		E(IPO)	$44.000m	
V(PUB)	**$210.725m**	**V(PUB)**		**$210.725m**

[a]ΔV(w/IPO) is the additional value created by the IPO decision; however, not all of this incremental value belongs to the original owners.

[5] $120,725,000 is the actual value calculated using the actual offer price without rounding it to three decimal digits.

[6] $44,000,000 is the actual value calculated using the actual number of new shares 2,915,718 and the actual offer price without rounding it to three decimal digits.

[7] $164,725,000 is the actual value calculated using the actual number of total shares (8,000,000 + 2,915,718) and the actual offer price without rounding to three decimal digits.

Case of No Underpricing

If there is no underpricing, the new shares will be placed at an offer price equal to the expected new price of the stock. To raise the planned gross proceeds of $40m, NTC will sell new shares with a market value of $40m. The value of the original shares with the IPO is now:

$$E_o(\text{PUB}) = V(\text{PUB}) - D(\text{PUB}) - E(\text{IPO}) = \$210.275m - \$46m - \$40m = \$124.725m.$$

To estimate the new price of the stock with the IPO, we write:

$$\text{Price(PUB)} = \frac{E_o(\text{PUB})}{\text{Old No. of Shares}} = \frac{\$124.725m}{8m} = \$15.591 \text{ per share.}$$

In this case, the offer price is also equal to $15.591. Therefore, to raise $40m, the firm needs to place $\frac{\$40,000,000}{\$15.591 \text{per share}} = 2,565,583 \text{shares}$[8]. This number is less than the 2,915,664 shares the firm had to issue when the underpricing was 10% of the offer price.

The net gain of the IPO decision is estimated as:

$$\text{GAIN(IPO)} = E_o(\text{PUB}) - E(\text{PRI}) = \$124.725m - \$80m = \$44.725m.$$

Without underpricing, the original shareholders have saved the $4m, they would otherwise leave on the table under the 10% underpricing. As a result of the zero-underpricing deal, the original shareholders will own 75.72% (i.e., $124.725m/$164.725m) and the new shareholders will own 24.28% (i.e., $40m/$164.725m) of the firm's public equity. Without underpricing, the original shareholders retain a greater fraction of the equity of the firm after going public.

---

[8] This number is 61 shares less than the actual number (2,565,644) due to rounding of the offer price ($15.591) to three decimal digits in our illustrative calculations.

15

Structuring Securities Offerings

New securities can be placed with investors in public or private markets and under a variety of registration rules, underwriting arrangements and contracts. Issuers also have choices with respect to the marketplace for the listing of the new securities. Finally, issuers need to decide on the firms that will serve, respectively, as the underwriter, auditor, and legal counsel for the new issue.

This and the next chapter discuss the choices issuers, and underwriters have to make in structuring the offer of securities and present the empirical findings that can provide guidance in relation to these choices.

Choices and Criteria for Evaluation

The List of Decisions

Once a firm has decided to raise capital through an initial public offering (IPO), seasoned equity offering (SEO), or debt offering, its management, and most often in collaboration with the underwriter, needs to structure the offering so that it maximizes the benefits to the firm and meets its goals. The decisions that must be analyzed are as follows:

- Private versus public offer,
- General cash offer versus rights offering,
- Traditional versus shelf-registration offering,
- Negotiated versus competitive offer,
- The type of underwriting contract,
- The postoffer ownership structure in the case of equity offers,
- The share price level,
- The marketplace for listing.

These choices will be covered in this chapter. Additional decisions the issuer must make are those that refer to the underwriter and the structure of the underwriting syndicate, the auditor, and the legal counsel. These decisions will be covered in the following chapter.

The Decision Criteria

The above decisions should be evaluated with respect to certain criteria. By that, we mean the impact the decisions are expected to have on the costs and benefits associated with the issuance of securities which ultimately affect the value of the issuing firm. These criteria include the following:

- The issue announcement effect on the stock price of the issuing firm.
- The underwriter's fees (gross spread) and other related issuance costs.

- The degree of underpricing or overpricing.
- The long-run return performance of the issuing firm's stock.

Private Versus Public Offerings

Pros and Cons of Private Offerings

The main benefits and costs private placements have in comparison to public offers are summarized below:

Lower issuance costs: Private offers cost less in preparation and compliance than public offers due to less regulation.

Speedy placement: The absence of a formal approval process by the SEC allows private offers to reach the market in a timely fashion, thus enabling issuers to exploit windows of favorable valuation conditions.

Flexibility of terms: Privately placed issues allow a more flexible design of the terms of new issues (especially in the case of debt issues) that better align the payoffs of the new securities to the cash-flow pattern expected by the issuer.

Informational advantage: Private placements afford a greater exchange of inside information between the issuer and buying investors unencumbered by the quiet period restrictions. This can reduce the information asymmetry between the issuer and the investors. Nonetheless, the need for greater information production by investors may have to be compensated through a lower offer price.

Reduced agency problems: Since privately placed securities can be bought in large blocks by strategic investors, they can include provisions that permit closer monitoring of management decisions, thus reducing agency-type problems and the associated costs.

Ability to recontract: Privately placed securities, in particular debt, can be restructured with greater ease and timeliness in the case the issuer encounters difficulties in meeting the obligations emanating from the new securities.

However, the above advantages come with several disadvantages compared to publicly placed and traded securities.

Restricted liquidity: The rules governing private placements put restrictions in the resale and trading privileges of security holders. This can add a liquidity premium to the cost of capital. However, Rule 144A provides considerable relief to the liquidity problem of privately placed securities, provided certain conditions are met.

Irregular pricing: The lack of continuous and transparent trading for privately placed securities deprives them of the benefit of up to date prices.

The Private Placement Decision

In general, firms that suffer from asymmetric information and hence would have difficulty issuing securities in the public market would prefer to raise funds in the private market.

Resolving asymmetric information problems is more cost-efficient in the private than the public markets since private firm-related information is shared with few investors.

Consistent with the informational advantages of private placement, Hertzel and Smith (1993) find that private equity offers are preferred by firms whose stock is undervalued and, hence, would obtain a better valuation following the communication of sensitive information to private investors. Private equity placements are also conducted by smaller, less known firms whose financial condition is more difficult to assess (Marciukaityte, Szewczyk, and Varma, 2005). Wu (2004) finds that private placement firms have high information asymmetry; are less likely to have been backed by venture capital (VC) firms in the IPO preceding the private placement; have equity held by fewer institutional investors; their stock trades at wider bid−ask spreads; and have smaller trading volumes and are covered by fewer analysts. In sum, these are firms with less publicly available information.

Blackwell and Kidwell (1988) find that firms that always issue in private markets are smaller and riskier, whereas those that occasionally issue in private markets are larger, less risky firms with less agency problems and access to both private and public markets. Huang and Ramírez (2010) report that the likelihood for a private placement increases in the case of convertibles bonds without credit rating (i.e., bonds with greater asymmetric information).

The private offering of securities has experienced a dramatic surge thanks to the creation of the Rule 144A market, and the main beneficiary has been the issuance of debt by firms that carry very high credit risk and are subject to severe asymmetric information problems. Contrary to the perception of private markets as the primary market venue of private nonreporting firms, Livingston and Zhou (2002) report that, as of the late 1990s, about two-thirds of Rule 144A issuers were public-reporting firms.

Huang and Ramírez (2010) report that the Rule 144A market accounted for 82% of all convertible bond issues and 83% of all high-yield bond issues by 2004. These trends confirm the greater importance of information production for high-risk debt that private markets can support. An important motivation for the majority of speculative issues to prefer the Rule 144A market is the participation of lenders that specialize in the valuation of high-risk debt. The study finds that 88% of convertible and 91% of straight debt issues are registered with the SEC after their private placement. The commitment to register with the SEC gives investors assurance that the resale restrictions will be lifted and the firm-specific information will become public so that investors will be able to more fully assess the firm's true quality.

A recent development that has expanded the allure of private funding is the growth of the private initial public offerings (PIPO) market. This market allows high-value young private firms to raise private equity funds that rival those of regular IPOs. Brown and Wiles (2015) had identified 142 private firms with equity valuations exceeding $1 billion (the so-called "unicorns") which had raised $625 billion as of 2015. The main reasons private firms prefer to be funded through a PIPO are: avoidance of the compliance costs imposed by the Sarbanes−Oxley Act; avoidance of public issuance costs; and the decline of analyst coverage for new public firms as a result of regulatory constraints imposed after the IPO market irregularities in the early 2000s.

Announcement Stock Price Effects

Several studies report that the announcement of private equity issues causes a positive market reaction, which stands opposite to the generally documented negative price reaction to announcements of public equity offers (Wruck, 1989; Hertzel and Smith, 1993; Goh, Gombola, Lee, and Liu, 1999; Hertzel, Lemmon, Linck, and Rees, 2002). Positive stock price reaction is also found upon the announcement of straight (Szewczyk and Varma, 1991) and convertible (Fields and Mais, 1991) private debt issues. Hertzel, Lemmon, Linck, and Rees (2002) also find a positive stock price reaction at the announcement of private equity issues when they are preceded by poor return performance by the issuer's stock.

A special class of private sale of equity is the private investment in public equity (PIPE). Finnerty (2013) reports that PIPEs with a commitment to register soon after the placement realize negative stock price reaction around the time of issue announcement, whereas offers without a similar registration commitment experience a positive stock price reaction. The negative stock price reaction of PIPEs with a shorter registration timetable reflects the market's perception the stock is overvalued, and hence, insiders plan to sell before the true value of the firm is revealed.

Initial Pricing

Equity Offers

Privately placed issues are found to carry lower offer prices than public issues. The difference is compensation for the restricted liquidity, the additional monitoring costs of investors, and the possibility of postissue underperformance if the issuer is indeed overvalued. Wruck (1989) reports an average (median) offer price discount of 13.5% (12.2%) for private equity issues versus 4.1% (1.8%) for public equity offers. Hertzel and Smith (1993) find even greater average (median) discounts of 20.14% (13.25%) compared to 5.29% (5.24%) for public equity issues. Further, the offer price discount is less when the firm places more shares with a single investor who can exert more efficient monitoring. However, Wu (2004) reports evidence that casts doubt on the monitoring effect on discounts. For example, informed investors, like VC and pension funds, seem to decrease their holdings, whereas other blockholders increase theirs following private equity offers. Interestingly, discounts tend to increase when the initial buyers are inside managers, an indication of preferential treatment.

Hertzel, Lemmon, Linck, and Rees (2002) find that privately placed equity offerings have average (median) discounts of 16.5% (13.4%) relative to the market price at the end of the month prior to the placement. The authors explain these sizable discounts as compensation for resale restrictions and a hedge against postissue underperformance in light of the average poor pre-issue price performance of the issuing firms.

In the case of Rule 144A and PIPEs, the issuer can commit to register the privately placed securities in order to expedite the public trading of the placed securities. A shorter time to registration reduces the cost of liquidity restrictions but it can signal that the firm is overvalued (i.e., insiders are eager to trade their overvalued shares). The firm can defer the registration to allow time for its true value to be revealed but at the cost of less liquidity. Using a sample of private investments in public equity (PIPEs), Finnerty (2013) finds that PIPEs registered within 30 days of the placement carry average discount of 15.32% compared to 25.14% for PIPEs registered later—a difference explained by the liquidity effect.

Debt Offers

Blackwell and Kidwell (1988) find evidence that issuers choose the placement market that minimizes the financing cost. Smaller and riskier firms are those that primarily benefit from the private market due to the information and agency problems they face. These authors find that should these firms had chosen to issue public debt their effective (bid) yields would have been higher than those they obtained by issuing private debt. Similar evidence is found by Emerick and White (1992) in the case of debt issuers that used the Rule 144A market. They report that, thanks to the interest of institutional investors willing to engage in price discovery, relatively unknown firms which would have attracted little interest from underwriters are able to issue private debt at lower yield spreads (i.e., at higher offer prices) than similar firms that executed public debt offers.

If information about the issuer matters, seasoned issuers should obtain higher offer prices than first-time issuers when both types of issuers tap the primary markets. Fenn (2000) finds that although reoffering yields of high-yield (high-risk) debt issues were higher for Rule 144A issues than similar public issues, the yield premium had disappeared by the end of the 1990s. Furthermore, first-time debt issuers were not charged higher offer yields on their high-yield debt issues placed under Rule 144A. The findings imply that the qualified institutional buyers (QIBs) that participate in the Rule 144A market are sophisticated enough so that the limited information produced by underwriters does not impose an "information" premium on yields. Livingston and Zhou (2002) report higher reoffering yields for Rule 144A than public debt offers, with first-time debt issuers paying higher yields. Reoffering yields are lower for investment grade debt and for offers with registration commitments. They find no evidence to support Fenn's (2000) claim that premiums have declined over time.

Huang and Ramírez (2010) also report higher reoffering yields for Rule 144A and nonshelf public debt issues than shelf-registered public straight bond offers. Reoffering yields are not though significantly different across shelf, nonshelf, and Rule 144A convertible debt issues.

Underwriting Gross Spreads

Although first-time issuers are charged greater underwriter fees than seasoned issuers, Livingston and Zhou (2002) do not find significant difference in the gross spreads of Rule 144A and public issues of nonconvertible debt after controlling for other factors. Huang and Ramírez (2010) report that underwriting spreads of straight debt issues are higher if they are placed under Rule 144A and traditional (nonshelf) registration than shelf-registration. In contrast, gross spreads are not found to be significantly different across shelf, nonshelf, and Rule 144A convertible bond issues.

General Cash Offers Versus Rights Offerings

General Cash Offers

General cash offers allow the issuer to place the new securities with the general public across pools of investors. This can increase the recognition factor for the issuing firm and attract more investor interest, which can contribute to the production of more information about the firm and its securities. General cash offers increase dispersion of stock ownership and may result in less effective monitoring of managers. General cash offers are normally executed either with a firm commitment contract or a "best efforts" contract. General cash offers can be placed with bookbuilding, the subscription method, or an auction.

Rights Offerings

Rights offerings give existing shareholders the right of first refusal regarding the purchase of new shares. Each existing shareholder is allocated rights equal to the number of shares owned. A new share can be bought by surrendering a prescribed number of rights (say, 5 rights) and paying the subscription or exercise price (say, $10 per share). Shareholders have normally 3 weeks to exercise the rights. Since a right represents an option to buy a security at a fixed price, right-holders exercise them only if the actual market price of the security is higher than the subscription price at the end of the subscription period. Alternatively, a shareholder may sell the rights to other investors who are interested in participating in the new equity offer. Shareholders who fail to exercise or sell their rights incur a wealth loss.

The choices shareholders have with respect to the disposition of the rights depend on the institutional setting of the market. Rights may be nontransferable or nontradable in which case the trading of rights is practically impossible. In the United States, only half of all rights are transferable and many of these are not tradable (Holderness and Pontiff, 2016). Rights can also be renounceable or nonrenounceable as, for example, in Australia. Renounceable rights can be sold by their holders, whereas nonrenounceable rights do not permit shareholders to sell the rights. In the latter case, a shareholder can either liquidate equivalent amount of stock to finance the exercise of rights or let them expire and lose their value (Balachandran, Faff, and Theobald, 2008).

Rights offers can be executed by the firm itself (uninsured rights offerings) or with the assistance of an underwriter. Underwritten (insured) rights offerings are executed through a contract called the stand-by agreement. In this case, the underwriter bears underwriting risk only for the portion of the issue that is not taken up by investors through the exercise of the rights. The underwriter is compensated by the stand-by fee assessed on the gross proceeds (i.e., shares issued times the exercise price) and a take-up fee assessed on the number of unsold shares covered by the underwriter (say, $0.50 per share). The take-up fee compensates the underwriter for the risk of having to carry unsold securities.

Issuers can avoid the use of an underwriter altogether by simply setting the exercise price low enough to guarantee the full exercise of the rights. Besides a sufficiently low exercise price, the success of uninsured rights offers also depends on the precommitments of insiders to exercise their rights and buy new shares. Insider participation is a potent positive signal about the viability of the firm and helps mitigate the adverse selection problem faced by outside investors.

Although in many countries, corporations are obliged by law to use rights in their seasoned equity offerings, in the United States, corporations have the right to choose either a general cash offer or a rights issue. Nonetheless, the use of rights in the United States has dramatically declined since the 1960s. A study by Holderness and Pontiff (2016) reports that only 64% of rights are exercised, at an average loss of 7% in rights value. Several reasons have been proposed to explain this decline. First, many rights in the United States are not tradable, forcing shareholders either to participate or forfeit the rights. Second, Smith (1977) mentions that the sale of rights imposes brokerage fees and may also have tax implications. A third reason advanced by Smith (1977) and Hansen (1988) is board of directors' bias in favor of the more expensive firm commitment contract due to connections to investment bankers. Finally, an agency-related explanation is that managers prefer general cash offers in order to increase stock ownership diffusion and lessen the monitoring of outside shareholders (Hansen and Pinkerton, 1982).

The Rights Offering Decision

An interesting question is: what types of firms should have a preference for a rights offering versus a general cash offer? In general, within an asymmetric information environment, low-quality firms prefer to issue equity through a general cash offer in order to benefit from the underwriter certification effect. Firms perceived by their management to be of higher quality prefer an underwritten rights offer because the underwriter's investigation can distinguish them from lower quality firms. Those that prefer an uninsured rights offer are firms of intermediate quality whose insiders are optimistic about the firm's prospects and are willing to participate and take up their share of offered shares. These firms signal quality through higher exercise prices (Heinkel and Schwartz, 1986). Indeed, Eckbo and Masulis (1992) find that uninsured rights offerings have higher rates of precommitment than underwritten rights offers.

Heron and Lie (2004) propose that rights offerings are a better choice for firms that believe their stock is undervalued and are in financial distress. Although undervalued firms have a motive to issue debt, financial distress would preclude them from doing so. Ursel (2006) finds uninsured rights offerings to be preferred by firms close to bankruptcy and with limited access to underwriters. These firms are found to realize improvement in their operating performance.

Announcement Stock Price Effects

Rights offers in general are associated with smaller negative or even insignificant announcement abnormal stock returns in contrast to an average 3% negative stock price reaction following announcements of firm commitment (general cash) offers (Smith, 1977). Hansen (1988) finds a negative stock price reaction (-2.61%), whereas Eckbo and Masulis (1992) find that while underwritten rights offers realize negative abnormal stock returns, uninsured rights offers produce insignificant announcement stock price reaction. However, uninsured rights offers are associated with stock price declines between the announcement day and the day before expiration. This means a downward adjustment in price beyond that justified by the lower exercise price.

Positive and greater stock price reaction following uninsured as opposed to underwritten rights offers have been reported in Norway (Bøhren, Eckbo, and Michalsen, 1997). Tsangarakis (1996) also reports significant positive announcement returns for uninsured rights offers completed by Greek firms. In both these studies, the stock price reaction is positively related to increasing stock ownership by insiders, which serves as a signal of confidence in the future of the firms. In contrast to these findings, Slovin, Sushka, and Lai (2000) find that uninsured rights offers in the United Kingdom are associated with more negative stock price reaction than insured rights around announcement time. The announcement performance of rights offers is worse for issues with lower shareholder take-up rates and lower subscription prices. The overall better returns of underwritten issues are attributed to the certification role of underwriters. Similarly, Balachandran, Faff, and Theobald (2008) find less negative price reaction to announcements of fully insured rights offers than to uninsured rights offers executed by Australian firms.

An interesting question is whether the stock price reaction is related to the subscription (or exercise) price of the rights. If existing shareholders buy all the new shares or sell their rights at fair prices, then there should be no transfer of wealth from the current to the new shareholders and the exercise price should not matter. However, a firm that is uncertain about the value of its stock at the rights expiration date would be inclined to choose a lower exercise price to ensure the success of the issue, thus inadvertently sending a negative signal. The studies of Eckbo and Masulis (1992), Bøhren, Eckbo, and Michalsen (1997), and Tsangarakis (1996) find no evidence of a relationship between stock price reaction and subscription price.

Issuance Costs

Smith (1977) reports that uninsured rights issues carry low flotation costs (2.45% on average) compared to underwritten rights issues (4.32%) and firm commitment general cash offers (5.02%). In more recent samples, average (median) gross spreads and other expenses have been found to be 5.53% (3.82%) for firm commitment, 3.32% (2.07%) for stand-by agreements, and 0.94% (0.22%) for uninsured rights offers (Eckbo and Masulis, 1992). Uninsured rights offers have also been found to be less expensive than insured rights offers in Norway (Bøhren, Eckbo, and Michalsen, 1997).

With respect to the price discount (i.e., the difference of offer price or subscription price to last trading price) in firm commitment offers and rights offers, Eckbo and Masulis (1992) report average (median) discounts of 0.44% (0.00%) for firm commitments, 20.4% (19.5%) for stand-by agreements, and 8.3% (14.3%) for uninsured rights offers completed in the 1960s and 1970s. Ursel (2006) reports average (median) discount of 13.5% (7.5%) for a sample of uninsured rights offers completed in the 1980s and 1990s.

Kothare (1997) documents one more disadvantage of rights offerings versus general cash offerings. Specifically, Kothare finds that the bid–ask spread (as percent of the midpoint of bid and ask prices) increases after rights offerings but declines after pubic underwritten offerings. The main reason appears to be the heavier stock ownership concentration that results when firms execute rights offerings.

Traditional Versus Shelf-Registration Offerings

All issues registered with Form S-3 and entitled to the delayed offering privileges of Rule 415 are referred to as shelf-registration offerings. New issues registered with Form S-1 (including all IPOs) are referred to as traditional or nonshelf offerings.

Shelf Versus Traditional Offerings

Shelf-registration issues enjoy simpler filing requirements and very short review periods. Shelf-registered offers can be also sold in whole or in part over a 3-year period after the registration statement becomes effective. Instead, traditional offers must produce fresh registration materials and undergo the full SEC review process. Hence, they have longer waiting periods. In addition, once the prospectus has been approved, the issue must be offered for sale or be withdrawn in the face of unexpected adverse conditions. As a result of these regulatory differences, shelf offers enjoy a number of benefits over nonshelf offers.

- Shelf issues have lower preparation and registration costs.
- Shelf issuers can bring issues to the market when valuations are high or interest rates are low; hence, exposure of issuer to waiting risk is minimal.
- Once the issue has been declared effective, issuers have the flexibility to redesign an issue before placing it in the market without further SEC review.
- Shelf-registration fosters competition among investment banks, which need to offer attractive terms (i.e., underwriting spreads, offer price) in order to win mandates.
- However, the issuer's ability to choose the time of sale leaves investment banks with little time to perform due diligence and price discovery.

The Shelf Versus Nonshelf Offer Decision

The lack of sufficient time for underwriters to engage in price discovery and bookbuilding activities are important concerns to firms which are less well-known, riskier, and undervalued. These firms stand to benefit more from information production than well-established firms. Thus, meeting the criteria for a Rule 415 offer is not sufficient for a firm to choose a shelf issue. In an early study, Denis (1993) found that equity issuers that qualified for shelf-registration registered with the short Form S-3 to reduce flotation costs but retained an underwriter to conduct a fully marketed offer. In contrast, in the case of debt issues (which are less beset by adverse selection problems), firms took full advantage of Rule 415 by registering on Form S-3 and conducting sales into the market.

Blackwell, Marr, and Spivey (1990) and Denis (1991) find shelf-registration is more likely in the case of less risky firms and firms with a greater public profile. Heron and Lie (2004) find that shelf issuers are more likely to have larger capitalization and leverage and have less value attributed to growth opportunities. Shelf issues are also less likely to coincide with a preoffer price run-up to avoid the impression of opportunistic timing that would increase the adverse selection concerns of investors.

Despite its advantages over traditional offers, the popularity of shelf-registration declined dramatically over time following its adoption in 1983. Sherman (1999) attributes this decline to diminished due diligence and underwriter reluctance to manage shelf issues of risky firms. But Autore, Kumar, and Shome (2008) note that after a period of decline, the number of shelf issues had started to recover from 0 to 8 issues annually for most of the 1990s to 26 to 84 issues in 1997–2003. They also confirm the pattern found in Denis (1993) that firms register under Rule 415 but conduct fully underwritten offerings for the benefit of due diligence. A recent study by Gustafson and Iliev (2017) finds that the use of accelerated, shelf registration issues has increased following the SEC relaxation of the $75 million of market capitalization requirement in 2008. This has given previously excluded firms greater access to public markets and significant reduction in price discounts and issuance fees for equity issues.

Announcement Stock Price Effects

Shelf equity issues have been found to generate less negative announcement stock price reaction than nonshelf issues (Bhagat, Marr, and Thompson, 1985). But Moore, Peterson, and Peterson (1986) find no difference in announcement returns between shelf and nonshelf issues. Denis (1991) reports higher negative announcement returns for shelf issues of more volatile stocks and attributes it to weaker underwriter certification compared to nonshelf issues. In more recent samples of new stock issues, Heron and Lie (2004) find a less negative announcement stock price reaction for shelf issuers (median value of -1.6%) compared to a median announcement return of -2.5% for nonshelf issuers. The same study reports postissue declines in the operating performance of traditional registration issuers but improvements for shelf issuers (another indication that shelf issuers do not engage in opportunistic timing of their shelf equity offers). Autore, Kumar, and Shome (2008) report that when a firm's past issuance of securities has been subject to the scrutiny of the markets (as in the case of an underwritten offering), announcements of shelf issues are followed by stock price reaction similar to that generated by traditional issues. On the contrary, first-time shelf issuers realize worse announcement stock returns due to undercertification.

Issuance Costs

Equity Offers

Early research on shelf equity offers showed that they enjoyed savings in underwriting spreads over nonshelf issues (Bhagat, Marr, and Thompson, 1985). Most of the cost savings of shelf-registration were realized by less risky issuers (Blackwell, Marr, and Spivey, 1990). Allen, Lamy, and Thompson (1990) and Denis (1993) find that those equity issuers who qualified for shelf-registration had not enjoyed any savings when they adopted the shelf-registration method. Nonetheless, these issuers enjoyed cost savings compared to nonqualifying issuers. This implies that the cost savings were mostly explained by differences in the profiles of issuers and not the shelf registration method itself. This cost neutrality does not seem to have persisted though. In more recent samples, Autore, Kumar, and Shome (2008) find that shelf equity issues are less expensive than nonshelf issues by the same issuers. Shelf issues by firms that have been scrutinized in prior financial deals also enjoy a cost advantage over those without a pre-issue certification record.

Debt Offers

Although gross spreads of shelf and traditional debt offers were found to be indistinguishable in Rogowski and Sorensen (1985), they were found to differ in favor of shelf issues in Kidwell, Marr, and Thompson (1984) and Foster (1989). Shelf debt issuers appear to benefit in the form of lower (higher) reoffering yields (offer prices) (e.g., Kidwell, Marr, and Thompson, 1984; Rogowski and Sorensen, 1985). In addition, Kadapakkam and Kon (1989) find evidence that due to their timing advantage, shelf issuers were able to issue debt at lower reoffering yields than traditional offer issuers. Fung and Rudd (1986) report higher reoffering yields for speculative grade bond issues if they are shelf-registered instead of being fully marketed by underwriters.

Negotiated Versus Competitive Offerings

In negotiated offerings, the issuer chooses the underwriting firm that can best meet the needs of the issue. The issuer and the underwriter negotiate the terms of the offer and work together to prepare the issue for registration and marketing to investors. In competitive offerings, the winning underwriter is the investment bank that submits the highest bid, that is, the price, net of underwriting costs, the underwriter must pay to buy the new issue.

Negotiated offerings allow the underwriter to engage in extensive investigation of the issuer's business and have time to market the issue and learn the investors' opinions regarding its value. A more thorough price discovery can lead to higher offer price but the greater effort extended by the underwriter and the syndicate can also result in a higher underwriting cost to compensate underwriters for due diligence effort and certification.

The advantage of competitive bids comes mainly from increased competition among investment banks. The net effect of competitive offerings on underwriting costs depends on the trade-off between less extensive information production and higher underwriter risk. By limiting the price discovery and due diligence effort, a competitive offering may leave the underwriter with greater uncertainty about the value of the issue. If the higher premium for underwriting risk exceeds the savings from reduced price discovery and marketing, gross spread would be higher than in a comparable negotiated issue. In many respects, competitive offerings resemble shelf or accelerated offerings.

The study of negotiated versus competitive offerings is usually done utilizing samples of new issues offered by utility firms. Rule 50 of the Public Utility Company Act of 1935 stipulates that all registered utility holding companies must use the competitive method to issue securities except during those periods the rule is suspended. The SEC grants the suspension in periods of high market volatility when investment banks would be reluctant to submit bids without the benefit of due diligence and price discovery.

When both methods are permitted, an issuer should choose the method that minimizes the effective cost of issuance, that is, the bid price or bid yield for debt, given the characteristics of the issuer and the market conditions. Accordingly, firms about which more is known and with easy to value operations (i.e., less information asymmetry and adverse selection problems) are more likely to choose the competitive offer. On the other hand, lower quality and riskier firms can benefit from the price discovery and underwriter certification of negotiated offers (Smith, 1987).

Announcement Stock Price Effects

There is limited evidence on how stock prices react to the issuance of negotiated or competitive bond offers. Bhagat (1986) finds when the SEC suspends Rule 50 utility firms experience a negative stock price reaction, whereas termination of the suspension generates positive stock price reaction. One explanation for the market's response is that the negotiated method is more expensive and consumes equity value. An alternative, not mutually exclusive, explanation is that, left to the managers' discretion, the choice of the offering method is motivated by benefits managers derive from preferential relationships with investment banks at the expense of value maximization.

Issuance Costs

Negotiated debt offers are associated with higher (lower) reoffering yields (prices) after accounting for differences in quality and other terms (Ederington, 1976; Sorensen, 1979; Smith, 1987). Bid yields (prices) are also found to be higher (lower) in negotiated than competitive offers (Sorensen, 1979). The same authors and Bhagat and Frost (1986) find that negotiated offers also carry higher gross spreads.

The evidence shows that the beneficial impact of competitive offers on yields and gross spreads increases with the number of competitive bids and declines with issue and market uncertainty. The competitive offer is also less advantageous than the negotiated offer in the case of lower quality debt or in the case of volatile markets. In these cases, gross spreads and yields are lower under the negotiated method (Fabozzi, Moran, and Ma, 1988; Smith, 1987).

The Underwriting Contract Decision

The choice of the underwriting contract is closely associated with the offering method the issuer chooses for the sale of the new securities. For example, an underwritten rights issue is handled with a stand-by agreement. A general cash offer in the United States can be executed under a firm commitment or a "best efforts" contract. As the stand-by agreement was discussed earlier in this chapter, below we evaluate the decision to use a firm commitment versus a "best efforts" contract.

The Firm Commitment Contract

This is a full-service contract. The underwriter agrees to buy the new issue from the issuer at the agreed bid price and then sells it at a higher fixed offer price. The spread between the offer and bid price compensates the syndicate for the underwriting services. The firm commitment contract gives the issuer the assurance that all the capital expected from the new issue (minus the spread) will be raised. The risk of failure lies with the underwriting syndicate. An escape clause gives the issuer and underwriter the option to withdraw the issue if they face unfavorable conditions.

The "Best Efforts" Contract

Under a "best efforts" contract, the underwriter provides the issuer origination, pricing, and distribution services but does not underwrite the placement risk. The issuer and the underwriter agree on the terms of the offer, mainly the bid and offer price, and the underwriter commits to a best effort to ensure the issue is placed with investors. Any unsold portion of the issue reverts to the issuer as the underwriter has no obligation to step in and buy the unsold part. Under this contract, the issuer bears the uncertainty about the proceeds from the issue. As with all new issues, the offer price may prove to be too high, in which case the issue may not be fully placed. To overcome this uncertainty, "best efforts" contracts often carry an "all-or-none" clause that gives the issuer the right to cancel the issue if placement of the whole issue at the fixed offer price fails. Alternatively, the contract may set a minimum and maximum number of shares to be sold, also referred to as the minimum sales constraint (MSC).

Decision Factors

Certification and price discovery: Under a firm commitment contract, the underwriter bears full responsibility for the placement of the issue; therefore, he/she has a keen interest in certifying its value by engaging in extended price discovery and due diligence. With the underwriting responsibility absent in "best efforts" contracts, the underwriter is less motivated to provide as strong a certification as under the firm commitment contract.

Probability of withdrawal: "Best efforts" contracts have higher probability of cancelation. The main reason is the uncertainty about their reception by investors and the "all-or-none" or MSC provisions. Higher likelihood of cancelation decreases the probability of execution and the realization of the compensation underwriters expect. This, in turn, can lead to higher underwriting charges. On the other hand, the escape provisions allow the issuer to set a higher offer price and test the receptivity of the market. Thus, unlike firm commitment contracts under which price discovery precedes pricing of the issue, in "best efforts" contracts, price discovery follows the pricing of the issue.

Proceeds and capital needs: When issue proceeds are purposed to meet important capital needs, the contract choice presents issuers with difficult trade-offs. A firm commitment contract in conjunction with the overallotment option (OAO) can reduce the issuance costs. For example, by increasing the OAO size, the underwriter can underprice the issue less because there are more securities to allocate to investors who produce and share information. The probability of raising the planned capital is also higher with an OAO because with more securities available for sale it is more likely the original proceeds target will be reached. Thus, a larger size OAO lowers the gross spread and the underpricing (Welch, 1991).

Issuers who choose the "best efforts" contract can attempt to raise a greater amount of proceeds by setting a higher MSC in order to motivate the underwriter to exert greater effort to avoid cancelation of the issue and loss of compensation. Although a higher MSC sends a positive signal about the quality of the issue, it also raises the probability of cancelation if the minimum level of proceeds is too big to place (Ritter, 1987).

Information production costs: Given the weaker motivation of underwriters to engage in full price discovery as well as the presence of escape provisions that may signal overpricing, interested investors have to bear a greater part of the information production effort in a "best efforts" offer. Hence, they may demand higher compensation in the form of lower offer prices to commit themselves to participate in "best efforts" offers (Sherman, 1992).

The Issuer's Perspective

In light of the above pros and cons, how should issuers choose between firm commitment and "best efforts" contracts? Firms considered to be undervalued would benefit more from greater certification and price discovery that would separate them from poor-quality firms. Thus, they would prefer the firm commitment contract (Bower, 1989). On the other hand, overvalued firms beset by relatively high information asymmetry concerning their value can benefit from the "best efforts" contract. Issuers can avoid heavy underpricing because under the escape clauses, the issue can be canceled if the offer price is too high to attract enough demand. The possibility of cancelation should the offer price proves to be too high also mitigates the adverse selection problem of uninformed investors (Ritter, 1987).

The most likely candidates for the "best efforts" contract are small issues by less well-known and riskier firms which are also less likely to attract prestigious underwriters. In these cases, the cost of price discovery and marketing may be nominally and proportionately too high under a firm commitment contract (Sherman, 1992).

In their survey, Brau and Fawcett (2006) find that Chief Financial Officers prefer the firm commitment contract. However, this contract is not easily available to speculative and low-quality issuers. Prestigious investment banks are, in general, averse to underwriting issues with high price uncertainty under the "best efforts" contract. Hence, the choice of contract and underwriter quality are not independent.

Issuance Costs

Judging by the gamut of services provided under each contract, one would expect firm commitment contracts to be more expensive than "best efforts" contracts. However, the opposite is true. The main explanation is that "best efforts" contracts are used by smaller and riskier firms and thus require greater effort to place the issue. In addition, "best efforts" issues have small investor base and thus require more market making support in the aftermarket (Chua, 1995).

Ritter (1987) finds average gross spread of 8.67% for firm commitment offers and 10.26% for "best efforts" offers. Other flotation costs are also higher for "best efforts" offers. In contrast, Welch (1991) finds that average underwriter compensation is lower for "best efforts" offerings. Both Ritter (1987) and Welch (1991) find that IPOs underwritten under the firm commitment contract had lower average initial return (14.8% in Ritter and 14.7% in Welch) compared to an average initial return (47.78% in Ritter and 46.5% in Welch) for "best efforts" contracts. Both studies find that underpricing declines with the size of the OAO (as expected) in firm commitment contracts, whereas underpricing increases with the minimum sales constraint (MSC) in "best efforts" contracts. The finding in connection to the MSC constraint is contrary to the expectation that this escape clause can lessen the degree of underpricing. Both Ritter (1987) and Welch (1991) find that although the OAO exerts a negative impact on gross spreads of firm commitment contracts, the gross spread increases with the MSC in "best efforts" offers. The latter relationship implies that offers with higher MSC are more expensive to market, and underwriters charge more. Ritter (1987) concludes that had the "best efforts" issuers switched to a firm commitment contract (for its apparently lower costs), they would have sustained higher underpricing and spreads than under the "best efforts" contract.

Using a more recent sample period, including the late 1990s, Chua (1995) reports that average fees are 8.87% for firm commitment and 11.89% for "best efforts" offerings, whereas underpricing averages 11.1% for firm commitment and 46.98% for "best efforts" offerings. Average issue size, age, offer price, and underwriter ranking are much lower for "best efforts" offers, whereas aftermarket bid−ask spread and volatility of returns are higher. The evidence is consistent with the general prediction that "best efforts" contracts are chosen by relatively small, risky, and less well-known firms whose offers would pose more severe adverse selection problems to investors and, hence, demand much greater marketing and pricing effort by underwriters.

Warrants as Underwriter Compensation

It is not uncommon for the underwriting contract to include warrants, especially when the issuer is a smaller and riskier firm. The warrants grant the underwriter the option to buy a fixed number of securities from the issuing firm at a fixed (exercise) price within a fixed time period. The warrants have value as long as there is a probability the price of the security will exceed the exercise price and the underwriter exercises them. Thus, warrants are an indirect compensation for the underwriter. It is estimated that the value of warrants is upward of 50% of the underwriter spread. Regulations prohibit the shares issued under warrants to exceed 10% of the IPO shares and the exercise of warrants within the first year.

Warrants provide complementary compensation to the underwriter in offers whose underwriting costs would suggest a gross spread deemed too high according to guidelines set by FINRA. Warrants can mitigate adverse selection problems because of their interaction with the offer price. As they enhance the underwriter's compensation, there is less reason to lower the offer price in order to lower the underwriting costs. On the other hand, to make warrants more valuable, the underwriter could underprice the issue more than necessary so that the exercise price—which cannot fall short of the offer price—is more likely to remain below the market price of the issue. Warrants can be also used to signal the underwriter's confidence in the future of the firm. Dunbar (1995) finds that the likelihood of including warrants decreases with the size of the secondary portion of the IPO (that is, the fraction of shares existing shareholders sell as part of the public offering), the offer price, firm value, and underwriter reputation. Ng and Smith (1996) also find that compared to nonwarrant users, warrant users are smaller and riskier issuers that raise lower proceeds and retain less prestigious underwriters.

Issuers should grant warrants only if they help reduce the overall issuance cost of the offer. Barry, Muscarella, and Vetsuypens (1991) find that 17% of 723 IPOs completed in 1983–1987 granted warrants to the underwriters. Dunbar (1995) finds evidence consistent with the cost minimization hypothesis. Total costs (underpricing, underwriting fees, and other expenses) are negatively related to the use of warrants. For warrant users, the total issuance cost is found to be 47% but without warrants the cost would have been 51%. Dunbar concludes that issuers rationally decide in favor or against warrants as a means to reduce issuance costs, and the use of warrants does not represent overcompensation of underwriters.

As warrants have value only if the stock price is likely to rise above the current value, warrants certify the underwriter's confidence in the future prospects of the firm. But for warrants to be a credible signal, the gross spread must be lower than the underwriter's costs—so that the positive value of the warrants complements the gross spread. Using a sample of SEOs, Ng and Smith (1996) find evidence that the gross spread and underpricing would have been higher had warrant users not used warrants, which is evidence that warrants represent complementary compensation. The evidence suggests that issuers make rational use of warrants in their effort to minimize costs and maximize proceeds.

Unit IPOs

The flotation costs can be also impacted by the presence of rights that allow investors to buy more of the issued security in the future at a presumably lower price. The joint sale of new shares and such rights or warrants at the offer price is referred to as a Unit IPO. The warrants, which represent call options, give the investor the right to buy a fixed number of shares of the issuing firm at a fixed (exercise) price within a fixed period of time. These warrants must be distinguished from warrants granted to underwriters as a form of supplemental compensation, though the incidence of unit IPOs correlates with the granting of warrants to underwriters. The warrants in unit offers often include antidilution provisions to prevent the firm rendering the warrants worthless. For example, if there is a stock split, the number of shares in the warrants is adjusted accordingly. Warrants may also include provisions that allow the issuing firm to keep the warrants alive through amendments that extend the expiration time, lower the exercise price, or both.

Raising capital with the use of unit offerings is considered to be a form of staged financing, which is especially appropriate for new startup firms (Schultz, 1993). New firms with uncertain prospects are exposed to moral hazard problems related to the possibility that insiders may squander or appropriate funds and thus hurt the firm's value. Warrants give the firm the opportunity to raise additional capital if its operations prove to be successful. Schultz (1993) finds that unit offers are more frequently used by smaller, younger, and riskier firms. Both underwriting fees and underpricing are higher for unit IPOs than shares-only IPOs.

Firms may choose to amend the terms of warrants in unit offers by either extending the expiration term or lowering the exercise price. Extension amendments allow firms that face capital constraints to fund future valuable growth opportunities. Thus, extending the expiration period is a positive signal. Although lowering the exercise price is a negative signal, it is still rational for firms that expect their valuation to improve in the future. Garner and Marshall (2004) find that half of their sample of firms with unit IPOs faced an "amend or expire" decision. The likelihood of extending the term of the warrants is greater for firms with greater cash needs and shorter expiration periods. The likelihood of lowering the exercise price also increases with greater cash needs and lower inside ownership (explained by the insiders' aversion to stock price dilution). Firms with better value prospects are also more likely to amend the exercise price downward in order to increase the probability the warrants will remain a potential source of capital.

Ownership Structure and Investor Clientele Decisions

Most IPOs and many SEOs have a secondary offering that allows current shareholders, including insiders, to liquidate a portion of their shareholdings in the firm. Thus, secondary offers can alter the ownership structure of equity in relation to existing and new shareholders. In addition, the issuing firm can structure the offer in ways that appeal primarily to large (mostly institutional) investors or to small (mostly individual investors). The preference for institutional versus individual investors is a choice about investor clientele. These decisions can have consequences for the cost of the offering and the value of the firm's securities.

The Secondary Offer Decision

What portion of their pre-issue equity holdings the current shareholders decide to retain and what portion they decide to sell in the secondary offering can have serious wealth consequences. These wealth effects are related to the degree of underpricing of the new shares. Selling shareholders sustain a direct loss when their shares are offered at an offer price below the market price of shares. Underpricing also results in floating more shares to raise a fixed amount of equity; hence, all pre-issue shareholders sustain a price dilution on their retained shares.

Specifically, we have seen in Chapter 14: The Decision to Issue Securities that if the firm places new shares at an offer price equal to the price implied by the value of equity with the decision to issue there is no price dilution. If, however, the new shares are sold at a lower offer price, there is dilution. Not accounting for the flotation expenses, the new price with dilution can be estimated as:

$$MP = \frac{NO \times PB + NN \times OP}{NO + NN},$$

where MP is the postdilution market price, NO is the number of old shares, PB is the predilution price, OP is the offer price, and NN is the number of new shares (Habib and Ljungqvist, 2001). The greater the size of the primary offer or the greater the underpricing, the lower the postdilution price is.

Habib and Ljungqvist (2001) estimate the wealth loss sustained by retaining and selling shareholders as:

$$\text{Wealth loss} = NR \times (PB - MP) + NS \times (PB - OP),$$

where NR is the number of retained shares, and NS is the number of secondary shares sold. The difference PB − MP is the dilution in relation to the postissue market price, whereas PB − OP is the dilution in relation to the offer price. Since with underpricing, OP < MP, the difference PB − MP is less than the difference PB − OP. Hence, it is clear that selling shareholders sustain a greater loss per share than the retaining shareholders.

Example: In Chapter 14: The Decision to Issue Securities, it was estimated that the predilution price of the stock with the various valuation effects was $15.59. The stock price with 2.916 million additional shares at an offer price of $13.72 was estimated to be $15.09. This price is also equal to (8 million × $15.59 + 2.916 million × $13.72)/(8 million + 2.916 million), where 8 million are the old shares and 2.916 million are the new shares. In this example, the old shares sustained a price dilution of $0.50 per share ($15.59 − $15.09). If the current shareholders sell 2 million out of their 8 million shares under a secondary offer, the wealth loss of the retaining and the selling shareholders is:

$$\text{Wealth loss} = 6 \text{ million} \times (\$15.59 - \$15.09) + 2 \text{ million} \times (\$15.59 - \$13.72)$$
$$= \$3 \text{ million} + \$3.74 \text{ million} = \$6.74 \text{ million}.$$

The relative loss of the retaining shareholders is: $3 million/(6 million × $15.59) = 3.2%. The relative loss of the selling shareholders is: $3.74 million/(2 million × $15.59) = 12%. If the underpricing were higher, the relative loss of the selling shareholders would rise.

Shareholders, especially insiders, that expect to sell a large fraction of their holdings in the secondary offer, have a strong incentive to bargain for as small an underpricing as possible. Or from a different perspective, when the degree of underpricing is expected to be high, current shareholders will be better off to limit the size of the secondary offer and retain more of the pre-issue shares. The ratio of retained shares to the primary shares is often defined as the "overhang." Dolvin and Jordan (2008) report that overhang for IPOs averaged around

2.60 in 1986–2004 but jumped to an average of 4.4 in the dot-com years of 1999–2000, when underpricing was extremely high.

In addition to losses because of underpricing, the issuing firm should also consider other value-related effects associated with the inclusion and the size of a secondary offer in the IPO or SEO.

Valuation Effects

The secondary part of an equity offer can include shares sold on behalf of insiders (i.e., owners in managerial positions) as well as shares sold on behalf of other owners that hold passive investments in the firm. Although the decision of major owners to sell shares matters for the valuation of the firm, the participation of insiders carries particular weight because of their more intimate knowledge about the current and future financial state of the firm. For this reason, the impact of secondary sales by insiders has received particular attention.

By tying up more of their wealth in the equity of one firm insiders bear the cost of reduced diversification and are, thus, more exposed to the idiosyncratic risk of the firm. Unless the performance of the firm is expected to compensate for the higher risk, insiders have no reason to raise their investment in their firms' equity (Leland and Pyle, 1977). Hence, greater retention is a positive signal. If insiders reduce their holdings, their wealth is dependent less on the value of the firm. In this case, insiders may be more inclined to engage in behavior that increases their private benefits at the expense of other shareholders. Therefore, a lower retention rate has a negative impact on firm value (Ritter, 1984).

Using samples of IPOs, Downes and Heinkel (1982) find evidence in favor of signaling, whereas Ritter (1984) finds evidence favoring the agency cost explanation regarding the positive relationship between owner retention and firm value. Recent evidence also supports that IPO firms obtain better offer prices and aftermarket values when retention rates are higher. The positive impact of retention is stronger for firms in high-tech sectors (including internet firms). Importantly, positive changes in the retention rates of insiders (i.e., CEOs, directors, and venture capital firms) are associated with higher valuation of IPO shares (Aggarwal, Bhagat, and Rangan, 2009; Xiao and Yung, 2015).

Higher participation rate of insiders in the secondary portion of SEOs is found to be associated with worse stock price reaction (Heron and Lie, 2004). There is no evidence though that firms attempt to sell overvalued equity, as firms that conduct secondary offers are found to realize improvement in their postoffer operating performance regardless of the size of equity stake sold by insiders. Similar findings are reported by Gokkaya and Highfield (2014) who find that announcement returns are more negative for SEOs with higher executive participation rate in secondary offerings. Long-run postissue returns are also worse when executives sell shares in secondary offers. However, Lee and Masulis (2009) argue that for a given size of proceeds, larger fractions of secondary offers reduce the size of the primary offer and thus less amount of capital flows to the firm. This reduces the agency problem that free cash flow may be wasted in nonvalue maximizing projects. Consistent with this conjecture, they find a slightly more favorable stock price reaction at the announcement of SEOs that have a larger fraction of secondary offer (though the overall stock price reaction is still negative).

Signaling Through Resale Restrictions

Besides the retention rate, insiders can convey their confidence in the value of the firm by deferring liquidation of their shares to allow sufficient time for all relevant information to emerge, thus mitigating the adverse selection risk of outside investors (Courteau, 1995). Extending the lockup period is also a valuable signal of insider confidence when the original size of the secondary offer is amended in response to strong preoffer demand that suggests a higher offer price. Ang and Brau (2003) find that in these cases, insiders accept longer lockup periods in order to blunt any negative signal due to the greater secondary sale. Interestingly, the degree of underpricing is related to the original size of the secondary offer; amendments that raise the fraction of the secondary offer have no relation to initial returns. It seems that the intention to sell more insider shares escapes the attention of the market or does not matter.

Zhang (2005) reports that 24% of firms that have an IPO with a lockup provision conduct an SEO before the lockup period expires. Insiders sell more shares in the follow-on SEO than in the IPO and the size of their selling varies directly with the degree of underpricing in the IPO. The size of the secondary offer in the follow-on SEO is inversely related to the size of the IPO and the insiders' participation in the IPO. These patterns suggest that insiders are mindful of the negative signal of secondary sales in IPOs and spread the liquidation of their holdings over successive offers in order to mitigate the negative information effects. Insiders also postpone their selling in order to avoid the cost of high underpricing.

Underpricing Effects

The size of the secondary offer (and conversely the retention rate) can also impact the degree of underpricing. In early research, Logue (1973a) reports an inverse relationship between the secondary fraction of IPO shares offered and degree of underpricing. He attributes this to greater insider interest in receiving a higher offer price on their shares. Habib and Ljungqvist (2001) report higher promotion costs and lower underpricing as the secondary offer fraction increases. Current shareholders can avoid losses on secondary sales by retaining more shares. The evidence confirms that higher share overhang (the ratio of retained shares to new shares offered) is positively associated with the degree of underpricing (Bradley and Jordan, 2002). Bradley, Cooney, Jordan, and Singh (2004) find that the positive relationship between overhang and underpricing became significant after 1990 as average underpricing started to rise. Interestingly, the size of the secondary offer by itself does not affect the degree of underpricing in their sample. Intintoli and Kahle (2010) report that SEOs with high proportion of secondary shares are less underpriced; they attribute this to firm's executives putting more pressure on underwriters, especially when the latter are of lower rank.

Underwriting Cost Effects

The positive valuation effect of insider holdings can also affect underwriting costs by enhancing confidence in the value of the firm. Indeed, Hansen and Torregrosa (1992) find that the gross spread is lower in SEOs executed by firms with greater managerial holdings. However, the size of secondary offers in SEOs is found by Lee and Masulis (2009) to have a negative impact on gross spreads which can be explained by their argument that a higher fraction of the secondary offer reduces the valuation uncertainty surrounding the use of new capital by issuing firms.

The Investor Clientele Decision

The decision concerning the allocation of new securities between large (better informed) investors and small (less informed) investors is related to the effects of corporate control and monitoring. Entrenched insiders prefer a widespread distribution of shares in order to minimize takeover threats and lessen the degree of monitoring by large outside investors. To achieve this, insiders are willing to accept a higher than necessary underpricing in order to attract mostly small investors. The alternative view argues that executives welcome outside monitoring in order to reduce agency problems and increase the firm's value. Stoughton and Zechner (1998) argue that firms with less known business histories and more complex assets and operations (e.g., high-tech firms) benefit more from outside monitoring by investors. These firms may have to accept higher underpricing in order to compensate large investors for the cost of information production implied by active monitoring. Mello and Parsons (1998) propose that to maximize total proceeds from the sale of equity, a firm should first sell to small investors and later sell larger blocks to large investors. By selling first to retail investors, the issuer can learn about its value and then negotiate the sale price with large investors. However, empirical evidence in Aruğaslan, Cook, and Kieschnick (2004) suggests that large institutional holdings are explained by issuing firm size and not the degree of underpricing. This implies that issuers do not necessarily set the degree of underpricing with the goal to influence postissue stock ownership in favor of large investors.

The Price Level Decision

The level of price a firm chooses for its shares following its IPO can have implications in relation to trading costs, attracting different investor clienteles, and eliciting analyst attention and coverage. The issuer can calibrate the price level by adjusting the number of total shares that will be outstanding after the IPO. Given the estimated total value of equity with the new issue, choosing a higher or lower number of outstanding shares adjusts the price to a lower or higher level. This is similar to adjusting the number of shares in a stock split in order to attain a preferred trading price range for the stock.

Example: Let us assume the equity value of the firm with the IPO has been estimated at $500 million. If the preferred market price is around $20, there should be 25 million shares outstanding following the IPO. If the firm needs to raise gross proceeds by selling shares with a market value of $100 million, the firm will issue 5 million new shares. Therefore, the existing shareholders will own the remaining 20 million shares. If these shareholders currently own 10 million shares, the firm will withdraw these old shares and distribute to the old shareholders 20 million new shares in a 2-for-1 exchange.

Setting the share price at a lower level has the following benefits:

- It attracts more retail investors and contributes to a more diffused and broader shareholders base.
- It attracts greater number of market makers because the bid–ask spread as percent of price increases as price drops.
- Market-making interest and higher turnover result in more analyst coverage by the securities firms that act as dealers on the stock.
- At a lower price, the value of round lots of shares is less thus making a stock "affordable" to retail investors given the lower brokerage fees of round lots.

The costs of low-priced stocks, on the other hand, include:

- The higher bid–ask spreads as percentage of price discourages both retail and institutional investors.

Relatively well-known and large firms that expect to attract sufficient analyst coverage may have less preference for a low price. Similarly, firms that need to improve the informational environment of their stock and expand the price discovery effort among institutional investors may prefer a higher price level. On the other hand, firms that wish to attain a wider spread of share ownership would prefer a lower trading price.

Fernando, Krishnamurthy, and Spindt (2004) find that high-price stocks attract more institutional than retail investors and are more likely to be managed by more reputable underwriters. Importantly, the study finds that underpricing exhibits a U-shaped relationship with offer price. Average (median) initial returns are 17% (8.3%) for stocks priced between $3 and $6; 9.5% (4%) for stocks priced between $6 and $15; and 18% (11%) for stocks priced over $15.

The Listing Choice

Marketplace Options

Firms executing IPOs must choose the market where the new security will be traded. Listing the security on a particular marketplace (e.g., NYSE or Nasdaq) is conditional on the firm's meeting the initial and continued listing criteria of the chosen trading venue. In some cases, the issuer may select both a domestic and a foreign market for a dual listing of the security. A firm may also bypass its domestic market and select a foreign market for the primary trading of its securities. Foreign issuers can list their securities in the United States either directly or through an ADR (American Depository Receipt) program.

Listing Decision Factors

Listing criteria: Listing criteria vary across market venues and even across segments of the same exchange. Currently, the NYSE and Nasdaq apply some common criteria (e.g., both require a minimum price per share of $4 and a minimum of 400 of round-lot shareholders or 2,200 shareholders otherwise) but differ in relation to other criteria like earnings, asset size, and market capitalization. The multitier structure of the Nasdaq market allows for different listing criteria depending on the segment in which the firm choses to list its stock. The Nasdaq Global Select Market imposes the strictest criteria, whereas the Nasdaq Capital Market (a trading venue for smaller and startup firms) requires the least strict requirements.

Listing fees: Listing firms must pay an application fee and the initial listing fees as well annual fees for continued listing. In general, listing fees (initial and annual) are higher on the NYSE than the Nasdaq market. In the latter market, the listing fees are higher for the Nasdaq Global Select Market than the Nasdaq National Market.

Prestige and valuation: Although the NYSE is older and more established, it does not mean that it is suitable to all firms. An issuing firm should choose the exchange where stocks of similar characteristics are traded, and as a result, they attract the attention of investors that specialize in this type of firms. This can generate information spillover effects conducive to more efficient valuation. For example, Nasdaq tends to attract technology intensive firms as well as startups.

Certification and value: By imposing minimum standards for initial and continued listing, an exchange can provide a certification effect regarding the value of the stock. The continued listing standards in particular provide a floor of firm performance below which the firm's stock listing could be jeopardized (Papaioannou, Travlos, and Viswanathan, 2009).

Liquidity: Trading liquidity is important because it is factored into the cost of capital associated with a security (Amihud and Mendelson, 1986). Earlier research had shown that liquidity was, in general, greater on the NYSE. However, this advantage has diminished over the years (Jain and Kim, 2006).

The Listing Decision and Issuance Costs

Affleck-Graves, Hegde, Miller, and Reilly (1993) have found no significant differences in spreads and underpricing for IPOs listed on the NYSE, AMEX, or Nasdaq market. In contrast, Corwin and Harris (2001) report average (median) underwriting spreads of 6.23% (6.25%) for IPOs listed on NYSE and 6.78% (7%) for IPOs listed on Nasdaq. Although underpricing was lower for NYSE-listed IPO stocks, it was not statistically different from that of Nasdaq-listed IPOs.

Datta, Iskandar-Datta, and Patel (1997) report lower underpricing for debt issues if listed on the NYSE or AMEX than the Nasdaq market. However, this relationship may be explained by the lower status of underwriters and the lower rating of debt issues listed on Nasdaq. They also found evidence that underwriting spreads were smaller for NYSE-listed seasoned equity offerings.

Many IPO firms are eligible to list on the NYSE or the Nasdaq, and yet they prefer one to the other. For example, Corwin and Harris (2001) find that 23.1% of 438 IPO firms that met both the NYSE and Nasdaq standards in the early 1990s were listed on Nasdaq. The listing decision in favor of the NYSE (hence, against Nasdaq) was positively influenced by equity capitalization and proportion of same industry firms listed on the NYSE and negatively by return volatility and whether the firm was in a high-technology sector.

Similarly, Anderson and Dyl (2008) find that Nasdaq is preferred by firms with lower offer price, smaller number of shares outstanding, lower quality underwriter, and by firms operating in high-technology sectors.

16

New Issue Decisions: The Underwriter, Syndicate, Auditor, and Legal Counsel

The previous chapter described the decisions the issuer has to make in relation to the structuring of the new issue deal. This chapter describes the decisions of the issuer in relation to choosing the lead underwriter, the structure of the syndicate, the auditing firm and the legal counsel.

The Underwriter Choice

Issuers should evaluate underwriting firms with respect to the skills and resources they bring to the management of a new issue. These include the following:

Certification power: This is the ability to certify the value of the new issue, and, in particular, its offer price. Underwriting firms develop certification power because they rely on repeat new issues business to generate revenue. Choosing a prestigious investment bank is a signal the issuer is willing to subject the issue and the firm to stricter scrutiny (Chemmanur and Fulghieri, 1994).

Valuation skills: An underwriter should possess the skills and capital market experience to produce reliable estimates of the value of a new security in order to correctly assess the underwriting costs and ensure that the placement is successful from the issuer's and investors' perspective.

Investor relationships and placement capabilities: Strong investor relationships contribute to a more thorough price discovery and successful placement of the new issue. Investment banks with strong placement power are more likely to price new issues more aggressively. Investment banks that operate wholesale and retail securities business are also better positioned to provide more complete placement services.

Analyst quality: Analysts provide research and information to investors that is necessary for the development of active secondary market trading; they also contribute to the valuation process.

Market making: Market making is especially important to IPO issuers. The lead manager and less so the comanagers must have strong presence in market making and trading so they can help the new security develop a robust secondary market.

Underwriting Services and the New Issues Market. DOI: http://dx.doi.org/10.1016/B978-0-12-803282-4.00016-X

Measuring Underwriter Reputation

The desired qualities for successful placement of new issues can be found in prestigious underwriters. The common criteria used to identify prestigious underwriters are described below.

Market share: For a particular class of new issues (e.g., seasoned equity offerings-SEOs), market power is measured by the percentage of total gross proceeds raised by an investment bank within a period of time, usually a year. The higher the fraction of proceeds in multiple underwriting markets raised by an investment bank, the more prestigious the bank is perceived to be. Underwriting rankings by market share of gross proceeds raised appear in the League Tables published by the *Investment Dealers' Digest*.

Frequency and position in the prospectus: As noted elsewhere in this book, investment banks are classified into brackets called bulge, major, submajor, and mezzanine. Classification into the various brackets depends on the frequency and the position of an underwriting firm in the lists of underwriters that appear in the new issue prospectuses and the old-style tombstone advertisements.

The Carter—Manaster (CM) ranking: This ranking method is a variation of the bracket classification method. It assigns each underwriting firm an explicit weight depending on the frequency with which an underwriter appears in each one of the brackets. Underwriting firms are then ranked according to their composite score (Carter and Manaster, 1990).

The modified CM ranking: This ranking method assigns bulge bracket firms a value of 3, major bracket firms a value of 2, submajor bracket firms a value of 1, and all other firms a value of 0 (Johnson and Miller, 1988). Carter and Dark (1992) show that the Carter—Manaster (CM) ranking has greater explanatory power as a prestige standard than the modified CM scale of Johnson and Miller.

The lead underwriter centrality: Bajo, Chemmanur, Simonyan, and Tehranian (2016) develop a more complex indicator of underwriter power that measures how centrally an underwriter is located in the network of underwriting firms and investors. The more centrally positioned an underwriter is the more extensive and more enduring relations the underwriter has with other underwriters and through them with networks of investors. Centrally located underwriters can attract more institutional investors and are able to extract more issue-related information, which can improve the performance of the new issue.

The Issuer's Decision Factors

Issuers can apply both deal-specific as well as long-term factors in deciding which underwriter to choose.

Deal-Specific Factors

Underwriting and other expenses: An issuer should choose the underwriter that will charge the lowest gross spread given the characteristics of the issuer and the issue.

Pricing and valuation: An issuer should also choose the underwriting firm that can place the new issue at the highest possible offer price. Low underpricing is not necessarily a sufficient condition to attain a higher offer price. The issue may be heavily underpriced and yet its offer price may exceed that of a less underpriced issue. In some instances, issuers are willing to accept a heavier underpricing in order to achieve other objectives that are consonant with firm value maximization. In these cases, the issuer has to ensure that the excess underpricing "buys" other benefits.

Distribution: Firms selling equity through an initial public offering (IPO) and seasoned firms with concentrated stock ownership have an interest to increase their investor base. Although higher equity concentration is associated with more effective monitoring, a narrow investor base may keep the cost of equity higher than otherwise. Hence, such a firm would prefer an investment bank that has strong retail investor relations and retail distributional capacity.

Long-Term Factors

Issuers can approach their choice of an underwriter from a transactional or a relationship banking perspective. In a transaction-based decision, the issuer chooses the bank that will deliver the most benefits in the specific deal. In a relationship banking decision, the issuer looks beyond the specific deal and aims to maximize benefits from an ongoing relationship with the investment bank.

An important advantage of relationship banking is the lower costs for price discovery. Doing repeat deals with an investment bank endows the latter with a more complete and private stock of information that can be used in future deals. This, in turn, enables the investment bank to more credibly certify the value of new issues by the issuer. Therefore, issuers interested in follow-on issues can enjoy savings in issuance costs.

If doing business within a relationship banking framework is of importance to an issuer, the types of deals should influence the underwriter choice. For example, issuers that are more likely to raise capital through debt offers should prefer investment banks with underwriting advantages in the debt markets. If the issuer is interested in executing mergers and acquisition (M&A) transactions, the preferred investment bank should be one that has a strong corporate finance division.

Finally, maintaining close ties with the issuer's underwriting firm also grants the issuer the privilege of "free" advice on various matters as the underwriter is eager to maintain the exchange of information alive in anticipation of prospective deals.

The underwriter decision has become more complicated in the post Glass—Steagall era that has seen the entry of commercial banks into the underwriting market. Issuers must now decide not only between wholesale or retail securities firms or between full-service and boutique securities firms, they must also decide between underwriting firms affiliated with commercial banks and independent underwriting firms.

The Evidence on Underwriter Impact

There is considerable evidence on how the underwriter choice impacts the underwriting costs and the pricing and valuation of new issues.

Underwriting Costs

Equity issues: The relationship between underwriting costs and underwriter prestige is not always clear. In the case, at least, of IPOs, the persistence of the 7% gross spread leaves little room for variability of spreads across underwriters for issues with proceeds below $80 to $100 million. Prestigious underwriters may be more cost efficient due to greater volume of business, but they may demand higher compensation because of more valuable certification and other aftermarket services they provide. The relationship may be also confounded by a selectivity bias. That is, high reputation underwriters tend to manage less risky issues of better-known firms. For example, Johnson and Miller (1988) find that after accounting for issue and issuer characteristics, there is no significant difference in underwriting costs for IPOs. A recent study of IPOs and SEOs finds that issuers pay higher dollar spread to prestigious underwriters. The excess spread appears to represent compensation for bigger syndicates, higher reputation and top analyst quality (Fernando, Gatchev, May, and Megginson, 2015). However, Kim, Palia, and Saunders (2008) report that underwriter reputation exerts an independent negative impact on the underwriting spreads of IPOs and SEOs but not on the spreads of debt offers.

Debt issues: Underwriting spreads are lower when straight bonds are underwritten by prestigious underwriters (Livingston and Miller, 2000). Fees are lower even after accounting for the higher quality of issues managed by prestigious underwriters. Despite the lower gross spread, prestigious underwriters still capture a spread premium over what less prestigious underwriters would have charged for the same issues. The fee premium compensates prestigious underwriters for the superior services they can deliver thanks to their larger scale of operations, investor networks and placement capabilities.

Underpricing

Equity issues: The selectivity bias also applies to the relationship between pricing and underwriter reputation. If prestigious underwriters prefer to manage issues with lower ex ante risk, underpricing is expected to be lower. Several studies find that after adjusting for other factors, underwriter prestige has no independent effect on the degree of underpricing (Johnson and Miller, 1988; Habib and Ljungqvist, 2001). Logue, Rogalski, Seward, and Foster-Johnson, (2002) propose that initial pricing and long-run returns of IPOs are better explained by how underwriters organize the various types of activities related to the flotation of IPOs than by differences in prestige. Thus, paying attention to the type and quality of services to be delivered by the investment bank is more important than the bank's status. Dolvin (2005) finds that while underpricing falls as underwriter rank rises, it increases with the market share of the underwriter. That implies that underwriters take advantage of their market power to impose heavier underpricing on issuers. Prestigious underwriters are associated with higher offer prices and lower discounts in SEOs, but this comes with greater gross spread (Fernando, Gatchev, May, and Megginson, 2015). Boeh and Dunbar (2016) find that underwriters with a heavy pipeline of IPO deals are associated with greater underpricing either because of lack of capacity to properly screen many IPOs within a limited time or because of market power. The same authors also find that the longer IPO deals remain in the pipeline for various administrative and market-related reasons the greater the underpricing is.

Debt issues: Prestigious underwriters are also associated with lower offering yields (higher offer prices) in straight bond issues even after accounting for other factors (Livingston and Miller, 2000; Fang, 2005). Prestigious underwriters appear to have an advantage over less prestigious underwriters in producing lower offering yields, especially in noninvestment grade bond issues. Prestigious underwriters also produce greater gross proceeds than what less prestigious underwriters would have produced for similar quality bonds. This implies that despite charging a fee premium, the higher offer prices enable issues to raise greater net proceeds (Fang, 2005).

Valuation

How does the market react to the announcement of a new issue in regards to the status of the underwriter? Several studies find that stock price reaction is more favorable when the lead manager is identified as a prestigious underwriting firm (McLaughlin, Safieddine, and Vasudevan, 2000; Helou and Park, 2001).

High-reputation underwriters are also found to produce higher offer prices and first after-market prices and this advantage holds in both hot and cold issue IPO markets (Chemmanur and Krishnan, 2012). Unlike the certification effect which emanates from the status of the lead manager, this valuation advantage is attributed to the market power prestigious underwriters have in regards to attracting comanagers and investor clienteles that can support superior valuation levels than those achieved by less prestigious underwriters. The same study finds that the valuation advantage of prestigious underwriters persisted through the 1990s despite evidence that IPOs managed by prestigious underwriters were more heavily underpriced than those managed by less prestigious underwriters.

Bajo, Chemmanur, Simonyan, and Tehranian (2016) find that underwriters more centrally positioned in the networks of underwriting firms are associated with higher valuation IPOs which also enjoy higher market prices in the secondary market. These IPOs also attract more analysts and have greater liquidity in the aftermarket.

The Evidence on the Underwriter Choice

In dealing with investment banks, issuers can adopt a transaction banking or a relationship banking approach. As stated above, transaction banking focuses on maximizing benefits from the transaction at hand. Relationship banking takes a longer term perspective on costs and benefits. The issuer's choice of underwriter is also affected by the preferences of underwriters. Reputable investment banks favor relationships with higher quality and larger issuers that are more likely to execute future securities offers or other corporate finance transactions (e.g., mergers).

In surveys of Chief Financial Officers whose firms had conducted IPOs, the top five criteria in selecting a high prestige underwriter were found to include underwriter status, quality of the research department, industry expertise, market making services, and institutional client base. In regards to selecting a less prestigious underwriter, the institutional client base is replaced by pricing and valuation promises. Those firms that choose low-rank underwriters are also more concerned with the underwriter's relationship with retail investor client base and with underwriting fees (Brau and Fawcett, 2006; Krigman, Shaw, and Womack, 2001).

Fang (2005) finds that debt issuers are more likely to do business with a reputable investment bank if they are bigger, issue investment grade debt, are more frequent debt issuers, and they have received more services from the lead underwriter in the past.

Fernando, Gatchev, and Spindt (2005) posit that issuers and underwriters mutually select each other by taking account of the characteristics that are likely to maximize their respective benefits from each transaction. Therefore, this is a transaction banking model of underwriter choice. Typically, the issuer-underwriter pairing develops along tiers of quality. As long as the issuer and underwriter remain in compatible tiers, the relationship is preserved; otherwise, the issuer is likely to switch to another underwriter of equal tier. For IPO deals, high quality pairs include issuing firms that are older and bigger, more profitable and less financially distressed, issue greater amounts and are VC-backed. Similar characteristics apply in top quality pairs for SEO deals. Lower quality issuers are more likely to pair up with a reputable underwriter in cold markets when there is a scarcity of new issues, while lower reputation underwriters are more likely to be matched with better quality issuers in hot markets because of the limited capacity of prestigious banks. Fernando, Gatchev, and Spindt (2005) find that the trend toward transaction banking has increased over time.

Switching Underwriters

Issuers do not necessarily retain the same investment bank for their follow-on new issues. They often choose to switch to another underwriter. Although charging lower gross spreads is one way to increase the probability of retention (Carter, 1992), this decision is more complicated as the empirical evidence shows.

Krigman, Shaw, and Womack (2001) find that the decision to switch to another underwriter after the firm's IPO is unrelated to the degree of underpricing, weak placement or extent of flipping. Switchers are more likely to be issuers that realized gross proceeds that fall short of their expectations based on the midpoint of the filing price range, i.e., the final offer price fell short of the offer price implied by the midpoint of the price range. The timeliness, extent, and quality of analyst coverage as well as the quality of market making were found to be the most serious execution-specific reasons. Firms that raise their profile are more likely to "trade up" (i.e., switch) to a more reputable underwriter. Securing better analyst coverage is an important criterion in choosing the next underwriter. Switching firms realize less negative price reaction if they graduate to a more prestigious underwriting firm, especially one with all-star analysts in its ranks. Underwriting fees seem to fare less in the switching decision. Nonswitchers have higher 1-year post-IPO returns and less negative 1-year post-SEO returns than switchers.

Cliff and Denis (2004) find that switching to another underwriter is more likely if the firm can retain a higher reputation underwriter for the follow-on SEO. Switching is less likely if the IPO offer price has been revised more positively from the midpoint of the filing range, the IPO underwriter was more reputable and the underwriter generated more coverage than expected.

Burch, Nanda, and Warther (2005) find that client-underwriter relationships have become more fluid in recent years. Underwriting fees decline with loyalty in equity issues but increase in debt issues. And firms that graduate to higher quality underwriters enjoy savings in fees for equity and debt issues, unless switching underwriters aims at getting better analyst coverage in equity issues. Loyalty matters more to issuers of speculative offers because of the importance of the information advantage the original underwriter enjoys over rival underwriting firms.

Ertugrul and Krishnan (2014) report that when firms retain the same investment bank to advise on acquisitions or to underwrite a debt or equity issue, they do not enjoy lower advisory fees or lower offering yields (for debt) or lower underpricing (for equity issues). Following this experience, most of these issuers switch to another investment bank.

Switching and Analyst Coverage
Analyst recommendations and coverage are valuable because they raise the firm's profile, expand its investor base and recognition, and increase the stock's liquidity. Insiders are also interested in analyst coverage that can boost the stock price so they can sell shares at higher prices in the post-IPO follow-on secondary issues. Cliff and Denis (2004) find a strong correlation between underpricing and both the frequency and the perceived quality of postissue analyst recommendations. Failure by the lead manager to provide analyst recommendations within a year of IPO increases the likelihood the issuer will switch to another underwriter. Cliff and Denis also find that the lead manager's analysts are also prone to making more favorable recommendations. The same authors report that analyst coverage increased from 93.7% of IPOs in 1993 to 100% in 2000. As a result, switching rates declined over the same period.

Ljungqvist, Marston, and Wilhelm (2006) investigate whether analyst recommendations influence underwriting mandates. They find no such evidence. Specifically, investment banks with a strong presence (and hence reputation) in the equity markets are associated with less aggressive analyst recommendations in order to maintain their credibility in resolving information asymmetries surrounding the valuation of equity issues. Although underwriting reputation and presence of star analysts is influential, the underwriter choice in equity issues is determined more by underwriting relationships and to a lesser degree by prior lending relationships. Debt issue mandates, on the other hand, are influenced by prior debt underwriting and lending relationships and the winning underwriter's debt and loan market share, but not by the presence of star analysts.

Clarke, Khorana, Patel, and Rau (2007) also find that when all-star analysts leave an underwriting firm, they are not found to engage in more optimistic or biased behavior in the new firm. New firm clients are drawn to the hiring underwriting firm because of the expectation they will be covered by all-star analysts and not because the new clients expect to receive more favorable recommendations.

Commercial Banks as Underwriters

Until 1989 (for debt) and 1990 (for equity), issuers could choose their underwriter from among the securities firms that operated underwriting divisions. Following the entry of commercial banks into the underwriting business in 1989, and especially after the full repeal of the Glass–Steagall act in 1999, the underwriter choices expanded to include commercial banks. Actually issuers had more choices in the 1990s before the large commercial banks took over most of the full service securities firms, with the exception of Goldman Sachs and Morgan Stanley. As a result of the great consolidation of the underwriting industry under the control of commercial banks, the choice between a securities firm and a commercial bank-affiliated underwriting firm has lost much of its practical importance.

Still though the choice between an independent underwriting firm and a commercial bank has implications in those cases a choice is available to the issuer in light of the still operating independent though smaller investment banks. It has also consequences from an operational efficiency point of view. That is, does the combination of bank lending and underwriting operations create economies of scope enabling commercial banks to offer more cost efficient underwriting services to issuers.

The choice for an issuer centers around the question: which type of underwriter can place new securities with less underpricing and at a lower underwriting compensation (gross spread)? Puri (1999) formalized the two possible effects related to a commercial bank acting as an underwriter.

The "certification" hypothesis: A bank that has a lending relationship with an issuer has more information about its client's business due to long standing relations and ongoing monitoring of the client's credit worthiness. This gives the bank a greater informational advantage over its investment bank competitors as a certifier of the new issue's value. Thus, the "certification" hypothesis predicts that new issues are less underpriced if the underwriter is their commercial bank. Moreover, this informational advantage increases with the uncertainty and riskiness surrounding the new issue, e.g., IPOs and low-grade bonds.

The "conflict of interest" hypothesis: At the same time, the lending relationship generates a conflict of interest if the issuer intends to use the proceeds to pay off or refinance loans it has with the bank that serves as the underwriter. The bank may be tempted to misrepresent the financial soundness of the issuer in order to complete the offering and recoup the loans. In this case, investors will demand a higher price discount in order to mitigate their adverse selection problem. Therefore, the "conflict of interest" hypothesis predicts higher underpricing for new issues underwritten by banks that have a lending relationship with the issuing firm.

The same arguments suggest that if the commercial bank faces lower costs in producing information about the issue and transfers all or part of the savings to the issuer, the underwriting fees will be lower compared to those charged by investment banks. However, the commercial bank may charge higher fees as a compensation for the higher offer price it produces for the issuer. It is only through empirical studies that we can have answers to these alternative possibilities.

The Decision to Choose a Commercial Bank

Schenone (2004) analyzes the assignment of IPO mandates to the firm's bank or another bank or securities firm in the post-1989 era. In the sample analyzed by Schenone, 30% of the firms with prior lending relationships went public with their commercial bank. Only 18% chose to switch to another investment bank. The rest had a relationship with a bank that could not execute the IPO for lack of a Section 20 securities affiliate.

Yasuda (2005) finds that in debt offers, bank relationships matter for the underwriter choice beyond their effects on underwriting fees. The importance of lower fees is less for securities with greater information asymmetry, like junk bonds and for first-time issuers, for which value certification is more important. The bank's prior record that matters is as originator and not just as participant to loans. A commercial bank is less likely to be retained if the firm had executed a debt offer prior to the current bond issue or the issue size is large.

Bharath, Dahiya, Saunders, and Srinivasan (2007) find higher probability of winning a debt issue or IPO underwriting mandate if the underwriter has had a lending relationship with the issuer. But lending relationships are not more important in influencing the underwriter choice in the case of SEOs since issuers are reporting firms and, as a result, more well known.

Narayanan, Rangan, and Rangan (2007) find that the likelihood to choose the issuer's own lending bank increases with the reputation of the bank in the syndicated and private placement markets and if the issue is a bond initial public offer (BIPOs) and decreases with the size of the bond issue. Investment banks are more likely to be selected if they have a higher presence in the bond underwriting market.

Following the deregulation of debt and equity underwriting in 1989–1990, extending lending to an underwriting client became a competitive practice. Commercial banks, in particular, were best placed to exploit this "pay-to-play" tactic. Drucker and Puri (2005) find that likely issuers for such joint transactions are mostly highly leveraged firms that issue noninvestment grade debt. They find that concurrent lending and debt underwriting result in lower fees and discounted yields on the loans. The savings are strongest for issuers of noninvestment grade debt. Investment grade issuers do not enjoy fee discounts. Prior lending relationships also contribute independently to fee discounts. Lending at the time of the SEO also positively influences the likelihood of retaining the same underwriter for subsequent SEOs. This influence persists even after accounting for analyst quality and underwriter reputation. Independent investment banks also compete for concurrent deals but more so through gross spread than loan yield.

Effects on Underwriting Spreads

IPOs and SEOs

Several studies have shown that deregulation of the underwriting business has not resulted in lower gross spreads for IPO deals (Gande, Puri, and Saunders, 1999; Chaplinsky and Erwin, 2001; Fields, Fraser, and Bhargava, 2003). Similar evidence has been found for SEOs

(Chaplinsky and Erwin, 2001). However, a more recent study by Kim, Palia, and Saunders (2008) finds that the entry of commercial banks into underwriting had reduced gross spreads for IPOs and SEOs.

Debt Issues

The entry of commercial banks into underwriting was expected to have a greater impact on the cost and pricing of debt issues, given the commercial banks' expertise in analyzing credit risks. Gande, Puri, and Saunders (1999) find that deregulation had depressed the underwriting fees for nonconvertible debt issues whether they were underwritten by commercial or investment banks without significant differences across type of underwriter. The savings have been especially pronounced in lower grade debt issues. There is also evidence of lower underwriting fees for noninvestment grade bond issues when the underwriter is a commercial bank (Rotten and Mullineaux, 2002; Yasuda, 2005). Narayanan, Rangan, and Rangan (2007) report lower gross spreads for nonconvertible bond issues managed by commercial banks with high reputation in the syndicated and private placement debt markets. The gross spread savings are greater if these banks also have a lending relationship with the issuer. Kim, Palia, and Saunders (2008) also find that the entry of commercial banks into underwriting had reduced gross spreads for nonconvertible bond issues.

Effects on Underpricing and Long-Run Price Performance

IPOs

The evidence is mixed in regards to the impact of commercial banks on the pricing of IPOs. Fields, Fraser, and Bhargava (2003) and Schenone (2004) find that underpricing is less in IPOs when the issuer has had a prior lending relationship with the underwriting bank. A similar effect on underpricing is reported in Hebb (2002) who also finds that using issue proceeds to refinance bank loans adds to underpricing.

Benzoni and Schenone (2010) examine the long-run stock return performance of IPOs managed by relationship banks and nonrelationship, independent, banks. They find no significant differences in the stock return performance of IPOs managed by relationship and independent banks, respectively.

Debt Issues

Gande, Puri, Saunders, and Walter (1997) find that pre-IPO lending relationships with the underwriting firm (i.e., commercial bank) help to reduce the reoffering yields of lower quality bonds. However, use of proceeds to refinance the bank loan adds to the yields of bond issues regardless of debt quality. Gande, Puri, and Saunders (1999) study fixed rate nonconvertible US corporate bond issues before the lifting of firewalls between the commercial and investment banking departments of banks in 1996. They find that the deregulation had caused offering yields to decline across all issues whether underwritten by a commercial or investment bank. Smaller more speculative issues were the main beneficiaries of the lower offering yields.

Roten and Mullineaux (2002) analyze bonds underwritten by commercial banks and securities firms in 1995–1997 before and after removal of firewalls. They find no significant difference in the reoffering yields of bond issues underwritten by commercial and investment banks, respectively, though low grade bonds appear to enjoy somewhat lower reoffering yields after the removal of firewalls.

Narayanan, Rangan, and Rangan (2007) argue that commercial banks that specialize in syndicated and privately placed debt possess skills that are good substitutes for the valuation and placement needed to execute underwritten public debt offers. They find that nonconvertible bonds carry lower reoffering yields if they are underwritten by banks with which the issuer has a lending relationship. However, using the issue proceeds to refinance the bank's loan adds to the reoffering yield. High reputation commercial banks produce additional savings in reoffering yields if they have a lending relationship with the issuer compared to high reputation banks without such a relationship.

The Syndicate Structure Choice

Choosing a syndicate with the structure and size that best serves the issuer's needs is critical to the success of the new offer. The most important part of the syndicate is the managing group that comprises the lead manager and the comanagers. There is strong evidence that the presence and the number of comanagers add value to the underwriting service. Comanagers contribute to information gathering and, if reputable, they enhance the certification power of the syndicate. Furthermore, comanagers expand market making capacity and generate broader analyst coverage. An issuer should also favor syndicates with members that have expertise in the firm's industry and have placement capabilities—wholesale versus retail—that are valuable to the type of the offered security. Bond issuers, for example, would favor wholesale distribution capacity to minimize the distribution cost, whereas equity issuers would favor retail distribution capacity to ensure a wide dispersion of ownership of the new shares.

Corwin and Schultz (2005) report that the number of comanagers and their allocations have increased in the period leading to 2002, though the syndicate size has decreased. As expected, greater size issues are associated with more underwriters and comanagers. Larger underwriting groups are also associated with greater price updates relative to the midpoint of the filing range. The disadvantage of large underwriting groups is the upward pressure placed on gross spreads. Large underwriting groups leave less money for the lead underwriter and as a result small size issues (that generate lower gross spread dollars) carry larger percentage spreads.

Given the differential advantages and disadvantages that commercial and investment banks bring to the table, the roles they assume in the managing group can influence the pricing of the issue. When the issuer retains its commercial bank with which it maintains a lending relationship, the conflict of interest may hurt the pricing of the issue. In these cases, the commercial bank may prefer to serve as a comanager and cede the lead manager's role to an investment bank or to another commercial bank without a lending relationship with the client. Such a syndicate structure is called a "hybrid" syndicate.

Song (2004) finds that smaller firms and those more dependent on bank financing favor a hybrid over a pure-investment bank syndicate that is led by an independent investment bank and comanaged by a commercial bank. The hybrid syndicate form is also favored in issues of lower quality (noninvestment grade) debt because of the greater information frictions that require credible certification of value. Compared to commercial bank-led syndicates, hybrid syndicates are also more likely to be chosen when the proceeds are slated to pay back the bank's loans. Hybrid syndicates are found to produce lower reoffering yields in bond issues thanks to the information synergies between investment and commercial banks.

Narayanan, Rangan, and Rangan (2004) also find that when the lending (commercial) bank comanages seasoned equity offerings of its loan clients with reputable independent investment banks as lead managers the underwriting fees are lower than if the lending bank is the lead-manager of the issue. However, the pricing of the issue is not affected by the role a lending bank assumes in the syndicate, that is, whether it serves as the issue's lead-manager or not. Thus, the total issuance cost (gross spread and underpricing) is lower when SEOs are comanaged by lending banks and investment banks. In these cases of hybrid syndicates, the lending bank is less likely to lead manage the issue if the issuer is larger and there is a lending relationship, since commercial bank certification is less valuable to large issuers.

The Auditor and Legal Counsel Choice

The choice of auditor and legal counsel has consequences for the underwriter compensation and the pricing of the issue. Retaining a reputable auditing or law firm signals that the registration statement and other disclosed materials are of high quality and more accurate. Since reputable auditors and legal advisers have more to lose in reputational capital, they have an interest to exercise greater due diligence and subject the issuing firm to greater scrutiny. Thus, reputable auditors and legal counsels can better certify the information that influences the value of the new issue.

As in the case of underwriters, reputable auditors build their reputational capital by carefully screening and exposing risks unbeknownst to the market. Titman and Trueman (1986) show that less risky and higher quality issuers prefer higher quality auditors because they need to separate themselves from low quality issuers.

The certification power of auditors can either complement the certification credentials of the underwriter or serve as a substitute for the lower certification provided by less reputable underwriters. In either case, the underwriter's risk is reduced and the market's confidence in the value of the offer is increased. As a result, the placement effort is easier and less costly. These effects should be reflected in the gross spread and the pricing of new issues.

Balvers, McDonald, and Miller (1988) argue that an underwriter may choose to select a reputable auditor and compensate the issuer with higher quality services for the excess cost of auditor reputation. They find that across issues more prestigious underwriters are more likely than less prestigious underwriters to be associated with prestigious auditors. Both, underwriter and auditor reputation are associated with less underpricing. However, the presence of a high-quality party reduces the marginal benefits derived from the high quality of the other party. Thus, combining top quality underwriters and auditors may result in overpayment in gross spread that is not recouped by lower underpricing.

Beatty (1989) finds that reputable auditors (identified with the big eight auditing firms at the time of the study) are associated with less underpriced but also less risky IPOs. The lower underpricing comes though at the cost of higher auditor fees. Michaely and Shaw (1995) also find that reputable auditing firms prefer less risky issuers in order to protect their reputation and reduce litigation risk. Less risky clients also align themselves with more reputable underwriters as predicted by Titman and Trueman (1986). IPOs audited by high quality auditors realize lower underpricing and better abnormal long-run stock returns (though still negative) than IPOs audited by lower quality auditors.

Beatty and Welch (1996) find that in the 1990s, smaller issuers who paid higher fees to retain reputable auditing and legal firms enjoyed savings in underwriting fees. This implies that the higher certification value of the auditing and legal services reduced the underwriting costs. Smaller issuers enjoyed less underpricing of their IPOs if both auditor and legal counsel were of higher quality, whereas larger issuers enjoyed less underpricing if only the auditor was of higher quality.

Rauterkus and Song (2005) provide strong evidence that auditor quality matters for price certification. They find that, in the aftermath of the Enron scandal, announcements of SEOs by firms that had been audited in the past by Arthur Andersen (the Enron's auditor) realized much greater negative price reaction than the SEOs of firms audited by other auditing firms.

References

Abrahamson, M., Jenkinson, T., & Jones, H. (2011). Why don't U.S. issuers demand European fees for IPOs? *The Journal of Finance, 66*(6), 2055–2082.

Affleck-Graves, J., Hegde, S., & Miller, R. E. (1996). Conditional price trends in the aftermarket for initial public offerings. *Financial Management, 25*(4), 25–40.

Affleck-Graves, J., Hegde, S. P., Miller, R. E., & Reilly, F. K. (1993). The effect of the trading system on the underpricing of initial public offerings. *Financial Management, 22*(1), 99–108.

Affleck-Graves, J., & Miller, R. E. (1989). Regulatory and procedural effects on the underpricing of initial public offerings. *Journal of Financial Research, 12*(3), 193–202.

Afterman, A. B. (1995). *SEC regulation of public companies.* Englewood Cliffs, N.J.: Prentice Hall.

Aggarwal, R. (2000). Stabilization activities by underwriters after initial public offerings. *The Journal of Finance, 55*(3), 1075–1103.

Aggarwal, R. (2003). Allocation of initial public offerings and flipping activity. *Journal of Financial Economics, 68*(1), 111–135.

Aggarwal, R., & Conroy, P. (2000). Price discovery in initial public offerings and the role of the lead underwriter. *The Journal of Finance, 55*(6), 2903–2922.

Aggarwal, R., Leal, R., & Hernandez, L. (1993). The aftermarket performance of initial public offerings in Latin America. *Financial Management, 22*(1), 42–53.

Aggarwal, R., Prabhala, N. R., & Puri, M. (2002). Institutional allocation in initial public offerings: Empirical evidence. *The Journal of Finance, 57*(3), 1421–1442.

Aggarwal, R., & Rivoli, P. (1990). Fads in the initial public offering market? *Financial Management, 19*(4), 45–57.

Aggarwal, R. K., Bhagat, S., & Rangan, S. (2009). The impact of fundamentals on IPO valuation. *Financial Management, 38*(2), 253–284.

Aggarwal, R. K., Krigman, L., & Womack, K. L. (2002). Strategic IPO underpricing, information momentum, and lockup expiration selling. *Journal of Financial Economics, 66*(1), 105–137.

Ahmad-Zaluki, N. A., Campbell, K., & Goodacre, A. (2007). The long run share price performance of Malaysian initial public offerings (IPOs). *Journal of Business Finance & Accounting, 34*(1–2), 78–110.

Akhigbe, A., & Madura, J. (2001). Motivation and performance of seasoned offerings by closed-end funds. *The Financial Review, 36*(3), 101–122.

Akyol, A. C., Cooper, T., Meoli, M., & Vismara, S. (2014). Do regulatory changes affect the underpricing of European IPOs? *Journal of Banking & Finance, 45*, 43–58.

Alderson, M. J., & Betker, B. L. (2000). The long-run performance of companies that withdraw seasoned equity offerings. *Journal of Financial Research, 23*(2), 157–178.

Allen, D. S., Lamy, R. E., & Thompson, G. R. (1990). The shelf registration of debt and self selection bias. *The Journal of Finance, 45*(1), 275–287.

Allen, F., & Faulhaber, G. R. (1989). Signalling by underpricing in the IPO market. *Journal of Financial Economics, 23*(2), 303–323.

Altınkılıç, O., & Hansen, R. S. (2000). Are there economies of scale in underwriting fees? Evidence of rising external financing costs. *Review of Financial Studies, 13*(1), 191–218.

Altınkılıç, O., & Hansen, R. S. (2003). Discounting and underpricing in seasoned equity offers. *Journal of Financial Economics, 69*(2), 285−323.

Amihud, Y., Hauser, S., & Kirsh, A. (2003). Allocations, adverse selection, and cascades in IPOs: Evidence from the Tel Aviv Stock Exchange. *Journal of Financial Economics, 68*(1), 137−158.

Amihud, Y., & Mendelson, H. (1986). Asset pricing and the bid-ask spread. *Journal of Financial Economics, 17*(2), 223−249.

Anderson, A. M., & Dyl, E. A. (2008). IPO listings: Where and why? *Financial Management, 37*(1), 23−43.

Anderson, S. C., Born, J. A., & Beard, T. R. (1991). An analysis of bond investment company initial public offerings: Past and present. *The Financial Review, 26*(2), 211−222.

Ang, J. S., & Brau, J. C. (2003). Concealing and confounding adverse signals: Insider wealth-maximizing behavior in the IPO process. *Journal of Financial Economics, 67*(1), 149−172.

Arnold, T., Fishe, R. P. H., & North, D. (2010). The effects of ambiguous information on initial and subsequent IPO returns. *Financial Management, 39*(4), 1497−1519.

Aruğaslan, O., Cook, D. O., & Kieschnick, R. (2004). Monitoring as a motivation for IPO underpricing. *The Journal of Finance, 59*(5), 2403−2420.

Aussenegg, W., Pichler, P., & Stomper, A. (2006). IPO pricing with bookbuilding and a when-issued market. *Journal of Financial and Quantitative Analysis, 41*(4), 829−862.

Autore, D. M., Kumar, R., & Shome, D. K. (2008). The revival of shelf-registered corporate equity offerings. *Journal of Corporate Finance, 14*(1), 32−50.

Bae, G. S., Jeong, J., Sun, H.-L., & Tang, A. P. (2002). Stock returns and operating performance of securities issuers. *Journal of Financial Research, 25*(3), 337−352.

Bae, S. C., & Levy, H. (1990). The valuation of firm commitment underwriting contracts for seasoned new equity issues: Theory and evidence. *Financial Management, 19*(2), 48−59.

Bajaj, M., Mazumdar, S. C., & Sarin, A. (2002). The costs of issuing preferred stock. *Journal of Financial Research, 25*(4), 577−592.

Bajo, E., Chemmanur, T. J., Simonyan, K., & Tehranian, H. (2016). Underwriter networks, investor attention, and initial public offerings. *Journal of Financial Economics, 122*(2), 376−408.

Baker, M., & Wurgler, J. (2000). The equity share in new issues and aggregate stock returns. *The Journal of Finance, 55*(5), 2219−2257.

Balachandran, B., Faff, R., & Theobald, M. (2008). Rights offerings, takeup, renounceability, and underwriting status. *Journal of Financial Economics, 89*(2), 328−346.

Balvers, R. J., McDonald, B., & Miller, R. E. (1988). Underpricing of new issues and the choice of auditor as a signal of investment banker reputation. *The Accounting Review, 63*(4), 605−622.

Barber, B. M., Lehavy, R., & Trueman, B. (2007). Comparing the stock recommendation performance of investment banks and independent research firms. *Journal of Financial Economics, 85*(2), 490−517.

Barber, B. M., & Lyon, J. D. (1996). Detecting abnormal operating performance: The empirical power and specification of test statistics. *Journal of Financial Economics, 41*(3), 359−399.

Barber, B. M., & Lyon, J. D. (1997). Detecting long-run abnormal stock returns: The empirical power and specification of test statistics. *Journal of Financial Economics, 43*(3), 341−372.

Baron, D. P. (1982). A model of the demand for investment banking advising and distribution services for new issues. *The Journal of Finance, 37*(4), 955−976.

Barry, C. B., & Jennings, R. H. (1993). The opening price performance of initial public offerings of common stock. *Financial Management, 22*(1), 54−63.

Barry, C. B., Muscarella, C. J., Peavy, J. W., & Vetsuypens, M. R. (1990). The role of venture capital in the creation of public companies. *Journal of Financial Economics, 27*(2), 447−471.

Barry, C. B., Muscarella, C. J., & Vetsuypens, M. R. (1991). Underwriter warrants, underwriter compensation, and the costs of going public. *Journal of Financial Economics, 29*(1), 113–135.

Bayless, M., & Chaplinsky, S. (1996). Is there a window of opportunity for seasoned equity issuance? *The Journal of Finance, 51*(1), 253–278.

Beatty, R. P. (1989). Auditor reputation and the pricing of initial public offerings. *The Accounting Review, 64*(4), 693–709.

Beatty, R. P., & Ritter, J. R. (1986). Investment banking, reputation, and the underpricing of initial public offerings. *Journal of Financial Economics, 15*(1–2), 213–232.

Beatty, R. P., & Welch, I. (1996). Issuer expenses and legal liability in initial public offerings. *The Journal of Law and Economics, 39*(2), 545–602.

Beckman, J., Garner, J., Marshall, B., & Okamura, H. (2001). The influence of underwriter reputation, keiretsu affiliation, and financial health on the underpricing of Japanese IPOs. *Pacific-Basin Finance Journal, 9*(5), 513–534.

Bengtsson, O., & Dai, N. (2014). Financial contracts in PIPE offerings: The role of expert placement agents. *Financial Management, 43*(4), 795–832.

Benveniste, L. M., & Busaba, W. Y. (1997). Bookbuilding vs. fixed price: An analysis of competing strategies for marketing IPOs. *Journal of Financial and Quantitative Analysis, 32*(4), 383–403.

Benveniste, L. M., Busaba, W. Y., & Wilhelm, W. J. (1996). Price stabilization as a bonding mechanism in new equity issues. *Journal of Financial Economics, 42*(2), 223–255.

Benveniste, L. M., Busaba, W. Y., & Wilhelm, W. J. (2002). Information externalities and the role of underwriters in primary equity markets. *Journal of Financial Intermediation, 11*(1), 61–86.

Benveniste, L. M., Ljungqvist, A., Wilhelm, W. J., & Yu, X. (2003). Evidence of information spillovers in the production of investment banking services. *The Journal of Finance, 58*(2), 577–608.

Benveniste, L. M., & Spindt, P. A. (1989). How investment bankers determine the offer price and allocation of new issues. *Journal of Financial Economics, 24*(2), 343–361.

Benveniste, L. M., & Wilhelm, W. J. (1990). A comparative analysis of IPO proceeds under alternative regulatory environments. *Journal of Financial Economics, 28*(1–2), 173–207.

Benzoni, L., & Schenone, C. (2010). Conflict of interest and certification in the U.S. IPO market. *Journal of Financial Intermediation, 19*(2), 235–254.

Bertoni, F., & Giudici, G. (2014). The strategic reallocation of IPO shares. *Journal of Banking & Finance, 39*, 211–222.

Berzins, J., Liu, C. H., & Trzcinka, C. (2013). Asset management and investment banking. *Journal of Financial Economics, 110*(1), 215–231.

Bhabra, H. S., & Pettway, R. H. (2003). IPO prospectus information and subsequent performance. *The Financial Review, 38*(3), 369–397.

Bhagat, S. (1986). The effect of management's choice between negotiated and competitive equity offerings on shareholder wealth. *Journal of Financial and Quantitative Analysis, 21*(2), 181–196.

Bhagat, S., & Frost, P. A. (1986). Issuing costs to existing shareholders in competitive and negotiated underwritten public utility equity offerings. *Journal of Financial Economics, 15*(1–2), 233–259.

Bhagat, S., Marr, M. W., & Thompson, G. R. (1985). The rule 415 experiment: Equity markets. *The Journal of Finance, 40*(5), 1385–1401.

Bharath, S., Dahiya, S., Saunders, A., & Srinivasan, A. (2007). So what do I get? The bank's view of lending relationships. *Journal of Financial Economics, 85*(2), 368–419.

Bharath, S. T., & Dittmar, A. K. (2010). Why do firms use private equity to opt out of public markets? *Review of Financial Studies, 23*(5), 1771–1818.

Billett, M. T., Flannery, M. J., & Garfinkel, J. A. (2011). Frequent issuers' influence on long-run post-issuance returns. *Journal of Financial Economics*, *99*(2), 349–364.

Blackwell, D. W., & Kidwell, D. S. (1988). An investigation of cost differences between public sales and private placements of debt. *Journal of Financial Economics*, *22*(2), 253–278.

Blackwell, D. W., Marr, M. W., & Spivey, M. F. (1990). Shelf registration and the reduced due diligence argument: Implications of the underwriter certification and the implicit insurance hypotheses. *Journal of Financial and Quantitative Analysis*, *25*(2), 245–259.

Blowers, S. C., Griffith, P. H., & Milan, T. L. (1999). *The Ernst & Young guide to the IPO value journey*. New York, NY: John Wiley & Sons.

Boeh, K. K., & Dunbar, C. (2016). Underwriter deal pipeline and the pricing of IPOs. *Journal of Financial Economics*, *120*(2), 383–399.

Boehmer, B., Boehmer, E., & Fishe, R. P. H. (2006). Do institutions receive favorable allocations in IPOs with better long-run returns? *Journal of Financial and Quantitative Analysis*, *41*(4), 809–828.

Boone, A. L., Floros, I. V., & Johnson, S. A. (2016). Redacting proprietary information at the initial public offering. *Journal of Financial Economics*, *120*(1), 102–123.

Booth, J. R., & Chua, L. (1996). Ownership dispersion, costly information, and IPO underpricing. *Journal of Financial Economics*, *41*(2), 291–310.

Booth, J. R., & Smith, R. L. (1986). Capital raising, underwriting and the certification hypothesis. *Journal of Financial Economics*, *15*(1–2), 261–281.

Bortolotti, B., Megginson, W., & Smart, S. B. (2008). The rise of accelerated seasoned equity underwritings. *Journal of Applied Corporate Finance*, *20*(3), 35–57.

Boubakri, N., & Cosset, J.-C. (1998). The financial and operating performance of newly privatized firms: Evidence from developing countries. *The Journal of Finance*, *53*(3), 1081–1110.

Boulton, T. J., Smart, S. B., & Zutter, C. J. (2010). Acquisition activity and IPO underpricing. *Financial Management*, *39*(4), 1521–1546.

Boutchkova, M. K., & Megginson, W. L. (2000). Privatization and the rise of global capital markets. *Financial Management*, *29*(4), 31–75.

Bouzouita, N., Gajewski, J.-F., & Gresse, C. (2015). Liquidity benefits from IPO underpricing: Ownership dispersion or information effect. *Financial Management*, *44*(4), 785–810.

Bower, N. L. (1989). Firm value and the choice of offering method in initial public offerings. *The Journal of Finance*, *44*(3), 647–662.

Bradley, D. J., Cooney, J. W., Jr., Dolvin, S. D., & Jordan, B. D. (2006). Penny stock IPOs. *Financial Management*, *35*(1), 5–29.

Bradley, D. J., Cooney, J. W., Jordan, B. D., & Singh, A. K. (2004). Negotiation and the IPO offer price: A comparison of integer vs. non-integer IPOs. *Journal of Financial and Quantitative Analysis*, *39*(3), 517–540.

Bradley, D. J., & Jordan, B. D. (2002). Partial adjustment to public information and IPO underpricing. *Journal of Financial and Quantitative Analysis*, *37*(4), 595–616.

Bradley, D. J., Jordan, B. D., & Ritter, J. R. (2003). The quiet period goes out with a bang. *The Journal of Finance*, *58*(1), 1–36.

Bradley, D. J., Jordan, B. D., & Ritter, J. R. (2008). Analyst behavior following IPOs: The "bubble period" evidence. *Review of Financial Studies*, *21*(1), 101–133.

Brau, J. C., & Fawcett, S. E. (2006). Initial public offerings: An analysis of theory and practice. *The Journal of Finance*, *61*(1), 399–436.

Brau, J. C., Lambson, V. E., & McQueen, G. (2005). Lockups revisited. *Journal of Financial and Quantitative Analysis*, *40*(3), 519–530.

Brau, J. C., Ryan, P. A., & DeGraw, I. (2006). Initial public offerings: CFO perceptions. *The Financial Review*, *41*(4), 483−511.

Brav, A., Geczy, C., & Gompers, P. A. (2000). Is the abnormal return following equity issuances anomalous? *Journal of Financial Economics*, *56*(2), 209−249.

Brav, A., & Gompers, P. A. (1997). Myth or reality? The long-run underperformance of initial public offerings: Evidence from venture and nonventure capital-backed companies. *The Journal of Finance*, *52*(5), 1791−1821.

Brav, A., & Gompers, P. A. (2003). The role of lockups in initial public offerings. *Review of Financial Studies*, *16*(1), 1−29.

Brennan, M. J., & Franks, J. (1997). Underpricing, ownership and control in initial public offerings of equity securities in the UK. *Journal of Financial Economics*, *45*(3), 391−413.

Brooks, R. M., Mathew, P. G., & Yang, J. J. (2014). When-issued trading in the Indian IPO market. *Journal of Financial Markets*, *19*, 170−196.

Brous, P. A. (1992). Common stock offerings and earnings expectations: A test of the release of unfavorable information. *The Journal of Finance*, *47*(4), 1517−1536.

Brous, P. A., Datar, V., & Kini, O. (2001). Is the market optimistic about the future earnings of seasoned equity offering firms? *Journal of Financial and Quantitative Analysis*, *36*(2), 141−168.

Brown, K. C., & Wiles, K. W. (2015). In search of unicorns: Private IPOs and the changing markets for private equity investments and corporate control. *Journal of Applied Corporate Finance*, *27*(3), 34−48.

Bruner, R., Chaplinsky, S., & Ramchand, L. (2004). US-bound IPOs: Issue costs and selective entry. *Financial Management*, *33*(3), 39−60.

Burch, T. R., Nanda, V., & Warther, V. (2005). Does it pay to be loyal? An empirical analysis of underwriting relationships and fees. *Journal of Financial Economics*, *77*(3), 673−699.

Busaba, W. Y., Benveniste, L. M., & Guo, R.-J. (2001). The option to withdraw IPOs during the premarket: Empirical analysis. *Journal of Financial Economics*, *60*(1), 73−102.

Butler, A. W., Grullon, G., & Weston, J. P. (2005). Stock market liquidity and the cost of issuing equity. *Journal of Financial and Quantitative Analysis*, *40*(2), 331−348.

Butler, A. W., & Wan, H. (2010). Stock market liquidity and the long-run stock performance of debt issuers. *Review of Financial Studies*, *23*(11), 3966−3995.

Bøhren, Ø., Eckbo, B. E., & Michalsen, D. (1997). Why underwrite rights offerings? Some new evidence. *Journal of Financial Economics*, *46*(2), 223−261.

Cai, K. N., Helwege, J., & Warga, A. (2007). Underpricing in the corporate bond market. *Review of Financial Studies*, *20*(6), 2021−2046.

Cai, K. N., Lee, H. W., & Sharma, V. (2011). Underpricing of IPOs that follow private placement. *Journal of Financial Research*, *34*(3), 441−459.

Cai, N., Ramchand, L., & Warga, A. (2004). The pricing of equity IPOs that follow public debt offerings. *Financial Management*, *33*(4), 5−26.

Cao, C., Field, L. C., & Hanka, G. (2004). Does insider trading impair market liquidity? Evidence from IPO lockup expirations. *Journal of Financial and Quantitative Analysis*, *39*(1), 25−46.

Cao, Q., Tang, Y., & Yuan, N. (2013). Venture capital certification and IPO underpricing. *Chinese Economy*, *46*(6), 50−66.

Carter, R. B. (1992). Underwriter reputation and repetitive public offerings. *Journal of Financial Research*, *15*(4), 341−354.

Carter, R. B., & Dark, F. H. (1990). The use of the over-allotment option in initial public offerings of equity: Risks and underwriter prestige. *Financial Management*, *19*(3), 55−64.

Carter, R. B., & Dark, F. H. (1992). An empirical examination of investment banking reputation measures. *The Financial Review, 27*(3), 355–374.

Carter, R. B., & Dark, F. H. (1993). Underwriter reputation and initial public offers: The detrimental effects of flippers. *The Financial Review, 28*(2), 279–301.

Carter, R. B., Dark, F. H., Floros, I. V., & Sapp, T. R. A. (2011). Characterizing the risk of IPO long-run returns: The impact of momentum, liquidity, skewness, and investment. *Financial Management, 40*(4), 1067–1086.

Carter, R. B., Dark, F. H., & Singh, A. K. (1998). Underwriter reputation, initial returns, and the long-run performance of IPO stocks. *The Journal of Finance, 53*(1), 285–311.

Carter, R., & Manaster, S. (1990). Initial public offerings and underwriter reputation. *The Journal of Finance, 45*(4), 1045–1067.

Chalmers, K., Haman, J., & Qu, W. (2014). China's securities reforms and IPO wealth loss. *Journal of Contemporary Accounting & Economics, 10*(3), 161–175.

Chambers, D., & Dimson, E. (2009). IPO underpricing over the very long run. *The Journal of Finance, 64*(3), 1407–1443.

Chan, K., & Chan, Y.-C. (2014). Price informativeness and stock return synchronicity: Evidence from the pricing of seasoned equity offerings. *Journal of Financial Economics, 114*(1), 36–53.

Chan, K., Cooney, J. W., Kim, J., & Singh, A. K. (2008). The IPO Derby: Are there consistent losers and winners on this track? *Financial Management, 37*(1), 45–79.

Chan, K., Wang, J., & Wei, K. C. J. (2004). Underpricing and long-term performance of IPOs in China. *Journal of Corporate Finance, 10*(3), 409–430.

Chan, Y.-C. (2010). Retail trading and IPO returns in the aftermarket. *Financial Management, 39*(4), 1475–1495.

Chang, H. H., Chen, A., Kao, L., & Wu, C. S. (2014). IPO price discovery efficiency under alternative regulatory constraints: Taiwan, Hong Kong and the U.S. *International Review of Economics and Finance, 29*, 83–96.

Chaplinsky, S. & Erwin, G., (2001). Great expectations: Banks as equity underwriters. Working paper, University of Virginia.

Chaplinsky, S., & Haushalter, D. (2010). Financing under extreme risk: Contract terms and returns to private investments in public equity. *Review of Financial Studies, 23*(7), 2789–2820.

Chaplinsky, S., & Ramchand, L. (2000). The impact of global equity offerings. *The Journal of Finance, 55*(6), 2767–2789.

Chaplinsky, S., & Ramchand, L. (2004). The impact of SEC rule 144A on corporate debt issuance by international firms. *The Journal of Business, 77*(4), 1073–1098.

Chemmanur, T. J. (1993). The pricing of initial public offerings: A dynamic model with information production. *The Journal of Finance, 48*(1), 285–304.

Chemmanur, T. J., & Fulghieri, P. (1994). Investment bank reputation, information production, and financial intermediation. *The Journal of Finance, 49*(1), 57–79.

Chemmanur, T. J., & He, J. (2011). IPO waves, product market competition, and the going public decision: Theory and evidence. *Journal of Financial Economics, 101*(2), 382–412.

Chemmanur, T. J., He, S., & Hu, G. (2009). The role of institutional investors in seasoned equity offerings. *Journal of Financial Economics, 94*(3), 384–411.

Chemmanur, T. J., He, S., & Nandy, D. K. (2010). The going-public decision and the product market. *Review of Financial Studies, 23*(5), 1855–1908.

Chemmanur, T. J., Hu, G., & Huang, J. (2010). The role of institutional investors in initial public offerings. *Review of Financial Studies, 23*(12), 4496–4540.

Chemmanur, T. J., & Krishnan, K. (2012). Heterogeneous beliefs, IPO valuation, and the economic role of the underwriter in IPOs. *Financial Management, 41*(4), 769–811.

Chemmanur, T. J., & Paeglis, I. (2005). Management quality, certification, and initial public offerings. *Journal of Financial Economics, 76*(2), 331–368.

Chen, C., Shi, H., & Xu, H. (2014). The IPO underwriting market share in China: Do ownership and quality matter? *Journal of Banking & Finance, 46*(1), 177–189.

Chen, H.-C., Chen, S.-S., & Huang, C.-W. (2012). Why do insiders sell shares following IPO lockups? *Financial Management, 41*(4), 813–847.

Chen, H.-C., Fauver, L., & Yang, P.-C. (2009). What do investment banks charge to underwrite American depositary receipts? *Journal of Banking & Finance, 33*(4), 609–618.

Chen, H.-C., & Ritter, J. R. (2000). The seven percent solution. *The Journal of Finance, 55*(3), 1105–1131.

Chen, Y., Wang, S. S., Li, W., Sun, Q., & Tong, W. H. S. (2015). Institutional environment, firm ownership, and IPO first-day returns: Evidence from China. *Journal of Corporate Finance, 32*, 150–168.

Chen, Z., Morrison, A., & Wilhelm, W. J. (2014). Another look at bookbuilding, auctions, and the future of the IPO process. *Journal of Applied Corporate Finance, 26*(2), 19–29.

Chen, Z., Morrison, A. D., & Wilhelm, W. J. (2015). Traders vs. relationship managers: Reputational conflicts in full-service investment banks. *Review of Financial Studies, 28*(4), 1153–1198.

Chi, J., Wang, C., & Young, M. (2010). Long-run outperformance of Chinese initial public offerings. *Chinese Economy, 43*(5), 62–88.

Chiang, Y.-M., Qian, Y., & Sherman, A. E. (2010). Endogenous entry and partial adjustment in IPO auctions: Are institutional investors better informed? *Review of Financial Studies, 23*(3), 1200–1230.

Chod, J., & Lyandres, E. (2011). Strategic IPOs and product market competition. *Journal of Financial Economics, 100*(1), 45–67.

Choe, H., Masulis, R. W., & Nanda, V. (1993). Common stock offerings across the business cycle: Theory and evidence. *Journal of Empirical Finance, 1*(1), 3–31.

Choi, S.-D., Lee, I., & Megginson, W. (2010). Do privatization IPOs outperform in the long run? *Financial Management, 39*(1), 153–185.

Chowdhry, B., & Nanda, V. (1996). Stabilization, syndication, and pricing of IPOs. *Journal of Financial and Quantitative Analysis, 31*(1), 25–42.

Chua, L. (1995). A reexamination of the costs of firm commitment and best efforts IPOs. *The Financial Review, 30*(2), 337–365.

Clarke, J., Dunbar, C., & Kahle, K. M. (2001). Long-run performance and insider trading in completed and canceled seasoned equity offerings. *Journal of Financial and Quantitative Analysis, 36*(4), 415–430.

Clarke, J., Khorana, A., Patel, A., & Rau, P. R. (2007). The impact of all-star analyst job changes on their coverage choices and investment banking deal flow. *Journal of Financial Economics, 84*(3), 713–737.

Cliff, M. T., & Denis, D. J. (2004). Do initial public offering firms purchase analyst coverage with underpricing? *The Journal of Finance, 59*(6), 2871–2901.

Cook, D. O., Kieschnick, R., & Van Ness, R. A. (2006). On the marketing of IPOs. *Journal of Financial Economics, 82*(1), 35–61.

Cornelli, F., & Goldreich, D. (2001). Bookbuilding and strategic allocation. *The Journal of Finance, 56*(6), 2337–2369.

Cornelli, F., & Goldreich, D. (2003). Bookbuilding: How informative is the order book? *The Journal of Finance, 58*(4), 1415–1443.

Cornelli, F., Goldreich, D., & Ljungqvist, A. (2006). Investor sentiment and pre-IPO markets. *The Journal of Finance, 61*(3), 1187–1216.

Cornett, M. M., & Travlos, N. G. (1989). Information effects associated with debt-for-equity and equity-for-debt exchange offers. *The Journal of Finance, 44*(2), 451–468.

Corwin, S. A. (2003). The determinants of underpricing for seasoned equity offers. *The Journal of Finance, 58* (5), 2249–2279.

Corwin, S. A., & Harris, J. H. (2001). The initial listing decisions of firms that go public. *Financial Management, 30*(1), 35–55.

Corwin, S. A., Harris, J. H., & Lipson, M. L. (2004). The development of secondary market liquidity for NYSE-listed IPOs. *The Journal of Finance, 59*(5), 2339–2374.

Corwin, S. A., & Schultz, P. (2005). The role of IPO underwriting syndicates: Pricing, information production, and underwriter competition. *The Journal of Finance, 60*(1), 443–486.

Courteau, L. (1995). Under-diversification and retention commitments in IPOs. *Journal of Financial and Quantitative Analysis, 30*(4), 487.

D'Mello, R., & Ferris, S. P. (2000). The information effects of analyst activity at the announcement of new equity issues. *Financial Management, 29*(1), 78–95.

D'Mello, R., Tawatnuntachai, O., & Yaman, D. (2003). Does the sequence of seasoned equity offerings matter? *Financial Management, 32*(4), 59–86.

D'Souza, J., & Megginson, W. L. (1999). The financial and operating performance of privatized firms during the 1990s. *The Journal of Finance, 54*(4), 1397–1438.

Dai, N., Jo, H., & Schatzberg, J. D. (2010). The quality and price of investment banks' service: Evidence from the PIPE market. *Financial Management, 39*(2), 585–612.

Dambra, M., Field, L. C., & Gustafson, M. T. (2015). The JOBS act and IPO volume: Evidence that disclosure costs affect the IPO decision. *Journal of Financial Economics, 116*(1), 121–143.

Das, S., Guo, R.-J., & Zhang, H. (2006). Analysts' selective coverage and subsequent performance of newly public firms. *The Journal of Finance, 61*(3), 1159–1185.

Datta, S., Iskandar-Datta, M., & Patel, A. (1997). The pricing of initial public offers of corporate straight debt. *The Journal of Finance, 52*(1), 379–396.

Datta, S., Iskandar-Datta, M., & Patel, A. (1999). Bank monitoring and the pricing of corporate public debt. *Journal of Financial Economics, 51*(3), 435–449.

Datta, S., Iskandar-Datta, M., & Patel, A. (2000). Some evidence on the uniqueness of initial public debt offerings. *The Journal of Finance, 55*(2), 715–743.

Davidson, W. N., Xie, B., & Xu, W. (2006). IPO placement risk and the number of co-managers. *The Financial Review, 41*(3), 405–418.

DeAngelo, H., DeAngelo, L., & Stulz, R. M. (2010). Seasoned equity offerings, market timing, and the corporate lifecycle. *Journal of Financial Economics, 95*(3), 275–295.

Degeorge, F., Derrien, F., & Womack, K. L. (2007). Analyst hype in IPOs: Explaining the popularity of book-building. *Review of Financial Studies, 20*(4), 1021–1058.

Degeorge, F., Derrien, F., & Womack, K. L. (2010). Auctioned IPOs: The US evidence. *Journal of Financial Economics, 98*(2), 177–194.

Degeorge, F., & Zeckhauser, R. (1993). The reverse LBO decision and firm performance: Theory and evidence. *The Journal of Finance, 48*(4), 1323–1348.

Demers, E., & Lewellen, K. (2003). The marketing role of IPOs: Evidence from internet stocks. *Journal of Financial Economics, 68*(3), 413–437.

Deng, Q., & Zhou, Z. (2015). Offline oversubscription, issue size, and market momentum: The driving forces for ChiNext IPOs' initial underpricing. *The Chinese Economy, 48*(2), 114–129.

Denis, D. J. (1991). Shelf registration and the market for seasoned equity offerings. *The Journal of Business, 64* (2), 189–212.

Denis, D. J. (1993). The costs of equity issues since rule 415: A closer look. *Journal of Financial Research, 16* (1), 77−88.

Denis, D. J., & Sarin, A. (2001). Is the market surprised by poor earnings realizations following seasoned equity offerings? *Journal of Financial and Quantitative Analysis, 36*(2), 169−193.

Derrien, F., & Kecskés, A. (2007). The initial public offerings of listed firms. *The Journal of Finance, 62*(1), 447−479.

Derrien, F., & Womack, K. L. (2003). Auctions vs. bookbuilding and the control of underpricing in hot IPO markets. *Review of Financial Studies, 16*(1), 31−61.

Dewenter, K. L., & Malatesta, P. H. (1997). Public offerings of state-owned and privately-owned enterprises: An international comparison. *The Journal of Finance, 52*(4), 1659−1679.

Dittmar, A., & Thakor, A. (2007). Why do firms issue equity? *The Journal of Finance, 62*(1), 1−54.

Dolvin, S. D. (2005). Market structure, changing incentives, and underwriter certification. *Journal of Financial Research, 28*(3), 403−419.

Dolvin, S. D., & Jordan, B. D. (2008). Underpricing, overhang, and the cost of going public to preexisting shareholders. *Journal of Business Finance & Accounting, 35*(3−4), 434−458.

Dong, M., Michel, J.-S., & Pandes, J. A. (2011). Underwriter quality and long-run IPO performance. *Financial Management, 40*(1), 219−251.

Downes, D. H., & Heinkel, R. (1982). Signaling and the valuation of unseasoned new issues. *The Journal of Finance, 37*(1), 1−10.

Drake, P. D., & Vetsuypens, M. R. (1993). IPO underpricing and insurance against legal liability. *Financial Management, 22*(1), 64−73.

Drucker, S., & Puri, M. (2005). On the benefits of concurrent lending and underwriting. *The Journal of Finance, 60*(6), 2763−2799.

Duarte-Silva, T. (2010). The market for certification by external parties: Evidence from underwriting and banking relationships. *Journal of Financial Economics, 98*(3), 568−582.

Dunbar, C. G. (1995). The use of warrants as underwriter compensation in initial public offerings. *Journal of Financial Economics, 38*(1), 59−78.

Dunbar, C. (2000). Factors affecting investment bank initial public offering market share. *Journal of Financial Economics, 55*(1), 3−41.

Dunbar, C. G., & Foerster, S. R. (2008). Second time lucky? Withdrawn IPOs that return to the market. *Journal of Financial Economics, 87*(3), 610−635.

Eberhart, A. C., & Siddique, A. (2002). The long-term performance of corporate bonds (and stocks) following seasoned equity offerings. *Review of Financial Studies, 15*(5), 1385−1406.

Eccles, R. G., & Crane, D. B. (1988). *Doing deals: Investment banks at work.* Boston, Mass: Harvard Business School Press.

Eckbo, B. E., & Masulis, R. W. (1992). Adverse selection and the rights offer paradox. *Journal of Financial Economics, 32*(3), 293−332.

Eckbo, B. E., Masulis, R. W., & Norli, Ø. (2000). Seasoned public offerings: Resolution of the "new issues puzzle". *Journal of Financial Economics, 56*(2), 251−291.

Eckbo, B. E., & Norli, Ø. (2005). Liquidity risk, leverage and long-run IPO returns. *Journal of Corporate Finance, 11*(1), 1−35.

Edelen, R. M., & Kadlec, G. B. (2005). Issuer surplus and the partial adjustment of IPO prices to public information. *Journal of Financial Economics, 77*(2), 347−373.

Ederington, L. H. (1976). Negotiated versus competitive underwritings of corporate bonds. *The Journal of Finance, 31*(1), 17−28.

Edwards, A. K., & Hanley, K. W. (2010). Short selling in initial public offerings. *Journal of Financial Economics, 98*(1), 21−39.

Ellis, K. (2006). Who trades IPOs? A close look at the first days of trading. *Journal of Financial Economics, 79* (2), 339−363.

Ellis, K., Michaely, R., & O'Hara, M. (2000). When the underwriter is the market maker: An examination of trading in the IPO aftermarket. *The Journal of Finance, 55*(3), 1039−1074.

Emerick, D., & White, W. (1992). The case for private placements: How sophisticated investors add value to corporate debt issuers. *Journal of Applied Corporate Finance, 5*(3), 83−91.

Ertugrul, M., & Krishnan, K. (2014). Investment banks in dual roles: Acquirer M&A advisors as underwriters. *Journal of Financial Research, 37*(2), 159−189.

Fabozzi, F. J., Moran, E., & Ma, C. K. (1988). Market uncertainty and the least-cost offering method of public utility debt: A note. *The Journal of Finance, 43*(4), 1025−1034.

Falconieri, S., Murphy, A., & Weaver, D. (2009). Underpricing and ex post value uncertainty. *Financial Management, 38*(2), 285−300.

Fama, E. F. (1998). Market efficiency, long-term returns, and behavioral finance. *Journal of Financial Economics, 49*(3), 283−306.

Fama, E. F., & French, K. R. (1993). Common risk factors in the returns on stocks and bonds. *Journal of Financial Economics, 33*(1), 3−56.

Fang, L. H. (2005). Investment bank reputation and the price and quality of underwriting services. *The Journal of Finance, 60*(6), 2729−2761.

Fenn, G. W. (2000). Speed of issuance and the adequacy of disclosure in the 144A high-yield debt market. *Journal of Financial Economics, 56*(3), 383−405.

Fernandes, N., Lel, U., & Miller, D. P. (2010). Escape from New York: The market impact of loosening disclosure requirements. *Journal of Financial Economics, 95*(2), 129−147.

Fernando, C. S., Gatchev, V. A., May, A. D., & Megginson, W. L. (2015). The value of reputation: Evidence from equity underwriting. *Journal of Applied Corporate Finance, 27*(3), 96−112.

Fernando, C. S., Gatchev, V. A., & Spindt, P. A. (2005). Wanna dance? How firms and underwriters choose each other. *The Journal of Finance, 60*(5), 2437−2469.

Fernando, C. S., Krishnamurthy, S., & Spindt, P. A. (2004). Are share price levels informative? Evidence from the ownership, pricing, turnover and performance of IPO firms. *Journal of Financial Markets, 7*(4), 377−403.

Field, L. C., & Hanka, G. (2001). The expiration of IPO share lockups. *The Journal of Finance, 56*(2), 471−500.

Field, L. C., & Karpoff, J. M. (2002). Takeover defenses of IPO firms. *The Journal of Finance, 57*(5), 1857−1889.

Fields, L. P., & Mais, E. L. (1991). The valuation effects of private placements of convertible debt. *The Journal of Finance, 46*(5), 1925−1932.

Fields, P., Fraser, D., & Bhargava, R. (2003). A comparison of underwriting costs of initial public offerings by investment and commercial banks. *Journal of Financial Research, 26*(4), 517−534.

Finnerty, J. D. (2013). The impact of stock transfer restrictions on the private placement discount. *Financial Management, 42*(3), 575−609.

Firth, M. (1997). An analysis of the stock market performance of new issues in New Zealand. *Pacific-Basin Finance Journal, 5*(1), 63−85.

Foster, F. D. (1989). Syndicate size, spreads, and market power during the introduction of shelf registration. *The Journal of Finance, 44*(1), 195−204.

Friday, H. S., Howton, S. D., & Howton, S. W. (2000). Anomalous evidence on operating performance following seasoned equity offerings: The case of REITs. *Financial Management, 29*(2), 76−87.

Fu, F. (2010). Overinvestment and the operating performance of SEO firms. *Financial Management, 39*(1), 249−272.

Fung, W. K. H., & Rudd, A. (1986). Pricing new corporate bond issues: An analysis of issue cost and seasoning effects. *The Journal of Finance, 41*(3), 633−643.

Galloway, T. M., Loderer, C. F., & Sheehan, D. P. (1998). What does the market learn from stock offering revisions? *Financial Management, 27*(1), 5−16.

Gande, A., Puri, M., & Saunders, A. (1999). Bank entry, competition, and the market for corporate securities underwriting. *Journal of Financial Economics, 54*(2), 165−195.

Gande, A., Puri, M., Saunders, A., & Walter, I. (1997). Bank underwriting of debt securities: Modern evidence. *Review of Financial Studies, 10*(4), 1175−1202.

Gao, X., & Ritter, J. R. (2010). The marketing of seasoned equity offerings. *Journal of Financial Economics, 97* (1), 33−52.

Gao, Y., Mao, C. X., & Zhong, R. (2006). Divergence of opinion and long-term performance of initial public offerings. *Journal of Financial Research, 29*(1), 113−129.

Garfinkel, J. A. (1993). IPO underpricing, insider selling and subsequent equity offerings: Is underpricing a signal of quality? *Financial Management, 22*(1), 74−83.

Garner, J. L., & Marshall, B. B. (2004). Unit IPOs: The who, when, and why of warrant amendment. *Journal of Financial Research, 27*(2), 217−233.

Ghosh, C., Petrova, M., Feng, Z., & Pattanapanchai, M. (2012). Does IPO pricing reflect public information? New insights from equity carve-outs. *Financial Management, 41*(1), 1−33.

Gibson, S., Safieddine, A., & Sonti, R. (2004). Smart investments by smart money: Evidence from seasoned equity offerings. *Journal of Financial Economics, 72*(3), 581−604.

Goh, J., Gombola, M. J., Lee, H. W., & Liu, F.-Y. (1999). Private placement of common equity and earnings expectations. *The Financial Review, 34*(3), 19−32.

Gokkaya, S., & Highfield, M. J. (2014). Sales of secondary shares in SEOs: A comparison across top managers, other insiders, and outsiders. *Financial Management, 43*(4), 757−794.

Gompers, P. A. (1996). Grandstanding in the venture capital industry. *Journal of Financial Economics, 42*(1), 133−156.

Gompers, P. A., & Lerner, J. (2003). The really long-run performance of initial public offerings: The pre-Nasdaq evidence. *The Journal of Finance, 58*(4), 1355−1392.

Gondat-Larralde, C., & James, K. R. (2008). IPO pricing and share allocation: The importance of being ignorant. *The Journal of Finance, 63*(1), 449−478.

Gonzalez, L., & James, C. (2007). Banks and bubbles: How good are bankers at spotting winners? *Journal of Financial Economics, 86*(1), 40−70.

Griffin, J. M., Harris, J. H., & Topaloglu, S. (2007). Why are IPO investors net buyers through lead underwriters? *Journal of Financial Economics, 85*(2), 518−551.

Grinblatt, M., & Hwang, C. Y. (1989). Signalling and the pricing of new issues. *The Journal of Finance, 44*(2), 393−420.

Gustafson, M. T., & Iliev, P. (2017). The effects of removing barriers to equity issuance. *Journal of Financial Economics, 124*(3), 580−598.

Güçbilmez, U. (2014). Why do some Chinese technology firms avoid ChiNext and go public in the US? *International Review of Financial Analysis, 36*(1), 179−194.

Habib, M. A., & Ljungqvist, A. P. (2001). Underpricing and entrepreneurial wealth losses in IPOs: Theory and evidence. *Review of Financial Studies, 14*(2), 433–458.

Hanley, K. W. (1993). The underpricing of initial public offerings and the partial adjustment phenomenon. *Journal of Financial Economics, 34*(2), 231–250.

Hanley, K. W., & Hoberg, G. (2010). The information content of IPO prospectuses. *Review of Financial Studies, 23*(7), 2821–2864.

Hanley, K. W., Kumar, A. A., & Seguin, P. J. (1993). Price stabilization in the market for new issues. *Journal of Financial Economics, 34*(2), 177–197.

Hanley, K. W., Lee, C. M. C., & Seguin, P. L. (1996). The marketing of closed-end fund IPOs: Evidence from transactions data. *Journal of Financial Intermediation, 5*(2), 127–159.

Hanley, K. W., & Wilhelm, W. J. (1995). Evidence on the strategic allocation of initial public offerings. *Journal of Financial Economics, 37*(2), 239–257.

Hansen, R. S. (1988). The demise of the rights issue. *Review of Financial Studies, 1*(3), 289–309.

Hansen, R. S. (2001). Do investment banks compete in IPOs?: The advent of the "7% plus Contract". *Journal of Financial Economics, 59*(3), 313–346.

Hansen, R. S., Fuller, B. R., & Janjigian, V. (1987). The over-allotment option and equity financing flotation costs: An empirical investigation. *Financial Management, 16*(2), 24–32.

Hansen, R. S., & Pinkerton, J. M. (1982). Direct equity financing: A resolution of a paradox. *The Journal of Finance, 37*(3), 651–665.

Hansen, R. S., & Torregrosa, P. (1992). Underwriter compensation and corporate monitoring. *The Journal of Finance, 47*(4), 1537–1555.

Hao, G. Q. (2007). Laddering in initial public offerings. *Journal of Financial Economics, 85*(1), 102–122.

Hao, G. Q. (2014). Institutional shareholder investment horizons and seasoned equity offerings. *Financial Management, 43*(1), 87–111.

Hao, X., Shi, J., & Yang, J. (2014). The differential impact of the bank–firm relationship on IPO underpricing: Evidence from China. *Pacific-Basin Finance Journal, 30*(1), 207–232.

Hass, J. J. (1998). Small issue public offerings conducted over the internet: Are they "suitable" for the retail investor? *Southern California Law Review, 72*(67), 68–103.

Hayes, S. (1979). The transformation of investment banking. *Harvard Business Review, 57*(1), 153–170.

Hayes, S. L., & Hubbard, P. M. (1990). *Investment banking: A tale of three cities*. Boston, MA: Harvard Business School Press.

Hebb, G. M. (2002). Conflict of interest in commercial bank equity underwriting. *The Financial Review, 37*(2), 185–205.

Heinkel, R., & Schwartz, E. S. (1986). Rights versus underwritten offerings: An asymmetric information approach. *The Journal of Finance, 41*(1), 1–18.

Helou, A., & Park, G. (2001). Is there a signaling effect of underwriter reputation? *Journal of Financial Research, 24*(1), 27–43.

Helwege, J., & Liang, N. (2004). Initial public offerings in hot and cold markets. *Journal of Financial and Quantitative Analysis, 39*(3), 541–569.

Henry, T. R., & Koski, J. L. (2010). Short selling around seasoned equity offerings. *Review of Financial Studies, 23*(12), 4389–4418.

Hensler, D. A., Rutherford, R. C., & Springer, T. M. (1997). The survival of initial public offerings in the after-market. *Journal of Financial Research, 20*(1), 93–110.

Heron, R., & Lie, E. (2004). A comparison of the motivations for and the information content of different types of equity offerings. *The Journal of Business, 77*(3), 605–632.

Hertzel, M., Lemmon, M., Linck, J. S., & Rees, L. (2002). Long-run performance following private placements of equity. *The Journal of Finance, 57*(6), 2595−2617.

Hertzel, M., & Smith, R. L. (1993). Market discounts and shareholder gains for placing equity privately. *The Journal of Finance, 48*(2), 459−485.

Higgins, E. J., Howton, S., & Howton, S. (2003). An analysis of closed-end fund seasoned equity offerings. *Journal of Financial Research, 26*(2), 243−257.

Hoberg, G. (2007). The underwriter persistence phenomenon. *The Journal of Finance, 62*(3), 1169−1206.

Holderness, C. G., & Pontiff, J. (2016). Shareholder nonparticipation in valuable rights offerings: New findings for an old puzzle. *Journal of Financial Economics, 120*(2), 252−268.

Hoque, H. (2014). Role of asymmetric information and moral hazard on IPO underpricing and lockup. *Journal of International Financial Markets, Institutions and Money, 30*(1), 81−105.

Hoque, H., & Lasfer, M. (2015). Directors' dealing and post-IPO performance. *European Financial Management, 21*(1), 178−204.

Houge, T., Loughran, T., Suchanek, G., & Yan, X. (2001). Divergence of opinion, uncertainty, and quality of initial public offerings. *Financial Management, 30*(4), 5−23.

Houston, J., James, C., & Karceski, J. (2006). What a difference a month makes: Stock analyst valuations following initial public offerings. *Journal of Financial and Quantitative Analysis, 41*(1), 111−138.

Hovakimian, A., & Hutton, I. (2010). Merger-motivated IPOs. *Financial Management, 39*(4), 1547−1573.

Howe, J. S., & Zhang, S. (2010). SEO cycles. *The Financial Review, 45*(3), 729−741.

Huang, R., & Ramírez, G. G. (2010). Speed of issuance, lender specialization, and the rise of the 144A debt market. *Financial Management, 39*(2), 643−673.

Huang, R., & Zhang, D. (2011). Managing underwriters and the marketing of seasoned equity offerings. *Journal of Financial and Quantitative Analysis, 46*(1), 141−170.

Hughes, P. J., & Thakor, A. V. (1992). Litigation risk, intermediation, and the underpricing of initial public offerings. *Review of Financial Studies, 5*(4), 709−742.

Hull, R. M., & Kerchner, R. (1996). Issue costs and common stock offerings. *Financial Management, 25*(4), 54−66.

Hunt-McCool, J., Koh, S. C., & Francis, B. B. (1996). Testing for deliberate underpricing in the IPO premarket: A stochastic frontier approach. *Review of Financial Studies, 9*(4), 1251−1269.

Ibbotson, R. G. (1975). Price performance of common stock new issues. *Journal of Financial Economics, 2*(3), 235−272.

Ibbotson, R. G., & Jaffe, J. F. (1975). "Hot Issue" markets. *The Journal of Finance, 30*(4), 1027−1042.

Ibbotson, R. G., Sindelar, J. L., & Ritter, J. R. (1988). Initial public offerings. *Journal of Applied Corporate Finance, 1*(2), 37−45.

Ibbotson, R. G., Sindelar, J. L., & Ritter, J. R. (1994). The market's problems with the pricing of initial public offerings. *Journal of Applied Corporate Finance, 7*(1), 66−74.

Intintoli, V. J., Jategaonkar, S. P., & Kahle, K. M. (2014). The effect of demand for shares on the timing and underpricing of seasoned equity offers. *Financial Management, 43*(1), 61−86.

Intintoli, V. J., & Kahle, K. M. (2010). Seasoned equity offers: The effect of insider ownership and float. *Financial Management, 39*(4), 1575−1599.

Jagannathan, R., & Sherman, A. E. (2005). Reforming the bookbuilding process for IPOs. *Journal of Applied Corporate Finance, 17*(1), 67−72.

Jain, B. A., & Kini, O. (1994). The post-issue operating performance of IPO firms. *The Journal of Finance, 49*(5), 1699−1726.

Jain, P. K., & Kim, J.-C. (2006). Investor recognition, liquidity, and exchange listings in the reformed markets. *Financial Management*, *35*(2), 21–42.

Jakobsen, J. B., & Sorensen, O. (2001). Decomposing and testing long-term returns: An application on Danish IPOs. *European Financial Management*, *7*(3), 393–417.

James, C., & Karceski, J. (2006). Strength of analyst coverage following IPOs. *Journal of Financial Economics*, *82*(1), 1–34.

Jeanneret, P. (2005). Use of the proceeds and long-term performance of French SEO firms. *European Financial Management*, *11*(1), 99–122.

Jegadeesh, N. (2000). Long-term performance of seasoned equity offerings: Benchmark errors and biases in expectations. *Financial Management*, *29*(3), 5–30.

Jegadeesh, N., Weinstein, M., & Welch, I. (1993). An empirical investigation of IPO returns and subsequent equity offerings. *Journal of Financial Economics*, *34*(2), 153–175.

Jenkinson, T., & Jones, H. (2004). Bids and allocations in European IPO bookbuilding. *The Journal of Finance*, *59*(5), 2309–2338.

Jenkinson, T., & Jones, H. (2009). IPO pricing and allocation: A survey of the views of institutional investors. *Review of Financial Studies*, *22*(4), 1477–1504.

Jenkinson, T., Morrison, A. D., & Wilhelm, W. J. (2006). Why are European IPOs so rarely priced outside the indicative price range? *Journal of Financial Economics*, *80*(1), 185–209.

Johnston, J., & Madura, J. (2009). The pricing of IPOs post-Sarbanes-Oxley. *The Financial Review*, *44*(2), 291–310.

Johnson, J. M., & Miller, R. E. (1988). Investment banker prestige and the underpricing of initial public offerings. *Financial Management*, *17*(2), 19–29.

Johnson, W. C., Kang, J.-K., & Yi, S. (2010). The certification role of large customers in the new issues market. *Financial Management*, *39*(4), 1425–1474.

Jones, S. L., Megginson, W. L., Nash, R. C., & Netter, J. M. (1999). Share issue privatizations as financial means to political and economic ends. *Journal of Financial Economics*, *53*(2), 217–253.

Kadan, O., Madureira, L., Wang, R., & Zach, T. (2009). Conflicts of interest and stock recommendations: The effects of the global settlement and related regulations. *Review of Financial Studies*, *22*(10), 4189–4217.

Kadapakkam, P.-R., & Kon, S. J. (1989). The value of shelf registration for new debt issues. *The Journal of Business*, *62*(2), 271–292.

Kaneko, T., & Pettway, R. H. (2003). Auctions versus book building of Japanese IPOs. *Pacific-Basin Finance Journal*, *11*(4), 439–462.

Kang, J.-K., & Lee, Y. W. (1996). The pricing of convertible debt offerings. *Journal of Financial Economics*, *41*(2), 231–248.

Kao, J. L., Wu, D., & Yang, Z. (2009). Regulations, earnings management, and post-IPO performance: The Chinese evidence. *Journal of Banking & Finance*, *33*(1), 63–76.

Kaustia, M., & Knüpfer, S. (2008). Do investors overweight personal experience? Evidence from IPO subscriptions. *The Journal of Finance*, *63*(6), 2679–2702.

Keloharju, M. (1993). The Winner's curse, legal liability, and the long-run price performance of initial public offerings in Finland. *Journal of Financial Economics*, *34*(2), 251–277.

Khanna, N., Noe, T. H., & Sonti, R. (2008). Good IPOs draw in bad: Inelastic banking capacity and hot markets. *Review of Financial Studies*, *21*(5), 1873–1906.

Khurshed, A., Paleari, S., Pande, A., & Vismara, S. (2014). Transparent bookbuilding, certification and initial public offerings. *Journal of Financial Markets*, *19*(1), 154–169.

Kidwell, D. S., Marr, M. W., & Thompson, G. R. (1984). SEC Rule 415: The ultimate competitive bid. *Journal of Financial and Quantitative Analysis, 19*(2), 183–195.

Kim, D., Palia, D., & Saunders, A., (2003). The long-run behavior of debt and equity underwriting spreads. Working paper, New York University.

Kim, D., Palia, D., & Saunders, A. (2008). The impact of commercial banks on underwriting spreads: Evidence from three decades. *Journal of Financial and Quantitative Analysis, 43*(4), 975–1000.

Kim, D., Palia, D., & Saunders, A. (2010). Are initial returns and underwriting spreads in equity issues complements or substitutes? *Financial Management, 39*(4), 1403–1423.

Kim, H. E., & Lee, Y. K. (1990). Issuing stocks in Korea. In R. Chang, & G. Rhee (Eds.), *Pacific-Basin Capital Markets Research* (pp. 243–253). North-Holland: Elsevier Science Publisher B.V.

Kim, K. A., & Shin, H.-H. (2004). The puzzling increase in the underpricing of seasoned equity offerings. *The Financial Review, 39*(3), 343–365.

Kim, W., & Weisbach, M. S. (2008). Motivations for public equity offers: An international perspective. *Journal of Financial Economics, 87*(2), 281–307.

Kiymaz, H. (2000). The initial and aftermarket performance of IPOs in an emerging market: Evidence from Istanbul stock exchange. *Journal of Multinational Financial Management, 10*(2), 213–227.

Koh, F., & Walter, T. (1989). A direct test of Rock's model of the pricing of unseasoned issues. *Journal of Financial Economics, 23*(2), 251–272.

Korajczyk, R. A., Lucas, D. J., & McDonald, R. L. (1991). The effect of information releases on the pricing and timing of equity issues. *Review of Financial Studies, 4*(4), 685–708.

Kothare, M. (1997). The effects of equity issues on ownership structure and stock liquidity: A comparison of rights and public offerings. *Journal of Financial Economics, 43*(1), 131–148.

Kothari, S. P., & Warner, J. B. (1997). Measuring long-horizon security price performance. *Journal of Financial Economics, 43*(3), 301–339.

Krigman, L., Shaw, W. H., & Womack, K. L. (1999). The persistence of IPO mispricing and the predictive power of flipping. *The Journal of Finance, 54*(3), 1015–1044.

Krigman, L., Shaw, W. H., & Womack, K. L. (2001). Why do firms switch underwriters? *Journal of Financial Economics, 60*(2–3), 245–284.

Kunimura, M., & Iihara, Y. (1985). Valuation of underwriting agreements for raising capital in the Japanese capital market. *Journal of Financial and Quantitative Analysis, 20*(2), 231–241.

Kutsuna, K., Smith, J. K., & Smith, R. L. (2009). Public information, IPO price formation, and long-run returns: Japanese evidence. *The Journal of Finance, 64*(1), 505–546.

Kutsuna, K., & Smith, R. (2004). Why does book building drive out auction methods of IPO issuance? Evidence from Japan. *Review of Financial Studies, 17*(4), 1129–1166.

Lee, G., & Masulis, R. W. (2009). Seasoned equity offerings: Quality of accounting information and expected flotation costs. *Journal of Financial Economics, 92*(3), 443–469.

Lee, I. (1997). Do firms knowingly sell overvalued equity? *The Journal of Finance, 52*(4), 1439–1466.

Lee, I., Lochhead, S., Ritter, J., & Zhao, Q. (1996). The costs of raising capital. *Journal of Financial Research, 19*(1), 59–74.

Lee, I., & Loughran, T. (1998). Performance following convertible bond issuance. *Journal of Corporate Finance, 4*(2), 185–207.

Lee, P. J., Taylor, S. L., & Walter, T. S. (1999). IPO underpricing explanations: Implications from investor application and allocation schedules. *Journal of Financial and Quantitative Analysis, 34*(4), 425–444.

Lee, P. M., & Wahal, S. (2004). Grandstanding, certification and the underpricing of venture capital backed IPOs. *Journal of Financial Economics, 73*(2), 375–407.

Leland, H. E., & Pyle, D. H. (1977). Informational asymmetries, financial structure, and financial intermedia-tion. *The Journal of Finance, 32*(2), 371–387.

Lerner, J. (1994). Venture capitalists and the decision to go public. *Journal of Financial Economics, 35*(3), 293–316.

Levis, M. (1993). The long-run performance of initial public offerings: The UK experience 1980–1988. *Financial Management, 22*(1), 28–41.

Lewellen, K. (2006). Risk, reputation, and IPO price support. *The Journal of Finance, 61*(2), 613–653.

Lewis, C. M., & Tan, Y. (2016). Debt-equity choices, R&D investment and market timing. *Journal of Financial Economics, 119*(3), 599–610.

Li, M., McInish, T. H., & Wongchoti, U. (2005). Asymmetric information in the IPO aftermarket. *The Financial Review, 40*(2), 131–153.

Lian, Q., & Wang, Q. (2009). Does the market incorporate previous IPO withdrawals when pricing second-time IPOs? *Financial Management, 38*(2), 357–380.

Lindvall, J. R. (1977). New issue corporate bonds, seasoned market efficiency and yield spreads. *The Journal of Finance, 32*(4), 1057–1067.

Ling, D. C., & Ryngaert, M. (1997). Valuation uncertainty, institutional involvement, and the underpricing of IPOs: The case of REITs. *Journal of Financial Economics, 43*(3), 433–456.

Liu, J., Uchida, K., & Gao, R. (2014). Legal protection and underpricing of IPOs: Evidence from China. *Pacific Basin Finance Journal, 27*(1), 163–187.

Liu, X., & Ritter, J. R. (2010). The economic consequences of IPO spinning. *Review of Financial Studies, 23*(5), 2024–2059.

Liu, X., & Ritter, J. R. (2011). Local underwriter oligopolies and IPO underpricing. *Journal of Financial Economics, 102*(3), 579–601.

Livingston, M., & Miller, R. E. (2000). Investment bank reputation and the underwriting of nonconvertible debt. *Financial Management, 29*(2), 21–34.

Livingston, M., & Zhou, L. (2002). The impact of rule 144A debt offerings upon bond yields and underwriter fees. *Financial Management, 31*(4), 5–27.

Ljungqvist, A., Marston, F., Starks, L. T., Wei, K. D., & Yan, H. (2007). Conflicts of interest in sell-side research and the moderating role of institutional investors. *Journal of Financial Economics, 85*(2), 420–456.

Ljungqvist, A., Marston, F., & Wilhelm, W. J. (2006). Competing for securities underwriting mandates: Banking relationships and analyst recommendations. *The Journal of Finance, 61*(1), 301–340.

Ljungqvist, A., Marston, F., & Wilhelm, W. J. (2009). Scaling the hierarchy: How and why investment banks compete for syndicate co-management appointments. *Review of Financial Studies, 22*(10), 3977–4007.

Ljungqvist, A., & Wilhelm, W. J. (2003). IPO pricing in the dot-com bubble. *The Journal of Finance, 58*(2), 723–752.

Ljungqvist, A., & Wilhelm, W. J. (2005). Does prospect theory explain IPO market behavior? *The Journal of Finance, 60*(4), 1759–1790.

Ljungqvist, A. P., Jenkinson, T., & Wilhelm, W. J. (2003). Global integration in primary equity markets: The role of U.S. banks and U.S. investors. *Review of Financial Studies, 16*(1), 63–99.

Ljungqvist, A. P., & Wilhelm, W. J. (2002). IPO allocations: Discriminatory or discretionary? *Journal of Financial Economics, 65*(2), 167–201.

Loderer, C. F., Sheehan, D. P., & Kadlec, G. B. (1991). The pricing of equity offerings. *Journal of Financial Economics, 29*(1), 35–57.

Logue, D. E. (1973a). On the pricing of unseasoned equity issues: 1965–1969. *Journal of Financial and Quantitative Analysis, 8*(1), 91–103.

Logue, D. E. (1973b). Premia on unseasoned equity issues. *Journal of Economics and Business, 25*(3), 133–141.

Logue, D. E., Rogalski, R. J., Seward, J. K., & Foster-Johnson, L. (2002). What is special about the roles of underwriter reputation and market activities in initial public offerings? *The Journal of Business, 75*(2), 213–243.

Loughran, T. (1993). NYSE vs NASDAQ returns: Market microstructure or the poor performance of initial public offerings? *Journal of Financial Economics, 33*(2), 241–260.

Loughran, T., & McDonald, B. (2013). IPO first-day returns, offer price revisions, volatility, and form S-1 language. *Journal of Financial Economics, 109*(2), 307–326.

Loughran, T., & Ritter, J. R. (1995). The new issues puzzle. *The Journal of Finance, 50*(1), 23–51.

Loughran, T., & Ritter, J. R. (1997). The operating performance of firms conducting seasoned equity offerings. *The Journal of Finance, 52*(5), 1823–1850.

Loughran, T., & Ritter, J. R. (2000). Uniformly least powerful tests of market efficiency. *Journal of Financial Economics, 55*(3), 361–389.

Loughran, T., & Ritter, J. R. (2002). Why don't issuers get upset about leaving money on the table in IPOs? *Review of Financial Studies, 15*(2), 413–444.

Loughran, T., & Ritter, J. R. (2004). Why has IPO underpricing changed over time? *Financial Management, 33* (3), 5–37.

Loughran, T., Ritter, J. R., & Rydqvist, K. (1994). Initial public offerings: International insights. *Pacific-Basin Finance Journal, 2*(2–3), 165–199.

Lowry, M. (2003). Why does IPO volume fluctuate so much? *Journal of Financial Economics, 67*(1), 3–40.

Lowry, M., Officer, M. S., & Schwert, G. W. (2010). The variability of IPO initial returns. *The Journal of Finance, 65*(2), 425–465.

Lowry, M., & Schwert, G. W. (2002). IPO market cycles: Bubbles or sequential learning? *The Journal of Finance, 57*(3), 1171–1200.

Lowry, M., & Schwert, G. W. (2004). Is the IPO pricing process efficient? *Journal of Financial Economics, 71* (1), 3–26.

Lowry, M., & Shu, S. (2002). Litigation risk and IPO underpricing. *Journal of Financial Economics, 65*(3), 309–335.

Lyandres, E., Sun, L., & Zhang, L. (2008). The new issues puzzle: Testing the investment-based explanation. *Review of Financial Studies, 21*(6), 2825–2855.

Lyn, E. O., & Zychowicz, E. J. (2003). The performance of new equity offerings in Hungary and Poland. *Global Finance Journal, 14*(2), 181–195.

Mandelker, G., & Raviv, A. (1977). Investment banking: An economic analysis of optimal underwriting contracts. *The Journal of Finance, 32*(3), 683–694.

Marciukaityte, D., Szewczyk, S. H., & Varma, R. (2005). Investor overoptimism and private equity placements. *Journal of Financial Research, 28*(4), 591–608.

Marr, M. W., & Thompson, G. R. (1984). The pricing of new convertible bond issues. *Financial Management, 13*(2), 31–37.

Martin, J. D., & Richards, R. M. (1981). The seasoning process for corporate bonds. *Financial Management, 10*(3), 41–48.

Mauer, D. C., & Senbet, L. W. (1992). The effect of the secondary market on the pricing of initial public offerings: Theory and evidence. *Journal of Financial and Quantitative Analysis, 27*(1), 55–79.

McDonald, J. G., & Fisher, A. K. (1972). New-issue stock price behavior. *The Journal of Finance, 27*(1), 97–102.

McLaughlin, R., Safieddine, A., & Vasudevan, G. K. (1996). The operating performance of seasoned equity issuers: Free cash flow and post-issue performance. *Financial Management, 25*(4), 41–53.

McLaughlin, R., Safieddine, A., & Vasudevan, G. K. (1998). The long-run performance of convertible debt issuers. *Journal of Financial Research, 21*(4), 373–388.

McLaughlin, R., Safieddine, A., & Vasudevan, G. K. (2000). Investment banker reputation and the performance of seasoned equity issuers. *Financial Management, 29*(1), 96–110.

Megginson, W. L., Nash, R. C., Netter, J. M., & Poulsen, A. B. (2004). The choice of private versus public capital markets: Evidence from privatizations. *The Journal of Finance, 59*(6), 2835–2870.

Megginson, W. L., Nash, R. C., Netter, J. M., & Schwartz, A. L. (2000). The long-run return to investors in share issue privatization. *Financial Management, 29*(1), 67–77.

Megginson, W. L., Nash, R. C., & Van Randenborgh, M. (1994). The financial and operating performance of newly privatized firms: An international empirical analysis. *The Journal of Finance, 49*(2), 403–452.

Megginson, W. L., & Weiss, K. A. (1991). Venture capitalist certification in initial public offerings. *The Journal of Finance, 46*(3), 879–903.

Mello, A. S., & Parsons, J. E. (1998). Going public and the ownership structure of the firm. *Journal of Financial Economics, 49*(1), 79–109.

Merton, R. C. (1987). A simple model of capital market equilibrium with incomplete information. *The Journal of Finance, 42*(3), 483–510.

Michaely, R., & Shaw, W. H. (1994). The pricing of initial public offerings: Tests of adverse-selection and signaling theories. *Review of Financial Studies, 7*(2), 279–319.

Michaely, R., & Shaw, W. H. (1995). Does the choice of auditor convey quality in an initial public offering? *Financial Management, 24*(4), 15–30.

Michaely, R., & Womack, K. L. (1999). Conflict of interest and the credibility of underwriter analyst recommendations. *Review of Financial Studies, 12*(4), 653–686.

Mikkelson, W. H., Megan Partch, M., & Shah, K. (1997). Ownership and operating performance of companies that go public. *Journal of Financial Economics, 44*(3), 281–307.

Miller, E. M. (1977). Risk, uncertainty, and divergence of opinion. *The Journal of Finance, 32*(4), 1151–1168.

Miller, M. H., & Rock, K. (1985). Dividend policy under asymmetric information. *The Journal of Finance, 40*(4), 1031–1051.

Miller, R. E., & Reilly, F. K. (1987). An examination of mispricing, returns, and uncertainty for initial public offerings. *Financial Management, 16*(2), 33–38.

Mohd Rashid, R., Abdul-Rahim, R., & Yong, O. (2014). The influence of lock-up provisions on IPO initial returns: Evidence from an emerging market. *Economic Systems, 38*(4), 487–501.

Mola, S., & Loughran, T. (2004). Discounting and clustering in seasoned equity offering prices. *Journal of Financial and Quantitative Analysis, 39*(1), 1–23.

Moore, N. H., Peterson, D. R., & Peterson, P. P. (1986). Shelf registrations and shareholder wealth: A comparison of shelf and traditional equity offerings. *The Journal of Finance, 41*(2), 451–463.

Morrison, A. D., & Wilhelm, W. J. (2007). Investment of banking: Past, present, and future. *Journal of Applied Corporate Finance, 19*(1), 42–54.

Morrison, A. D., & Wilhelm, W. J. (2008). The demise of investment banking partnerships: Theory and evidence. *The Journal of Finance, 63*(1), 311–350.

Muscarella, C. J. (1988). Price performance of initial public offerings of master limited partnership units. *The Financial Review, 23*(4), 513–521.

Muscarella, C. J., Peavy, J. W., & Vetsuypens, M. R. (1992). Optimal exercise of the over-allotment option in IPOs. *Financial Analysts Journal, 48*(3), 76−81.

Muscarella, C. J., & Vetsuypens, M. R. (1989). A simple test of Baron's model of IPO underpricing. *Journal of Financial Economics, 24*(1), 125−135.

Myers, S. C., & Majluf, N. S. (1984). Corporate financing and investment decisions when firms have information that investors do not have. *Journal of Financial Economics, 13*(2), 187−221.

Nanda, V., & Yun, Y. (1997). Reputation and financial intermediation: An empirical investigation of the impact of IPO mispricing on underwriter market value. *Journal of Financial Intermediation, 6*(1), 39−63.

Narayanan, R. P., Rangan, K. P., & Rangan, N. K. (2004). The role of syndicate structure in bank underwriting. *Journal of Financial Economics, 72*(3), 555−580.

Narayanan, R. P., Rangan, K. P., & Rangan, N. K. (2007). The effect of private-debt-underwriting reputation on bank public-debt underwriting. *Review of Financial Studies, 20*(3), 597−618.

Ng, C. K., & Smith, R. L. (1996). Determinants of contract choice: The use of warrants to compensate underwriters of seasoned equity issues. *The Journal of Finance, 51*(1), 363−380.

Nimalendran, M., Ritter, J. R., & Zhang, D. (2007). Do today's trades affect tomorrow's IPO allocations? *Journal of Financial Economics, 84*(1), 87−109.

Ofek, E., & Richardson, M. (2003). DotCom mania: The rise and fall of internet stock prices. *The Journal of Finance, 58*(3), 1113−1137.

Pagano, M., Panetta, F., & Zingales, L. (1998). Why do companies go public? An empirical analysis. *The Journal of Finance, 53*(1), 27−64.

Papaioannou, G. J. (1996). Financing corporate growth by going public. *Corporate Finance Review, 1*(1), 28−31.

Papaioannou, G. J. (2011). Competing for underwriting market share: The case of commercial banks and securities firms. *Journal of Financial Services Marketing, 16*(2), 153−169.

Papaioannou, G. J., Travlos, N. G., & Viswanathan, K. G. (2009). Visibility effects and timing in stock listing changes: Evidence from operating performance. *The Quarterly Review of Economics and Finance, 49*(2), 357−377.

Parsons, J. E., & Raviv, A. (1985). Underpricing of seasoned issues. *Journal of Financial Economics, 14*(3), 377−397.

Pástor, L'., Taylor, L. A., & Veronesi, P. (2009). Entrepreneurial learning, the IPO decision, and the post-IPO drop in firm profitability. *Review of Financial Studies, 22*(8), 3005−3046.

Peavy, J. W. (1990). Returns on initial public offerings of closed-end funds. *Review of Financial Studies, 3*(4), 695−708.

Perotti, E. C. (1995). Credible privatization. *The American Economic Review, 85*(4), 847−859.

Perotti, E. C., & Guney, S. E. (1993). The structure of privatization plans. *Financial Management, 22*(1), 84−98.

Pettway, R. H., & Kaneko, T. (1996). The effects of removing price limits and introducing auctions upon short-term IPO returns: The case of Japanese IPOs. *Pacific-Basin Finance Journal, 4*(2), 241−258.

Pichler, P., & Wilhelm, W. (2001). A theory of the syndicate: Form follows function. *The Journal of Finance, 56*(6), 2237−2264.

Popescu, M., & Xu, Z. (2011). Co-managers, information, and the secondary market liquidity of initial public offerings. *Financial Management, 40*(1), 199−218.

Poulsen, A. B., & Stegemoller, M. (2008). Moving from private to public ownership: Selling out to public firms versus initial public offerings. *Financial Management, 37*(1), 81−101.

Pukthuanthong-Le, K., & Varaiya, N. (2007). IPO pricing, block sales, and long-term performance. *The Financial Review, 42*(3), 319−348.

Puri, M. (1999). Commercial banks as underwriters: Implications for the going public process. *Journal of Financial Economics, 54*(2), 133−163.

Puri, M., & Rocholl, J. (2008). On the importance of retail banking relationships. *Journal of Financial Economics, 89*(2), 253−267.

Rajan, R., & Servaes, H. (1997). Analyst following of initial public offerings. *The Journal of Finance, 52*(2), 507−529.

Rangan, S. (1998). Earnings management and the performance of seasoned equity offerings. *Journal of Financial Economics, 50*(1), 101−122.

Rauterkus, S. Y., & Song, K. R. (2005). Auditor's reputation and equity offerings: The case of Arthur Andersen. *Financial Management, 34*(4), 121−135.

Reilly, F. K. (1977). New issues revisited. *Financial Management, 6*(4), 28−42.

Reilly, F. K., & Hatfield, K. (1969). Investor experience with new stock issues. *Financial Analysts Journal, 25* (5), 73−80.

Reuter, J. (2006). Are IPO allocations for sale? Evidence from mutual funds. *The Journal of Finance, 61*(5), 2289−2324.

Ritter, J. R. (1984a). Signaling and the valuation of unseasoned new issues: A comment. *The Journal of Finance, 39*(4), 1231−1237.

Ritter, J. R. (1984b). The "Hot Issue" market of 1980. *The Journal of Business, 57*(2), 215−240.

Ritter, J. R. (1987). The costs of going public. *Journal of Financial Economics, 19*(2), 269−281.

Ritter, J. R. (1991). The long-run performance of initial public offerings. *The Journal of Finance, 46*(1), 3−27.

Ritter, J. R. (2003). Differences between European and American IPO markets. *European Financial Management, 9*(4), 421−434.

Ritter, J. R. (2015). Growth capital-backed IPOs. *The Financial Review, 50*(4), 481−515.

Ritter, J. R., & Zhang, D. (2007). Affiliated mutual funds and the allocation of initial public offerings. *Journal of Financial Economics, 86*(2), 337−368.

Rock, K. (1986). Why new issues are underpriced. *Journal of Financial Economics, 15*(1−2), 187−212.

Rogowski, R. J., & Sorensen, E. H. (1985). Deregulation in investment banking: Shelf registrations, structure, and performance. *Financial Management, 14*(1), 5−15.

Roten, I. C., & Mullineaux, D. J. (2002). Debt underwriting by commercial bank-affiliated firms and investment banks: More evidence. *Journal of Banking & Finance, 26*(4), 689−718.

Safieddine, A., & Wilhelm, W. J. (1996). An empirical investigation of short-selling activity prior to seasoned equity offerings. *The Journal of Finance, 51*(2), 729−749.

Schenone, C. (2004). The effect of banking relationships on the firm's IPO underpricing. *The Journal of Finance, 59*(6), 2903−2958.

Schultz, P. (1993). Unit initial public offerings. *Journal of Financial Economics, 34*(2), 199−229.

Schultz, P. (2003). Pseudo market timing and the long-run underperformance of IPOs. *The Journal of Finance, 58*(2), 483−517.

Schultz, P. H., & Zaman, M. A. (1994). Aftermarket support and underpricing of initial public offerings. *Journal of Financial Economics, 35*(2), 199−219.

Sherman, A. E. (1999). Underwriter certification and the effect of shelf registration on due diligence. *Financial Management, 28*(1), 5−19.

Sherman, A. E. (2000). IPOs and long-term relationships: An advantage of book building. *Review of Financial Studies, 13*(3), 697−714.

Sherman, A. E. (2005). Global trends in IPO methods: Book building versus auctions with endogenous entry. *Journal of Financial Economics, 78*(3), 615−649.

Sherman, A. E., & Titman, S. (2002). Building the IPO order book: Underpricing and participation limits with costly information. *Journal of Financial Economics, 65*(1), 3−29.

Sherman, A. G. (1992). The pricing of best efforts new issues. *The Journal of Finance, 47*(2), 781−790.

da Silva Rosa, R., Velayuthen, G., & Walter, T. (2003). The sharemarket performance of Australian venture capital-backed and non-venture capital-backed IPOs. *Pacific-Basin Finance Journal, 11*(2), 197−218.

Skousen, K. F. (1983). *An introduction* to the SEC (3rd ed). Cincinnati: South-Western Pub. Co.

Slovin, M., Sushka, M., & Lai, K. W. (2000). Alternative flotation methods, adverse selection, and ownership structure: Evidence from seasoned equity issuance in the U.K. *Journal of Financial Economics, 57*(2), 157−190.

Smart, S. B., & Zutter, C. J. (2003). Control as a motivation for underpricing: A comparison of dual and single-class IPOs. *Journal of Financial Economics, 69*(1), 85−110.

Smart, S. B., & Zutter, C. J. (2008). Dual class IPOs are underpriced less severely. *The Financial Review, 43*(1), 85−106.

Smith, C. W. (1977). Alternative methods for raising capital. *Journal of Financial Economics, 5*(3), 273−307.

Smith, C. W. (1986). Raising capital: Theory and evidence. *Midland Corporate Finance Journal, 4*(1), 6−22.

Smith, R. L. (1987). The choice of issuance procedure and the cost of competitive and negotiated underwriting: An examination of the impact of rule 50. *The Journal of Finance, 42*(3), 703−720.

Song, S., Tan, J., & Yi, Y. (2014). IPO initial returns in China: Underpricing or overvaluation? *China Journal of Accounting Research, 7*(1), 31−49.

Song, W.-L. (2004). Competition and coalition among underwriters: The decision to join a syndicate. *The Journal of Finance, 59*(5), 2421−2444.

Sorensen, E. H. (1979). The impact of underwriting method and bidder competition upon corporate bond interest cost. *The Journal of Finance, 34*(4), 863−870.

Sorensen, E. H. (1982). On the seasoning process of new bonds: Some are more seasoned than others. *Journal of Financial and Quantitative Analysis, 17*(2), 195−208.

Spiess, D. K., & Affleck-Graves, J. (1995). Underperformance in long-run stock returns following seasoned equity offerings. *Journal of Financial Economics, 38*(3), 243−267.

Spiess, D. K., & Affleck-Graves, J. (1999). The long-run performance of stock returns following debt offerings. *Journal of Financial Economics, 54*(1), 45−73.

Stehle, R., Ehrhardt, O., & Przyborowsky, R. (2000). Long-run stock performance of German initial public offerings and seasoned equity issues. *European Financial Management, 6*(2), 173−196.

Stoll, H. K. (1976). Pricing of underwritten offerings of listed common-stocks and compensation of underwriters. *Journal of Economics and Business, 28*(2), 96−103.

Stoughton, N. M., & Zechner, J. (1998). IPO-mechanisms, monitoring and ownership structure. *Journal of Financial Economics, 49*(1), 45−77.

Su, D. (2004). Adverse-selection versus signaling: Evidence from the pricing of Chinese IPOs. *Journal of Economics and Business, 56*(1), 1−19.

Sullivan, M. J., & Unite, A. A. (2001). The influence of group affiliation and the underwriting process on emerging market IPOs: The case of the Philippines. *Pacific-Basin Finance Journal, 9*(5), 487−512.

Sun, Q., & Tong, W. H. (2003). China share issue privatization: The extent of its success. *Journal of Financial Economics, 70*(2), 183−222.

Sun, Y., Uchida, K., & Matsumoto, M. (2013). The dark side of independent venture capitalists: Evidence from Japan. *Pacific-Basin Finance Journal, 24*, 279–300.

Szewczyk, S. H., & Varma, R. (1991). Raising capital with private placements of debt. *Journal of Financial Research, 14*(1), 1–13.

Teoh, S. H., Welch, I., & Wong, T. J. (1998). Earnings management and the long-run market performance of initial public offerings. *The Journal of Finance, 53*(6), 1935–1974.

Teoh, S. H., & Wong, T. J. (2002). Why new issues and high-accrual firms underperform: The role of analysts' credulity. *Review of Financial Studies, 15*(3), 869–900.

Thomadakis, S., Gounopoulos, D., Nounis, C., & Merikas, A. (2016). Collateral regulation and IPO-specific liberalisation: The case of price limits in the Athens stock exchange. *European Financial Management, 22*(2), 276–312.

Thomadakis, S., Nounis, C., & Gounopoulos, D. (2012). Long-term performance of Greek IPOs. *European Financial Management, 18*(1), 117–141.

Tiniç, S. M. (1988). Anatomy of initial public offerings of common stock. *The Journal of Finance, 43*(4), 789–822.

Titman, S., & Trueman, B. (1986). Information quality and the valuation of new issues. *Journal of Accounting and Economics, 8*(2), 159–172.

Torstila, S. (2001). The distribution of fees within the IPO syndicate. *Financial Management, 30*(4), 25–43.

Torstila, S. (2003). The clustering of IPO gross spreads: International evidence. *Journal of Financial and Quantitative Analysis, 38*(3), 673–694.

Tsangarakis, N. V. (1996). Shareholder wealth effects of equity issues in emerging markets: Evidence from rights offerings in Greece. *Financial Management, 25*(3), 21–32.

Ursel, N. D. (2006). Rights offerings and corporate financial condition. *Financial Management, 35*(1), 31–52.

Vismara, S., Signori, A., & Paleari, S. (2015). Changes in underwriters' selection of comparable firms pre- and post-IPO: Same bank, same company, different peers. *Journal of Corporate Finance, 34*(1), 235–250.

Wang, K., Chan, S. H., & Gau, G. W. (1992). Initial public offerings of equity securities. *Journal of Financial Economics, 31*(3), 381–410.

Wang, Q., & Ligon, J. A. (2009). The underpricing of insurance IPOs. *Financial Management, 38*(2), 301–322.

Wang, X., Cao, J., Liu, Q., Tang, J., & Tian, G. G. (2015). Disproportionate ownership structure and IPO long-run performance of non-SOEs in China. *China Economic Review, 32*, 27–42.

Wei, Z., Varela, O., D'Souza, J., & Hassan, M. K. (2003). The financial and operating performance of China's newly privatized firms. *Financial Management, 32*(2), 107–126.

Weinstein, M. I. (1978). The seasoning process of new corporate bond issues. *The Journal of Finance, 33*(5), 1343–1354.

Weiss, K. (1989). The post-offering price performance of closed-end funds. *Financial Management, 18*(3), 57–67.

Welch, I. (1989). Seasoned offerings, imitation costs, and the underpricing of initial public offerings. *The Journal of Finance, 44*(2), 421–449.

Welch, I. (1991). An empirical examination of models of contract choice in initial public offerings. *Journal of Financial and Quantitative Analysis, 26*(4), 497.

Welch, I. (1992). Sequential sales, learning, and cascades. *The Journal of Finance, 47*(2), 695–732.

Wilhelm, W. J. (1999). Internet investment banking: The impact of information technology on relationship banking. *Journal of Applied Corporate Finance, 12*(1), 21–27.

Wilhelm, W. J. (2005). Bookbuilding, auctions, and the future of the IPO process. *Journal of Applied Corporate Finance, 17*(1), 55–66.

Wruck, K. H. (1989). Equity ownership concentration and firm value: Evidence from private equity financings. *Journal of Financial Economics, 23*(1), 3–28.

Wu, C., & Kwok, C. C. Y. (2002). Why do US firms choose global equity offerings? *Financial Management, 31* (2), 47–65.

Wu, Y. (2004). The choice of equity-selling mechanisms. *Journal of Financial Economics, 74*(1), 93–119.

Xiao, Y., & Yung, C. (2015). Extrapolation errors in IPOs. *Financial management, 44*(4), 713–751.

Yasuda, A. (2005). Do bank relationships affect the firm's underwriter choice in the corporate-bond underwriting market? *The Journal of Finance, 60*(3), 1259–1292.

Yeoman, J. C. (2001). The optimal spread and offering price for underwritten securities. *Journal of Financial Economics, 62*(1), 169–198.

Yung, C., Çolak, G., & Wang, W. (2008). Cycles in the IPO market. *Journal of Financial Economics, 89*(1), 192–208.

Zhang, S. (2005). Underpricing, share overhang, and insider selling in follow-on offerings. *The Financial Review, 40*(3), 409–428.

Zhu, Y. (Ellen) (2009). The relation between IPO underpricing and litigation risk revisited: Changes between 1990 and 2002. *Financial Management, 38*(2), 323–355.

Index

Printed in the United States
By Bookmasters